BUILDING
A
SUCCESSFUL MARRIAGE

BUILDING A SUCCESSFUL MARRIAGE

Second Edition

JUDSON T. LANDIS
University of California at Berkeley

and

MARY G. LANDIS

New York
PRENTICE-HALL, INC.

PRENTICE-HALL SOCIOLOGY SERIES

HERBERT BLUMER, EDITOR

Library of Congress Catalog Card No.: 53-7671

First printing .... May, 1953
Second printing .... September, 1953
Third printing .... March, 1954

PRINTED IN THE UNITED STATES OF AMERICA

To

J.R.L. and J.F.L.

PREFACE

MOST of the readers of this book will be either approaching marriage or already married and learning that marriage is a process of growth that constantly requires new understandings and adjustments. Our purpose is to present in readable form the scientific knowledge that exists about mate selection, courtship, and the adjustment problems of marriage. We hope that the book will continue to prove useful to readers who are seeking to build successful marriages.

In this revised edition, we have tried to retain all the materials from the first edition that have stood the test of objectivity, scientific validity, and usefulness in meeting the special needs of young people. But we have rewritten many sections in the light of our further thinking and experience with young people and in view of new and enlightening research.

The first edition included certain chapters that were in direct response to needs expressed by young people. Revised versions of these chapters appear in the present edition. They include: Mixed Marriages, Premarital Sex Relations, Buying Life Insurance, In-Laws and Marriage Adjustment, Finances and Adjustment in Marriage, and Sex Education of Children. The chapters that deal with adjustment in marriage should help readers to achieve a more objective and realistic understanding of what marriage is all about. They should serve as a valuable guide for those who are in the courtship period and in the process of selecting mates. Included also are two new chapters pertinent to the experience of today's generations. These are: Changing Sex Roles, and Marriages Under Special Circumstances (Marriage While in College, Marriage and Military Separation, Marriage to a Previously Married Person).

New research findings have been added on dating and courtship, premarital sex standards, husband-wife adjustment to pregnancy, and other topics. Many of the research findings concerning maturation and dating reported in the first edition of this book were retested through research among college students in a wide variety of colleges and universities in 1952. The newer findings are included in this edition.

We appreciate the cooperation of the teachers and students in marriage and family courses who supplied information for the research on maturation and dating in 1952.

This study of student dating in eleven colleges was possible only because of the generous cooperation of the following: Eugene P. Link, State University of New York, New Paltz; Kenneth Cannon and Fern Brown, University of Nebraska; Gus Turbeville, University of Minnesota, Duluth Branch; B. F. Timmons, University of Illinois; Freda Wallin, Stanford University; J. Shailer Arnold, Fullerton Junior College; Marion B. Smith, Louisiana State University; Lawrence S. Bee, University of Kansas; Arlie E. McGuire, University of Dubuque; and Charles B. Spaulding, Whittier College.

We are grateful to others for the valuable contributions they have made either directly or indirectly. We are indebted specifically to the 212 couples who gave their histories of adjustment to first pregnancy, the 544 couples who cooperated in the study of problems of early marriage, and the 409 couples of the older generation who supplied information on the length of time required after marriage to adjust in various relationships. We are also indebted to the many thousands of students who have contributed to our knowledge and our thinking by their discussions in classes and by their evaluations of the text and lecture materials, and to all colleagues who have helped with criticisms or evaluations of the first edition.

In addition to Alvin Ahern, Charles R. Hoffer, and Wilda F. Bolles, who helped our work by reading parts of the manuscript of the first edition and giving us the benefit of their comments, we would mention Eleanor B. Easley, M.D., obstetrician of Durham, North Carolina, who aided in the preparation of the revised edition by her critical reading of the chapter on Reproduction, and R. Wilfred Kelsey, of the Institute of Life Insurance, who provided constructive criticisms of the life-insurance material.

Several graduate students have assisted in the various research studies reported. We are especially grateful for the work of Anna Laura Kennedy on the study of 409 older-generation marriages; of Lois V. Pratt on the study of 544 marriages of shorter duration; and of Thomas and Shirley Poffenberger on the study of adjustment to first pregnancy.

We appreciate the faithful and competent assistance of Everett M. Sims, Coordinating Editor, of Prentice-Hall, Inc., who has worked with us throughout the publishing of both the first and second editions of this book.

Judson T. Landis
Berkeley, California *Mary G. Landis*

CONTENTS

I. SUCCESSFUL MARRIAGE 1

II. ROLE CONCEPTS AND SEX DIFFERENCES . 12

III. CHANGING SEX ROLES 27

IV. WHY PEOPLE MARRY OR DO NOT MARRY . 38

V. THE COURTSHIP PERIOD 63

VI. MARRIAGEABILITY 88

VII. MARRIAGE UNDER SPECIAL CIRCUMSTANCES 113

VIII. PREMARITAL SEXUAL RELATIONS . . . 130

IX. MIXED MARRIAGES 146

X. ENGAGEMENT 177

XI. LEGAL CONTROL OF MARRIAGE . . . 220

XII. ACHIEVING ADJUSTMENT IN MARRIAGE . 253

XIII. SEX ADJUSTMENT IN MARRIAGE . . . 281

XIV. IN-LAWS AND MARRIAGE ADJUSTMENT . 302

XV. RELIGIOUS ATTITUDES AND FAMILY LIFE . 321

XVI. FINANCES AND ADJUSTMENT IN MARRIAGE 330

XVII. GETTING YOUR MONEY'S WORTH . . . 341

XVIII. BUYING LIFE INSURANCE 354

XIX. FAMILY PLANNING 375

XX. REPRODUCTION 408

XXI. WHEN CHILDREN COME 441

XXII. BRINGING UP CHILDREN 459

XXIII. SEX EDUCATION 476

APPENDIX A: MARRIAGE COUNSELING AGENCIES . 497

APPENDIX B: SELECTED READINGS ON MARRIAGE AND FAMILY RELATIONS . . . 499

APPENDIX C: REVIEW QUESTIONS, SUGGESTED READINGS, SPECIAL PROBLEMS AND ACTIVITIES, SOCIO-DRAMAS . 511

APPENDIX D: SOURCES OF MOTION PICTURES . 553

INDEX 554

Chapter I

SUCCESSFUL MARRIAGE

THIS YEAR MORE THAN 3,000,000 Americans will say the words of the marriage ceremony and begin married life. For many of them the wedding will mark the beginning of a life of growing and expanding happiness, of a fulfillment which will enrich their lives and contribute to the welfare of society. A certain proportion of the marriages, however, will not be successful; they will end in divorce—the official acknowledgment of failure.

Many things affect the future of any marriage: the personality traits of the two individuals, their family backgrounds, and, perhaps most important of all, the attitudes which they hold on a number of subjects. Strange as it may seem, their attitudes will have far more to do with their success in marriage than will the intensity of the love they feel for each other at the time of their wedding. Their conception of what marriage is, what it will require of them, and what they may hope to receive from the relationship, will be of fundamental importance to their success.

Successful marriage

Poets, cynics, and philosophers have all attempted epigrammatic summaries of marriage, but what marriage is cannot be told in a sentence. In this chapter we will discuss a concept of successful marriage. The rest of the book will explore the many aspects of marriage that require practical consideration by those who would build successful marriages.

A successful marriage is one in which two people have intelligently committed themselves to a lifetime together, in which each seeks to enrich the life of the other as well as his own. In a successful marriage each partner, because of the marriage, stands as a more integrated person, better able to meet and cope adequately with the vicissitudes of life. Such a marriage is based upon cooperation and includes the most rewarding comradeship. In a good marriage each partner is all that he himself is capable of being; moreover, his personality expands and takes on, in a measure, the attributes and capacities of the partner. Both are conscious that an interdependence exists by which the two stand together, so that pleasures are enhanced through the sharing, and blows which life may offer are cushioned.

This union of personalities is not a gift that is presented by fate to people who are lucky in love. It is not a benefit that is conferred by the final words of the wedding ceremony. It must be created by the partners in marriage, and can be achieved only through cooperative effort over a period of time. It will not be grasped by people who, although united legally in marriage, are striving each to go his own way and to retain his individual freedom. No absolute freedom exists for anyone either outside or inside marriage. But within marriage one gives up a measure of his personal freedom in exchange for the element of togetherness that is one of the permanent values of marriage.

Young people approaching marriage usually hope to be happy as a pair; they are seldom aware that the scope of marriage is broader than the two who marry. Yet individuals who can build a good marriage are contributing a positive good to the world about them. They will be more effective in all life's relationships. They are not the problem individuals who trouble society.

A successful marriage usually means children and a happy

home life for the children. Marriage happiness is extended and perpetuated through the children. Students of marriage have learned that successful marriages run in families. Hence the couple who marry with an intelligent understanding that they have committed themselves to living together in harmony, with tolerance for each other's faults, and with respect for each other's virtues, and who abide by their decision unalterably, are setting a pattern for the successful marriages of their children.

Attitude toward permanence of marriage

One of the important elements in this pattern is commitment to a permanent union. Successful marriages do not result when people go into marriage with reservations. Some couples go through the marriage ceremony, repeating the words, "I take thee . . . for better, for worse, for richer, for poorer, in sickness and in health . . . until death . . . ," but even while they are speaking they hold the thought that perhaps the marriage will not work, that marriage is a gamble anyway, but that if it fails to work out, a ready-made escape is at hand, thanks to modern divorce laws. Those who marry with confidence in the thought that divorce is easy are already steering toward divorce. The swimmer who starts to swim across a river, but is careful to stay close enough to shore so that his feet can always touch bottom in case he should change his mind and wish to walk back to dry land, will never make the crossing. He has set limitations upon his effort which eliminate all chance of success. It is just so with marriage. Successful cooperation is not possible when limitations are set upon it. Today, when divorce is relatively easy, it may seem surprising to advocate taking the marriage vows literally—"for better, for worse, until death." But that is the only logical starting point from which successful marriage can be built.

Let us illustrate the point with the experience of two couples. Two engaged girls compared their attitudes toward marriage and divorce. Helen said, "John and I have decided to wait until autumn to be married. Both of us have divorced parents and we know that divorce doesn't necessarily solve the problems of an unhappy marriage; so we have agreed that after we marry, no matter what comes up we will work our way through it together. Once we marry, we intend it to be for life."

Ruth said, "Tom and I don't feel that way at all. We are going to be married at once because we think the only way we can find out how we like married life is to try it. If we don't get along, we'll just call the whole thing off."

So Tom and Ruth were married, and in the normal course of events disagreements arose. Some were only minor; others required both to make serious adjustments. But according to their thinking, why should either of them make the effort to change or compromise? They both felt that if their marriage was not going to succeed they should find it out while they were still young enough to make a fresh start with someone else. Therefore, when differences arose they very logically braced themselves for battle and tried to force concessions from each other. Their marriage lasted a year. Both were disillusioned to find that the divorce involved more unhappiness and bitterness than they had anticipated; they could not end their marriage with as much nonchalance as they had thought.

Helen and John continued dating through the ten months following their engagement and were married in the fall. They also found points on which they disagreed. But after ten years of married life Helen said, "We figured that since we were together for life, the sooner we reached agreement on the points where we differed the happier we would be. We always understood each other better and had more respect for each other's viewpoint after we had talked over our differences. Sometimes one of us changed to the other's way of thinking, but more often we compromised." Their marriage was outstandingly successful.

It is true that in both these marriages personality traits and other factors contributed in part to the success or failure. However, there were no insurmountable barriers to happiness in either case. The crucial factor was the willingness or unwillingness to work at creating a successful marriage. In the one case the will to succeed outweighed differences.

Divorce a hazard

In a sense, then, easy divorce as it exists in our society is a hazard to successful marriage. People are deluded into thinking of it as a ready and acceptable solution to problems that arise in marriage. The prospect of escape through divorce often prevents people from facing in a mature manner the problems of marriage. Yet these problems, through the solving, might well become stepping stones to deeper and more lasting happiness. The point is sometimes made that in former times, when divorce was not socially acceptable, many people suffered through life in unhappy marriages because they had no escape. That is true. It is also true that many marriages now end in divorce that formerly would have been successful. If they had no easy way out, the partners in these marriages would recognize the necessity for working through problems to success.

One of the things which people contemplating marriage need to know in their preparation for marriage is that divorce is seldom a solution to problems. The emotional traumas involved for the individual and the damage done to personality by the experience of failure which divorce represents are often far worse than the difficulties in marriage from which people attempt to escape through divorce. Certainly, where marriage has failed beyond any possibility of recovery, divorce may be the only course of action. Many such failures occur in hastily contracted marriages between people who believe that to be violently in love is the only prerequisite for successful marriage. More realistic preparation for marriage, with a conception of marriage as a permanent relationship, should lead to more careful and rational mate selection and to less haste in entering marriage.

Marriage as a way of life

Almost all people who want to achieve success in marriage can do so if they are prepared for their task. They must realize that all marriages include the pleasant and the unpleasant, the happy and the unhappy, and hard work and commonplace, everyday living as well as ecstasy. A misplaced emphasis is often

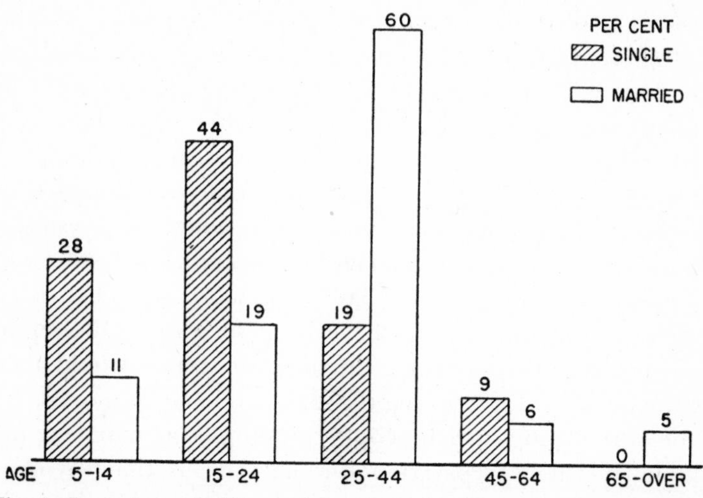

Fig. 1. Percentage of 450 married and single old people choosing different periods in life as the happiest. When a large group of old people between the ages of 65 and 100 were asked at what time they had been happiest in life, over half said the best years were those when they were married and had children at home. The comments indicated that their happiness in life was closely related to marriage and family living. The unmarried felt the happiest years had been during childhood and youth. Data from Judson T. Landis, "What Is the Happiest Period in Life?" *School and Society,* 55:1432 (June 6, 1942), 643-645.

made upon "happiness," so that many young people approach marriage expecting married life to be one long emotional spree. Disappointment is inevitable for them. None of us could endure for long a life made up of nothing but parties. Party clothes, party conversation, and party food would soon become intolerable to us. For life to be interesting and worth while we must have also the commonplace, the difficult, and even the drab. Old clothes are comfortable; real companionship is not dependent upon scintillating conversation; desserts and sweets simply embellish the plain food we require for nourishment. Whether we are married or not, if our attention is fixed upon only the garnitures, we may limit the development in our lives of the things which give permanent zest to living.

Marriage is simply a way of life. It requires much of the individual. How well an individual understands himself and his own personality needs, and how well he habitually gets along with himself and with others will have much to do with the success of his marriage. Marriage does not change basic personality. Sometimes people marry with the expectation that marriage will work miracles in their lives, that it will bring them happiness when they lack the habit of happiness, and that it will resolve all their maladjustments. That is expecting too much of marriage. Those who marry with an intelligent understanding of their own marriageability and an appreciation of their obligations as well as their privileges are likely to achieve greater success and happiness.

Social changes and marriage stability

It is true today as never before that the outcome is in our own hands when we marry. In former generations individual choice and responsibility were not so great. The institutional aspects of marriage exerted pressures that are almost nonexistent today. Law, tradition, religion, and social custom all operated as external controls to give permanence to marriage. The marriage relationship was carefully defined and regulated by society. Since tradition and social pressure favored male domination in marriage, adjustment was not necessarily shared equally by husband and wife.

Moreover, life was predominantly rural. In 1880, 70 per cent of our people lived in rural areas. Consequently, families were generally held together by many bonds that no longer exert a strong influence. A family worked together in rural areas to produce a living. Their isolated mode of life made it possible for all members of the family to be held readily accountable for their goings and comings. Members of the family were dependent upon each other for recreation and social life. In many ways the family was forced by circumstances to build together all that was worth while in life.

These conditions have changed. Man's position as the dominant head of the family no longer goes unchallenged. Our population is no longer predominantly rural. In 1950, 64 per cent of our people were living in urban areas. The conditions under which people live in cities make it more difficult for them to maintain a stable family life. Crowded living conditions, the anonymity of the individual, freedom from social controls, the opportunities for varied recreational activities which separate rather than unite the family, and the lack of any necessity or opportunity for working together to produce a living, all affect the stability of marriage.

Formerly, practical considerations helped maintain the permanence of a marriage. A man had to depend upon a wife to keep his clothes in order, to prepare his food, to make a home for his aged parents, and to rear his children. A woman had to have a husband to support her and to give her the social standing that was impossible for a spinster to attain. Now a man no longer needs a wife to care for his clothes; the cleaner and the tailor can do the job more efficiently. He can eat in restaurants. The state will provide for his aged parents through old age assistance, or they may provide for themselves through social security. As for the woman, the many lines of work now open to her mean that she can earn her own living. Although marriage still has a greater prestige value than spinsterhood, the stigma of spinsterhood has greatly decreased. Actually, some career women prefer single independence to marriage. The total effect of all these changes is that the reasons for present-day marriage are different from what they used to be.

Independent of economic or social needs, or considerations of personal convenience in the daily circumstances of living, monogamous marriage meets a fundamental affectional need of human beings in our culture. The very changes that have decreased the power of outer controls on marriage stability have emphasized and served to give greater force to the affectional function of marriage. Greater population mobility, the anonymity of the individual in the city, the loosening of bonds with family members, all these factors emphasize for the individual his need for some one person with whom he can build a life of comradeship and understanding.

Fig. 2. Ratio of marriages to divorces in 1952. For every three couples applying for marriage licenses, one married couple applied for a divorce.

Young people have ample opportunity to observe the instability of the relationships of others and the unhappiness and failure that many people make of marriage. The present generation of young people is looking for new light on the subject of marriage. Many of them are not willing to take a leap in the dark or to trust to luck for success in marriage.

Divorce is the public acknowledgment of failure, whatever may be the reason for the failure. It is sometimes the inevitable result of circumstances or events beyond the control of the individual. In other cases the divorce is evidence that the partners were not willing to expend the effort required to create a successful marriage. They turn to divorce if fate or luck fails to present them with marital happiness as a finished product. It is safe to assume that legal divorces will continue to be fairly easy to secure. Our emphasis, then, must be upon preparation for those who desire the permanent and unequaled satisfactions of a successful marriage, and who are willing to commit themselves to the building of such a marriage.

Education for marriage

Young people of college age are in the process of selecting mates. Some are consciously seeking a future husband or wife. Others have not established a rational course of action directed toward the goal of marriage. The latter are content to date and to enjoy association with the opposite sex, but they give little thought to the choice of a permanent mate. However, studies of college alumni show that a large majority of them marry someone whom they dated in college.

Since most young people plan to marry eventually, no training can be of more practical value to them than training in preparation for marriage and family living. It is our purpose to present in later chapters of this book the helpful, scientific information about marriage which is now available. Although many of the changes which have taken place in our society are threats to the stability of marriage, people who marry now have opportunities to prepare for marriage that were not available to couples in the past. Research among married people and scientific study of the problems of family living are providing much information that will help in the building of good marriages. People are now able to approach marriage intelligently, relatively well prepared with an understanding of the physical, psychological, and social scope and implications of marriage.

Education for marriage is relatively new in the colleges and universities of our country. Although courses in the family had been offered before 1927, the late professor Ernest R. Groves of the University of North Carolina offered the first college course in preparation for marriage in that year. Probably no other course has grown more rapidly in the college curriculum during the last 20 years. Colleges have introduced credit and non-credit courses in marriage, the family, and family relationships. Each year brings an increasing demand from students for courses in marriage and family living, and such courses are now being offered in most of the colleges.

With more widespread preparation for marriage, the proportion of marriage failures should decrease, and it would be reasonable to expect that more people should find greater happiness in marriage.

Chapter II

ROLE CONCEPTS AND SEX DIFFERENCES

IN THE PRECEDING CHAPTER we suggested the importance of the attitudes that young people hold concerning the nature of marriage, its demands upon the individual, and the rewards it offers. We emphasized also the necessity for looking upon the wedding as a commitment binding both partners to permanent cooperation, and offering no limiting escape clause. Important also is the attitude each individual holds concerning his or her role in life. What rights, privileges, and obligations are mine because I was born a male? Or what rights, privileges, and obligations are mine because I was born a female? The success of some marriages is jeopardized at the outset because the partners hold set prejudices concerning man's place or woman's place in life. No final answer can be given to many of the questions that will be raised in this and the following chapter; our purpose will be to present facts and ideas which may help the reader to evaluate his attitudes concerning sex roles in modern life. Unprejudiced viewpoints based upon scientific facts are of practical value to those contemplating marriage.

Changing status of women

In early American history no higher education was open to women; they had few opportunities for training for work other than household tasks, and therefore were dependent economically upon the men of their families. Until fairly recently only a small minority of American women could vote, and their legal rights as individuals were few. The mores of American life still followed the pattern favored by the bachelor Paul: "If the woman would know anything let her go home and ask her husband."

The accepted attitude toward women was expressed in a book published in 1881, *Decorum: A Practical Treatise on Etiquette and Dress of the Best American Society*. The author offers the following advice to gentlemen: "When addressing ladies, pay them the compliment of seeming to consider them capable of an equal understanding with gentlemen . . . they will appreciate the delicate compliment." In the same treatise on decorum the author states, "Young married ladies must never appear in any public place unattended by their husbands or by elder ladies. This rule must never be infringed." And, "Of late years ladies have taken to rowing; this can be managed in a quiet river or private pond but it is scarcely to be attempted in the . . . public parts of our rivers unless superintended by a gentleman." For the edification of all concerned, he comments, "Most women are naturally amiable, gentle and complying."

Perhaps the author of *Decorum* was whistling in the dark, for despite the amiability and gentleness of women, some able women have, in the last 75 years, devoted their lives to battling for the "rights" of women. Much has been written and said about sex equality. And attitudes have changed concerning the place of women. Nowhere in our country are there now any limitations placed on women's right to vote. Most universities are open to women on an equal basis with men, although university education is still geared to train for typically masculine achievement. Nevertheless, women can train themselves for almost any occupation or profession if they so choose. It has now become the accepted custom for unmarried American women to hold jobs outside the home. Formerly, it was proper for the unmarried woman to make herself useful within the shelter of the home of her parents or brothers. Now, however, even among married women, 50 per cent hold outside jobs during the first year of marriage.[1]

Yet laws that discriminate against women still remain on the statute books of several states. In some states women are barred from holding certain public offices; in others they may not sign contracts without the husband's consent. In most states, however, women are free to enter almost all occupations, but disparities often exist between the pay received by women and by men of equal training.

All inequalities that still exist are targets for those who are battling for complete freedom, or equality, for women. A proposed amendment to the federal Constitution reads: "Men and women shall have equal rights throughout the United States and every place subject to its jurisdiction." The amendment is supported by powerful groups of organized women, such as the National Federation of Business and Professional Women. It is opposed by some equally intelligent and powerful groups, such as the League of Women Voters.

Some of those who oppose such an amendment do so because they believe that to enforce complete "equality" would actually be to discriminate against women. It would place upon them equal responsibility with men, and would deprive them of certain protections that now exist. It would fail to recognize that certain inescapable obligations and responsibilities have already been placed upon women by nature. Men will never have to share these obligations equally with women. These obligations require for women exemptions from some of the responsibilities borne by men.

Sex dissimilarities

The picture is a complicated one. Some of the restrictions placed upon women by our moral and economic double standard have no justification; they are simply relics from less en-

[1] Metropolitan Life Insurance Company, *Statistical Bulletin,* 32:4 (April, 1951), 1.

lightened times. Others have a logical and firm basis in the scheme of things as set up by nature, and legislating against them or agitating about them will not alter the basic facts. The facts concerning the nature, physical make-up, and functioning of men and of women point neither to equality nor inequality. Those terms become inapplicable. The more proper concept is that major dissimilarities between the sexes exist; in make-up, functions, and behavior each shows capacities and abilities different from the other. Not only from the viewpoint of society, but also from that of the individual, the sexes are complementary to each other; an acceptance of their biological and cultural differences is important to a constructive and happy fulfillment of their roles.

Traditionally, woman has been thought of as the weaker sex. But careful study of children and adults in all phases of their growth and achievement forces a redefining of concepts. It is now known that in rate of development, both physical and mental, the female leads. In muscular strength, the male leads. In resistance to disease and death, the female has a great advantage over the male. The female also has greater ability to withstand or endure emotional pressure. Also, the differences in body chemistry of the two sexes may account for behavior dissimilarities. We will consider in more detail some of these basic differences.

Mortality and morbidity

Women have been known to remark of their husbands, "He doesn't get sick very often, but when he does, things seem to hit him so hard!" Wives who make that observation are not just describing an individual husband's reaction to illness; they have discovered a fact well known to the medical profession. Men are not sick so often as women, but when illness strikes, it does hit them harder. The death rates for males are higher from the time of conception on through every age. Biologists tell us that at least 120 males are conceived to every 100 females, yet the sex ratio at birth is 105.5 boys to 100 girls. The great surplus of males conceived do not survive to be born. During the first four months of pregnancy, at least four times as many males as females die. The proportion gradually changes until the eighth month of pregnancy, when the average is 55 males to 45 females. During the first year after birth, one-fourth more boys die than girls. Vital statistics records show this ratio to occur quite consistently year after year. When conditions are improved so that the total infant mortality rate is lowered, as it has been in America during this century, the proportion of male to female deaths becomes even greater. In other words, the greater resistance of the female enables her to profit more by better environment than the male is able to do. Mothers usually assume that girls are more delicate than boys. They are unaware that in reality boys have less resistance to disease and

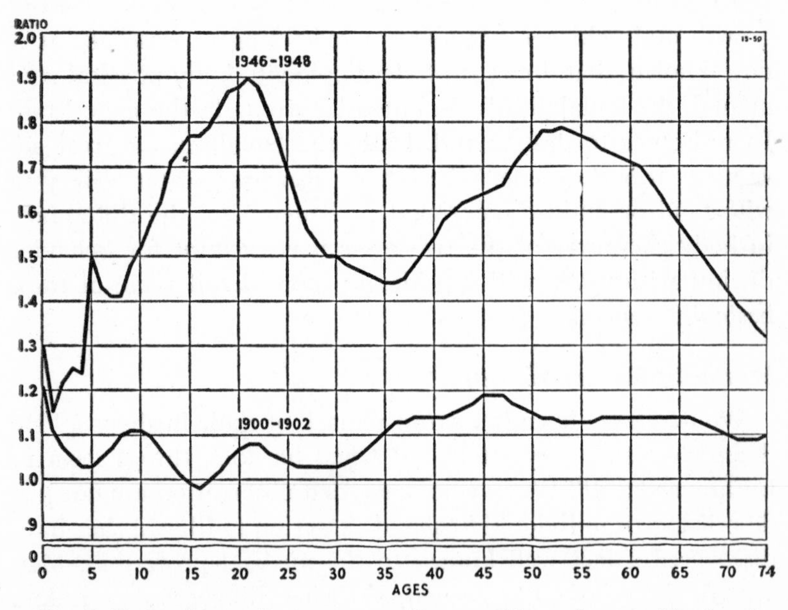

Fig. 3. Ratio of mortality rates at each age, white males to white females, United States 1900-02 and 1946-48. In reading the chart remember that line 1.0 represents female death rates, the other two lines are male rates for the two periods of time. Male death rates at all ages were higher *in proportion* to female rates in 1946-48 than in 1900-02. From Metropolitan Insurance Company, *Statistical Bulletin,* 31:9 (September, 1950), 8.

are in more serious danger when disease strikes than are girls.

In adulthood, more women than men have occasion to consult doctors. Many of the occasions arise from conditions resulting from the reproductive processes. It seems that women may have quite a few things wrong with them which necessitate medical attention, but may still be in fairly good health. With men the picture is different. They have fewer illnesses than women but they are susceptible to the more serious diseases, and, once ill, they are much more likely to succumb.

Figure 3 shows the ratio of male to female deaths at all ages. It is evident that females have benefited more than males from improved medical care during the past 50 years.

Various explanations have been advanced for the higher mortality rates of males. The fact is cited that their lives naturally expose them to greater dangers. But their higher mortality in the early months following conception as well as during the first twelve months after birth, and the fact that they fall victim to almost all the major diseases in greater numbers than females do, force the conclusion that males simply have been equipped by nature with less ability than females to resist or survive illness and infection. The difference in the mortality rates of men and women is reflected in the greater life expectancy for women. The life expectancy for a woman is more than five years greater than that for a man today. Her life expectancy is approaching 72 years, his 66 years. Should we say that males are the "weaker" sex?

Differences in muscular strength and coordination

Although females show from the beginning a natural ability to withstand illness, males from early infancy show development of a different type of strength. Those observers who have tested large numbers of infants and young children report that boys consistently show greater muscular strength than do girls during the pre-school years. Girls during this time have been developing a finer motor coordination. They are able to do things that require use of fingers, such as buttoning clothing, but boys can lift heavier articles and can throw and climb more easily.

It is sometimes believed that the difference in performance between the sexes, particularly the difference in their play activities, is all due to conditioning. That is, that the girl is given dolls and encouraged to dress them and play with them, whereas the boy is given blocks to build with, or trucks and wagons. The theory is that since boys are shamed if they wish to play with dolls they become conditioned to play in boyish ways. Certainly all human beings are in some degree conditioned by the culture in which they live. But it seems more logical to accept the fact that inherent biological differences account for some of the sex differences in performance. Since the boy's larger muscles are growing and developing strength at a greater rate than are the girl's, it is natural for him to feel the need for pushing, lifting, climbing, or entering into the type of play activity that makes use of his muscular strength. The girl's muscles are not so strong but they are more finely coordinated, hence she enjoys activities which make use of the finer coordination. In other words, she may like to string beads or dress and

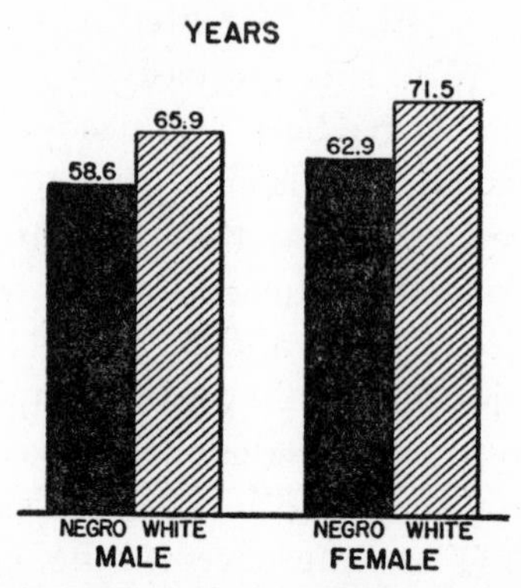

Fig. 4. Life expectancy for males and females, non-white and white, United States, 1949. Among both white and non-white, the weaker sex lives longer than the male. Data from Metropolitan Life Insurance Company, *Statistical Bulletin,* 32:11 (November, 1951), 4.

undress dolls. Those in charge of nursery schools report that little girls like to tie and untie their shoes and usually learn to lace their shoes considerably earlier than little boys do. While the girl works at lacing her shoes, her brother may be busy lining up the chairs and pushing them about in imitation of a train. It has been observed that in institutions where there are blind and deaf children who have no contact with a normal social environment sex differences in activities are even greater than with normal children.

Rate of growth

While the average little boy is developing muscular strength, his sister is growing at a faster rate. From infancy until middle adolescence girls on the average show a faster rate of physical growth, with accompanying differences in emotional and mental development. (See Figure 5.) At birth the average male is slightly taller than the average female. By age eleven, girls have caught up with boys in size, and at thirteen the average girl is almost an inch taller than the boys her age, and slightly heavier. She will continue to be taller until about the fifteenth year, when the boy will pass her in height. She will pass the boy in weight at about the twelfth year and continue to outweigh him until about the eighteenth year. The most marked difference in rate of development is evident during the years of early adolescence. Girls of twelve and thirteen are usually well into puberty, with their figures showing evidence of their developing physical maturity. They are also "boy conscious" at this age and are chagrined over the fact that most of the boys are not only smaller than they, but also are totally uninterested in girls as such. The average boy does not enter puberty until he is approximately fourteen. His most rapid growth will come between the years of fifteen and eighteen to twenty, and some boys continue growing as late as twenty-two or twenty-three.

Society recognizes the earlier physical maturity of the girl by setting the legal age for marriage at an earlier age for women than for men.

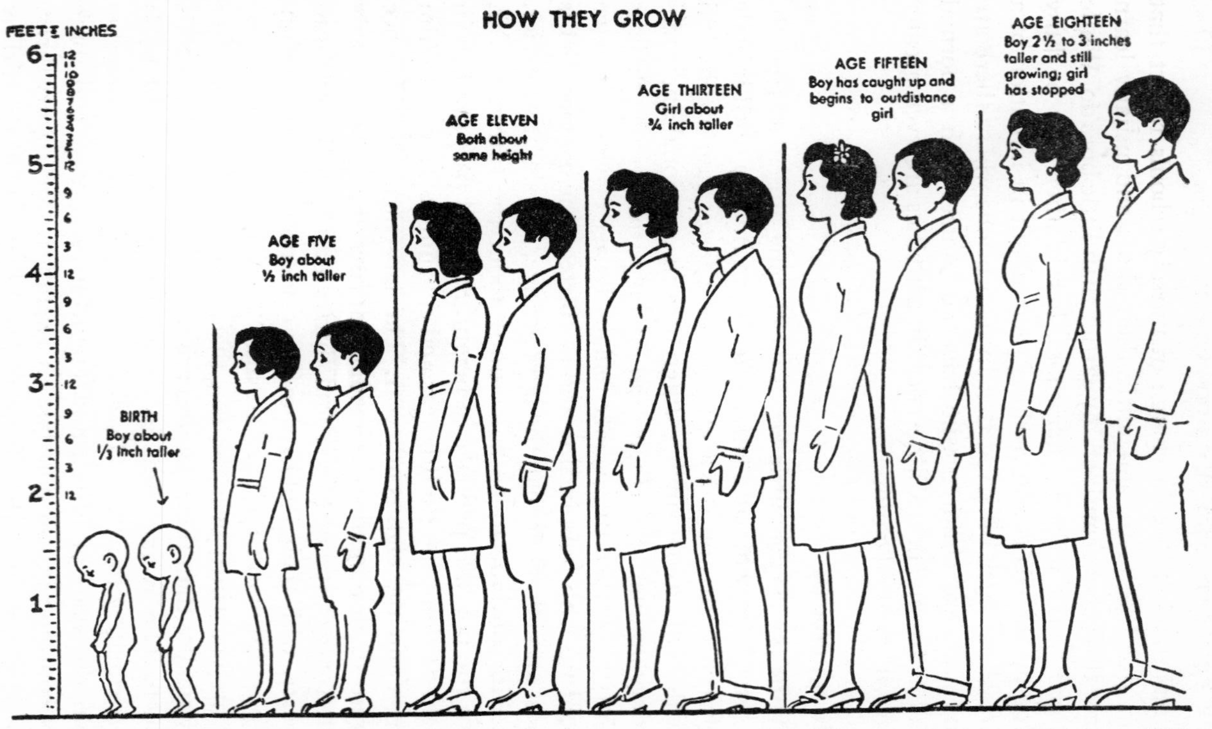

Fig. 5. *By permission,* Amram Scheinfeld, *Women and Men,* p. 54. New York: Harcourt, Brace and Company, 1943.

Psychological differences

Tradition has accorded mental superiority to the male. In our own generation a tendency still exists to give each sex a blanket rating of either superior or inferior. But what are to be used as standards for determining superiority or inferiority? There are sex differences in aptitudes which begin to show themselves in early childhood and which become more pronounced as individuals mature. Tests which attempt to measure intelligence bring out these differences. Boys consistently make better scores in the phases of the tests that have to do with mechanical ability, mathematical reasoning, comprehension of abstract meanings; girls do better in phases that test memory, those having to do with language skills, hand skills, and in phases with social connotations. College entrance examinations show the same differences. Boys excel in mathematics and the sciences, and girls excel in language ability as shown in word tests and in knowledge of foreign languages. Girls seem to reach their peak in mental development, as in physical, at an earlier age than boys.

A study of the results of mental tests emphasizes chiefly the fact that the sexes think differently. It would be a difficult if not impossible task to determine how much of the difference is due to capacity and how much is due to the cultural environment. Some of the most significant differences cannot be tested. It is difficult to test some of the forms of social intelligence in which women most strongly excel.

Observers who have worked closely with children are able to note differences and similarities that are not brought to light by the regulation mental tests. The Yale Clinic of Child Development has contributed much to knowledge of the characteristics of children at each age. Some varying characteristics are reported by Gesell and Ilg in their discussion of the child from five to ten.[2] They state that girls are more advanced and more

[2] See Arnold Gesell and Frances L. Ilg, *The Child from Five to Ten,* pp. 176-177. New York: Harper & Brothers, 1946.

generalized in some types of behavior. Boys are more intense and more channelized. Obsessive interest is more common in boys. Girls are more balanced and diversified in their play interests. At the age of six, girls are usually better in reading, writing, and drawing, whereas boys are better in number work and in listening to stories. Girls may advance more rapidly in the early grades. Girls (at eight) are more inquisitive and more demanding of facts about sex than boys—girls may think the subject through far enough to ask more specific questions than boys will ask. Boys are more apt to learn about sex from observing the mating of animals. However, they may be slow to transfer their accidental knowledge about animals to the human field. Gesell and Ilg state also that at ten years sex differences are pronounced. The psychology of a ten-year-old girl is significantly distinguishable from that of a ten-year-old boy of equivalent breeding and experience. The girl has more poise, more folk wisdom, and more interest in matters pertaining to marriage and the family. Comparing girls and boys as groups, girls tend to show a more precocious interest in sex than do boys. Their questions are more comprehensive, and less dependent upon the stimulus of information picked up from other children. The questions seem to come from a more integrated curiosity.[3]

The foregoing statements give a partial picture of some of the characteristics that emphasize differences between the sexes. The over-all picture does not indicate superiority or inferiority of either sex.

Rather, the evidence suggests the inadvisability of attempting to compare the characteristics of the sexes, or to measure their differing characteristics by identical standards.

Achievement differences

Another phase of the subject which cannot be overlooked is that in many types of achievement, the males seem to have the advantage. Although girls advance more rapidly than boys and

[3] *Ibid.*, p. 317.

maintain higher averages of scholastic achievement throughout many of the years of their schooling, during the years of late adolescence the boys catch up and forge ahead. The girls seem to reach a leveling-off period.

One of the best illustrations of this process is to be found in the study made by Terman of 1300 superior children. The careers of these gifted children, who were in the elementary grades at the time of the study in 1921-22, have been followed ever since. In this group it was found that the girls began to fall behind in relative achievement during adolescence. Three times as many boys continued their high level of achievement. The subsequent careers of these children have shown far greater achievement among the men in proportion to their numbers than among the women.

Similar results have been found by others studying achievement records of children.[4] A look at the names of those who have achieved greatness in almost all fields of endeavor throughout the past and in our own times shows the list to be made up largely of men. The great artists, musicians, and scientists of the past have been men.

Reasons for achievement differences

Many explanations have been offered for this relative monopoly in the field of achievement by men. The one most acceptable to the male ego is the traditional explanation that man is intellectually superior. But the explanation is not that simple. Terman says, "The woman who is a potential poet, novelist, lawyer, physician or scientist usually gives up any professional ambition she may have had and devotes herself to home, husband, and children. The exclusive devotion of women to domestic pursuits robs the arts and sciences of a large fraction of the genius that might otherwise be dedicated to them. Data strongly suggest that this loss must be debited to motivational causes

[4] According to studies made at Harvard under Dr. Psyche Cattell, and a study of musical talent by Amram Scheinfeld, girls show musical talent earlier, but develop it less later on.

and to limitations of opportunity rather than to lack of ability." [5] Others have attempted to explain the difference in terms of "drive." They believe that man's drive to achieve is related to his sex drive, and hence is not subject to the limitations placed upon woman by her sex. It must be recognized that although "drive" may be continuous in the male, the recurring changes in hormone balance and physical functioning that accompany menstruation and childbirth periodically lessen or eliminate "drive" in the female.

Undoubtedly the traditional concept itself of man as the superior being who must do great things in the world serves as a stimulus toward achievement for the male. Conversely, the traditional concept of the place of woman cannot but serve as an inhibiting influence upon achievement in the lives of a great many women. This influence may be the reason for the intellectual lag observed in girls during later adolescence. At this time girls become acutely aware of what is expected of them by the opposite sex. Perceptive girls recognize that intellectual superiority is not always an advantage to them; they sense that if they show mental ability beyond that of the male, they injure his masculine ego.

Some comments by college girls are illuminating in this connection.[6] One girl said, "When a girl asks me what marks I got last semester I answer, "Not so good, only one 'A.' " When a boys asks the same question, I say very brightly with a note of surprise, "Imagine, I got an 'A'!" Another said, "I was always fearful lest I say too much in class or answer questions which the boys I dated couldn't answer." And another, "My brother writes, 'Cover up that high forehead and act a little dumb once in a while.' "

Thus, in order to conform to the roles expected by the group, the boy will do his best to excel, whereas the girl will not have

[5] Lewis M. Terman, "Psychological Approach to the Biography of Genius," *Science*, Vol. 92 (Oct. 4, 1940), 293-301.

[6] Mirra Komarovsky, "Cultural Contradictions and Sex Roles," *American Journal of Sociology*, 52:3 (November, 1946), 184-189.

such a strong impetus to excellence, except within certain well-defined feminine areas.

The double standard and biological factors

A careful look at some of the differences between the sexes will raise the question of whether it is possible to elminate entirely the so-called double standard. Girls sometimes resent the fact that their brothers are so much freer to come and go at will, to be on the street later at night, and, in general, to act with less restriction. It is true that the male has greater freedom of action. The biological results of sexual freedom will not affect his life to the same extent that they will affect the life of the female. Then too, the unprotected female is simply not as safe as the male. She has less physical strength with which to protect herself.

Another factor is that, although modern social institutions have taken over some of the functions formerly performed by mothers, the child still is more closely associated with the mother than with the father. The mother's physical connection with the child before birth and his dependence upon her in the early months of his life are arrangements made by nature. These arrangements do limit the mother's freedom more than they limit the father's. It seems logical that with the greater freedom of the father should go a greater responsibility for the support and protection of his wife and children.

The problem of the proponents of sex equality is to distinguish between laws which are purely discriminatory and those which have a basis in nature. The changing status of women has already placed upon them many added responsibilities which may or may not have been balanced by the removal of certain restrictions. In some states women are now equally responsible with men for the support of the children. In others they are subject to the same alimony requirements that men are subject to, in case of divorce. Clearly, confusion exists in the thinking of those who attempt to legislate concerning equality between the sexes.

A better understanding is needed of the biological as well as the social facts about sex differences. It is even more necessary, if individual marriages are to be successful, that men and women approaching marriage discard outmoded ideas about the superiority or inferiority of either sex and understand not only the physical differences that exist, but also the cultural changes that are affecting man-woman relationships. The next chapter will explore further some cultural trends in sex roles, and their effect upon marriage success.

Chapter III

CHANGING SEX ROLES

A MULTITUDE OF WORDS has been written in the last decade about the problems of modern women, their "conflicts," "confusion," and "frustrations." All sorts of solutions have been offered, ranging from suggestions that colleges and universities stop educating women to compete in the same fields with men, to suggested plans for providing nursery schools or mother's helpers so that no woman need be tied to her home any more than her husband is.

Since young people approaching marriage today often are not aware that the roles of husbands and wives are in a stage of transition, it is important that some aspects of the subject of changing roles be presented early in this book. Attitudes and views concerning roles will have many implications for wise mate selection and will have much to do with how two people adjust in marriage. Today many young couples find after they are married that they are far apart in their views concerning what role each may expect of the other in marriage.

Fixed roles of husband and wives in the past

Conflict over who plays what role in the family is relatively new. In the past, roles were fixed; each partner knew what was expected. The girl grew up knowing that if she married she would play the role of wife-and-mother. She knew she was to spend her time doing household tasks, caring for a family, making clothes, preserving food, helping to grow the food, and in being a helpmate for her husband in whatever he did. She did not need formal education, or need to keep up in the realm of politics, economics, or world affairs; that was a man's world. This was an "honored role" for women of the past.

Men also had definite roles to play. The man was head of the family and was looked upon as the provider. It was not his place to care for the children or to do household tasks. He ran the farm or made the living by doing work outside the home. Any work connected with the home was feminine. The man was supposed to know the ways of the world and to have superior knowledge in financial matters. If anyone in the family had a formal education, it was the husband. A good wife was supposed to recognize and respect her husband's place as head of the family. Both received ego satisfaction in fulfilling these expected roles. Husbands honored wives who were diligent, thrifty, and devoted to their families, especially those wives who were adept at making the husband feel the importance and superiority of his role as head of the family.

The roles of husband and wife in transition

For some years, the roles of men and women have been shifting and changing so that today lines are not so clearly drawn. Roles are no longer so well defined. With the establishment of the democratic educational system over 100 years ago, both sexes started going to school. Gradually the educational system has absorbed more and more women, so that today a high-school education for all is obligatory and a college education is considered desirable for girls as well as for boys. Meanwhile, the educational system has not changed; it continues to have the same emphasis as in the days when only men were educated. All who go to college are offered training that will help them to rise socially and economically in the business and professional world. Standards of achievement have begun to approach similarity for both women and men. A woman's success is no longer dependent solely upon her feminine achievements as wife-and-mother. She can also rise in the same way that the man achieves status. The emphasis in education has often been upon getting ahead economically, not upon getting an education in order to live a better life.

Thus the "successful" woman may need to compete with men in the business or professional world.

At the same time that women have been educated to com-

Fig. 6. "Sure, I'm in favor of women having equal rights; but you'll never get them back to that!" Reproduced courtesy of *Ladies' Home Journal* © C.P. Co.

pete in a man's world, other changes have affected the nature of the work to be done in the home. The birth rate has fallen, so there are fewer children to care for. Many services once performed in the home by the wife are now done outside the home. Sewing, canning, baking, cleaning, washing, and pressing are often not considered a part of the work of the housewife. Labor-saving devices shorten the time required for the work that still is done in the home.

Youth and the changing roles

The average person sees evidence of the changes that have taken place, but he may still cling to inherited traditional attitudes about man's place and woman's place in life. Boys know that they have had to compete with girls for grades all the way through their school years, yet many of them, without giving serious thought to the matter, confidently believe that when they marry the role situation of a generation ago will exist in their home. Girls also, when they look ahead to marriage in the future, are likely to think that they will be perfectly content when they get the man, the little home, and the children to care for.

Purdue University, through its polling of young people in all sections of the country, has found that 63 per cent of the boys and 46 per cent of the girls say that homemaking and family raising is the best career for girls.[1] Twenty per cent of the boys and 36 per cent of the girls thought a combination of homemaking and a career would be best. The study shows that boys are more traditional than girls, but that both express conservative attitudes. It is difficult for people to look ahead and know what their true feelings will be when they became involved in a situation that is still only hypothetical. After marriage many girls are satisfied playing the wife-and-mother role for a time, but sooner or later they may become dissatisfied and feel that they must "do something" outside the home. To be other than a wife-and-mother becomes a psychological necessity.

Wife-and-mother role not sufficiently respected by society. How often have you heard the woman being interviewed on the radio who responds to the question, "And what do you do?" with, "Oh, I'm just a housewife." The tone indicates that she feels that she must apologize for wasting her time. She may be working full time taking good care of her family, as homemaker, chauffeur for husband and children, den mother for the cub scouts, P.T.A. program chairman, and general flunky for the

[1] *The Purdue Opinion Poll for Young People,* 7:3 (April, 1948), 21.

family. But she feels that according to the standards by which she was educated and by which society judges her she is not really "doing" anything.

A mass of evidence could be assembled to show that the role of housewife is as important and basic to family existence as it has ever been, and that for every back-breaking task that has been eliminated by a modern invention, some new tension-producing or energy-absorbing responsibility has been added. And it might be pointed out that the true measure of a successful homemaker, now as in the past, is not so much in her efficiency as a houseworker, as in her ability to promote harmony and happy family relationships, and a sense of well-being in each family member.

But to insist that homemaking is still of essential importance and should not be undervalued does not get at the problem; it merely explains one kind of pressure to which modern women react either consciously or unconsciously.

Wife-and-mother role not respected by the husband. Although many men think they want the wife to play a traditional role, they actually do not have a high regard for that role. They place a higher value upon work in a competitive world than they do upon homemaking. Their attitude is a logical result of the social changes in our culture. With the urbanization of our population, many of the values that were formerly attached to homemaking no longer seem to have validity. In a predominantly rural society the wife's work contribution was certainly valued as highly as was the husband's. The gardening, cooking, sewing, home nursing, canning and preserving of farm products, and many other tasks that were the wife's responsibility were respected as basic to the existence of the family. But with economic changes in America, that is no longer true. It has become the custom to think of the work that provides the income as the only work that is really basic to family survival. One woman explained her feelings this way, "My husband just thought of me as 'the little woman.' He didn't seem to think anything I did was of any real importance until I went out and got a job. No matter how much I accomplished at home, he seemed to think my days were just a breeze. He wanted me to stay at home and be a housewife, but he certainly puts more value on what I'm doing now." This un-

Fig. 7. Modern woman as housewife and worker. In 1951, 19,000,000 women were working outside the home. Currently, about one-third of the total labor force is composed of women, and almost one-half of these are married. Chart adapted from *A Chart Book, Children and Youth at the Midcentury.* Washington, D.C.: Midcentury White House Conference on Children and Youth, 1950.

dervaluing of the housewife's role puts strains upon husband-wife understanding, especially because basic differences in viewpoint or inconsistencies in attitudes are not clearly defined in the mind of either husband or wife.

Changing roles and courtship

In our highly mobile population two young people who date and marry may come from two families whose attitudes and experience concerning roles will be at opposite poles. A boy from a traditionally patriarchal family, of which there are still a great many, and a girl from an extremely equalitarian family, or one that is mother-dominated, may have a hard time reaching a satisfactory understanding in their expectations of each other in marriage. Each tends to accept as "right" whatever situation he has grown up with. Many people, in the years before they marry, view the matter as one that can be rather easily settled by a simple decision about whether or not married women should work outside the home. Whether or not a wife will have an outside job is not the basic problem. The important consideration is whether or not the husband and wife agree or can harmonize their feelings about roles. A girl who has a strong drive toward achievement and a desire for personal recognition, and a boy whose ego needs are such that he must be the dominant-superior one in the family, would be likely to be an unhappy match, whether or not the wife ever held a job outside the home. But a couple who are cooperative and who can accord to one another recognition and respect for ability or achievement in whatever line it may be, would have a good chance of happiness regardless of whether the wife held an outside job or devoted herself to homemaking.

During courtship and dating years, couples need to try to understand each other's true attitudes, recognizing that true attitudes toward others are not necessarily the same as the opinions one may express when discussing man-woman relationships.

Some girls believe that the problem of man-woman roles can be taken care of if a girl is adept at playing up to masculine egos. Such a girl is quoted in Komarovsky's study of cultural contradictions and sex roles.[2] This girl explains that she transferred to a woman's college from a state university because she was a good student and in the coeducational university a girl's social life was hurt if she became known as a "brain." This girl says, "Now I am engaged to a southern boy who doesn't think too much of woman's intellect. . . . I play up to his theories because the less one knows and does the more he does for you and thinks you 'cute' into the bargain. . . . I allow him . . . to treat me as a child in financial matters. I let my fiancé make most of the decisions when we are out. It annoys me but he prefers it."

The problem may seem to be solved for this couple at the moment. The man is happy in his feeling of superiority and the girl is fairly content to let him enjoy his false security, since she is in love with him and intends to marry him. But what will the situation be after they have been married a few years? Will

[2] Mirra Komarovsky, "Cultural Contradictions and Sex Roles," *The American Journal of Sociology*, 52:3 (November, 1946), 184-189.

the "annoyance" the girl now feels later be an outright unwillingness or inability to play a role of assumed inferiority? How long will she be content to "play dumb" so that her husband will think her cute? And when the inevitable happens and she begins to be her natural self and act according to her natural abilities, what will happen to her husband's ego?

In other generations such a husband would have less difficulty than now, for he could fall back upon his traditionally accepted male prerogatives. His wife would be forced by social pressure to continue to use whatever abilities she had in ways that were accepted as exclusively and typically feminine. But today men are forced to do far more adjusting than was formerly necessary. We are in a process of shifting and rearranging our concepts concerning the roles of *both men and women.* The problem is not solely a problem of women or a question of "problem women." Men and women both are often confused and frustrated because the circumstances of their lives do not seem to fit with their concepts of what role they had thought they would play after marriage. It is impossible for a major social change to affect only one sex and not the other. Many men struggle to live according to the role expectations they had for themselves and to force their wives to fit a preconceived mold. The tendency to view the situation as a problem only of women clouds the issues and contributes to misunderstandings and conflicts in many marriages.

Changing roles and marriage adjustment

Clifford Kirkpatrick has developed some sound theories on conflicts that arise from inconsistencies in the attitudes of both men and women concerning roles. His views are pertinent here. He recognizes that cultural change has opened a wide range of roles to women other than the traditionally accepted wife-and-mother role, and that men are confronted with the necessity for adjusting to life in a role far more complicated or different from the traditional role as dominant family-head. Kirkpatrick's hypothesis is that in this situation both sexes are inconsistent:

women tend to want to have the privileges and rewards of several major roles, such as wife and mother, companion, and partner, while accepting the obligations of only one; and men are inclined to want their wives to accept the responsibilities of several roles while they are willing to accord them the privileges and rewards of only one or two. Kirkpatrick points out that unfairness results in cases where wives claim and get the privileges of more than one role without accepting the corresponding obligations, or where they accept the obligations of several roles without receiving corresponding privileges.[3] Some wives expect to be treated as if they were the mothers of a half dozen well brought up children in a well-kept home, although they have no children and actually contribute little to the comfort, well-being, or economic success of their husbands. Other wives may rear children, carry the full load of homemaking and, in addition, earn almost as much as the husband does, without receiving any special recognition from their husbands for their contribution. Kirkpatrick says, "Naturally it is easy for husbands and wives to regard the distribution of obligations and privileges from different points of view."

Jacobson found in a study of 100 divorced and 100 married couples that divorced couples show a greater disparity in their attitudes toward the roles of the husband and wife in marriage than do married couples. He found also that both divorced and married men tend to favor the male dominant or traditional role, while women, especially divorced women, approached the extreme in approving equality in roles.[4]

People naturally see situations in the light of their own personal desires, and in marriage it is easy to be concerned with only our own needs and expectations without being able to see

[3] For a report of Kirkpatrick's research, see: Clifford Kirkpatrick, "Inconsistencies in Marriage Roles and Marriage Conflict." Reprinted in Judson T. Landis and Mary G. Landis, *Readings in Marriage and the Family,* 386-392. New York: Prentice-Hall, Inc., 1952.

[4] Alver Hilding Jacobson, "Conflict of Attitudes Toward the Roles of the Husband and Wife in Marriage," *American Sociological Review,* 17:2 (April, 1952), 146-150.

the other side of the question. If we can recognize at the outset that we are likely to be inconsistent in what we require of our mates and what we are willing to concede in return, marriage will have a better chance of success.

The attitudes that people hold concerning their roles in life and their expectations for themselves and from those they marry will certainly affect the happiness and success of their marriage. Flexibility in attitudes is a most important factor. The feeling that many women have after a few years of marriage that their work as housewife is undervalued as compared with other types of work, and their observation of other women who seem to be respected as wives and also as workers in a man's world, may begin to exert a pressure toward dissatisfaction. Points that both husband and wife thought were settled before marriage will have to be reconsidered. Every individual, whether man or woman, in order to remain mentally and emotionally healthy, must feel that he or she is of worth, that the way he is expending his emotional and physical energy is of value and importance to others as well as to himself.

Transition in roles and ego satisfactions

If a wife feels undervalued, or if she is dissatisfied with the role that her marriage seems to require of her, she may retaliate by subtly undermining her husband's self-esteem and his satisfaction with his own role. Even though her retaliation is without rational intention, it may still be effective in undermining her husband's self-confidence or puncturing his ego. The result may be mounting conflict in various areas of the marriage, with neither partner able to diagnose the trouble.

Of course a husband may consciously or unconsciously undermine his wife's ego because he does not value highly her work as a housewife. But it can work the other way too. The husband's self-esteem may be threatened by many situations. Some men will develop feelings of inadequacy and suffer ego damage if: (a) the wife makes more money; (b) the husband feels his wife is more intelligent; (c) the wife has to get a job to support or help support the family; (d) the wife has greater capacity for sexual enjoyment; (e) the wife has more education; (f) the wife plays the partner role but is superior to her husband; (g) the husband expects the wife to get her ego satisfaction and status through living in his shadow, but she feels that she must achieve these satisfactions independently of him.

In a period of changing roles when there are no longer any fixed and well-defined ways through which the sexes can meet each other's ego needs, it becomes increasingly important for husbands and wives to be aware of the necessity for understanding this phase of their relationship. Couples contemplating marriage need to give thought to how well they understand each other and to what is tolerable or intolerable to each. A competitive attitude toward each other during courtship may be an indication of conflict in role expectation. The young woman who has a strong drive to achieve on her own should consider whether her prospective husband is one who could accept her achievement or one who would consider her achievements a threat to his own self-esteem.

Objectivity is needed on the part of both men and women in interpreting the contribution that each can make in any individual marriage. Women will always need a few special privileges because of the requirements that nature has placed upon them. And men can no longer withdraw to the safety of their traditional role in their relationships with women. Young people going into marriage will have a better chance for happiness if they can discard prejudices and simply realize that the sexes are different, that they have different potentialities and needs, but that neither is born to dominate or be dominated, neither is inherently superior or inferior, and that no set boundaries delineate what is man's place or man's work and what is woman's place or woman's work. The two sexes are mutually dependent; successful relationships depend on cooperation, not on dominance or subservience.

Chapter IV

WHY PEOPLE MARRY OR DO NOT MARRY

IN OUR SOCIETY, marriage is not as inevitable for an individual as death, but it runs a close second. In 1951, 93 per cent of the women and 92 per cent of the men at ages of 45 and over in the United States were married or had been married. The percentage of women who marry is higher in the United States than in any other country in the Western world.

American young people marry at an earlier age than do the young people in other Western countries. Over 32 per cent of the young women in the United States and 7 per cent of the

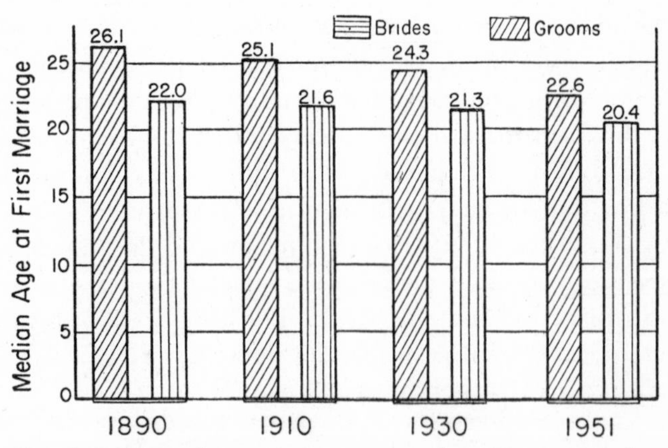

Fig. 8. Brides and grooms are younger than they used to be.

young men have married before the age of 20.[1] The median age at marriage in the United States has been decreasing for the last 60 years. In 1890 the median age at first marriage for males was 26.1; in 1951 it was 22.6. The median age at first marriage for females was 22.0 in 1890 and 20.4 in 1951. As much decrease in age at marriage took place between 1940 and 1951 as had taken place in the previous 50 years.

The percentage of people who marry has been steadily increasing. In 1890, 55.3 per cent of the population 14 years old and over was married; this figure had increased to 68 per cent in 1952.[2] In the period from 1940 to 1952 the number of families increased by almost one-fourth, from 32,000,000 to over 40,000,000, and the number of single people decreased to the lowest in our history.

Part of the increase in the percentage of the population married is explained by the aging of the population. Today a larger proportion of the population is of marriageable age than was the case in 1890. Earlier in our history, a larger proportion of the population was made up of children under marriageable age. Another factor in the higher marriage rate is growing prosperity. Marriage rates tend to vary directly with economic depression and prosperity. In times of depression, young people may wish to marry but the difficulty of earning an adequate income may force postponement of marriages. Part of the increased marriage rate may also be due to the more widespread knowledge of and acceptance of contraception. Many young people are ready to marry before they are ready for parenthood, and with the prevalence of contraception they may now feel that they can marry but postpone parenthood until they are economically able to support children. The uncertainty over the future which has characterized recent years may also have caused many young people to marry earlier than they would have if

[1] Bureau of the Census, Current Population Reports, Population Characteristics, Series P-20, No. 38, April, 1952.

[2] Bureau of the Census, Current Population Reports, Population Characteristics, Series P-20, No. 41, October, 1952.

there had been no war or threat of war. Moreover, girls may now look more favorably upon early marriage because they feel there may be a scarcity of husbands later on, and boys are willing to marry in an attempt to win some security in a world that offers little security in the future.

More marriages are taking place

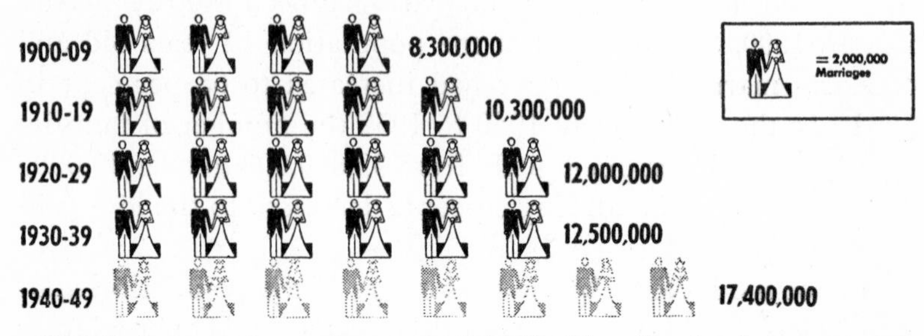

Fig. 9. Increase in marriage rate, 1900-49. War, threats of war, economic prosperity, the uncertain future, all contributed to a high marriage rate during the decade of the 'forties. From *A Chart Book, Children and Youth at the Mid-century,* Washington, D.C.: Midcentury White House Conference on Children and Youth, 1950.

One basic reason why people marry is to satisfy their need for affectional response. However, some people marry for social position, for economic status, or because society is organized for married people and social pressure is exerted toward marriage. A more complete analysis of why some people marry and others do not follows.

An analysis of affectional needs

People have certain affectional needs that require satisfaction from birth throughout life. The greater part of the desire for affection is satisfied within the framework of marriage and the family. Babies respond to caressing, fondling, and being held close in the mother's arms. The fulfilling of this need for intimate response on the part of the baby is vital to the normal physical and mental development of the child. Studies show that children are sometimes retarded because of failure to have affectional needs satisfied through normal family relationships. Children in institutions, when placed in the care of older girls who took time to "mother" them, developed more rapidly than those who did not receive mothering. As the baby matures, it learns to bestow as well as to receive affection, and its love nature expands to include others as well as itself.

Fig. 10. "I shut my eyes during the kissing scene and make believe he's choking her." By permission, Ray Helle and *The Saturday Evening Post.*

The love object of the child changes as he matures. At first the mother is the chief love object, then other members of the family are included in the affectional pattern. In the preadolescent years, boys and girls have reached a preheterosexual stage in their affectional desires. Boys want to be with boys in the gang or the play group and wish to have nothing to do with girls. Girls wish to be with girls and are not interested in boys.

Fig. 11. *By permission,* Amram Scheinfeld, *Women and Men,* p. 133. New York: Harcourt, Brace and Company, 1943.

With the biological maturity that comes at puberty, a new development begins in the affectional needs of the individual. The desire arises for a mature type of affectional response. The young person's attention now begins to turn to members of the opposite sex outside the immediate family. Normally, interests and activities begin to be centered around boy-girl relationships.

During the teen-age period, then, the young person normally goes through a period of growing away from a family group which for years has satisfied his emotional needs. The family group no longer meets all basic needs and the drive for intimate response forces young people along the road to matrimory. In marriage their basic sex urges are satisfied. Normally, they decide later on that their lives are still not complete and they begin to desire children. Thus the cycle goes on as a new family is started and the "affectional stream" continues its course in the babies of the new family.

After the children leave home, the parents must again secure affectional satisfaction through each other more exclusively than while the children were at home. In most cases they are not entirely cut off from their children after the children leave home, and a measure of affectional fulfillment continues. In-law friction sometimes develops after the children marry because the parents continue to seek affection and attention from their children, or because children continue to look to the parents with more dependence than their mates will tolerate. (A discussion of in-law relationships will be found in Chapter XIV.)

Why people marry

A number of different interacting factors and conditions impel people to marry. We shall discuss some of the considerations that are effective as a basis for decisions to marry.

Marriage for love. The accepted belief is that people marry because they are in love. Folsom gives an extensive discussion of love feelings and their objects in his text.[3] The interested

[3] Joseph Kirk Folsom, *The Family and Democratic Society,* pp. 365-409. New York: John Wiley & Sons, Inc., 1943.

student may wish to read that discussion. For our purpose, a general definition of the type of love that usually leads to marriage and a discussion of some phases of misplaced emphasis on love will be sufficient. The love which we shall be discussing in the next few chapters involves mutual attraction and feelings of tenderness and affection between two individuals of opposite sex. It differs from love of parents, siblings, or friends in the following three characteristics: it includes an acknowledged sex element; society is interested in the love behavior; a permanent union through marriage may result.

Much controversy exists over how love comes into one's life. Some people believe it is something that strikes suddenly: two people see each other and experience an instantaneous revelation that they are meant for each other. Such love at first sight is highly advertised in romantic literature. It is true that sometimes two people will feel a strong mutual attraction at their first meeting. However, the love relationship results only after a period of association; it requires time to mature and develop.

Love at first sight. Most young people have some idea of the type of person they would like to marry. If by chance two people meet whose ideal types are complementary, and mutual interest is aroused, they may consider this interest love at first sight, especially if the powerful element of physical attraction is involved.

Occasionally, happily married couples declare that their love experience was one in which both fell desperately in love at sight. What actually happened in such cases was that the couple experienced strong mutual attraction at first sight, and upon getting acquainted found that they had many things in common, such as similar beliefs, attitudes, social standards, and tastes. These common interests made it possible for them to continue an association which grew into love and a happy marriage. Some of these couples do not know at what point in their association they passed the phase of purely sexual attraction and progressed into a relationship enriched by other elements necessary to love.

The cases of "love at first sight" that do not end in happy marriage are probably far more numerous than those that do. They receive less attention, however, for when the affair turns out to be a passing thing those involved forget that it was "love at first sight" and relegate it to its place with other short-lived infatuations. In other words, the emotional response was not love; the elements necessary for the growth of love were not present.

Most of us will recall times when we were strongly attracted to a member of the opposite sex, but upon acquaintance we

Fig. 12. "Pardon me, sir—I resent your statement that all other loves pale into insignificance beside yours." *By permission,* Salo Roth and *The Saturday Evening Post.*

found that the individual was undesirable in many respects. We often see people who are physically attractive but who have personalities, mannerisms, or attitudes which become intolerable upon longer acquaintance.

When 735 college students were asked whether they believed in "falling in love at first sight," 34 per cent of the men and 50 per cent of the women said they did not; but 39 per cent of the men and 34 per cent of the women said they did. The rest were undecided.[4] The fact that over half of a group of present-day college students say either that they believe in love at first sight or that they are undecided in their conception of love indicates that romantic literature, movies, and "folk tales" continue to have a strong influence on thinking about love. Waller states that instead of idealizing and treating it in a tender way, we should look upon "love at first sight" as pathological and symbolic of disorders of the love life.[5] The sudden falling in love while on the rebound from a broken love affair with someone else is typical of such emotional disorder.

Love which leads to happy marriage may begin with a physical attraction that impels a couple to seek association with each other. That is only the starting point. Necessary to the development of love is the discovery of mutual interests, enjoyment of each other's company, a certain measure of agreement on life goals and values, and the absence of personality traits that cause irritation or quarrels between the two. When all the necessary elements are present, the couple usually finds that they are "in love," and logically they begin to consider marriage.

Other factors also contribute to the decision to marry. The contributing factors are so interrelated that it would hardly be possible to say of any marriage, "For this one reason they married." Most people either are, or believe themselves to be, in love when they marry. One or both may be aware of other motives entering into the decision, but they would usually find it difficult to assign exact ratings of relative importance to the different reasons prompting them to marry.

Social status. In many marriages the chief motivating force for the woman is her desire to rise socially. Marriage is one of the chief means available to women who wish to rise socially in our society. Some men improve their social standing through marriage, but there are other ways in which men can rise in the social world, such as achievement in a profession, in the army,

[4] Unpublished study by Judson Landis.

[5] Willard Waller, *The Family* (revised by Reuben Hill), p. 200. New York: The Dryden Press, 1951.

in the business world, or through education. Since a wife is usually accorded the social position of her husband, marriage is a simple and effective way for her to achieve a desired social position. Without disparaging love, women are inclined to be more realistic than men in taking cognizance of the advantages or disadvantages involved in a marriage.

"—'and for richer'—I like that!"

Fig. 13. *By permission,* George Wolfe and *Collier's.*

Economic status. Romantic literature offers the love stories in which the poor girl falls in love with the wealthy prince, but the stories never hint that she marries the prince for his money. Romantically, they marry because they are in love; money is incidental. In real life, when poverty marries wealth the economic considerations cannot but enter in. In some marriages the desire of one partner for the economic standing of the other is an important factor. Our society places great emphasis upon economic wealth, and the one who is successful in marrying wealth is often accorded respect for having made a "good marriage." If parents condition their children to value money and material possessions more than the affectional satisfactions of marriage, the children will judge prospective mates by their material possessions rather than by the qualities which would make for happiness in marriage.

Of course, some individuals will make economic considerations the deciding factors in choosing a mate, whereas others, though conscious of economic advantages or disadvantages, may be swayed by other motives and may still marry in spite of the doubtful economic future indicated. Still others may be quite unconscious of financial considerations.

Social expectancy. A strong force compelling many people to marry is social expectancy. Our society has been set up and organized on the assumption that people will marry and establish families. It is recognized as the normal thing to do. Society looks askance at those who do not marry. In Puritan New England the unmarried were required either to live with their families or with some respectable family who could vouch for their behavior. Additional taxes have been used in modern times to force people into marriage. The more important factor is, without doubt, the thinking of the group about those who do not marry. It is assumed that all women would like to marry and that if they do not it is because they have not had the opportunity. When a woman fails to marry, her acquaintances explain it in different ways: she is too aggressive in trying to get a man; she is too efficient; she drives men away; or she doesn't attract men. An awareness of the attitudes directed toward the spinster forces into marriage many women who would not marry if the position of the single woman were comparable to that of the married woman. Many marry in self-defense, to demonstrate their normality, and not because of intense love feelings.

One unattractive girl, doomed to spinsterhood in her own community, went to the city and there met a man whom she married. Soon after the marriage her husband was arrested; she discovered that he had a criminal record. She had also contracted a venereal disease from him. She secured a divorce and returned to her home community. When a friend began to commiserate with her over her unfortunate marriage, she replied, "Oh, no. I proved that I could get married. It is much more comfortable to be a divorcee than to be a spinster. I'll never be called an old maid now." This is an extreme case, but it illustrates the force of social pressure as an impellent toward marriage.

The bachelor fares better than the spinster, for it is assumed that the man has a choice in the matter and that if he stays single it may be because he prefers the single state. His friends may ridicule him and call him a "poor old bachelor," but he can parry their gibes with references to the lost freedom of his married friends. Nevertheless, the bachelor still is subject to the pressure toward marriage because he recognizes that all who know him are seeking explanations for his bachelorhood. His friends may explain it in any of several ways: he is a mama's boy; he is afraid of the girls; he is too selfish to marry; he fancies himself as too charming to settle down with any one girl; he is afraid he cannot support a family; or he is just not attractive to women. There is no doubt that the influence of the 92 per cent of the males who do marry is powerful in exerting pressure upon the bachelor.

Loneliness. After people have left home and are "on their own," many are inclined to consider marriage more seriously because they feel alone in the world. Their friends are married and they are conscious of their lack of any permanent ties. One wife who had been married for 25 years summed up her experience in this way, "I did not marry for love or for money. The man loved me and had many of the expected qualifications. We belonged to the same church and our families approved and encouraged the match. I not only did not love him, but in a physical sense he was unattractive to me. Yet being lonely, and with no close friends, I decided it might be a good thing to help establish the home which both of us seemed to want."

This particular marriage was not a happy one. The decision

to marry because of a conscious need for companionship should also include some willingness to work to make the marriage successful. This woman seemed to lack that willingness.

Marriage as an escape. Girls who come from homes in which they find living unpleasant may use marriage as an escape. If they feel that they have to work too hard or that the parents treat them as children, or if there is constant conflict with the parents, marriage may seem to be the only release from an unpleasant environment. Other girls who are working outside the home supporting themselves may find their work monotonous and so look to marriage as an escape. Girls who have been trained for a career may find that the career is less stimulating and involves more drudgery than they had anticipated. For these people marriage may seem attractive as a way of gaining economic support.

Many who go into marriage as an escape from some other situation become disillusioned when they find that marriage also requires work and self-discipline. If their dissatisfaction with the former environment was due to faults within themselves, they will not be any better satisfied with marriage. It is possible, however, even for the girl who marries as an escape to make a fortunate choice of a mate and to value what she finds in marriage sufficiently so that she will work to make a success of it.

Personality needs and marriage. Marriage serves to satisfy certain personality needs which individuals find difficult to satisfy outside marriage. Strauss asked 173 men and 200 women who were engaged or who had been married less than a year to list the personality needs which they hoped to have satisfied in the marriage.[6] (See Table 1 for summary.) It will be noticed that the things that men and women desire from marriage do not differ greatly. A greater percentage of the women expressed felt personality needs. This may indicate that while both sexes have the same needs, women are more conscious of their needs than men are.

[6] Ernest W. Burgess and Harvey J. Locke, *The Family,* p. 420. New York: American Book Company, 1945.

The happy marriages are those in which both husband and wife find fulfillment of a majority of these needs. In many marriages both partners either consciously or unconsciously seek to give to each other the love, understanding, and moral support that enable the spouse to feel that he counts for something. In many marriages enough of these needs are met so that both partners are fairly well satisfied with the bargain, and the

TABLE 1

PERCENTAGES OF 373 MEN AND WOMEN STATING VARIOUS PERSONALITY NEEDS WHICH THEY HOPED TO HAVE SATISFIED THROUGH MARRIAGE

Personality Need	Men	Women
Someone to love me	36.4%	53.5%
Someone to confide in	30.6	40.0
Someone to show affection	20.8	30.0
Someone to respect my ideals	26.0	26.0
Someone to appreciate what I wish to achieve	28.3	24.0
Someone to understand my moods	23.1	27.5
Someone to help make my decisions	15.0	32.5
Someone to stimulate my ambition	26.6	21.0
Someone to look up to	16.2	29.0
Someone to give me self-confidence	19.6	24.0
Someone to back me in difficulty	16.2	25.5
Someone to appreciate me just as I am	20.2	20.5
Someone to admire my ability	18.5	19.5
Someone to make me feel important	20.8	17.0
Someone to relieve my loneliness	18.5	18.5

marriage may be called successful. In other marriages one or the other may seem to take pleasure in puncturing the self-esteem of the spouse, or may be entirely unconscious of the personality needs of the mate and make no effort to contribute to their satisfaction. The consciousness of these needs, nevertheless, impels people toward marriage.

Those who do not marry

Among the reasons why some people do not marry are (1) failure to meet eligible prospects, (2) failure to interest the opposite sex, (3) failure to achieve emotional independence,

(4) failure to take advantage of opportunities, and (5) physical or psychological defects.

Failure to meet eligible prospects. Many people find it difficult to meet eligible prospects in the marriage market because of the unequal number of men and women of marriageable age, the unequal distribution of the sexes in different parts of the country, and the problems involved in meeting eligible people in the modern city environment.

The sex ratio. The daily press often refers to the prospect that many women may have to go without husbands because of the altering sex ratio. In one city it was reported that a group of women were organizing to bring pressure upon army authorities to prevent military personnel from marrying foreign wives, believing that war brides brought here mean fewer chances for American girls to marry.

Just how serious a problem does the present sex ratio create for those who wish to marry? In Chapter II, we noted that 105.5 boys are born for each 100 girls and that the death rate for men at each age is higher than for women. It has been estimated that by middle age the sexes are equalized in number because the surplus of males has died by that time. In a stationary population there would be enough members of each sex so that most could marry. The United States had a surplus of men in the past because of the migration of men from other countries. In 1910 the sex ratio for our country was 106 men to 100 women, but in 1951 the sex ratio was 98.6 men to 100 women. Although there are now 1,500,000 more women than men in the United States, most of the surplus women are in the older age groups and are not a threat to young women who wish to marry. It is becoming increasingly difficult for older women to marry because the longer average life of women means a surplus of widows, and of single and divorced women in the older age groups. Women past 45 years who might wish to marry outnumber unmarried men by almost three to one.

For young people of marriageable age the sex ratios are sufficiently equal so that from a numerical point of view most should be able to find mates. However, numbers do not tell the whole story. A larger percentage of males than of females of marrying age are unmarriageable for physical, mental, or emotional reasons.

Another factor which complicates marriage chances and makes the sex ratio unfavorable to women is that men marry women who are younger. The average man of 35 marries a woman 6½ years younger, and there are more women in the age group from 25 to 29 than there are men in the age group from 30 to 34.

Rural and urban sex ratios. Young women leave the farms and go to the cities in order to find work. If the young men leave the farm, they leave at a later age. This migration leaves a surplus of marriageable men in the rural regions and a dearth of marriageable men in most of the cities. The exception is found

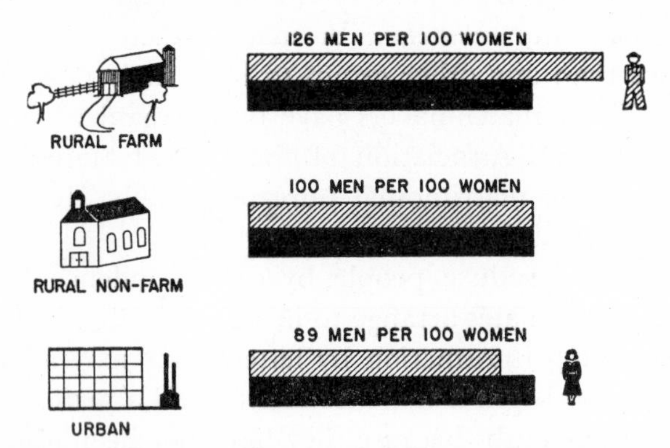

Fig. 14. Ratios of men to women ages 20-24 in urban, rural non-farm, and rural farm areas, United States, 1940.

in certain highly industrialized cities which attract more males. Gary, Detroit, and Hoboken are typical of cities with a higher proportion of males. At the other extreme, Pasadena and Washington, D.C. are cities with a preponderance of females. This imbalance in the sex ratio in different regions, states, and cities undoubtedly depresses the marriage rate. Professor Ogburn estimates that cities lower the percentage married by at least 10 per cent.[7] That is, at least 10 per cent more people of comparable age would be married if they lived in rural areas.

Conditions in cities, with their heterogeneous religions, occupations, and nationalities, make it difficult for those interested in marriage to become acquainted with other interested people of the same socio-economic backgrounds. It takes effort on the part of single persons in the city to engage in activities which will enable them to meet eligible mates. The woman who is timid or backward faces a real handicap in a marriage market where there are not enough eligible males. Women engaged in certain occupations, such as teaching, library work, and social work, have less opportunity to meet eligible men among their associates than have women in some other occupations.

Matrimonial agencies and the urban sex ratio. In order to help solve the problem of meeting eligible mates, clubs have been organized in the larger cities to bring people together. The Jews, through the *schatchen* or matchmaker, have probably done more than any other group to help their people get acquainted. Their matchmakers have been organized into "The Marriage Brokers Association of the United States." Among other groups are matrimonial bureaus, Lonely Hearts Clubs, Cupid's Arrow Clubs, and many others.

Such clubs introduce people by correspondence for a fee. The prospective mates arrange to meet personally, if they wish, after exchanging information by letter. This may seem like a peculiar way to begin a romance and to find a mate, but thousands join these clubs because they have not been able to find eligible persons in the usual way. Some unscrupulous people have started "Lonely Hearts Clubs" for the purpose of exploiting lonely persons. Many of those who join such clubs wish to keep their membership and their interest in matrimony secret from those who know them; so if they are swindled through a club, they do not go to the police for fear of publicity. The fact that marriage clubs are a profitable field for swindling indicates

[7] W. F. Ogburn, with the assistance of Clark Tibbits, *Recent Social Trends in the United States*, p. 681. New York: McGraw-Hill Book Company, Inc., 1933.

a felt need for such agencies. European countries have recognized the need for marriage clubs and have supervised them more carefully.

Failure to interest the opposite sex. Another reason why people do not marry is that many never learn the technique of getting along with members of the other sex. Girls who have grown up with several brothers in a home where relationships are happy usually have an advantage in getting along with men. Men who have had sisters and a happy family life have the same advantage when it comes to associating with women. Some adults have been so conditioned that they find it impossible to understand the other sex and to have the type of pleasant associations with them that will lead to marriage. Some women eliminate their chances because they have not learned to play the role that is most effective in man-woman relationships. In general, the most successful women with men are those who are sensitive to men's ego needs.

The girl who is too anxious for marriage and who shows indications of aggressiveness in her behavior with men is likely to decrease her chances for marriage. Some men respond favorably to pursuit by the girl, but many feel that they must do the pursuing and are wary of overly aggressive women. However, many girls know how to pursue in a subtle way so that the man either believes he is taking the initiative or enjoys being pursued.

Some men and women cannot hold the interest of members of the other sex because they are too timid to act with naturalness and ease when they are with them. They feel inadequate and withdraw into themselves. Others have not developed conversational ability and are hindered by their ineptness in all social techniques.

The fact that a woman has a college degree limits her opportunities for marriage if she does not make acquaintances in college which will lead to matrimony. Some men with a high-school education or less feel inferior and insecure when dating a girl who has more education. In one study of student thinking on courtship (see Table 3) only 9 per cent of the men said they would want their mate to have more education than they themselves had. It is noteworthy that 82 per cent said they would like to marry a girl with the same education as theirs. The girl, then, who gets a college degree has limited the field from which she can pick a mate after leaving college.

Failure to achieve emotional independence. A factor which must be taken into consideration in explaining the unmarried is that many people fail to achieve emotional independence in their relationship with their parents. This failure may be the fault of dominating parents, or it may be due to personality traits in the child himself. The child may form an intense attachment for one parent and fail to mature to where he can become interested in a member of the opposite sex outside the family. His affectional development has been arrested at an immature level. In some such cases the individuals may later marry. Sometimes they in effect marry the parent through their marriage to someone having many of the parental characteristics.

Some parents consistently dominate the child and demand undivided devotion. Their children are so impressed from earliest childhood with their obligations to the parent that it is hard for them ever to break away and marry. Parents of this type are selfish and immature in their own behavior. They have refused to recognize that it is a part of life for children to grow up, to leave home, and to establish homes of their own.

Other parents, because of their own disillusionment with marriage, feel that they are doing right to condition their children against marriage. One young man patiently courted a girl from a family where the mother had done everything in her power to condition the girl against marriage. The marriage was held up for 10 years by the mother. Every time the wedding was planned, the mother would become ill and the wedding would have to be postponed. Finally, after several attempts, the couple married in spite of the heart attack which the mother was having. After the wedding, the mother recovered from her attack.

The fact that she was able to prevent the marriage for so long showed that this was not a one-sided attachment; the daughter was immature in her extreme devotion and submission to the will of the mother. The husband desired children, but the wife postponed having them year after year so that she could be free to care for her mother during her frequent illnesses. A convenient time never came about for her to have a child. Such cases as this are not at all infrequent. Most adults could cite some from among their acquaintances.

The most interesting case of parent-child attachment we have observed was one in which a couple had been married 40 years but had never lived together. They married with the understanding that the wife was to continue living with her mother as long as her mother needed her. The husband had a business in another town and was to live there, since the mother-in-law would not leave the farm to live in his home. When we met the couple they were still living apart. The mother-in-law was in her late nineties, the young folks in their late sixties.

Some young people do not become interested in marriage because they are content with an already satisfying emotional relationship with someone such as a parent, a brother, or a sister. The security that they feel in the established relationship prevents their feeling a need for cultivating heterosexual relationships outside the family. Sometimes the strong reliance placed upon the secure relationship within the family may be based in part on fears of sex or of marriage or upon a lack of confidence in associating with the other sex. They cling to a relationship that they feel adequate for, and accept it as a satisfactory substitute for other relationships.

Lack of self-confidence is undoubtedly an important reason for the failure of some women and men to marry. Some girls grow up feeling that they are not attractive or that they have nothing to offer that would inspire a man to want to marry them. So they occupy themselves with other interests that preclude romance.

Failure to take advantage of opportunities. Some people do not marry because they fail to take advantage of the opportunities that they have. Certain young women may be sincere when they say that they wish to have a career other than marriage. They prepare for the career and either refuse to become seriously involved in courtship or do not accept the proposals of marriage that are made. They may engage in a profession for

Fig. 15. "There's always hope . . . My mom didn't hook anyone till she was twenty-three!" *By permission,* Consolidated News Features, *San Francisco Chronicle,* and Marty Links.

some time and then discover that when they are ready for marriage it is too late. They have passed the time when most girls marry and it is no longer easy to find eligible mates. If they have been successful in a career, they may have developed aggressive characteristics in working with men which do not attract men in an affectional way.

Other girls mature late in their attitudes toward marriage and even though they are not interested in a career, they pass up opportunities for marriage. They do not become interested in marrying at the time when opportunities are presented. Many modern spinsters quite freely express regret that they did not take advantage of earlier opportunities for marriage. They can see that some of those whom they disregarded earlier would have made fine husbands had they themselves been mature enough at the time to recognize a good marital prospect.

Physical and psychological reasons. The failure of some people to marry may have a physical or psychological basis. Men and women with physical disabilities may decide that they should not consider marriage. Single men have higher death, insanity, and suicide rates than married men. The Metropolitan Life Insurance Company found that little difference exists between the death rates of single and married women of ages 25 to 50, but that the death rate of single men is twice that of married men for these ages.[8] These statistics might seem to prove that the marriage state is more healthful for men. No great difference in the longevity or the suicide and insanity rates of single and married women is indicated.

Marriage may contribute to longevity and mental balance slightly if it means that a man has someone to care for him and if he lives a more normal life, but the larger factor is that those who are the most normal physically and who have the best mental balance are apt to marry. Those who are physically abnormal, insane, feeble-minded, or psychoneurotic are excluded from marriage or are less likely to marry. This selection explains

[8] Metropolitan Life Insurance Company, *Statistical Bulletin,* 24:7 (July, 1943), 6.

the difference in personality disorganization and longevity between the married and unmarried male. Since even in present-day society, with its changing courtship customs, men still have an advantage in choosing mates, these selective factors operate more effectively with men than with women. Women who do not marry are not necessarily the emotionally and physically inferior ones to the extent that may be true of men. In fact, women who would be excellent wives and mothers are frequently overlooked and remain unmarried because they have less opportunity than men to seek a mate openly.

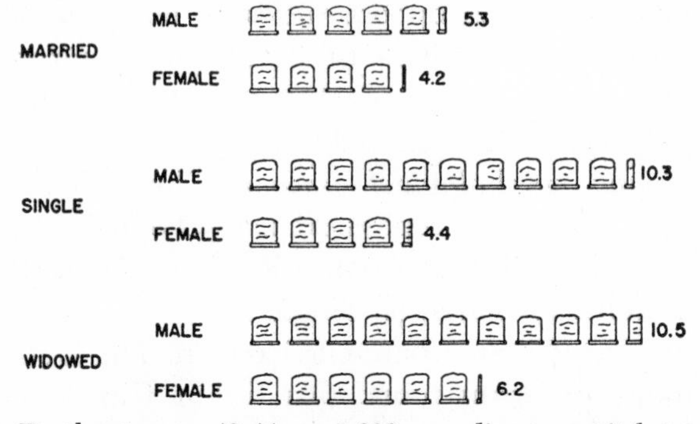

Fig. 16. Death rates age 40-44 per 1,000 according to marital status and sex. New York State, exclusive of New York City, 1939-1941. Data from Metropolitan Life Insurance Company, *Statistical Bulletin,* 24:7 (July, 1943), 6.

The *mating gradient* is a term used to refer to the fact that on the average men tend to marry beneath them in social and economic status. Evidence seems to indicate that men also tend to select mates who are physically and emotionally less fit than themselves. Folsom suggests that the operation of the mating gradient would seem to leave an unmarried residue on the upper rungs of the female ladder and on the lower rungs of the male ladder.[9] This selective factor would certainly be a partial explanation of the difference in the longevity and mental balance of the single female and the single male. The less able

[9] Joseph Kirk Folsom, *The Family and Democratic Society,* pp. 490-491. New York: John Wiley & Sons, Inc., 1943.

males tend to be among the permanently single, but that is not true of females.

We have discussed the more common reasons why people do not marry. Other less common circumstances operate to prevent marriage in individual cases. When all these factors are considered, it is not surprising that about 10 per cent of our people fail to marry.

Who should marry

Without doubt, many people who should never marry are forced into marriage by social pressure, or by a consciousness of society's attitude toward the unmarried. Some individuals are not suited for marriage and cannot make a success of such a

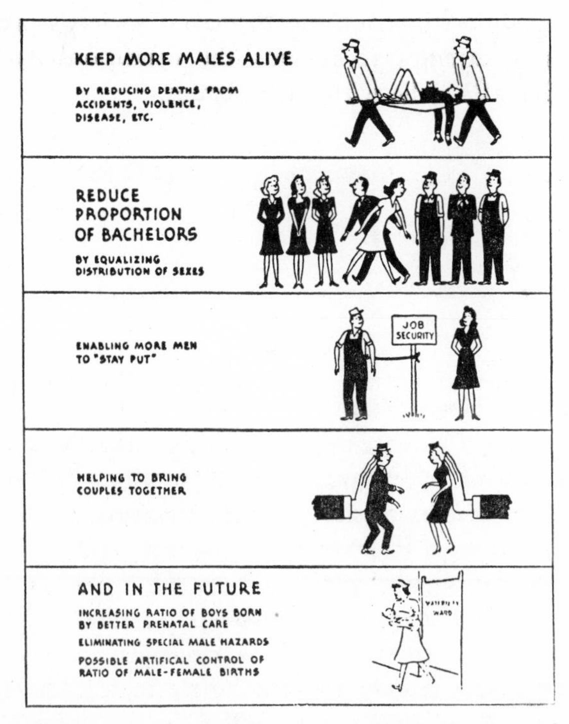

Fig. 17. Possible ways to provide more eligible husbands in the marriage market. *By permission,* Tony Barlow and *Collier's.*

relationship. If a woman's chief interests are in a career outside the home rather than in a home and family, it should not be necessary for her to marry in order to establish status. With the changing sex ratio in our country, the problem becomes one of inducing those who are best suited for marriage to marry.

Girls have been conditioned to think of marriage as a desirable goal in life, whereas boys have not been so conditioned. With the changing sex ratio, however, it would be desirable if the conditioning could be reversed. The potential husband supply might be increased if boys were brought up to think of marriage as an inevitable and desirable part of adulthood. At the same time, more emphasis in the upbringing of girls might be placed upon the opportunity for worth-while living that does not necessarily include marriage. As long as nature continues to function, people will continue to marry; society's problem at present is to attempt to remedy the conditions that permit qualified females to be without husbands.

Chapter V

THE COURTSHIP PERIOD

BROADLY SPEAKING, the courtship period includes the entire time during which a young person is going through the process of shifting his center of affection from his own parents and family to a member of the other sex in another family. The process begins with the first date and ends with marriage. When the very young start dating, they give little thought to marriage as an end result of the dating; to the older, however, the dating may be a rational step in the direction of marriage.

Dating and courtship

A distinction is sometimes made between dating and courtship. The term dating is limited to associations in which the chief motive is to get acquainted with members of the other sex; marriage is out of the question in these associations because the people are too young, have not finished school, or are not economically established. The term is used to apply to young people who date with no thought of marriage. Such dating is simply a pleasurable activity growing out of developing social nature.

However, it is almost impossible to draw a line between dating and courtship because a dating period usually occurs in all courtships. Through a hit-and-miss process of dating, young people eventually find one with whom dating becomes courtship. The dating-courtship period starts for many young people at around 15 and is over by the time they are 19 or 20. Over 32 per cent of all girls marry before they are 20, and one-half are married before they are 21. As a rule, boys do not start dating as soon as girls do, but their average courtship period is longer, since half are not married until the age of 22.6.

Dating among young people of high-school age seems to be much more common than it was a few years ago. However, there is much variation from one place to another. In some communities, little steady dating is done, but in others a large percentage of high-school young people are "going steady," and quite a large percentage marry soon after graduation. Starting the courtship period at an earlier age than ever before has probably contributed to the lowering of the average age at marriage.

Ideally, the first part of the courtship period is a time in which the youth becomes acquainted with many members of the other sex. If he does little "steady" dating, he can become acquainted with different types of personalities. During this "browsing" period the young person may gain some understanding of the other sex. It is a time when the young person can develop his skills in getting along with people and can find those who get along with him and enjoy his company. As he matures, he will come to recognize that there are a great many types of personalities: some are congenial, others repel him; some are fun on dates but would be poor wives or husbands; others, after longer acquaintance, prove to be selfish and self-centered and would take the joy out of life for any mate. After he has dated for some time, he should be better able to use intelligence in selecting the type of person with whom he can make a good marriage. This is the ideal, but not the usual, pattern followed in early or later dating.

Going steady. In a study of the dating behavior of 1600 students in 11 colleges in all sections of the United States, the students were asked whether at present they preferred to go steady or to date with a number of different people.[1] Approxi-

[1] In later chapters reference will be made to our study, "Background Factors Related to Maturation and Dating." The study was carried out in the spring of 1952 in the following schools: University of Illinois, University of Nebraska,

mately two out of three of the 1,000 students who were not engaged or married said that they preferred "to date the field." This percentage is surprisingly high, but it suggests that these students are taking the courtship period seriously and that they do not wish to limit their dating to one person until they find someone who may be a suitable mate. A national study of opinion on steady dating among high-school students[2] showed more young people of high-school age in favor of steady dating and fewer opposed than did the college study.

The fact that high-school students have had less experience and so may have less confidence in their ability to get and hold good "dates" may exert pressure toward steady dating among the younger group. A "steady" represents dating security. Many of the steady-dating high-school students do not associate steady dating with any idea of marriage. The steady dating is a temporary arrangement which meets basic needs of youthful daters. College students, as a group, are more mature, more at ease in getting and holding dates; they can be freer in "dating the field," but if they do go steady it is often with some awareness that the dating may lead to a serious involvement and marriage.

Of course, some college students are not beyond the high-school level in their maturation. And they may make the mistake of going steady before they have acquired an adequate understanding of other people, of their own sex as well as of the other sex.

Monopoly in the early dating period serves a function: it may

---

Louisiana State University, State University of New York (New Paltz), University of Minnesota (Duluth Branch), University of Kansas, Stanford University, University of Dubuque, Whittier College, Fullerton Junior College, University of California (Berkeley). Most of those participating in the study were enrolled in marriage and family classes. Of the sample, 12 per cent were freshmen, 20 per cent sophomores, 24 per cent juniors, 40 per cent seniors, and 4 per cent graduates. Ten per cent were married, 15 per cent formally engaged, and 15 per cent had an "understanding to be engaged." Most of the remainder were dating. The students in the study were probably a fairly representative sample of college people who elected a marriage and family course in the second semester of 1952. We do not know how or whether students in marriage and family classes differ from the total student body.

[2] *The Purdue Opinion Poll for Young People,* 8:1 (November, 1948), 26.

help a young person to grow toward finding his emotional satisfactions in heterosexual relationships rather than so exclusively in his parental family as he did in his childhood. But it should be a passing phase of youthful dating. People need to be free to date more widely if they are to make an intelligent choice of a mate. Steady dating at later ages, then, is of a different nature; it represents a more serious consideration of the dating partner as a possible marriage prospect. However, since all levels of maturity and immaturity exist among people, there are many college students who, after a few dates with one person, settle into steady dating simply as the line of least resistance. They are falling back upon the steady date for "dating security," just as more youthful daters do. Many of these couples drift into marriages which may not prove desirable.

Criticisms of dating behavior

When we asked students in our classes to give their chief criticisms of the dating behavior of the other sex on campus, we found the following patterns. Girls listed:

1. Lack of respect and courtesy; rudeness, inconsiderate behavior.
2. Overindulgence in or overemphasis on drinking.
3. Failure to plan for the date, leaving it up to the girl to decide.
4. Prevalence of attempts to neck, especially on first dates; attitudes that suggest a pattern of sexual exploitation.
5. Too much conceit, boastfulness, and self-centeredness.

Boys gave the following as their most common criticisms of girls:

1. Too hard to please; act conceited, self-centered, and artificial.
2. Too expensive, they are "gold diggers."
3. Too much emphasis on "rating" in choice of dates.
4. Insist that we must ask too far in advance for dates.
5. They are habitually late for dates.

All the criticisms given suggest a background of lack of confidence in the dating relationship and a lack of finesse in social situations. Is an overemphasis on drinking an indication that the boy feels ill at ease? Is artificial, aloof, and self-centered behavior on the part of the girl a defense for feelings of uncertainty? Are girls "gold diggers," or is it that the boys do not know how to suggest entertainments within their budgets? Is the boy being thoughtful or thoughtless when he lets his date plan the activities for the evening?

Petting. A universal problem of the courtship period is how far to go in necking and petting. With the greater freedom now existing in the association between the sexes, this problem exists from the first date until young people marry.

A generation or so ago almost any caressing before marriage was frowned upon. A kiss meant engagement, and any other familiarities were reserved for after marriage. In a recent meeting of high-school young people, in which dating problems were being discussed, attention centered around whether a girl should permit and whether a boy should expect a kiss on the first date. Such a discussion points up the change from attitudes of former generations.

Many young people whose sex education has included a fairly good understanding of physical phases of growing up have little understanding of the emotional phase of sex functioning. Parents and others working with young people in the early years of dating should help youth to understand that petting is not only an expression of affection for another person but, according to nature's plan, it is also preparation for sexual intercourse, and the more extreme the petting the more difficult is control. Girls are not usually so easily aroused sexually as boys are, and what seems to girls to be relatively safe petting may lead the boy beyond the point of his self-control. The girl herself may be aroused to an emotional response that is new to her, and many girls mistake this new response for love.

It must be recognized that responsiveness to others and the ability to give and to receive expressions of affection are important parts of an integrated personality. The person who is over-inhibited, excessively prudish, or unresponsive to the extent that he or she cannot or will not tolerate overt expressions of affection from a member of the other sex has just as great a problem as the person who aggressively goes as far as possible in petting on all dates. Both types of behavior indicate undesirable attitudes toward heterosexual relationships.

GRIN AND BEAR IT — By Lichty

"Why shouldn't he be smooth—he's got a half dozen technical experts and a director standing right there telling HIM how!"

Fig. 18. *By permission,* George Lichty and Chicago Sun-Times Syndicate.

The general acceptance of the free expression of affection during the courtship period places a greater responsibility than ever before upon individuals. There are indications that young people recognize this responsibility and are forming codes to regulate courtship behavior. A redefining of the term petting in terms of acceptable and unacceptable behavior is an indication of the thinking of youth. Although definitions differ in different communities and sections of the country, young people tend to distinguish in their own minds between what is acceptable and unacceptable during dating and courtship. Acceptable behavior such as holding hands and relatively unstimulating kissing and embracing is termed "necking," while "petting" is usually used to refer to a more extreme type of behavior. Whether consciously or unconsciously, petting, as the term is commonly used, is directed toward sexual excitation.

In questioning college students in 1952 we found that men

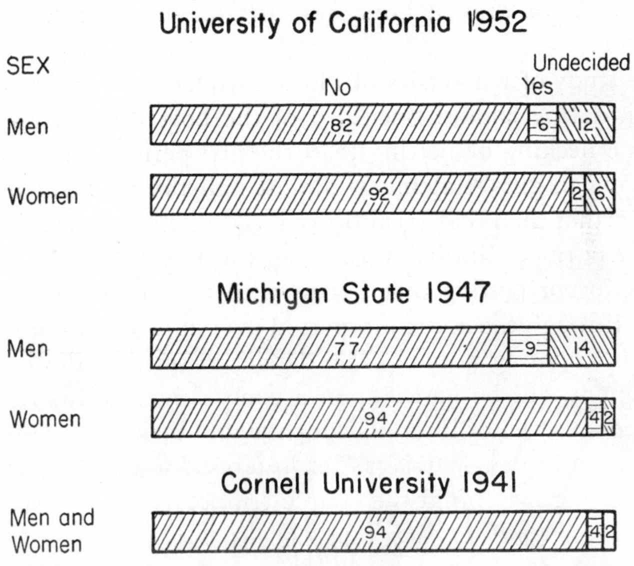

Fig. 19. Percentages of three different student generations expressing different opinions on the statement, "A girl must 'pet' on dates if she is to be popular." (2,000 of our students at Michigan State College in 1947, 450 at the University of California in 1952, and 364 students of Lemo Rockwood and Mary Ford at Cornell University in 1941).

and women were almost unanimous in expressing the opinion that a girl did not have to "pet" to be popular. (See Fig. 19.) However, 38 per cent of the men and 18 per cent of the women thought a girl who would not "neck" would not be popular. Further, one girl in five said she preferred to date a boy who expected to do some "necking," while only two girls out of 100 preferred to date a boy who expected to "pet." [3] An acceptable pattern of behavior may eventually evolve which will be far different from the code of grandmother's day but which will serve to maintain satisfactory standards.

In response to the statement, "It is as much the responsibility of the boy as the girl to determine where the line should be drawn while petting on dates," 88 per cent of the college boys queried agreed and only 12 per cent disagreed.[4] This response may indicate that men are willing to take more responsibility in controlling extreme petting than is generally supposed. Of course, the all-important question may remain as to *where* the line should be drawn; boys and girls may differ radically on this point.

In a study of University of Florida students, Ehrmann found that in dating, almost one-third of the boys tried to do more extreme necking or petting than the girl permitted. However, according to girls' statements almost half the boys did not try to go farther than the girl approved. Apparently men also recognize their responsibility in drawing the line.[5]

Necking or petting that begins with the first date and continues through the courtship period overemphasizes the sex element in choosing a mate. The danger arises that the couple's attachment will be based upon a compulsive sex interest and not upon a series of interests which would make for permanent companionship in marriage. Sex interest increased by continuous petting may blind the couple temporarily to the fact that

[3] Attitudes of 450 University of California students in 1952.
[4] *Ibid.*
[5] Winston W. Ehrmann, "Student Cooperation in a Study of Dating Behavior," *Marriage and Family Living,* 14:4 (November, 1952), 322-326.

they have few other interests in common. A marriage based upon sex attraction alone has small chance for success.

In querying students on the question of dating behavior we have found quite wide differences between the responses of the boys and the girls. For example, among a large group of students, 36 per cent of the boys agreed that "Girls expect a man to pet on dates," and 32 per cent disagreed. Only 6 per cent of the girls agreed, and 91 per cent disagreed. These percentages certainly suggest a misunderstanding of each other's true attitudes. Many boys, no doubt, make their first petting advances because they feel it is expected and they would not want to be thought slow. Girls may accept the advances for the same reason. The girl may believe that her acceptance is expected and she does not want to be thought old-fashioned or prudish. Both may be acting contrary to their personal codes, a situation that could be avoided if people better understood one another's true attitudes.

Suggestions to help minimize the sex element in courtship

In order that the sex element will not be overstressed during courtship, the individuals involved usually have to pursue a positive program so that dates will not always end in necking or petting parties. For young people who are mature enough so that they have a conscious desire eventually to make a good marriage that will mean permanent happiness, the problem is simplified. They will be able to maintain a measure of perspective in relationships, recognizing that the period of courtship is relatively short. They will make an effort to include a broad range of activities and interests during the courtship period so that sex interest keeps its proportionate place.

It is important to make quite definite plans for activities on a date. Men may ask for a date to go to a movie or to a dance and have nothing planned for the hours after the event. Girls who wish to avoid extensive petting will recognize this possibility and will have plans in reserve to take care of the remainder of the evening. The most popular girls are those who have many different interests and can enjoy varied activities. These interests and activities are what boys are thinking of when they say it is not necessary for a girl to pet. Couples who wish to avoid too extensive petting often plan activities with others. Double dates with those who are in agreement on the subject are good solutions. Attending parties and other planned social activities also minimizes the time when there is nothing to do.

Exploitation

During the courtship period some individuals indulge in exploitative behavior. Certain circumstances or conditions, such as differences in social class, differences in age, and traumas of courtship, are conducive to an unfair or unjust utilization of an individual by one of the other sex.[5] In general, our society has had a double standard for men and women. Boys have been permitted to do more experimenting in the realm of sex without so much loss of standing. This double standard makes exploitation possible. Exploitation usually indicates a one-sided emotional involvement. The exploited one is emotionally involved, but the other is after selfish gratification.

Social class. Men from a higher social class are in a position to exploit women from the lower social classes. White men can sometimes exploit Negro women. College men sometimes use their position to exploit non-college girls. In the study of University of Florida students, Ehrmann found that when college men dated girls of a lower social class they were more apt to go as far as they could with the girl. On the other hand, if they were dating girls of their own social class they did not try to go farther than the girl thought was right.[5a]

Age. Younger women may exploit older men in order to gain economic advantages. Older, experienced men may exploit

[5] See Willard Waller, *The Family* (revised by Reuben Hill), pp. 159-173. New York: The Dryden Press, 1951.

[5a] *Op. cit.*, p. 326.

the affections of young girls to gain selfish gratification. Because society recognizes that older men may exploit young girls, it protects girls until a certain age through laws on statutory rape. After the girl reaches the specified age, she is supposed to be worldly-wise enough to be able to protect her affectional interests from exploitation. Boys are not protected by law from exploitation by older women, but cases of this type of exploitation certainly occur.

Courtship desirability. Some individuals who are highly desirable as dates are in a position to exploit others. Studies made on college campuses show that certain students who rate on the campus are the ones most desired as dates. The man who is a good dancer and who has a car and plenty of money may rate. Women wish to date him not only for a good time but because dating a man who rates on the campus has great prestige value. The football hero may be able to date anyone he wants to because of his rating. Those who rate are in a position to exploit those whom they date.

Exploitative behavior is carried on by women as well as by men. A young woman of much physical charm may keep several men involved emotionally. As in other cases of exploitation, the emotional involvement is usually one-sided. The feminine exploiter may take advantage of the emotional involvement of the men not only to have the convenience of their devotion but to exploit them economically in the "gold-digger" manner. Men exploit usually to gain sexual gratification. Women exploit to gain prestige, status, or economic advantages.

The influence of one-sex groups. Before boys mature enough to become interested in girls, they form gangs and companionship groups of their own sex; they may have quite hostile attitudes toward girls. Many boys carry over into adulthood some of this immature behavior pattern of hostility to girls and loyalty to boys. They take the attitude that it is smart to exploit girls, and to have sex relations if possible, while remaining free of any affectional involvements. These boys may boast to their friends about the number of conquests they have made and they may report current progress in each affair. It is often true, however, that the person who boasts of his conquests has made few.

Sex ratio. In areas where a scarcity of one sex exists the exploitative pattern is likely to be more common. It is quite common in European countries, with their deficiency of men. Sex morality has been altered. Since the women in these countries are in surplus, they can do little to set the moral standards.

During World War II, so few men were left on college campuses that they were in positions to take advantage of the girls. In the post-war years the sex ratio on campuses suddenly changed, so that college girls found themselves in a position to resist exploitation.

Any attempt to say to what extent exploitation takes place would be guesswork, but it occurs in varying degrees. Not all such behavior, of course, is consciously exploitative. However, it is well for young people during the courtship years to learn to recognize such behavior for what it is, in order to avoid becoming victims of it.

Rating and dating

Some years ago, Willard Waller presented a theory concerning the dating behavior of college students.[6] From his observations and research he concluded that students want to date those who rate on campus, and that the rating of an individual is a major factor in the choice of dates. It is true that certain factors cause a student to "rate" on campus, and that the important factors vary somewhat among colleges. On most campuses, reputation as an athlete, membership in certain fraternities or sororities, and certain social skills, especially dancing, contribute to a higher rating. Among students on the campuses Waller had observed, men with plenty of money and a car had a distinct advantage in rating over other students, and a girl's rating depended upon popularity as a date, good clothes and

[6] Willard Waller, "The Rating and Dating Complex," *American Sociological Review,* 2:5 (Oct. 1937), 727-734.

attractive appearance, and some other factors such as conformity to dating customs.

College students are at the age when dating very often results in marriage. The person who is B.M.O.C. may or may not have the personality traits that make for happiness in marriage. One's rating on campus may have little relationship to one's desirability or undesirability as a permanent mate. If the college years are spent in trying to date those whom others consider good dates, one runs the danger of wasting the most favorable part of the dating period. This is especially true of college girls, since their chances for marriage are greatly reduced if they do not make a permanent attachment during the college years. Men are older when they marry, so if they do not find a suitable mate while in college their chances of marrying are not seriously reduced.

Some people who have worked with college students on university campuses for a number of years believe that rating has less to do with dating now than it did formerly. Although there will always be some people who strive to date those who rate, evidence seems to indicate that today a larger proportion of college students are aware of the implications of their dating. Since they are seriously interested in finding a good marriage partner, the rating of the partner on campus does not overshadow other qualities that may be more important in mate choice. Among large numbers of University of California students who were queried on their date choices, only 17 per cent said that they chose dates simply as dates, with no consideration for qualities desirable in a possible mate.[7]

In 1950, William M. Smith made a study among students of X College, a college in which Waller had analyzed student dating behavior, and upon which Waller had based many of his earlier conclusions concerning rating and dating. Smith's findings agree with our view that students today are likely to give more consideration to personality factors than to rating in their date choices, and to recognize that dating is a sort of screening

[7] Students queried by J. Landis in 1952.

process leading to courtship and marriage. Smith found that popularity, good appearance, good clothes, social skills, and sorority or fraternity membership are still assets. But he says, "A frequent reaction of the (1950) students to the list of characteristics suggested by Waller was that 'these are not essential on this campus and do not insure popularity. They help if the person has the right personality.' "[8]

Professor Lowrie[9] of Bowling Green University in Ohio has found in his research among almost 2,000 high-school and college students that the most common reasons given for dating are to find affection, to choose a mate, to learn to get along with others, and to gain poise or ease in associating with the other sex. Seventy per cent of the young people gave these reasons for dating, while only a small percentage gave as the chief reason anything that could be considered as based upon rating or prestige.

Getting dates

When the sexes are fairly equally distributed at courtship age, young people usually have little difficulty in getting acquainted with members of the opposite sex. As women pass the age of 25, however, it becomes increasingly difficult for them to meet eligible men because of the dearth of marriageable men in the age groups over 25. The first thing the person who wishes to date must do is to mingle in groups that present eligible prospects. The college boy or girl who sits in his or her room night after night should not feel resentful because of lack of dates. The office girl who spends her evenings at home or at a boarding club with other girls will meet few eligible males. When insurance companies hire a new salesman, one requirement is that the salesmen must interview a given number of prospects each day. The company knows that if a man sees

[8] William M. Smith, Jr., "Rating and Dating: A Re-study," *Marriage and Family Living,* 14:4 (November, 1952), 312-316.

[9] Samuel Harman Lowrie, "Dating Theories and Student Responses," *American Sociological Review,* 16:3 (June, 1951), 335-340.

enough prospects, sales are sure to result. However, if he sits behind his desk and worries about making his contacts, he will make few sales.

The same rule applies to people who are interested in finding mates. They will have to circulate where they will meet members of the other sex. College students should go to dances, informal parties, the union, the student coke bar, athletic events, and the many other places where students congregate. Conditions in many of the larger educational institutions make it rather difficult for the sexes to meet under circumstances where they can get dates. Large numbers of the students may commute from home to school, there may be few dormitories, and heavy enrollments may make it difficult to have many all-college functions for students. Even in small schools the students who commute often find it difficult to get acquainted, since they are seldom on campus except during classes.

We asked students at the University of California, where one-third of the students commute, what the best ways were for meeting the other sex on campus. They gave their answers in this order:

1. In regular classes and in the library.
2. In activities related to school.
3. At parties and dances (going stag).
4. Introduced by friends or relatives.
5. By having blind dates.
6. At fraternity-sorority functions.
7. Through campus organizations.
8. At religious group functions.
9. At living group (dormitory) functions.
10. At student "hangouts" or sports events.

Students who commute and who wish to date should join activities which will bring them into contact with others who are interested in dating. Over four-fifths of the California students queried felt that to belong to a fraternity or sorority gave one an advantage in getting dates. Students in any type of living group felt that they had a distinct advantage over those living alone or at home.

Young people not in college should become active participants in the community groups for which they are eligible. If a woman is working in a place where there are no unattached men, or in an occupation in which it is impossible to meet men, she may well change jobs or move to a new community. Certainly one should be as realistic about meeting good marital prospects as the insurance salesman is in trying to meet prospective buyers.

Where people meet

A study of 544 couples in the early years of marriage showed that the most common place of meeting was in high school or college, and that the most common method of being brought together was through mutual friends or the family. Since in all these marriages the husbands were students, this was actually a study of where college students met their prospective mates.

Lamson's study of the marriages of coeds at the University of Maine between 1879 and 1938 showed that approximately 45 per cent married University of Maine men. Table 2 shows a distribution of the pairings between classes. Eighty-seven per cent of those who married, married men who were in college

TABLE 2

MARRIAGE OF UNIVERSITY OF MAINE COEDS TO FELLOW-STUDENTS BY DIFFERENCES IN COLLEGE CLASSES
(Classes 1879-1938)

	Percentage	Husband	Wife
Husband in same class	30.0	senior	senior
Husband one year ahead	16.7	senior	junior
Husband two years ahead	14.2	senior	sophomore
Husband one class behind	13.4	junior	senior
Husband three classes ahead	5.0	senior	freshman
Husband two classes behind	4.5	sophomore	senior
Husband three years behind	3.0	freshman	senior

at the same time.[10] A study of Bryn Mawr graduates reveals that 90 per cent of those who married, married college graduates or alumni. The marriages of college students at other colleges and universities would probably be comparable to those of these schools.

Popenoe made a study of the place of meeting of married couples and classified the meeting places according to primary and secondary group contacts. His study indicates that people in the lower educational and class levels are more likely to have married people they met in secondary contacts such as commercial places of recreation, business, or travel, whereas those in the upper-middle class were more likely to have married those they met for the first time in primary social contacts, such as private homes, church organizations, or educational institutions. The educational system is by far the most common place of meeting for the upper-middle class group.[11]

Assortative mating

The tendency for people to select mates who are fairly similar to themselves in physical, psychological, or social traits is called assortative mating or homogamy. This process may be largely unconscious, or it may be conscious. It has been a common belief that opposites attract, with a tendency for fat men to marry slender women, or for brunettes to prefer blonds. The opposite is more nearly true. Fat men are more apt to marry fat women and brunettes are more likely to marry brunettes. Burgess and Locke report that approximately 100 studies have been made of assortative mating and that the majority of these studies show the tendency to be in the direction of homogamy. Some have thought that studies of married couples were not conclusive, since married couples may become more alike after marriage. However, in one study of 1,000 engaged couples the same tendency was observed. People tend to choose mates who

[10] Herbert D. Lamson, "Marriage of Coeds to Fellow-Students," *Marriage and the Family,* 8:2 (May, 1946), 27-28.

[11] Ernest W. Burgess and Harvey J. Locke, *The Family,* pp. 408-409. New York: American Book Company, 1945.

are like themselves in the following characteristics: intelligence, race, nationality, religion, age, socio-economic status, drinking and smoking habits, and leisure time activites.[12]

Fig. 20. "Do you believe the silly superstition that daughters instinctively look for boys who resemble their fathers?" *By permission,* Consolidated News Features, *San Francisco Chronicle,* and Marty Links.

Assortative mating is partially the result of the tendency for people of the same nationality, race, and religion, and the same

[12] Burgess and Locke, *op. cit.,* p. 422.

educational and socio-economic levels to mingle with their own groups and in many cases to live in the same communities. Social pressure is exerted to get young people to marry within their own religious and nationality group. Another factor leading toward assortative mating is that since one's ideal of a mate is influenced by one's parents and friends, their characteristics may be sought in a mate. Ethnocentrism is quite universal; children are led to believe that their family is superior in all respects, including appearance. A combination of these factors doubtless explains the more than accidental attraction of likes for likes.

There is a fair chance that young people will marry someone who lives close to where they live, even in the large city. Professor Bossard [13] arrived at this conclusion after studying the residential addresses of some 5,000 applicants for marriage licenses in the city of Philadelphia. The study revealed that approximately half lived within 20 blocks of each other, one-fourth within two blocks, and one-third within five blocks. Marvin's study[14] of 49,000 marriages in Philadelphia reveals that the tendency for people to marry within the same occupational group is much greater than would come about by chance. This tendency may be due to occupational propinquity, or an occupation may serve to draw a couple together even though they do not work at the same place of employment.

These studies emphasize the importance of a family's living in the type of neighborhood where the children will be in contact with those who would make desirable mates. If Protestant young people live in a predominantly Catholic neighborhood, there is a good chance that Protestants will marry Catholics and vice versa. Nationality groups wishing to preserve their identity should continue to live in segregated neighborhoods. In the interest of eliminating racial segregation and religious preju-

[13] James H. S. Bossard, "Residential Propinquity as a Factor in Marriage Selection," *American Journal of Sociology*, Vol. 38 (1932-1933), 219-224.

[14] Donald M. Marvin, "Occupational Propinquity as a Factor in Marriage Selection," *Journal of The American Statistical Association*, Vol. 16 (1918-1919), 131-150.

dice, intermarriage between differing groups might be encouraged, but in our present discussion we are speaking only in terms of the individual who seeks to make a happy marriage. And in general there are fewer hazards to happiness in marriages which are between those with similar backgrounds. Extreme differences in race, religion, or nationality will increase the problems of marital adjustment. (See Chapter IX.)

Student attitudes on mate selection

Young people approaching marriageable age seem to have rather well-defined ideas about the personality and family characteristics they will consider when selecting a mate. Whether they consciously consider these factors when they do select a

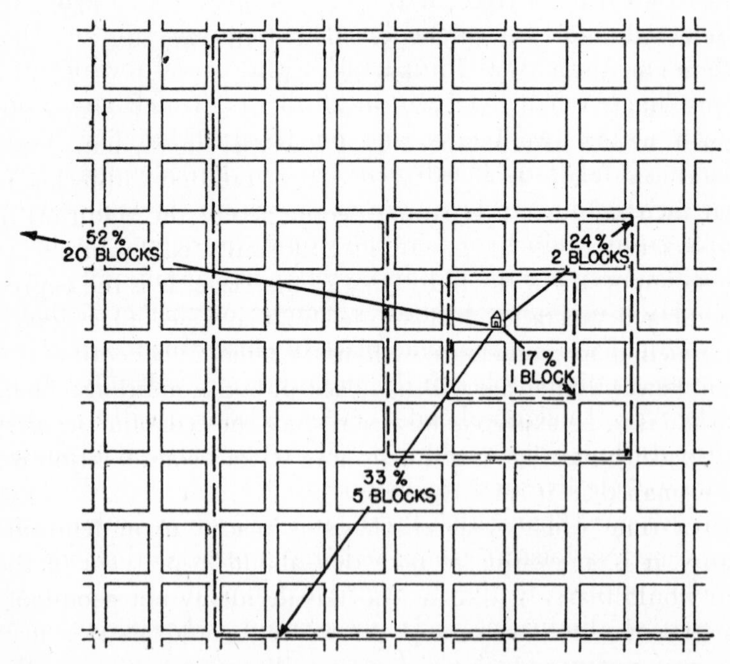

Fig. 21. Residential propinquity and mate selection. Young people in the city find a mate within a relatively short distance from their home. One-third marry someone within a distance of five blocks. Data from James H. S. Bossard, "Residential Propinquity as a Factor in Marriage Selection," *American Journal of Sociology,* Vol. 38 (1932-1933), 219-224.

mate we cannot be certain. Several studies have been made among high-school and college students to determine what traits they consider desirable. One of the most interesting of these studies was carried out over a period of years during the early 1930's by Ray E. Baber. After the nine items that students rated highest as bases for mate selection had been determined, a check list was prepared and submitted to 642 college students in their junior and senior years.

In 1947 we submitted these questions to 2,000 students at Michigan State College and, in 1952, to 1600 students at 11 colleges, to see whether student opinion had changed over the years. Table 3 gives a summary of the responses in the three studies. No great change had taken place in the attitudes of the three student generations over a period of 20 years. The findings suggest that cultural factors affecting the thinking of young people about marriage are slow to change.

The fact that approximately three out of four of the men and women would marry a person of lower economic rank or a person who came from a family they considered inferior to their own indicates that young people accept the tradition in our society that social, economic, and family backgrounds are not so important as the individual in marriage. It is the expression of a democratic ideal applied to marriage. The women are much more conservative than the men in accepting this ideal. Fewer women are willing to accept both conditions. Their attitude is to be expected, however, since the economic security provided by marriage is a much more serious consideration for the woman than it is for the man.

In a time when great emphasis is placed upon feminine beauty, it is interesting to note that about 39 per cent of the men would marry a woman who was decidedly not good-looking. Seventy-three per cent of the women would marry a man who was not good-looking. Beauty still matters more to the men than to the women, but a large percentage of both seem to subscribe to the idea that beauty is only skin deep. Baber

TABLE 3

ATTITUDES ON MATE SELECTION, 1600 STUDENTS FROM 11 COLLEGES IN 1952, 2,000 STUDENTS OF A MIDWESTERN COLLEGE IN 1947, AND 642 STUDENTS OF AN EASTERN UNIVERSITY IN THE EARLY 1930's[a]

Questions	Men, Percentage Answering Yes			Women, Percentage Answering Yes		
	1952	1947	1930	1952	1947	1930
All other factors being satisfactory would you marry:						
1. A person of lower economic rank?	93	94	93	76	69	82
2. A person from a family you consider inferior to your own?	79	79	78	61	58	75
3. A person decidedly not good looking?	38	39	32	73	74	79
4. A person of unattractive disposition and personality?	—	2	2	—	2	4
5. A person of lower moral standards than your own?	17	11	29	9	4	20
6. A person of a different religious faith (Catholic, Jewish, Protestant) than your own?	51	47	58	53	59	42
If so, would you be willing to adopt his faith?	12	25	9	20	40	5
7. A person of less intelligence and (or) education than your own?	81	83	76	42	37	18
8. A person who had had premarital sex relations?	73	67		71	48	
9. A person who had been divorced?	56	54		48	48	
10. A person who would not have children?	26	21		14	23	
11. Would you want your mate to have less education than you have, the same education you have, or more education than you have?	Less, 9 Same, 82 More, 9		17 78 5	Less, 1 Same, 18 More, 81		0 36 64
12. Do you want your mate to be older than yourself, the same age, or younger?	Older, 1 Same, 25 Younger, 74		1 24 75	Older, 86 Same, 11 Younger, 3		94 6 0

[a] Adapted by permission from *Marriage and the Family* by R. E. Baber, Copyrighted, 1939, by McGraw-Hill Book Co., Inc., p. 149. 1930 information from Baber; 1947, 1952 information from studies by J. Landis. All students answered "yes" or "no" to the first ten questions. The "no" answers are omitted in order to make the table less complicated.

suggests that women might be bowing gracefully to the inevitable.[15]

Students agreed almost unanimously that they would not marry a person of unattractive disposition and personality. Fortunately, there is little agreement as to what constitutes an unattractive disposition and personality. Otherwise a great many marriageable people would be shut out of the marriage market. Although ideas of appearance may find more agreement, many people do not have the perception to detect an unattractive personality.

Refusal to have children rates third on the list of barriers to marriage according to both the men and women. The question arises of whether young people seriously try to find out the true attitude of the prospective spouse toward having children. It seems probable that in a great many courtships the subject is given little consideration. The tendency is for all interest to be centered in present enjoyment of each other; if the thought of future children enters in at all, it is passed off with the assumption that all normal people will want children eventually. However, many go into marriage today with the attitude that they will not willingly have children. Since anything is fair in love and war, those who hold that attitude can easily avoid letting their true feelings be known before marriage. Even if objection to having children is expressed in an attempt to be honest with the fiancé, there is a strong tendency for the partner to minimize its significance by assuring himself that surely such an attitude will change after marriage.

Although about the same percentage of the three student generations is willing to marry across religious lines, a much larger percentage of the 1947 group is willing to accept the faith of the spouse if a mixed marriage is made.

Four-fifths of the women hope to marry a man with more education than their own. Only one-tenth of the men wish to

[15] Ray E. Baber, *Marriage and the Family,* p. 149. New York: McGraw-Hill Book Company, Inc., 1938.

marry women with more education than theirs. Four-fifths of the men say they would like to marry women who have the same education as themselves, but the same proportion *would* marry women with less intelligence and education (questions 7 and 11). Approximately one-third of the women *would* marry a man with less intelligence or education, but 99 per cent say that would not be their wish. They would want the man to have the same or more education. These answers indicate two things. First, that college men prefer to marry women whose qualifications are approximately equal to their own, but that if there is to be a difference in education and intelligence, they want to be the superior one. In the second place, the responses indicate that women accept the traditional idea that the husband should have more education. It is not clear whether they are motivated by a consciousness of masculine ego needs or an awareness of the greater security provided through marriage to a man having more education.

Three out of four of the men state that they would like the wife to be younger; more than four out of five women want the man to be older. On an average, the men want the wife to be two years younger and the women want the husband to be three years older. In actual practice, men average three years older than their wives. The man's ego and the wife's desire for greater security are doubtless the chief factors in explaining this culturalized expression on the part of young people. Age represents maturity, superiority, and dominance—all of which the man wants to feel are his if there is to be any difference at all between himself and his spouse. The wife accepts the pattern because it is traditional; she may also feel greater security because of the age difference.

On an average, women live five years longer than men. Since they marry men three years older, the average wife spends eight years in widowhood. From this viewpoint, a reversal of our present thinking about the proper ages of husbands and wives might be desirable.

Baber[16] submitted the same questions that we have been discussing to the parents of the students in his study and asked them to check the statements as they applied to their sons and daughters. In general, the same pattern was found among the parents as among the children; however, some sharp differences on moral standards, marrying into an inferior family, and marrying someone of a different faith were indicated. The children were more willing to marry someone with lower moral standards, an inferior family, and a different religion. Baber's study suggests that children's attitudes on mate selection are gained largely from the parents. Children may have greater tolerance of moral and religious differences because of greater moral and religious tolerance in their generation. It is possible that the parent generation has become more intolerant of moral and religious differences because experience has forced them to recognize the importance of these factors in making for success or failure in marriage.

[16] Baber, *op. cit.*, p. 154.

Chapter VI

MARRIAGEABILITY

WITH ALMOST one-fourth as many divorce decrees as marriage licenses being granted each year, more and more young people are questioning whether the hit-and-miss system of falling in love and marrying results in "living happily ever after."

Although most people hope to make good marriages, many have concepts that verge on the superstitious. They go on the assumption that marriage can only be a leap in the dark; that one responds to an irresistible attraction or an indefinable emotion called love, and makes the fatal plunge, devoutly hoping he will be lucky-in-love and end up happily married.

Personality traits and successful marriage

Those who have studied successful marriage know that a marriage can be no better than the two personalities that go into it. People who have undesirable traits before marriage will not suddenly lose these traits. Marriage does not change basic personality structure. If anything, people revert after marriage to their real selves, which may have been suppressed or controlled during courtship. From earliest childhood, people are subjected to many different types of social conditioning, all of which affect the various facets of personality. The particular personality traits we take into marriage will determine to a great degree our success or failure in marriage. They will also determine our degree of success in getting along with friends and business associates and with ourselves. There is nothing mysterious about this fundamental fact. Through self-analysis and special effort some individuals will improve their personalities, but it is safer for those choosing mates to assume that little change in personality will occur after marriage. Many people find it hard to admit weaknesses or faults. Criticism deflates their ego and they react by building fences around it to protect it from those who might endanger it in the future rather than by trying to make changes in themselves or in their ways.

Personality traits of happy and unhappy husbands and wives

Attempts have been made to compile lists of rules to follow in choosing a mate, with special emphasis upon personality traits. It is impossible to make a list which could be followed universally, since great individual differences exist. Traits which would make one man happy might ruin another man's happiness. We often see happy marriages which seem impossible to outsiders. The wife has personality traits which might be intolerable to us, yet the husband apparently does not mind at all. He may wonder how we can stand certain personality traits which we may consider attractive in our spouses. It is fortunate that people have different likes and dislikes, since a much greater proportion thus may marry. The important thing is for people to be properly paired so that the personality needs of each are met.

Although it is impossible to make universally applicable rules, it is possible to point out traits which in general characterize happy and unhappy married men and women. Some people are definitely more marriageable than others. They would have a better than average chance of making a success of any marriage they might enter. Others would have difficulty no matter whom they married; they are not marriageable personalities. Professor Terman made a careful analysis of the personality traits of 792 couples to find which traits were more common among those who were happily married and among those who were not happily married.[1] The happily married women were more likely to be of this type:

1. Have kindly attitudes toward others.
2. Expect kindly attitudes from others.
3. Do not easily take offense.
4. Not unduly concerned about the impressions they make upon others.
5. Do not look upon social relationships as rivalry situations.
6. Are cooperative.
7. Do not object to subordinate roles.
8. Are not annoyed by advice from others.
9. Frequently have missionary and ministering attitudes.
10. Enjoy activities that bring educational and pleasurable opportunities to others.
11. Like to do things for the dependent or underprivileged.
12. Are methodical and painstaking in their work.
13. Are careful in regard to money.
14. In religion, morals, and politics tend to be conservative and conventional.
15. Have expressed attitudes that imply a quiet self-assurance and a decidedly optimistic outlook upon life.

The unhappily married women showed a different set of personality characteristics. In general, they were as follows:

1. Are characterized by emotional tenseness.
2. Inclined toward ups and downs of moods.
3. Give evidence of deep-seated inferiority feelings to which they react by aggressive attitudes rather than by timidity.

[1] Lewis M. Terman, *Psychological Factors in Marital Happiness,* pp. 142-166. New York: McGraw-Hill Book Company, 1938. Terman and his associates made a study of 792 couples, who were in the middle and upper-middle classes, living in urban and semi-urban California. The couples had been married varying lengths of time, from less than one year to more than 30 years, the average being 11 years. Approximately one-third (38 per cent) were college graduates. Each spouse was asked to fill out a detailed questionnaire independently of the other. The study was anonymous. The chief purpose was to determine what psychological factors are associated with marital happiness. Data were collected in the early and middle 1930's. We shall refer to the Terman study occasionally throughout this book.

4. Are inclined to be irritable and dictatorial.

5. Have compensatory mechanisms resulting in restive striving, as evidenced by becoming active joiners, aggressive in business, and over-anxious in social life.

6. Strive for wide circle of acquaintances; are more concerned with being important than being liked.

7. Are egocentric.

8. Have little interest in benevolent and welfare activities unless these activities offer personal recognition.

9. Like activities fraught with opportunities for romance.

10. Are more inclined to be conciliatory in attitudes toward men than toward women.

11. Are impatient and fitful workers.

12. Dislike cautious or methodical people.

13. Dislike types of work that require methodical and painstaking effort.

14. In politics, religion, and social ethics are more often radical.

Terman found that happy husbands were inclined to have the following characteristics:

1. Have even and stable emotional tone.
2. Are cooperative.
3. Show attitude toward women that reflects equalitarian ideals.
4. Have benevolent attitude toward inferiors and the underprivileged.
5. Tend to be unselfconscious and somewhat extroverted.
6. Show superior initiative.
7. Have a greater tendency to take responsibility.
8. Show greater willingness to give close attention to detail.
9. Like methodical procedures and methodical people.
10. Are saving and cautious in money matters.
11. Hold conservative attitudes.
12. Have a favorable attitude toward religion.
13. Strongly uphold the sex mores and other social conventions.

Unhappy husbands showed personality characteristics which were somewhat comparable to those of the unhappy wives, although not the same in all cases:

1. Are inclined to be moody and somewhat neurotic.
2. Are prone to feelings of social inferiority.
3. Dislike being conspicuous in public.
4. Are highly reactive to social opinion.
5. Often compensate for a sense of social insecurity by domineering attitudes.
6. Take pleasure in commanding roles over business dependents or women.
7. Withdraw from playing inferior role or competing with superiors.
8. Often compensate by daydreams and power fantasies.
9. Are sporadic and irregular in their habits of work.
10. Dislike detail and methodical attitude.
11. Dislike saving money.
12. Like to wager.
13. More often express irreligious attitudes.
14. More inclined to radicalism in sex morals and politics.

If the student will make a careful study of the personality characteristics in these four classifications, he will see that the lists simply summarize characteristics of people who are well adjusted within themselves and those who are not. Those who were unhappy in marriage had characteristics which would make them unhappy in their associations whether they were married or single. The marriage relationship is not so different from many of our other associations. We do not choose friends who are non-cooperative, selfish, moody, and aggressive. We like people who show more positive attitudes, those who are willing to share, and those who are dependable from day to day. Friendships which are not based upon mutually satisfactory personality traits usually do not endure. People who lack desirable traits have difficulty in making and sustaining friendships. However, in the courtship process the elements of sex attraction and love fantasy may so affect an association between two people that they may become emotionally involved with each other and be quite unconscious of personality incompatibility. The emotional involvement sweeps them toward marriage without their having enough companionship-association to do much objective evaluating of each other's personality traits. After marriage, they may awaken to the fact that they not only have little in common but that serious personality faults are present.

Personality traits and marriage

Some 2350 case histories recorded by the American Institute of Family Relations[2] were analyzed to determine the differences in personality characteristics of 250 men and women who had failed in two marriages and 1500 who had failed or were failing in their first marriages. The failures were compared with 600 young people approaching marriage. Using the Johnson Temperament test as a measure of certain personality characteristics, it was found that those who had failed in two marriages, when compared with the unmarried group, were more impulsive and lacking in self-mastery; tended to take little part in community affairs; were tense, nervous, irritable, gloomy, and uncooperative; and were given to nagging, whining, complaining, and fault-finding. The traits of those who failed in one marriage were similar to those of the two-time failures, although their undesirable traits were not so extreme.

Husband-wife grievances

In order to find what common grievances married people hold against their spouses, Terman had his 792 couples rank 57 common grievances according to their seriousness in the marriage. The 28 most serious are given in Table 4.

It will be noticed that these grievances have little to do with the conditions of the marriage; rather, they are almost entirely personality faults. Terman points out that this holds for the first 20 complaints on the husbands' list and for all but one of the first 20 on the wives' list. "A majority of the faults are of the kind commonly thought to be indicative of emotional in-

[2] Shirley Raines, "Personality Traits of Persons Who Divorced and Remarried," *Family Life,* 10:6 (June, 1950), 1-2.

stability, neurotic tendency, or marked introversion, as these terms are used in the current literature of personality psychology."[3]

TABLE 4

RANK ORDER OF MARITAL GRIEVANCES ACCORDING TO SERIOUSNESS AS GIVEN BY 792 HUSBANDS AND 792 WIVES[a]

Order for husbands	Order for wives
1. W. nags me	1. H. selfish and inconsiderate
2. W. not affectionate	2. H. unsuccessful in business
3. W. selfish and inconsiderate	3. H. is untruthful
4. W. complains too much	4. H. complains too much
5. W. interferes with hobbies	5. H. does not show his affection
6. W. slovenly in appearance	6. H. does not talk things over
7. W. is quick-tempered	7. H. harsh with children
8. W. interferes with my discipline	8. H. touchy
9. W. conceited	9. H. has no interest in children
10. W. is insincere	10. H. not interested in home
11. W.'s feelings too easily hurt	11. H. not affectionate
12. W. criticizes me	12. H. rude
13. W. narrow-minded	13. H. lacks ambition
14. W. neglects the children	14. H. nervous or impatient
15. W. a poor housekeeper	15. H. criticizes me
16. W. argumentative	16. H.'s poor management of income
17. W. has annoying habits	17. H. narrow-minded
18. W. untruthful	18. H. not faithful to me
19. W. interferes in my business	19. H. lazy
20. W. spoils the children	20. H. bored with my small talk
21. W.'s poor management of income	21. In-laws
22. In-laws	22. H. easily influenced by others
23. Insufficient income	23. H. tight with money
24. W. nervous or emotional	24. H. argumentative
25. W. easily influenced by others	25. H.'s insufficient income
26. W. jealous	26. H. has no backbone
27. W. lazy	27. H. dislikes to go out with me
28. W. gossips indiscreetly	28. H. pays attention to other women

[a] By permission from *Psychological Factors in Marital Happiness* by L. M. Terman, Copyrighted, 1938, by McGraw-Hill Book Co., Inc., p. 99.

The most serious grievances from the husbands' point of view are that the wives nag, are not affectionate, are selfish and inconsiderate, complain too much, interfere with hobbies, are slovenly in appearance, and are quick-tempered. The wives

[3] Terman, *op. cit.*, p. 101.

counter that their husbands are too selfish and inconsiderate, are unsuccessful in business, are untruthful, complain too much, do not show affection, do not talk things over, and are too harsh with the children.

It is interesting to note that among the first eight grievances three are the same on both lists. The husbands put in third order and the wives in first order that the other is selfish and inconsiderate. One-third of the least happy husbands and wives, but only 3 per cent of the more happy spouses listed this complaint. Selfishness is not a trait that suddenly afflicts people after they marry. The trait was doubtless much in evidence before marriage to those who are not involved emotionally. But people caught up in the whirlwind of love may be truly blind when it comes to seeing personality traits before marriage.

Complaining is in fourth place on both lists. Again, the complaining attitude toward life is something which develops long before marriage. It is a trait that wins few friends outside marriage because few people care to listen to complainers. Chronic complainers usually do not recognize that they are complaining; the habit reflects an attitude toward life which may be traceable to some other personality difficulty.

One-third of the less happy husbands and wives said that the spouse was not affectionate enough. The fact that people do not show affection may be due to selfishness or thoughtlessness; or it may be because people have been conditioned as children to show little affection. In some families the family pattern does not include demonstration of affection; caresses between parents and children are rare in these families and the children do not have the habit of showing affection. This pattern is carried over into marriage. When a person marries who was brought up in a family where there were constant demonstrations of affection, he or she will expect this outward demonstration of affection in marriage. The lack of such expression may cause the person to feel insecure and uncertain of the love of the spouse.

Many of the grievances listed are simply the outward indications of unhappy temperaments. One of the most important characteristics of a marriageable person is the *habit of happiness.* It would be impossible to overestimate the value of cultivating this trait in oneself and of seeking it in a marriage partner.

Specific traits and time to adjust in marriage

In our study of 409 couples who had been married for an average of 20 years, personality traits were rated high as contributors to a successful or unsuccessful marriage.[4] The couples were asked to list the most serious problems they had encountered in achieving happiness in marriage. Economic, sex, and in-law adjustments were listed most often, but after those came a series of personality traits which had caused most difficulty. The following were mentioned most often: bad temper, intolerance, selfishness, lack of confidence in partner, lack of consideration, impatience, moodiness.

Next the couples mentioned most frequently as sources of difficulty difference in temperaments and difference in interests.

When these same couples were asked to tell what had made for success in their marriages, both the husbands and wives explained their success largely in terms of desirable personality traits possessed by the spouse. These personality traits are given in Table 5. It will be noticed that in general husbands and wives list the traits in the same order. However, there are some notable exceptions. The wives consider talking things over as much more important to their happiness than the husbands do. It will be remembered that the wives in the Terman study

[4] This study was an analysis of the experience of 409 couples to determine how long it takes to work out adjustments after marriage and to find what factors are associated with happiness in marriage. The couples had been married from three to 40 years, an average of 20 years. All were still married. Each spouse was asked to fill out a questionnaire independently of the other. The study was anonymous. Many of the couples were the parents of college students; they were largely residents of the Middle West, Michigan, and Illinois; and they were of the middle or upper class economically. One-third of the participants were college graduates. Data were collected in 1945. For a summary of the study see: Judson T. Landis, "Length of Time Required To Achieve Adjustment in Marriage," *American Sociological Review,* 11:6 (December, 1946), 666-677.

considered failure to talk things over as the sixth most serious grievance against their husbands. This trait in the American husband is probably a relic of the traditional viewpoint of former generations, when it was man's prerogative to make all

TABLE 5

RANK ORDER OF FACTORS ACCORDING TO IMPORTANCE IN MAKING FOR SUCCESS IN MARRIAGE AS GIVEN BY 409 HUSBANDS AND 409 WIVES

Rank order for husbands			*Rank order for wives*
Affection	1	1	Affection
Understanding	2	2	Mutual interests
Give and take	3	3	Cooperation
Cooperation	4	4	Give and take
Children	5	5	Understanding
Mutual interests	6	6	Talking things over
Religion	7	7	Religion
Tolerance	8	8	Desire for success
Desire for success	9	9	Respect
Well acquainted before marriage	10	10	Children
Hard work	11	11	Tolerance
No financial problems	12	12	Similar backgrounds
Talking things over	13	13	Consideration
Patience	14	14	Even temper
Respect	15	15	Well acquainted before marriage
Common sense	16	16	Old enough to marry
Trust	17	17	No financial problems
Faith	18	18	Common sense
Holding temper	19	19	Faith
Similar backgrounds	20	20	Hard work
Consideration	21	21	Holding temper
Old enough to marry	22	22	Compromise
Honest	23	23	Sense of humor
Compromise	24	24	Honesty
Sense of humor	25	25	Patience

decisions and woman's place to accept them without question. With the change in the status of women, this old pattern is no longer acceptable and wives resent a husband's failure to talk things over.

Comments by married couples on this point indicate that when differences in viewpoint exist, husbands are inclined to look upon discussing the differences as quarreling or having an argument, whereas wives more often feel that the differences might be eliminated if they could be discussed. Wives also feel that a husband's unwillingness to talk over differences means either that he does not consider the differences important, or that he is determined not to change his viewpoint. One wife who had been married for 27 years expressed her feelings thus: "I never know where my husband stands on a given subject. He always assumes that everything is all right and that there is no need to talk anything over. He is blind to the problems about which I raise a question and will say 'yes' to anything rather than face a problem and discuss it frankly. He considers talking things over in the same category with having an argument, so is always agreeable but is never any help in working out problems."

In the more successful marriages the couples are able to talk things over without quarreling, and to reach an understanding on common problems.

Both the husbands and wives list as most important expression of affection, understanding, cooperation, give and take, tolerance, and a desire for the success of the marriage. It is worth while for young people considering marriage to give thought to their own traits and to the type of personality that would fit with theirs and help make a happy marriage. We must realize that it is often difficult to become acquainted with the real personality of the person being courted; that personality traits which cause annoyance before marriage will be intensified after marriage; and that it is difficult to "change" or "reform" personalities. All the research on personality and happiness in marriage shows that one of the best guarantees of happiness in marriage is to make a wise choice of a marriage partner. Marry a person who has few personality quirks and a happy temperament. And give some thought also to the questions,

"Am I a marriageable person? If not, what can I be doing about it?"

As Terman sums it up: "What comes out of marriage depends upon what goes into it, and among the most important things going into it are the attitudes, preferences, aversions, habit patterns, and emotional-response patterns which give or

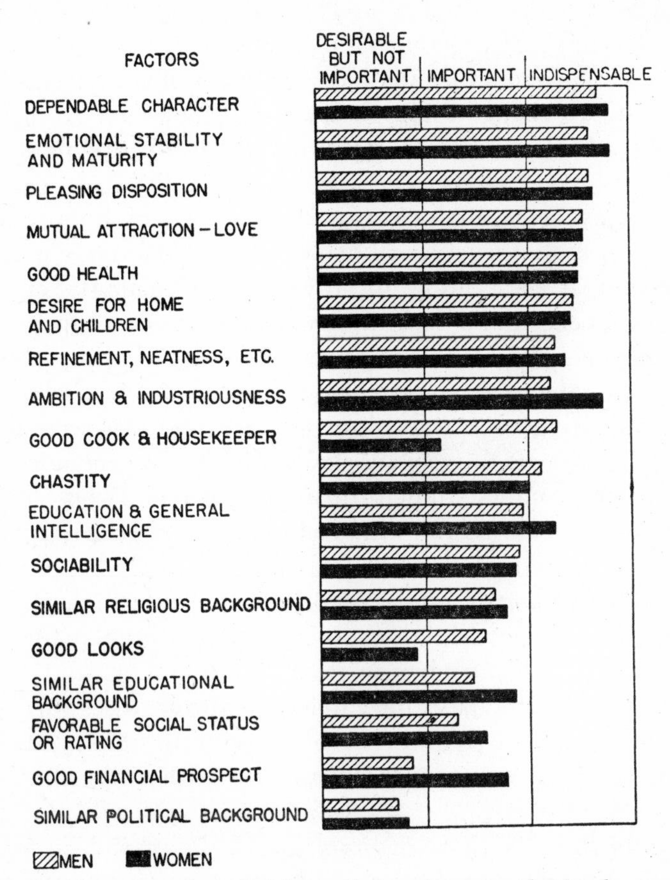

Fig. 22. Average rating of eighteen factors in mate selection by men and women students. Are the factors listed by the students before marriage important to marital happiness after marriage? *By permission,* Reuben Hill, "Campus Values in Mate Selection," *Journal of Home Economics,* 37:9 (November, 1945), 557.

deny to one the aptitude of compatibility. In a large proportion of unsuccessful marriages it is possible to discover either in the husband or the wife, or perhaps both, numerous elements of the unhappy temperament and evidence that these elements have played a causal role." [5]

Adaptability. Those young people who have been brought up in such a way that they find it easy to adjust to new situations and to many different kinds of people will fit more easily into marriage. Some people have rigid personalities; they find it difficult to change their ways, to accept new ways, to make new friends, or to fit into any situation that is different from what they have always been used to. Since marriage requires many adjustments, the person who does not look upon change as a threat to his security will make the better marriage partner.

In comparing a group of divorced and happily married couples, Locke found that the happily married group of men and women rated higher on adaptability. He considered those more adaptable who could "give in" in arguments, who were not dominating, who were slow to anger, and who were quick to get over anger. Burgess and Wallin have also concluded that some of the couples studied during engagement who had low marital-prediction scores still made happy marriages, possibly because of a high rating on general adaptability.

Ability to identify. Marriageable people rate high in their ability to identify with others. Identification is the quality that enables us to put ourselves in the place of another and to feel as he feels. It is the basis for empathy and tolerance. Successful marriage constantly requires each spouse to be able to identify with the other. Some people grow up with little ability to identify with others.

Ability to work through problems. A desire and an ability to work through problems are important personality traits in marriage. Some people have never formulated a positive program of attack for facing problems. Instead, they give up easily or regress to some former state of adjustment. Others find it

[5] Terman, *op. cit.*, 110-111.

impossible to see problems clearly. They become frustrated and filled with emotional tension, but they have no understanding of what is wrong or of what they can do about the trouble. Those who can see problems clearly, face them realistically, and seek intelligent solutions are likely to build satisfying relationships in marriage.

Family background and happiness in marriage

Both Terman and Burgess were interested to learn whether it is possible to predict the marital success or failure of young people before they enter marriage. The statement is sometimes made that a child is headed for a happy marriage or for the divorce court by the time he is ten years old because of the training and conditioning he has received up to that time. Burgess and Terman tested this hypothesis by investigating the background factors in the lives of people and attempting to relate these to success in marriage. Both concluded that young people are usually conditioned early in life in ways that will make them good or bad risks in marriage. Although the studies were made in different parts of the country, they produced many of the same conclusions concerning the background factors which make for happiness in marriage. Terman[6] found the following ten circumstances most predictive of marital happiness:

1. Superior happiness of parents.
2. Childhood happiness.
3. Lack of conflict with mother.
4. Home discipline that was firm, not harsh.
5. Strong attachment to mother.
6. Strong attachment to father.
7. Lack of conflict with father.
8. Parental frankness about matters of sex.
9. Infrequency and mildness of childhood punishment.
10. Premarital attitude free from disgust or aversion toward sex.

[6] Terman, *op. cit.*, pp. 110-111.

Terman believes that anyone who passes on all ten of these points is a distinctly better-than-average marital risk. Burgess

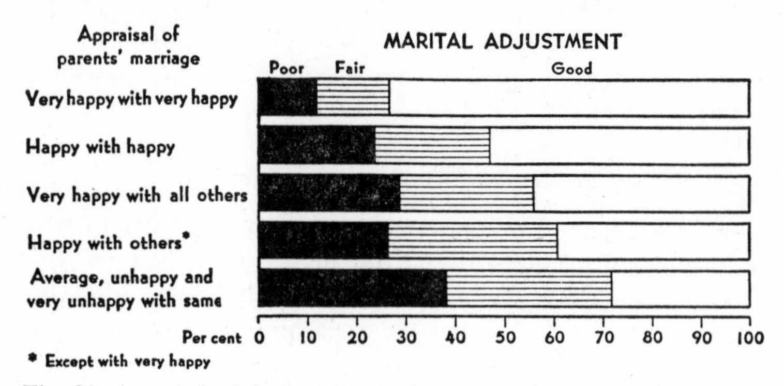

Fig. 23. Appraisal of the happiness of parents' marriage (combined ratings) and adjustment of their children in marriage. If both sets of parents had very happy marriages, the children have a much better chance for happiness in marriage. From E. W. Burgess and L. S. Cottrell, *Predicting Success or Failure in Marriage,* p. 101. New York: Prentice-Hall, Inc., 1939.

and Cottrell [7] found the following background factors most important in predicting success in marriage:

1. Happiness of parents' marriage.
2. Superior family background of husbands and wives.
3. Similarity of family backgrounds.
4. Husband and wife not "only" children.
5. Husband closely attached to father and having little or no conflict with mother.

[7] Ernest W. Burgess and Leonard S. Cottrell, *Predicting Success or Failure in Marriage.* New York: Prentice-Hall, Inc., 1939. Burgess and Cottrell conducted a study of 526 middle-class couples living in and about Chicago. The couples had been married from one to six years, an average of three years. Approximately 60 per cent had some education beyond high school. Married, separated, and divorced couples were included in the study. In most cases, the wife completed the questionnaire. The chief purpose of the study was to determine the factors and personality traits predictive of success or failure in marriage. The data for the Burgess-Cottrell studies were collected during the early 1930's. Charles E. King repeated the Burgess-Cottrell study in a group of 466 Negro couples and found the same relationships between premarital factors and marital adjustments. See Charles E. King, "The Burgess-Cottrell Method of Measuring Marital Adjustment Applied to a Non-White Southern Urban Population," *Marriage and Family Living,* 14:4 (November, 1952), 280-285.

6. Wife's close attachment to mother.
7. Husband and wife reared in country.
8. Husband and wife attended Sunday School beyond 18 years of age (as adults).
9. Husband and wife had several friends of the same and the opposite sex.
10. Parental approval of marriage.

These two lists agree in the main. Both are concerned with the happiness of the parents' marriage and the relationship of the child with his parents. People from homes where the parents had happy marriages and homes in which a satisfactory relationship existed between the parents and their children are good risks in marriage. They will have developed more of the desirable personality traits which make adjustment in marriages less difficult. People reared in homes in which the parents were unhappy and in which there was constant parent-child friction have some handicaps for successful marriage. In a study of more than 4,000 married men and women, Popenoe found that nearly half of the unhappy husbands and wives had been reared by parents who had been unhappy in their marriages. Few of the happy husbands and wives had come from unhappy homes.[8] Our study of 544 student couples revealed that those whose parents were still married were happier in their marriages than those whose parents had been divorced.[9]

The research evidence shows, then, that young people are conditioned by background factors which determine to a large degree whether they will be good or bad matrimonial risks. It

[8] Paul Popenoe and Donna Wicks, "Marital Happiness in Two Generations," *Mental Hygiene,* Vol. 21 (1937), 218-223.

[9] Judson T. Landis, "On the Campus," *Survey Midmonthly,* 84:1 (January, 1948), 17-19. The purpose of this study was to determine the special adjustment problems of the early years of marriage and to determine what factors are more closely related to happiness in marriage. The 544 couples had been married from less than a month to as long as six years. At least one member of each couple was a student. Most of their homes were in the Midwest, although many states were represented. Each spouse was asked to complete a questionnaire independently of the other. The study was anonymous. The data for this study were taken during 1946 and 1947.

suggests the advisability of learning about the family background of the person one considers marrying.

However, it should be understood that we are speaking of statistical averages: people from unhappy homes are, on the average, poorer marital risks than people from happy homes. But that does not mean that all children reared in unhappy homes are doomed to unhappiness in their marriages. Some young people are determined to put more than ordinary effort into building a successful marriage because of the unhappiness of their own childhood home. If they have been able to analyze the effects of the unhappy background upon their own attitudes

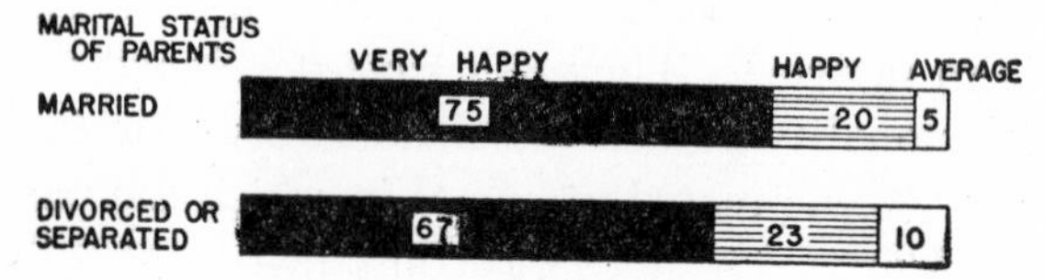

Fig. 24. Marital status of parents and happiness of their children in marriage.

toward marriage, and if they can make an objective appraisal of the factors which contributed to their parents' failure, they can overcome their handicap. One couple, both of whom were from unhappy homes, explained the success of their marriage in this way: "We had a mutual desire to establish a happier home than our parents had achieved. Both of us were convinced that happiness in marriage doesn't just happen and we were willing to work at it." This couple had been married for 24 years. In their case, the unhappy home background had served as an incentive for building a good marriage.

Occupation and success in marriage

Occupations may have something to do with the stability of marriage. In general, men engaged in occupations which take them away from home frequently and for extended periods of time have a higher divorce rate, especially if their work brings them in contact with women under conditions that are not closely controlled by the community. Studies of divorce show that commercial travelers (salesmen), actors, musicians, physicians, and stenographers have the highest divorce rate, whereas miners, manufacturers, clergymen, carpenters, and farmers have the lowest divorce rate.

Physical factors and happiness

Good health is a contributing factor to personal happiness throughout life. It does not guarantee happiness, nor does the lack of it necessarily preclude happiness. However, other things being equal, good health is important for good adjustment. In selecting mates men frequently fail to give the health factor enough consideration. It may appeal to their desire for dominance to marry women who are not robust. Burgess and Cottrell found that the health of the husband is of slight importance to happiness in marriage. However, the couples in the Burgess-Cottrell study were all in the early years of marriage. Such couples would have had little occasion to reckon with poor health as a factor in marital happiness. As time passes and as couples grow older, health problems arise more frequently, and new adjustments are required. The fact that health is closely related to happiness in marriage is revealed by a study of marriages of longer duration. Our study of marriages that had lasted for an average of 20 years showed a significant relationship between health and the happiness of the marriage.

Here, as in many other areas of living, attitudes are important. The marriageable person lives sanely, with the purpose of building and maintaining good health, but he is not unduly concerned about health matters or imagined ills. Moreover, the healthy personality does not escape into illness when life presents problems. In grandmother's day it may have been accepted as a feminine prerogative for a wife to take to her bed whenever the going was rough. But for a modern person, whether man or woman, to make it a habit to become ill in the face of disappointment or difficulty is usually evidence of neurotic tendencies. The prospective mate of such a person should take warning.

Age for marriage

Young people of the courtship age are interested in knowing whether there is a "best" age for marriage. Because of the many variables which must be taken into consideration, it is difficult to isolate the age factor. To illustrate, college people seem to have happier marriages than non-college people, and college graduates marry at a later age than non-college graduates. Is it the age at marriage or the college experience which results in happier marriages among college graduates? Professional people are more likely to be college graduates, to marry later, and

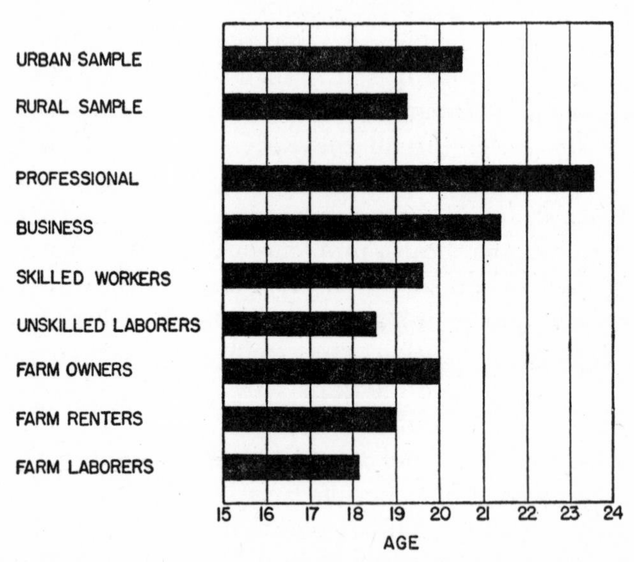

Fig. 25. Modal age of wife at marriage by place of residence and occupation of the husband. Data from Frank W. Notestein, "Differential Rate of Increase Among Social Classes of the American Population," *Social Forces,* Vol. 12, October, 1933, p. 23.

to be of a higher socio-economic group. Which factor or factors would explain the greater marital success of professional people? Although it is difficult to isolate the age factor, nevertheless evidence indicates that the better marriages are not the very youthful marriages.

Studies made of the relationship between age at marriage and happiness in marriage are summarized in Table 6.

TABLE 6

STUDIES OF THE BEST AGE FOR MARRIAGE AS JUDGED BY MARITAL SUCCESS AND FAILURE

	Poor	Good	Excellent
Burgess-Cottrell (526 marriages)			
Men:	Under 22	22-27; 31 and over	28-30
Women:	Under 19	19-27	28 and over
Hart-Shields (500 marriages)			
Men:	Under 24	24-28	29
Women:	Under 21	21-23	24
Terman (792 marriages)			
Men:	Under 22	22 and over	22 and over
Women:	Under 20	20 and over	20 and over
Landis (409 marriages)			
Men:	Under 20	20-29	30 and over
Women:	Under 20	25 and over	20-24
Landis (544 marriages)			
Men:	Under 20	20 and over	20 and over
Women:	Under 18	18-21	22-27

All the studies show that the chances for happiness in marriage are less when men marry before the age of 20 and when women marry before the age of 18. The studies are not in exact agreement as to what is the best age for marriage. In general, they show that the best age for women to marry seems to be between the ages of 21 and 25. Three of the studies show that men who married as they approached their thirties were more likely to find happiness in marriage than those who married at younger ages.

In our study of the 409 older-generation couples, we found that it took longer for the men and women married under the age of 20 to work out adjustments in sex relations, spending the income, associating with mutual friends, in-law relationships, and in social activities and recreation. The couples who were 20 years old or over when they married made the adjustments in less time, and, ir general, those who were married at 30 and over made the adjustments in less time than any other age group. The men who married at an early age had much more difficulty than the women in adjusting, and the men who married at 30 years and over had less difficulty than the women. Only 47 per cent of the men who married under 20 said the sex adjustment was satisfactory from the beginning of the marriage, whereas 83 per cent of the men who were 30 and over when they married said the adjustment was satisfactory from the beginning. In general, this is the pattern existing between age at marriage and adjustments that take place after marriage.

Studies of divorce show that youthful marriages are much more likely to end in divorce. Locke found in his study of divorced and happily married couples in Indiana that a much larger percentage of the divorced women had married before the age of 18 and of the divorced men before the age of 21. With reference to the two groups, he found the best age for marriage for women to be between 21 and 29 and for men between 24 and 29. The divorced women had on an average married two years younger and the divorced men one year younger than the happily married women and men.[10]

Figure 26 summarizes our study of the divorce rate in 1051 marriages. All the couples in this study were the parents of college students and therefore would not represent a cross section of the population. The divorce rate decreased in these families as the age at marriage increased. The divorce rate was six times higher in the marriages where both spouses were under 21 than in the marriages in which both spouses were 31 or over at marriage. If one spouse was under 20 and the other over 20 at marriage, the divorce rate was higher than if both were over 20 years old at marriage.

As we suggested earlier, age alone cannot be credited with sole responsibility for the higher proportion of failures among youthful marriages. Those who marry at a very early age may

[10] Harvey J. Locke, *Predicting Adjustment in Marriage: A Comparison of a Divorced and a Happily Married Group*, pp. 101-102. New York: Henry Holt and Company, 1951.

have emotional characteristics which would increase the probability of unhappiness in their marriages at any age. As Popenoe suggests, "Emotionally unstable, headstrong, self-willed young people, determined to have their own way at any cost . . . are not likely to marry successfully at any age, but if they do marry, are perhaps more likely to do so at twenty than at thirty."[11] One hypothesis is that more of those who marry early do so to escape unhappy home surroundings or to defy parental dominance than is true of those who marry later. Undoubtedly, some

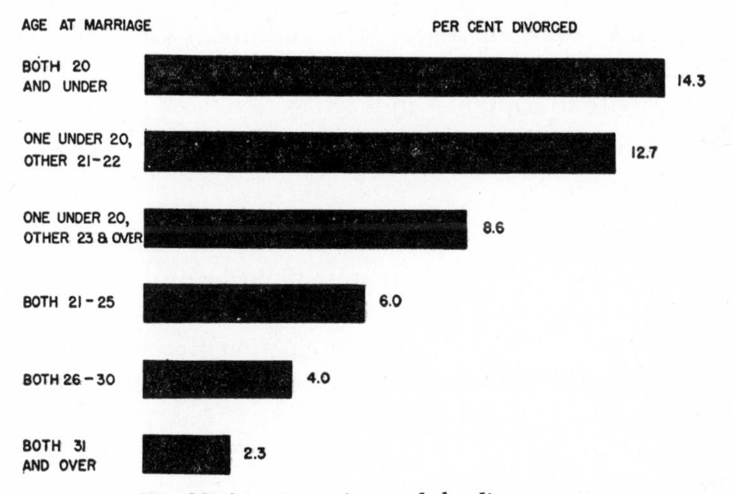

Fig. 26. Age at marriage and the divorce rate.

early marriages are handicapped at the outset by the fact that they are entered into hastily after short acquaintance, often without due consideration of the realities that will have to be faced after marriage.

It is often believed that people who are older when they marry will have greater difficulty in marital adjustments because they have become "set" in their ways. However, the studies on age for marriage do not indicate that this is a handicap to marriage. The older person will have had occasion to learn much which

[11] Paul Popenoe, "Should College Students Marry?" *Parents Magazine,* Vol. 13 (July, 1938), 18-19.

can make it easier for him to adjust. He has had opportunity to observe the marriage failures of his friends. It is possible to learn a great deal from observing the mistakes of others. The older person has had opportunity to read scientific material on marriage, and may have a rational rather than a romantic view of marriage. Since his sex drive is not so strong, he is less apt to base his selection solely upon sex appeal. His marriage will often have a broader companionship base. The woman who marries at a later age knows what it is to be a single adult and she has had time to decide whether she is willing to work at achieving a happy marriage. The additional knowledge, the rational approach to marriage, the more mature point of view, all contribute to happiness in marriage for those who marry at a later age.

Emotional maturity

One factor of great importance in youthful marriages is immaturity. The couple may be mature biologically, but biological maturity is only one of the considerations in determining readiness for marriage. Marriage is for emotionally mature adults. Some individuals achieve emotional maturity at an early age, but others never mature.

In our country dating starts at an early age. Early dating results in emotional involvements which may lead to early marriages. Many of those who marry young would, a few years later, choose an entirely different type of spouse from the one chosen at 18. Between the ages of 16 and 22, the individual's conception of a desirable spouse will change as much as, or more than, his ideas about a vocation. If the 16-year-old takes a job, he is more apt to drift into it, but the 22-year-old has given his vocation more serious thought and can approach some special field with greater certainty and confidence. It is strange that in some states the law assumes that a young person of 14 is mature enough to pick a lifetime mate but that he will not be mature enough to vote until he is 21 years old.

Following is a list of criteria of mature and immature behavior. If people under 20 years old do not measure up to all these criteria, it is no cause for alarm. Complete emotional maturity is achieved by relatively few people. However, failure on

Criteria of mature behavior	*Criteria of immature behavior*
The mature person:	The immature person:
1. is able to be objective.	1. blames others for his failures.
2. is emotionally independent of parents.	2. is dependent upon parents.
3. makes decisions for himself.	3. reverts to childish behavior.
4. acknowledges and takes responsibility for his mistakes.	4. refuses to accept his chronological age.
5. is heterosexual in his sex interests.	5. lets others make his decisions.
6. accepts his chronological age.	6. is selfish.
7. is willing to wait for future pleasures.	7. is aggressive and domineering.
8. profits by his mistakes.	8. is quick to judge others.
9. accepts the moral codes.	9. defies social codes.
10. tries to understand others.	10. requires immediate satisfaction.
11. gets along with other people.	11. holds a fantasy conception of mate selection.
12. accepts the present and looks to the future.	12. sees sex as vulgar and dirty, or as the chief end and interest in life.
13. sees sex expression as a normal and satisfying phase of life.	13. shows lack of consideration for others.
14. is willing to use reason rather than fantasy in mate selection.	14. is self-centered.
15. can evaluate himself and his motives.	

too many points indicates a general immaturity. If regressive types of behavior are the customary response to the difficult circumstances that arise in life, the individual is not mature enough for marriage, no matter what his chronological age may be.

One of the most important criteria of emotional maturity is objectivity, the ability to get outside ourselves and see ourselves and our interests realistically, to look at outward facts as separate from our feelings about them. Small children view most of the circumstances of their lives subjectively. They are self-centered. But with increased maturity comes the ability to see things in their proper relationships, the ability to stand aside, as it were, and judge events more impartially. The extent to which we are able to do this is a measure of our objectivity. Without objectivity, an individual will have distorted ideas of himself and his needs and "rights." He will constantly misjudge others and fail to evaluate his own motives. Few people can be completely objective, but it is an attribute worth cultivating.

In this chapter we have discussed a number of different considerations that have to do with marriageability. The most important aspects of marriageability are related to personality and to one's habitual ways of meeting life situations. Such habits and personality patterns are, of course, closely related to the family background and life experiences of the individual, but can, nevertheless, be modified.

Chapter VII

MARRIAGE UNDER SPECIAL CIRCUMSTANCES

ACCORDING TO THE AMERICAN STEREOTYPE, two young people grow up, finish their education, the man gets a job so he can begin to support a family, and they marry. The wife may work at an outside job for a few months or a year, but it is understood that shortly she will give up her job and devote all her time to caring for the home and children and advancing her husband's and family's interests as much as she can through her social and community activities.

Although that is the stereotype, more and more present-day marriages do not conform to the pattern. Cultural changes in our society, and military requirements that affect the marriage plans of a great many couples, mean that large numbers of marriages are made under special circumstances. These marriages may require special adjustments if they are to be successful. People need to recognize what some of the problems are and to consider their ability to cope with them. This chapter will discuss marriages that require special adjustments.

Marriage while in college

Many students in college now face the problem of whether to marry immediately or to postpone marriage until their education is completed. Before World War II, marriage while in college was rare. College student marriages were generally disapproved by parents and college administrators. Some colleges automatically dropped students who married before graduation. But with the influx into the colleges of the war veterans a change came. One G.I. in four married while he was still pursuing his studies, and almost half of these had children before graduation day. College administrations came to see the advantages of having married students on campus, and several studies made in Midwestern colleges revealed that married students were making better grades than the single students. Riemer found that the married students with children made better grades than any other students! [1]

Attitudes toward college marriages have clearly changed, although for various reasons the majority of students still prefer to remain single while in college. In 1952, we asked 450 of the students in our marriage classes, "If you found the one you hoped to marry eventually, would you marry while an undergraduate?" One-fifth of the boys and half of the girls said that they would marry while they were undergraduates. Four out of five men and women said that they would marry if they were in graduate school. The students expressed the belief that their parents are in approximate agreement with them about marriage while in college, that is, about the same percentages felt that their parents would approve if they chose to marry while in college.

Some advantages of college marriages. In 1947, we attempted to learn some of the advantages and disadvantages of college marriages by means of a detailed study of 544 college married couples.[2] Most of the men in these marriages were G.I.'s, so it was an older group of men and women than the average college population. However, some of the findings are applicable to any college marriage. Many of the advantages the married students listed had to do with the emotional security which marriage had provided. Many of the men felt that marriage gave more

[1] Svend Riemer, "Married Students Are Good Students," *Marriage and Family Living*, 9:1 (February, 1947), 11-12.

[2] Judson T. Landis, "On the Campus," *Survey Midmonthly*, 84:1 (January, 1948), 17-19.

stability to their lives, made life more purposeful, and made it easier for them to settle down to work. This feeling of stability might have had something to do with the higher grade average made by the married students. Almost all the husbands felt that a wife was a help in college rather than a hindrance. A few complained that the wives had too much company, interrupted study, or wanted to go out evenings. However, most were not critical. Almost half the wives in this study were working to help support the family, so they were a help in more ways than one.

Success of college marriages. Two studies, ours in 1947 and one by Christensen and Philbrick[3] at Purdue University in 1950 (346 couples), asked married students this question, "Knowing what you know now, would you marry before finishing college if you were unmarried?" In both studies, three-fourths of the couples said that they would marry while in college if they had it to do over again. The one-fourth who would not or who were uncertain felt there had been too many difficulties in earning a living, in finding housing, and in doing satisfactory college work. Although these were the reasons given by those who would hesitate to try a college marriage if they had it to do over again, other factors revealed by the research studies suggest that the real reasons may have been deeper. Many of the couples who doubted the wisdom of their college marriage felt that perhaps they had made a marriage which might end in failure. If they had waited to marry and had become better acquainted, they might not have married each other at all. The Christensen-Philbrick study showed a much lower happiness rating among those who would hesitate to marry while in college if they had it to do over again.[4]

It is difficult to get accurate information on the success of college marriages. In our study, 95 per cent of the couples gave a self rating of happy or very happy. Since all were in the very early years of marriage, a high happiness rating is to be ex-

[3] Harold T. Christensen and Robert E. Philbrick, "Family Size as a Factor in the Marital Adjustments of College Students," *American Sociological Review*, 17:3 (June, 1952), 306-312.

[4] *Ibid.*, p. 310.

pected; ratings by the same couples might have been different after more years of marriage. However, Riemer, who has made several studies of student marriages at the University of Wisconsin, found in one study of students in a student housing project that the divorce rate was lower than the usual rate during the first four years of marriage among a college-educated group.[5] Although some of the evidence seems to indicate that students who marry while in college make a better than average success of their marriages, it must also be recognized that their success may be achieved only because they are making more than an average effort at building good marriages.

Problems to be considered in college marriages

Many of the factors that are important in contributing to success in marriage are about the same whether people marry in college or after college. But additional problems arise in college marriages which are not necessarily present in other marriages.

Willingness to give up life of a single student. Most young people look forward to the enjoyment of the social side of college life. In the process of dating and enjoying college social life they may find one person whom they want to marry, but they may still not be ready to sacrifice their other activities for marriage. These students are not ready to settle down to marriage even if they are in love. A common complaint that single college girls make about the married men on campus is that the men "don't act like they're married." The man who is not ready to give up his single habits is not ready for marriage. Since college marriages are so generally accepted, couples may be swept along into marriage after a short engagement without facing realistically what it will mean to be married on campus.

Readiness for parenthood. Although most of the couples who marry in college may plan to postpone having children until

[5] Svend Riemer, "Youthful Marriages," Paper delivered at the Annual Meeting of the National Council on Family Relations, Lake Geneva, Wisconsin, September, 1951.

after graduation, they should face reality and accept the eventuality of parenthood. The girl who said, "We are not going to have a baby for three years, since it will be that long before my

"I feel sort of funny, getting a bachelor's degree!"

Fig. 27. *By permission,* Bo Brown and *The Saturday Evening Post.*

husband finishes his graduate work," expressed the confident philosophy of many couples approaching marriage. In studying 212 college couples at Michigan State College who had had their first baby,[6] we found that only slightly over one-third had

[6] Shirley Poffenberger, Thomas Poffenberger, and Judson T. Landis, "Intent Toward Conception and the Pregnancy Experience," *American Sociological Review,* 17:5 (October, 1952), 616-620.

definitely planned the first pregnancy. Christensen and Philbrick found the same percentage of planned pregnancies among the 346 couples studied at Purdue University.[7] Since the wife often works to supplement the income or is also a student, an unplanned pregnancy may upset carefully devised plans. People who cannot accept and adjust to such an upset are not ready for marriage. Many college people prefer to postpone marriage until they feel more adequate to cope with any eventuality.

Willingness of the husband to help the wife. When both members of a married couple are attending classes, and perhaps working part-time, or when one is in school and the other working, life becomes pretty busy. If, in addition, there are children to care for, couples need to be supermen and superwomen if they are to meet all their responsibilities adequately. The success of college marriages means that many young couples are adequate for all these requirements. But a man who expects to be waited upon at home, who considers it beneath him to do dishes, scrub floors, and diaper babies, is likely to be a problem husband in a college marriage. And a girl who wants to be a queen, above hard work and struggle, and who cannot be happy if she has to miss any of the whirl of college social life, should not marry while she is still in college. For even if there is plenty of money, working together at marriage while both are students requires much of men and women.

Present income and financial backing. Economic conditions and opportunities for part-time employment will have much to do with how frequent college marriages continue to be. In recent years it has been possible for most students to earn their living by holding part-time jobs. Most couples have been able to support themselves without having to depend upon their parents. In 1947, it cost an average of $148 per month for the college couples in our study to live. Most of these couples were living in college housing projects. In 1952, we found that the average had advanced to $222 per month.

Students thinking of marriage often reason that since their

[7] *Op. cit.*, p. 309.

parents support them while they are single, why shouldn't the support continue after marriage? The traditionally accepted viewpoint is that marriage means the end of parental support, especially for the girl. Once married, she is to be supported by the husband. Many parents still feel that this should be the case, and that when people marry, even in college, they should be ready and able to stand on their own feet. Parents who continue to support their children after marriage usually expect to have at least a measure of control and direction in the lives of the children as long as they support them, married or single.

Attitudes of both parents and children on whether or not parental support should continue after marriage may be changing, however. Some parents now express a willingness to support their children at least through college, if they can, whether or not the children marry. But few of the parents can look upon their children as independent married adults as long as they are contributing a major part to their children's support. In-law problems may easily arise in such cases.

Many cases have come to our attention in which the young people are willing to accept the parental support, but they are not willing to take the control and direction that may come with it. If there is to be parental subsidy, parents and children need to be objective about the situation. Otherwise, misunderstandings may bring disillusionment and disappointment to parents and unhappiness to children. Many of the married students who try to face problems realistically feel that they must earn their own way after they marry.

Most student husbands today are willing for the wife to work. Nevertheless, when 450 of our students were asked the question, "Should parents continue to support the daughter who married and continues in college?" almost half the men and one-fourth of the women said yes.

The precedent has been set, and young people will continue to marry while in college, especially as long as economic conditions are favorable. The more general acceptance of the fact that married women may continue indefinitely to work outside the home, the tendency for people to marry at younger ages than formerly, widespread knowledge of contraception, and a gradual change in the attitudes of parents toward continuing to help support sons or daughters after marriage—these and other factors will operate to establish the custom of college marriages more firmly within our mores.

Nevertheless, those who are considering such marriages need to be realistic in recognizing that they face certain alternatives which do not usually confront couples who marry after their education is complete. If they want to live as responsible adults, independent of outside financial help, they will have to work harder than couples who marry later. If, on the other hand, they marry expecting help from parents or others, they may expect during their college years to be in something of an interim state—no longer mere dependent children, but not independent married adults either. They also need to face the fact that *both* will have to be willing to work at all household tasks and to care for any children that may come.

Marriages involving separation

For a number of years—ever since Pearl Harbor was attacked on December 7, 1941—large numbers of young American men of marriageable age have been in military service, and that situation is likely to continue during the foreseeable future. This means that great numbers of young couples are faced with the question of whether to marry before the man enters the military service and endure the separation involved, or to postpone marriage and accept the resulting uncertainties. College people are more likely to face this decision than are young people not in college, since the college man may be deferred from military service until he completes his education. And during his college years he often finds the girl he wishes to marry.

People who are in love and who face separation because of military service or any other unavoidable circumstance naturally feel impelled to win some measure of future security by marrying quickly and having a honeymoon, no matter how short.

The present generations of college students bring this problem to their counselors very frequently. "He's going to leave soon, and probably will be gone for two years. We are in love. Ordinarily we'd want to wait a little longer before marrying, but we haven't time. Isn't it better to marry now so that we can know we have each other to come back to and so that our future will be settled?"

No absolute answer can be given. But certain considerations enter into every marriage which is to involve early separation.

Effect of postponing adjustments. When there is to be a separation soon after marriage, the adjustments which inevitably must be made in learning to live with each other are postponed. Time passes. A couple may be married two years or more without having had a chance, or the necessity, for making adjustments that are usually made very soon after marriage. Usually when a married couple are together during the first year of marriage they go almost everywhere together; they try their best to please each other in every way possible. And in the process they tend to grow closer together in their habits and ways of reacting to situations. They may never again have quite so strong an urge to work at giving their marriage a good start. With couples who undergo early separation, the situation is different. After their separation has ended, and they come together to begin life as a married couple, they learn that the interim has not been a blank; both have necessarily continued to live and grow, but not together. Even if they have been completely faithful to each other and have kept in touch with each other through frequent letters, they now face the task of starting in to build a marriage as a bride and groom when they are no longer bride and groom. The love affair that was climaxed by their wedding is now history, and society does not give them the help toward a good marital start that is so willingly extended to brides and grooms.

Many couples who have had to be separated soon after marriage say that they have never got to "feeling married." Therefore, while they are apart they are tempted to date others as much as if they were in fact single. The temptation may be increased by the loneliness arising from the separation. Many people cannot endure the strain of long-continued loneliness; their emotional balance may depend upon their ability to push their love for the absent one back into the periphery of their lives and thoughts. Thus the two will inevitably be farther apart when they are reunited.

These aspects of separation should be faced with as much realism as possible by any couple who are considering a marriage that would involve temporary separation. One college girl, faced with the decision, said, "I believe that John and I would make a really successful marriage if we could marry and start together, now. But I know myself well enough to know that I can't stand being lonely and on my own. I don't think we'd have a chance of surviving if we married now and were apart while he is overseas." These two young people decided not to marry, but to try to wait for each other. Both dated others while they were apart, but as time passed neither found anyone else so desirable, and after the boy's return they married. The fact that they were free to date others with no sense of guilt or obligation seemed to help make the separation more endurable. It is probable that their marriage got off to a better start because they did not marry before the separation. The temperament and attitudes of the two people involved will have much to do with what decision should be made. Of course, some couples do not marry when the man returns. They have grown too far apart.

Length of acquaintance. A reasonably long acquaintance is important to the success of all marriages, but long and thorough acquaintance is much more important before marriages that are to be followed by separation. Since absence does not always make the heart grow fonder, such couples need to have time to know each other well and to be sure of their love for each other before they marry, so that when the natural doubts arise later during separation they will have the confidence that comes with a long and deep understanding of each other. During war years many marriages fail because people marry hastily after a short acquaintance. Even if a marriage is a potentially good one, there is no basis of understanding and confidence to tide the couple over the periods of doubt and uncertainty that inevitably follow separation.

Age. The age of the young people is very important in these situations. All the handicaps that ordinarily exert pressure on the marriages of the very young will be intensified by separation. (See discussion of youthful marriages, Chapter V.) A high divorce rate can be expected among high-school girls who marry their high-school sweethearts before the boys go into military service at eighteen and a half or nineteen.

Emotional factors. Couples contemplating such a marriage should be very sure that they are looking at marriage as a lifetime proposition and that they are not being impelled into it by the emotional turmoil of the impending separation. The girl may feel sorry for the boy and wish to comfort him and to give him complete sexual satisfaction before he goes. He, in turn, is fighting separation from home, friends, and family; the future looks uncertain and he grasps for some sort of security. Marriage may seem to offer an answer. During the courtship the couple may give little attention to the basic factors which are important in a successful marriage, concentrating instead upon the upheaval that threatens them.

Alternatives to be faced. Some couples feel they should marry before separation because they are afraid they will lose each other if they do not. This may be true. But would their love survive if they were married? The fact of a wedding ceremony will not necessarily insure the survival of an emotional attachment. If their love for each other is not well established, it might be safer for them to part as an engaged rather than as a married couple. Sometimes questionable behavior during a separation can be accepted and forgiven by an engaged couple, while it would be grounds for divorce if they were married.

If they can survive an engagement apart, they have a better chance of making a success of marriage once they are together. If they cannot survive such an engagement, at least less damage will have been done than if they had married and their separation had resulted in a broken marriage.

Parenthood and separation. Marriage results in children even with the contraceptive information available today. Many couples who know that a child needs both parents decide to wait to marry until they can rear their children together. If a child is born after the father is gone, an adjustment for all three—father, mother, and child—is necessary after the father's return. At best, all are cheated of the privilege of growing to understand one another during the child's infancy.

Thus far our discussion seems to have presented only the negative aspects of marriages that involve separation. Those negative aspects are facts that have to be faced, even though most people would rather not face them when they contemplate such a marriage. However, after these aspects of the question have been faced, there is another side to the question.

Should the girl wait? If a couple are mature, well acquainted, sure that they meet each other's personality needs, and believe that if no separation loomed they would have no serious doubts about their marriage, then they ought to be able to marry and survive the separation. In such a case would it be fair for the man to expect the girl to wait a year or two, unmarried, for his return? Her best years for marriage are in the early twenties; if she waits faithfully for him to return, she will pass up her best opportunities to date and to find another suitable husband. The chance he would be taking would not be nearly so great, for men in their late twenties or in their thirties can usually find desirable and suitable younger girls to marry. Since, as far as chances for marriage are concerned, waiting favors the man rather than the woman, the girl facing the choice of whether to marry or to wait would seem wise to marry if she is sure the marriage is potentially a good one, or to wait only if she is free from any binding obligation to refrain from dating. The man who asks a girl to wait for him unmarried should let her feel as free to date others and perhaps to find another man for a husband while he is gone, as he will be to find another woman for a wife when he returns, in case his feelings for her have changed in the meantime.

Marrying someone who has been divorced

With the present divorce rates, a considerable proportion of marriages involve one member who has been married before. An analysis of remarriage by Bossard reveals that the divorced have a tendency to marry those who have also been divorced. However, many people marrying for the first time marry divorced people. Are there special problems in marriages of this type? How may a previous divorce affect a second marriage?

A young woman went to a marriage counselor for what she considered to be a routine premarital consultation. She told the counselor happily about her plans for her wedding and asked for any advice he might give her to help her make a good beginning in her marriage. Incidentally, she mentioned that her mother had not yet been told of her engagement because it was something of a problem to know how to break the news that the fiancé had only recently been divorced. There had never been a divorce in the girl's family and she felt that her mother might be prejudiced and doubtful about her daughter's marriage to a divorced person. The girl said to the counselor, "I feel that my future husband's having been divorced is of absolutely no importance as far as our happiness is concerned. All that is in the past. It was not his fault in any way and now that divorces are so common, it would be silly for anyone to attach any importance to whether or not one has been married before."

That view is often expressed by young people contemplating marriage to a divorced person. Nevertheless, the truth is that marriage to a divorced person does include special factors that differentiate such marriages from first marriages for both partners. These marriages differ in the following ways.

They differ in social approval. "All the world loves a lover." So public custom is to smile with approval upon "first" marriages. The wedding is acknowledged, approved, supported, and celebrated with an enthusiasm that is not always readily given when one partner has previously been married and divorced. The difference may be only slight, but it is represented by the attitudes of some ministers who will not officiate at a wedding if one partner has been divorced. Even if there is no disapproval from any source, many of the couple's friends may assume an attitude of watchful waiting to see how it turns out, in contrast to the attitude of optimistic acceptance that usually accompanies the wedding that is a first for both.

Families have doubts. Family doubts or outright opposition, which are factors to be reckoned with in the success or failure of any marriage, are more likely to be present when one partner has been divorced. The family of the one with no previous marital record is likely to view the marriage with mingled hope and fear for the future, whether or not the fears are justified by the circumstances of the previous marriage.

Comparisons with the past. The family of the divorced partner cannot help but make comparisons between the new spouse and the former one. Is the new choice better or worse? Views will vary, depending on family attitudes toward the circumstances of the first marriage and divorce. Consequently, the first marriage and divorce are one of the facts of life that will enter into in-law relationships and associations with friends, even when it is possible for the married pair to feel honestly that "all that is past."

How much did the divorced person learn through marriage failure?

The above factors are usually present. There are other points concerning marriage with a divorced person which can be answered only by the individuals involved. Perhaps the most important of these is the attitude of the person who has been divorced. If he (or she) feels sure that he was wholly blameless in the marriage failure that occurred, there is good reason to question whether he is good material for a second marriage. For marriage failure, like marriage success, can be achieved only by two working at it together. We have often wondered at the naïveté of young people who say, "I know he'll make a wonderful husband (or she'll make a wonderful wife). He had a rough time in his first marriage, but none of it was his fault in any way." The divorced person who has learned from his experience and is able to see where he himself failed and so contributed to the first marriage failure is far more likely to make a success of a second marriage. Many people do learn by bitter experience—not how to control the second mate better—but how to understand their own weaknesses and strengths, how to choose more wisely a second time, and how to work more effectively at building a successful marriage.

Among the people who make a success of a second marriage are those who have achieved greater maturity by the time they marry the second time, or who have been able to learn from their mistakes, whether the mistakes were in the choice of a mate or in meeting problems. They are able to do better in a second marriage. In the very unhappy group of those who fail a second time may be found those who could not accept any of the responsibility for the first failure but blamed the mate for all their problems. When they make a later marriage they will expect the next mate to make up for all their early troubles; they will set impossible standards for the mate and none for themselves. A young person considering marriage with a person previously married and divorced should ask above all, "What has he learned that might have helped in his first marriage and that would help make a better thing of our future marriage?"

Blithely to brush aside the thought of the former marriage and to tell oneself, "All that is of absolutely no importance to our happiness," is to invite unhappiness.

Success in second marriages

Some of the earlier research studies were inconclusive on the success of second marriages. However, recent evidence seems to leave little doubt here. Two states, Iowa and Missouri, now keep records on number of times married for all couples who make application for a marriage license. Monahan has made a detailed analysis of the data in these two states and has found that second marriages are not so enduring or so successful as first marriages. He also found that the divorce rate increases with successive marriages.[8] This finding is supported by information collected by the Bureau of the Census on previous marital status. The census data reveal a much higher failure rate in second marriages, 20.5 per cent of divorced men and 23.0 per cent of divorced women having had two or more marriages. Only 13.5 per cent of married people living with spouses had had a previous marriage ended either by death or divorce.[9]

Some reasons explaining a higher failure rate in marriages after divorce may be these: (a) Divorced persons tend to marry other divorced persons. Therefore both people in the marriage may have traits that make it difficult for them to adjust in marriage. (b) Any moral compunctions one might have against divorce would have been faced and overcome at the time of the first divorce, so there might be less hesitation to resort to divorce a second time. (c) Divorce may represent an attitude of trying to escape problem situations in marriage rather than the habit of working through problems to solutions other than divorce. (d) Divorce is often a traumatic experience. Marriages made after divorce may be the result of "rebound," or of conditions unfavorable to a wise choice.

This chapter has considered three kinds of marriages under special circumstances. The choice of whether or not to marry

[8] Thomas P. Monahan, "How Stable Are Remarriages?," *American Sociological Review*, 58:3 (November, 1952), 280-288.

[9] Bureau of the Census, Current Population Reports, Population Characteristics, Series P-20, No. 21, December, 1948.

under these circumstances confronts many college students today. Each person so confronted must consider the factors involved and the alternatives open to him as an individual. Many people are able to make a success of marriage under even the most difficult of circumstances. Whether circumstances are difficult or not is not so important as whether the individual is able to view the situation realistically and to evaluate accurately his own ability to cope with eventualities before making a lifetime decision.

Chapter VIII

PREMARITAL SEXUAL RELATIONS

A PROBLEM WHICH ARISES with increasing frequency among all groups of young people is the necessity for making decisions on the question of sex conduct before marriage. A great many young people who are sincerely interested in making good marriages, and who hope to avoid mistakes which they might regret at a later time, have questions concerning premarital coitus. The questions place emphasis upon moral, ethical, and empirical considerations in varying degrees. Is premarital sexual intercourse wrong? Is it good preparation for marriage? Is there danger to future happiness from emotional pressures resulting from over-repression of sexual drives? What is society's true attitude today toward sex experimentation before marriage? This chapter will outline considerations and point out facts which may be helpful in answering these questions.

Society's attitude toward premarital sex union

The present adult generation has seen many changes in the mores concerning marriage and the family. The most sensational of these has been the widespread acceptance of divorce as an alternative to coping with the common problems of marriage. Another change has been the greater freedom in the association of the sexes, with the virtual disappearance of chaperonage. Some observers of American life have superficially concluded that all standards have changed equally and that premarital sex union is no longer contrary to our mores. However, the majority of children in American families are still brought up believing that sexual intercourse is to be reserved for marriage and that sexual promiscuity is a deviation from acceptable moral standards.

In a way, our society has done many things to make it easier for young people to be sexually promiscuous. Formerly, society took great pains to control actions before marriage; girls were carefully chaperoned. Today a minimum of chaperonage exists. The sexes associate more freely and for more years before marriage because of earlier dating. Young people today are on their own morally during courtship. Yet society is not consistent, for although it no longer controls, and in fact makes it easy for people to break the rules, it still has not changed the penalties for people who do fail to live up to socially approved standards. Public opinion still condemns premarital coitus as a serious form of antisocial behavior for women; pregnancy before marriage is still looked upon as a great tragedy and disgrace in the middle and upper-middle class family. And there has been little change in social attitudes toward the unwed mother and her child; in all except two states the child still does not have equal legal rights with other children.

Conformity or nonconformity to moral codes

Various attempts have been made to determine how prevalent among young people is the disregarding of standards concerning sex conduct. In 1938, Terman, after attempting to compare sex behavior of older and younger generations, concluded that there had been a steady increase in premarital sex contacts among people born in four successive decades. Assuming that the trend would continue at an uninterrupted or at an accelerated rate, he predicted that virginity at marriage would be a thing of the past among those born around 1950. Kinsey's study of sex behavior among present-day Americans contradicts some of the findings of the Terman study in that the Kinsey report concludes that the incidence of premarital intercourse is not increasing but has remained stable for 20 or 30 years. The Kinsey report states that within a generation ". . . the number of persons who go to college has materially increased and since this is the group that has the least premarital coitus, this means that there is now a distinctly larger portion of the population which is going without premarital coitus than there was when Terman made his prediction ten years ago."[1] Studies made by Professor Ehrmann of the University of Florida,[2] and our study of 1600 students in 11 colleges and universities in 1952, show that a high percentage of university girls (from 88 to 91 per cent) say that they have refrained from having premarital sex relations. The accuracy of the responses would seem to be fairly reliable, since the anonymity of those responding was protected.

It is possible to offer an imposing array of facts and figures to prove either side of the question of increasing or decreasing nonconformity to approved sex standards. The question, however, with which we are concerned is not prevalence or nonprevalence of any activity, except insofar as such prevalence might affect the individual who must formulate his own behavior codes. In citing the results of studies on prevalence of premarital sexual experience it is often assumed that if a practice seems to be on the increase it must be becoming socially acceptable and therefore desirable for the individual. Some authorities urge that moral teachings be revised to fall into line with behavior if it can be known just what is the norm of behavior.

Because transition is evident in many phases of life, some people hastily conclude that sex behavior that was once considered undesirable or abnormal has now become acceptable. As yet, we have no absolutely reliable information concerning

[1] Alfred Kinsey, Wardell B. Pomeroy, and Clyde E. Martin, *Sexual Behavior in the Human Male,* p. 557. Philadelphia: W. B. Saunders Company, 1948.

[2] Winston W. Ehrmann, "Two Methods of Measuring the Individual's Control of Pre-marital Dating Behavior." Paper delivered at Annual Meeting of the National Council on Family Relations, Lake Geneva, Wisconsin, August 29, 1951. Winston W. Ehrmann, "Student Cooperation in a Study of Dating Behavior," *Marriage and Family Living,* 14:4 (November, 1952), 322-326.

the changes which may be taking place in behavior patterns. But even such information as is available does not indicate that a lowering of standards is desirable. Walter Waggoner's[3] comment that we need to be careful not to "confuse the ailment with the desired state of health, or change the temperature scales on the thermometer to make the fever 'normal,'" is pertinent. Although shifts occur in the mores concerning various types of behavior, the changes are not always in the direction of removal of taboos. In moral standards there is a tendency for reaction to occur after periods of greater laxity.

Attitudes of young people on premarital conduct

Between 1940 and 1952 three studies were made of the opinion of college students on sex standards for men and women outside marriage. The students were asked to check one of four statements that most nearly represented their opinion. The first study was made of 173 students at Cornell in 1940-41 by Rockwood and Ford.[4] We made a similar study among 2,000 students at Michigan State College in 1947, and repeated it in 1952 with 1600 students in 11 colleges. Table 7 summarizes the results.

It is interesting to note that in all three student generations approximately two out of three students stated that they believed in no sexual relations for either outside marriage, three-fourths of the girls and over half of the boys holding to this belief. If sex standards have been greatly modified by the social changes of recent years, the change is not revealed in these studies.

Investigation into the sex conduct of great numbers of men[5, 6] has revealed that indulgence in sexual relations before marriage is considerably less common among men with more

[3] Nieman Fellow at Harvard University.

[4] Lemo D. Rockwood and Mary E. Ford, *Youth, Marriage and Parenthood,* p. 40. New York: John Wiley & Sons, Inc., 1945.

[5] Alfred C. Kinsey, *op. cit.*

[6] Leslie B. Hohman and Bertram Schaffner, "The Sex Lives of Unmarried Men," *The American Journal of Sociology,* 52:6 (May, 1947), 501-507.

education than among men with less education. The percentage of men who have had premarital sex experience decreases with each rise in educational level. Indulgence is most prevalent among those with a grade-school education only, and least prevalent among those with some years of college. Studies among young women reveal that the same differences exist, that is, promiscuity becomes progressively less prevalent among girls as years of schooling increase.

TABLE 7

PERCENTAGES OF STUDENTS CHECKING EACH OF FOUR STATEMENTS REPRESENTING ATTITUDES ON PREMARITAL SEX STANDARDS, 1600 STUDENTS IN 11 COLLEGES IN 1952, 2,000 MICHIGAN STATE COLLEGE STUDENTS IN 1947, 173 CORNELL UNIVERSITY STUDENTS, 1940-41

	Men			Women		
Approved standard	11 Colleges 1952	M.S.C. 1947	Cornell 1940	11 Colleges 1952	M.S.C. 1947	Cornell 1940
Sexual relations:						
For both	19%	16%	15%	4%	2%	6%
None for either	57	59	49	70	76	76
For men only	9	10	23	19	15	11
Between engaged persons only	15	15	11	7	7	6

Regardless of how emancipated young women may be, few of them can indulge freely in premarital coitus without mental and emotional conflict. Since girls are quite universally conscious of the attitudes of their parents and families toward their sex conduct, few are happy in relationships that they fear will bring sorrow or disgrace to their families. Two studies of this subject over a period of 12 years show that approximately two out of three of the girls of each college generation give as their reason for refraining from premarital sex experimentation "family training" or "sorrow of parents." (See Table 8.) In the 1952 study, men who had refrained from premarital coitus also gave this as the second most common reason for their virginity.

It is possible that so few students in the later studies check fear of pregnancy not because they had no fear but because they felt there were better reasons than fear. They had a more positive reason for maintaining virginity before marriage. In collecting dating and courtship histories we have noticed that engaged couples are frank to say that they do heavy petting and that they are having difficulty in refraining from sexual relations, but that a great many of them also say "that is one

TABLE 8

PERCENTAGES OF 231 COLLEGE MEN AND 922 COLLEGE WOMEN FROM 11 COLLEGES IN 1952, AND 174 CORNELL WOMEN IN 1940, GIVING VARIOUS REASONS FOR HAVING REFRAINED FROM PREMARITAL SEX RELATIONS

Reason for chastity	Men 11 Colleges 1952	Women 11 Colleges 1952	Women Cornell 1940-41
I want to wait until married	47%	71%	—
Family training	42	66	71%
Religious beliefs	36	31	21
Fear of pregnancy (causing)	25	28	68
Fear that sexual relations will stand in the way of marriage	18	23	42
Fear of social ostracism	13	19	22
Other	8	3	—

thing we wish to save for marriage." Because this statement had been made to us over and over again in conferences with young couples, we put the statement "I want to wait until married" in our 1952 study. Among both men and women this was the most common reason chosen; 47 per cent of the men and 71 per cent of the women checked it.

The positive motivation for this idealism concerning sex and marriage has its source in family attitudes and teachings, in religion, in a conscious desire to have a good marriage, and an awareness of society's standards and expectations. The negative motivations, such as fear of venereal disease, fear of pregnancy, and fear of social ostracism, still exert pressure but they have lost a measure of the force they exerted in former generations. The positive motivations and the basic idealism of young people are now the major factors.

Premarital experience related to marital adjustment

Many people are especially interested to learn whether premarital experience has any effect upon later marital happiness. Research studies have attempted to find the final answer to that question. Although some findings seem to indicate that those who have had premarital experience are less well adjusted in marriage, it is not possible to establish a causal relationship between the premarital experience and the poor marital adjustment because of the fact that so many complicating factors are related to premarital experience as well as to marital adjustment.

To illustrate: A couple steady-dating during their senior year in high school indulged occasionally in sexual intercourse. Just after graduation, when they were both seventeen, the girl learned that she was pregnant. When they told their parents that they intended to be married, both families objected strenuously. The boy's family felt that the girl was from an undesirable family, a family of less wealth and social standing. The girl's family had had high hopes for the future of their daughter, since she had made a brilliant scholastic record in high school. She had talked of becoming a doctor and her family was anxious to help her toward her goal. Both families agreed to the wedding only when they were finally told of the pregnancy.

After five years of marriage this couple was extremely unhappy. The wife held a deep resentment because she had not been able to go to college or prepare for the career she had hoped for. She also had rejected her baby from the time of its birth, and it had developed into an unhappy problem child. She had been unable to respond sexually to her husband throughout almost all the marriage, although she had enjoyed coitus before marriage. An off-hand diagnosis would seem to be that the premarital coitus and resulting forced marriage were the whole cause of the trouble, since the wife had rejected everything associated with the premarital experience. But analysis of the factors involved in the case brought to light other circumstances that made diagnosis much less simple. Although the wife's mother seemed conscientious and anxious to help her daughters, this daughter, at 22, confessed that for as long as she could remember she had felt a bitter antagonism toward her mother. She was intensely attached to her father and said she had always resented being a girl and wished she were a man. Moreover, all through the young couple's marriage a violent antagonism had persisted between the two parent-in-law families, both of whom blamed the child-in-law for all the marital difficulties, as well as for the original sexual activity that had forced the marriage.

The young couple had also been plagued with financial difficulties, for the husband had trouble holding a job. His family sympathized with him in his job difficulties, always making excuses for his failures and blaming circumstances or other people. They were willing to help him with gifts of money, and they resented the fact that his wife was critical of her husband and felt that he ought to be able to support her and the baby without financial help from his parents.

Would it be possible to isolate any one factor and say that it was solely or largely responsible for this marriage failure? The case illustrates the difficulty of determining what causal relationship exists between premarital experience and later success or failure in marriage. Certain types of personality weaknesses or maladjustments may contribute to excessive sexual emphasis before marriage and these same factors may contribute to failure in marriage. Couples having difficulty in marriage may also tend to focus upon the premarital experience as the cause of marital troubles, whether or not the premarital experience significantly affected later marital adjustment.

Experimentation as preparation for marriage

Because studies have shown that the sex adjustment in marriage is often difficult, some young people believe it would be wise to experiment before marriage in order to learn whether or not they are well mated. But such experimentation may create doubts that have no sound basis. The experimentation can only tell people that they are physically fit for mating. This they may safely assume without experimentation, since only an extremely small percentage of human beings are not biologically equipped to mate. There is the possibility that the experimenting before marriage will be disappointing because of the conditions under which such experimentation must take place. The couple may conclude they are not well matched whereas, if they had waited until they could start their sex life under the more ideal conditions of marriage they would have found the experience mutually successful. The problems that are basic in difficult sex adjustments after marriage are not biological but psychological; and the psychic elements in sex adjustment require time and patience if a happy and permanently good sex adjustment is to be achieved. Those who are experimenting before marriage are not building a relationship which meets the emotional and psychic needs of both. Premarital intercourse must of necessity be chiefly on the physical level, characterized by selfishness rather than mutuality. If it is between a couple who later marry, there is a strong possibility that their ability to achieve psychic union as well as physical after marriage will be limited by the fact that their relationship has been fixed at a physical level before marriage.

A major objection to premarital coitus as preparation for marriage is that it is almost impossible for a couple to achieve, outside marriage, sexual union which is complete in all its psychic and emotional aspects. Couples who indulge in sex relations outside marriage fail to understand the possible completeness of a sex relationship. Such factors as the necessity for haste, the fear of discovery, embarrassment, the fear of pregnancy, and sordid surroundings are often influential. Couples whose marriage to each other might have had the possibility of great happiness may become disillusioned and doubtful after they have experimented sexually. In some of these cases the disillusionment results in the breaking off of a love affair that might have led to a successful marriage. Although it is true that any two people may not be equal in sex drive, there is no way before marriage for a couple to determine whether or not they match in sex drive. The moral training and psychological conditioning of young people in our society make it necessary for them to live together under the suitable conditions of marriage before it is possible to know the true nature of their sexual responses; these may be modified by the social environment. Fortunately, as time passes, couples in marriage are able to adjust and cope with differences in sex drive. This could not be done outside marriage. But in marriage they can study each other's responses and learn effective cooperation.

Premarital pregnancy

The ratio of illegitimate births to legitimate births continues about the same in our population from year to year, regardless of advances in contraceptive knowledge. Whatever attitudes may be held about premarital pregnancies, they are eventualities that can hardly be faced realistically ahead of time. When the situation is purely hypothetical, it is not hard for a couple to think of themselves as handling the situation in a modern and emancipated way. But when the case is no longer hypothetical and a girl finds or suspects that she is pregnant, serious decisions must be made and no happy solution is possible. The least unhappy solution is to be found in marriage, *if* the man and woman are suitable marriage partners. In a great many cases, however, marriage for couples caught in these circumstances would only mean the beginning of permanent unhappiness, for their sex interest may be their only bond. The girl may consider abortion, which not only means extreme risk to her life and health but involves moral considerations for most young people. Legal definition may distinguish between abortion and infanticide, but the girl who is involved lives with her own concepts of the difference. The other alternative is to try to make plans which will enable the girl to go safely through the pregnancy and give birth to the baby. This solution means that the parents must be trusted to help.

Many girls will not hesitate to give the baby for adoption, believing that that would be best for the baby and for themselves. Adoption is probably best for the baby, for he can be given the advantages of a happy home and loving parents. Under the best possible circumstances, parents or friends may be able to make the whole experience fairly smooth, with a minimum of publicity for the mother. After the baby is adopted, the mother may feel that the entire experience is in the past. But if she later marries happily and has other children, her love for them will bring her an awareness of the one that had to be given away. The finer her children, the more painful will be the thought of the first-born whom she was not able to know. Young people may be totally unconscious of this side of unmarried parenthood during the time when a premarital pregnancy is only a problem to be solved, but it is a consideration that becomes effective later and inevitably means sorrow. Later sorrow and mental conflict operate also in the case of the illegitimate father.

Numerous other considerations enter into the situation once a premarital pregnancy occurs, so that even among the most emancipated groups in present-day America premarital pregnancies are tragic for all concerned. This is a practical reason why many young people choose to adhere to socially approved standards of sexual conduct.

Hindrance to chances for marriage

Another major reason that young women cite for refraining from premarital unions is the possible "injury to chances for marriage afterwards." What about this reason? Although there are dangers for the boy as well as for the girl in premarital sexual intercourse, young men are somewhat less aware of these dangers. So it is usually the young man who is desirous of premarital coitus and who promotes the idea. It is the girl upon whom the responsibility falls for the final decision in the matter, and many girls who consent to coitus do so in the belief that their chances for marriage with the man in the case will be increased thereby. In some cases the boy may feel an obligation to marry the girl, but the more realistic attitude is probably that expressed by the girls in the Cornell study who believed that sex relations before marriage hindered chances for marriage.

We cite the case of one modern young man. He had been reared in an upper-class home, was intelligent and above average in personality and appearance. He considered his standards of conduct average or above. He stated that it was important to him to marry a girl whose standards of conduct were high and in whom he could have complete confidence. Therefore, in his dating, if he liked a girl and found her attractive he went as far as possible in his petting. He said, "If she permits coitus with me, I can usually be pretty sure I am not the only one, so I look for another girl." His problem was that he had at last found a girl with whom he was seriously in love. He hoped to marry her, but in pursuance of his usual policy he had finally, after having become engaged to her, succeeded in having coitus. He now found himself overwhelmed with doubts and unhappy about the planned marriage, even though she assured him that he was the only man with whom she had ever been intimate and that only because they were engaged had she consented to it. He broke the engagement but was extremely unhappy about it, as was the girl.

Most girls will be indignant at the unfair attitude of the young man in this case, but his attitude is more common than many girls would like to believe. Boys will express what they believe to be modern rational attitudes, especially late at night when the moon is bright and there has been extensive necking or petting. However, they often react emotionally in another way when they are faced with the situation in their own marriage, that is, after they have become married to a girl whom they know to be a non-virgin. There are many other situations in which we can express a rational attitude toward or acceptance of a fact, yet be unable to accept it on an emotional level. In the study of 1600 students in 11 colleges three men out of four could say rationally that, other factors being satisfactory, they would marry a girl who had had premarital coitus. It is doubtful, however, whether that large a percentage would emotionally accept previous non-virginity in their wives. Three out of four men students queried say they would not marry a girl who had had premarital sexual relations with *several* different people, and two out of three women state this opinion about men.[7] Neither sex can rationalize acceptance of promiscuity, but both can express more willingness to accept as a spouse a person who has made only one or a few "mistakes."

Overemphasis on sex

Our discussion thus far may seem to have been primarily from the viewpoint of the woman, but most of the considerations are of as much importance for the man who wishes to make a successful marriage. From the viewpoint of the young man, one of the chief hazards of premarital coitus, aside from the danger of being forced into a marriage with a girl whom he would not choose for his wife, is the danger of exaggerating the sex element in courtship to the neglect of other important considerations. It is easy to become so involved in obsessive sex interest with a girl who permits extreme petting or intimate relations that it is impossible to judge accurately whether or not there are other common interests which will make possible a happy marriage.

In Chapter VI we discussed the objectives which should be accomplished in courtship as a preliminary to a permanently successful marriage. Marriage counselors are constantly called upon for help by troubled couples who have been carried into marriage by an overwhelming sex interest only to find later that they have nothing else in common. The danger here is greater for the young man than for the girl because, in our society, since boys are less inhibited than girls they are more

[7] Attitudes of 450 University of California students answering questionnaire in 1952.

interested sexually. Thus boys are more easily blinded to other qualities if a girl provides sexual response. Therefore, the boy who hopes to make a good marriage needs to avoid obsessive sex interest and to be realistic in looking for other qualities. The best marriages are made by those couples who avoid becoming involved in premarital sexual intimacies while they look for personality traits and common interests which are important to a good marriage.

Premarital coitus and necessity for reeducation after marriage

In terms of successful marriage, an unfortunate effect of premarital experimentation on the part of the man is that such experience constitutes a type of education and fixes a set of habit patterns almost all of which will have to be unlearned or discarded if he is to be successful in marriage later. The major if not the total emphasis of the premarital experiences is self-centered sex gratification; physical techniques are developed which simply emphasize the one goal, satisfaction, or release from a physical pressure. There is neither awareness of the need for, nor desirability for the presence of, sympathy and identification with a loved personality as one of the satisfying essentials of sexual union. The more premarital experience a man has had, the more fixed will become his pattern of sex expression. After marriage it will be exceedingly difficult for him even to realize the need for a wider and more inclusive emphasis. Since his conception of marital consummation will be exclusively physical, if the physical response of his wife is not exactly according to his premarital pattern he may be disillusioned and inclined to seek physical response elsewhere, thus destroying the possibility of the physical and psychic identification which is one of the permanently satisfying aspects of successful marriage.

Deferred marriage

There is currently much discussion of the problems of those who, because of early dating, have become ready to marry, but who are not able to marry because they may have several years of professional training ahead of them, or because they may not have reached the point of financial independence that will allow them to marry. Various solutions have been suggested. A certain school of thought assumes that young people are faced with exactly three alternatives: they must either (1) marry immediately, (2) have sex expression through promiscuity or premarital relationships, or (3) inhibit their natural urges to the point of dangerous self-repression which may result in inability to adjust to normal marriage later. Several fallacies exist in such reasoning. The first major one is the assumption that marriage is only legal sexual indulgence; in other words, if sex urges are strong, young people are to marry young, with no consideration given to the fact that in general very young marriages are not as successful as those made after maturity has been achieved.

The second major fallacy is the assumption that the alternative is either premarital indulgence or dangerous repression. That assumption ignores the possibility of developing absorbing interests, cultivating a wide range of associations, and engaging in activities that preclude concentration on sex urges. It does not recognize the existence of self-control as distinguished from over-repression or dangerous inhibition. That viewpoint seems to be an underrating of modern young people. Are they all totally uninhibited, spoiled children who must have immediate and complete satisfaction of all urges? Or are they normal human beings, with urges, certainly, but with a reasonable measure of perspective on life needs and with the ability to plan and build for permanent happiness?

The third fallacy of those who hold that youth must either marry early, be promiscuous, or be over-repressed, is too widely accepted. It is argued that control of sex impulses before marriage leads to over-repression that may handicap later marital adjustment. It is true that marital adjustment is often handicapped by the strong inhibitions of one partner or the other, but these inhibitions are developed early in childhood and are usually due to the faults in our system of sex education of young children. If overly strong inhibitions are present, they have been built up long before later adolescence. They can usually be broken down gradually by intelligent effort in marriage, but to attempt to throw aside control and indulge in sexual experimentation before marriage would only result in greater mental conflict for the inhibited individuals.

Normally well-adjusted young people will suffer no ill effects from following a plan which includes self-control and emphasizes avoidance of excessive sex interest until they can marry. The advantages are all on the side of this course of action. Here, as in many other phases of marital and premarital experience, the long-time viewpoint is of fundamental importance. What is most desirable for life as a whole? The permanent happiness of a good marriage must be weighed against other considerations.

Chapter IX

MIXED MARRIAGES

OPPOSITES are commonly believed to attract each other. The novelty of extreme differences in background or personality make-up of two individuals is believed conducive to romance. Among groups of young people discussing marriage or courtship these questions often arise, "How much does it matter whether we are of the same nationality or religion? Why

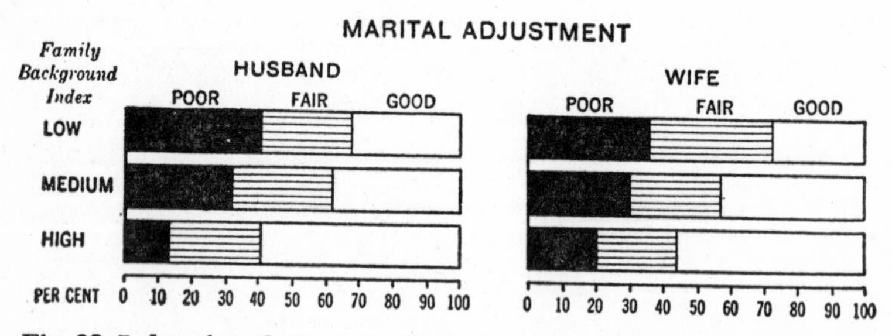

Fig. 28. Index of similarity in family background and adjustment in marriage. Young people who come from similar backgrounds have fewer handicaps to happiness in marriage. From E. W. Burgess and L. S. Cottrell, *Predicting Success or Failure in Marriage,* p. 79. New York: Prentice-Hall, Inc., 1939.

are parents often opposed to their children marrying across religious lines? Is it all just prejudice? How great do differences have to be to constitute a 'mixed marriage'?"

The time to consider these questions is before the final choice of a mate has been made. Many marriages take place between people of widely different backgrounds; the success of such marriages varies with the individuals who make them. The chance for success is greater if those who marry across lines of difference are aware at the outset that they will have to work harder for success than they would have to if they married someone with a background similar to their own. All couples have some problems after they marry; in the mixed marriage the number of problems is increased and some problems which would normally exist are intensified. Any marriage that involves extreme differences may be called a mixed marriage, although the term is usually applied to those in which there is a difference in race, nationality, or religion, since these differences show the problems of mixture most clearly.

In this chapter we shall consider several types of mixed marriages. We shall present the results of research studies which have provided information concerning the chances for success or probability of failure in such marriages.

Mixed religious marriages

Although greater religious tolerance exists in America today than ever before, there are still enough differences among the teachings of the Protestant, Catholic, and Jewish faiths to make interfaith marriages one of the more difficult types of mixed marriages. Since our population is heterogeneous religiously, interfaith marriages are common. Our population is made up of approximately 54,000,000 Protestants, 28,000,000 Catholics, 5,000,000 Jews, and 67,000,000 who have no religious affiliation. The latter group is largely of Protestant background; many are children who are not old enough to become church members, since most Protestant churches do not receive children as members until they are 10 or 12 years old. Although the religions are alike in many respects, they also include radical differences. Interfaith marriages are opposed by all three faiths for what they consider to be good reasons. We shall first discuss Protestant-Catholic marriages.

Protestant-Catholic marriages—denominational attitude. Opposition to interfaith marriages began with the intense religious hatreds and wars between Catholics and Protestants during the period of the Reformation. At that time each faith was convinced that the other was a heresy and each believed that no measure to destroy the heresy was too strong. The Thirty Years' War in Europe (1618-1648) was in part a religious war between the Protestants and Catholics.

Today many devout members of both faiths still look upon those who leave the church as lost souls. This conviction is probably the chief reason for church opposition to interfaith marriages. Protestants fear that if a Protestant marries a Catholic, the children born will be brought up to be Catholic and so will be lost to Protestantism. Catholics fear that the Catholic who marries a Protestant will become a lukewarm church member and that the children may be lost to the faith.

The Catholic church has been more aggressive in its program to prevent interfaith marriages and to guarantee that if such marriages are made the children will remain in the Catholic church. Catholic literature devotes considerable space to shaping the attitudes of their young people against interfaith marriages. In stating the Catholic point of view, Edgar Schmiedeler, Director of the Family Life Bureau of the National Catholic Welfare Conference, says, "Mixed marriages lead in many ways to a watered-down type of religion; and a watered-down type of religion does not make a cement which firmly and effectively binds the family group together. Since courtship is the beginning which leads ultimately to a marriage contract, the sound starting point toward this goal will be to avoid courtship with any and all non-Catholics." [1]

If a Catholic decides to marry a Protestant in spite of church pressure, the church asks that the Protestant take instruction in the Catholic faith. Classes are arranged for this purpose. The marriage must be performed by the Catholic church to be valid in the eyes of the church. Before marriage the Protestant member must sign an agreement that the children will be brought up in the Catholic faith, that the marriage will not

[1] Edgar Schmiedeler, *Marriage and the Family,* pp. 111-112. New York: McGraw-Hill Book Company, Inc., 1946.

be broken until death, and that no other marriage ceremony will be held. The agreement is reprinted here:

Ante-Nuptial Agreement

To Be Signed by Applicants for Dispensation from Impediment of Mixed Religion or Disparity of Cult.

Non-Catholic Party

I, the undersigned ________________ of ________________, not a member of the Catholic Church, desiring to contract marriage with ________________ of ________________, who is a member of the Catholic Church, propose to do so with the understanding that the marriage bond thus contracted can be broken only by death.

And thereupon in consideration of such marriage, I, the said ________________ do hereby covenant, promise, and agree to and with the said ________________ that he (she), the said ________________ shall be permitted the free exercise of religion according to the Catholic faith without hindrance or adverse comment and that all the children of either sex born of such marriage, shall be baptized and educated only in the faith and according to the teachings of the Roman Catholic Church, even if the said ________________ shall die first.

I hereby promise that no other marriage ceremony than that by the Catholic priest shall take place.

I furthermore realize the holiness of the use of marriage according to the teaching of the Catholic Church which condemns birth control and similar abuses of marriage. I shall have due respect for the religious principles and convictions of my Catholic partner.

Witness my hand this ______ day of ________________19______ at ______________ in the County of ______________, and State of

Signed in the presence of
Rev.________________________ ________________________

Signature of Non-Catholic

Catholic Party

I, the undersigned ________________ a member of the Catholic Church, of ________________ Parish, ________________, wishing to contract marriage with ____________________, a non-Catholic, hereby solemnly promise to have all the children of either sex, born of this marriage, baptized and reared only in the Catholic faith.

Furthermore, I promise that no other marriage ceremony than that by the Catholic priest shall take place.

I also realize my obligation in conscience to practice my religion faithfully and prudently to endeavor by prayer, good example and the reception of the Sacraments, to induce my life partner to investigate seriously the teachings of the Catholic Church in the hope that such investigation may lead to conversion.

Witness my hand this _______ day of ________________19____ at ______________ in the County of _______________, and State of

Signed in the presence of
Rev._______________________ _______________________
Signature of Catholic

So we see that the Catholic church, considering interfaith marriages a major problem, has developed a program to deal with such marriages.

What is the attitude of the Protestant church? The majority of the some 250 different Protestant denominations frown upon interfaith marriages, but go little further. They do not, as denominations, devote much time to discouraging their young people from marrying Catholics, they do not require the Catholic to agree that the children will be brought up in the Protestant faith, and they do recognize the validity of marriages performed by the Catholic church. The Protestant denominations are without doubt as much opposed to interfaith marriages as the Catholics are. From the viewpoint of holding their members, they have reason to be more opposed because of the definite program of the Catholics for seeing that the children of interfaith marriages are brought up Catholic. The Protestants' lack of a planned program to prevent or control interfaith marriages is due in part to the lack of organization among the many Protestant denominations.

Contrasts in beliefs. Although the churches emphasize that interfaith marriages lead to lukewarm religious attitudes and oppose them on that basis, other factors are involved which are of concern to those interested in the stability of marriage and family life. The difference in belief between Catholics and Protestants concerning birth control, for example, is a potential hazard to the success of an interfaith marriage. A couple might be able to differ on points of religious belief without the differences having any major effect upon marital happiness, but several Catholic-Protestant differences are vitally associated with marital relationships. These differences intrude into daily living and force some kind of adjustment. Chief of these are opposing views over (1) birth control, (2) nature of the marriage, (3) divorce, and (4) the wedding ceremony.

The Catholic church does not recognize the use of contraceptives for any reason. Although some Protestant churches do not approve of birth control, very few of them officially frown upon the use of contraceptives. The majority of the larger denominations have officially recognized birth control as not only right but desirable in marriage. (See Chapter XIX.) This difference in scriptural interpretation is of profound importance in a day when people have so generally accepted the idea of planned parenthood.

In the Catholic church, marriage is a sacrament, and as such it is believed to be ordained by God. Protestants consider marriage as having sacred implications but they do not consider it a sacrament. From the beginning of the Protestant movement, marriage has been looked upon as a civil contract. Since the Catholic church considers marriage a sacrament, it does not permit divorce under any circumstances. Under certain conditions marriages may be annulled. Separations may also be granted with special permission, but separated individuals cannot remarry. The Catholic church does not recognize civil divorces granted to Catholics. The position taken by Protestant churches is that divorces are permissible under certain conditions; the trend has been toward recognizing more conditions justifying divorce.

Protestants recognize the marriage ceremony as binding

whether performed by the church or by the state; the Catholics do not recognize marriage of Catholics by any other than the Catholic church.

Attitudes of Catholic and Protestant young people on mixed marriages. We might ask how all this controversy on the part of the elders in the churches has affected Catholic and Protestant young people. Would they cross church boundaries and marry? In a study of students' attitudes on marriage we found that over 50 per cent of 2,000 students said that other things being equal they would marry into a different faith. There was little difference between responses of Catholics and Protestants. One-third of those who would marry outside their faith would be willing to change to the faith of the partners. Protestant students expressed more willingness to change than Catholics.

This study seems to indicate that younger people are more sympathetic toward other faiths than are the church officials, and that young people do not consider themselves bound by the official attitudes of the church. Students who do not accept official statements from the church as controlling factors when it comes to choosing a marriage partner are nevertheless deeply interested in the findings of research concerning the chances for success in Catholic-Protestant marriages. In states with a large Catholic population young people are constantly asking for the facts about these marriages.

In a study of ecclesiastically valid mixed marriages in all sections of the country, Thomas found that in some dioceses three-fourths of all Roman Catholics marry outside their own church and that for the country as a whole more than one Catholic in four marries outside the church, the greater proportion of mixed marriages being contracted by Catholics of higher educational and socio-economic status.[2]

Divorce rates in mixed and non-mixed marriages. Three large studies have been made to determine the divorce rate in mixed Catholic-Protestant marriages. These studies did not

[2] John L. Thomas, "The Factor of Religion in the Selection of Marriage Mates," *American Sociological Review,* 16:4 (August, 1951), 487-491.

distinguish between ecclesiastically valid marriages (those sanctioned and performed by the Catholic church) and marriages in which the parties were of different faiths but married without the sanction of the Catholic church. One of these studies was our analysis of data from 4,108 mixed and non-mixed marriages among the parents of college students in Michigan. Special attention was given to: conflict situations resulting from religious differences; types of solutions attempted for the conflicts; the adjustments reached by the parents on the religious training of the children; and the eventual denominational choice of the children. Using separation and divorce as an index of failure, the study showed that mixed marriages in which both husband and wife hold to their separate religious faiths have a much higher rate of failure than other marriages. Where both parents were Catholic the divorce rate was lowest, only 4.4 per cent of the marriages ending in divorce; if both were Protestant, 6.0 per cent ended in divorce. If neither was religious, 17.9 per cent ended in divorce. The highest divorce rate of all existed in marriages in which the husband was Catholic and the wife Protestant. Of this group 20.6 per cent were divorced (see Figure 29).

The two other studies of mixed marriages were made in widely separated parts of the country and show approximately the same results. These studies did not analyze the divorce rate by the different possible combinations, that is, by whether the father was Catholic or Protestant and by the divorce rate when one spouse drops his religion and takes up the religion of the other. Ashley Weeks analyzed the marital status of 6,548 families of public and parochial school children in Spokane, Washington. He found a divorce rate of 3.8 among Catholics, 10.0 among Protestants, 17.4 in mixed marriages, and 23.9 if there was no religion.[3] Howard Bell analyzed the marital status of 13,528 families of mixed and non-mixed marriages in Maryland, and found a divorce rate of 6.4 among Catholics, 4.6

[3] H. Ashley Weeks, "Differential Divorce Rates by Occupation," *Social Forces*, 21:3 (March, 1943), 336.

among Jews, 6.8 among Protestants, 15.2 in mixed marriages, and 16.7 if there was no religion in the home.[4] All these studies seem to show that both Catholic and Protestant authorities are justified from the viewpoint of family stability in discouraging young people from entering mixed marriages. However, the research studies on mixed religious marriages have dealt with couples who have children. It is possible that the divorce rate is no higher than average in mixed marriages where there are

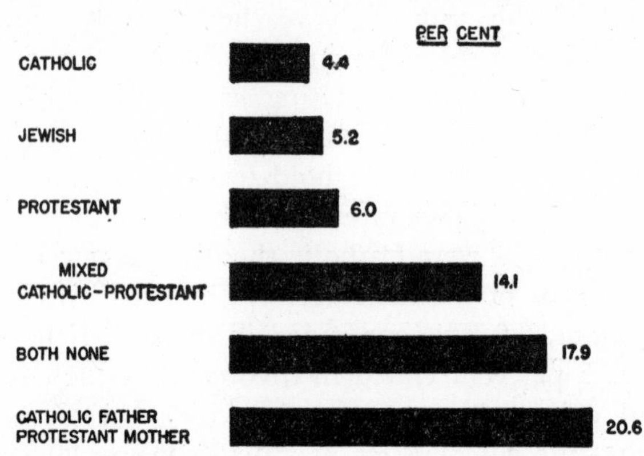

Fig. 29. Religious affiliation and percentage of marriages broken by divorce or separation (4,108 marriages).

no children. On this point existing data are as yet insufficient.

Tentative explanation of higher divorce rate. What are the explanations for the higher divorce rate in mixed marriages? One factor is that during the period of courtship it is hard to be realistic about marriage and easy to minimize the difficulties ahead. A man will sign away his birthright and that of his children under the influence of love, but he may regret it later. Religion may not seem important to young people, but it may become more important as they grow older, especially as they have children. Professor Baber, who has made a number of case studies of mixed marriages, has found that one-half of the conflicts which occur in Protestant-Catholic marriages are over religion, and that often these conflicts center around the training of the

[4] Howard M. Bell, *Youth Tell Their Story,* p. 21. Washington, D.C.: American Council on Education, 1938.

children. He found that the mixed marriages in which the parents were "indifferent" to religion were almost as likely to have conflict over religion as those in which the parents were "devout." [5] Although a person may not be much interested in religion, if he has been exposed to the religious teachings of a certain faith for a period of years it is difficult for him to forget this training. It is also difficult for him to be entirely indifferent about the training of his children. He may never bother to give his children religious training in his own faith, but he will often resent their being brought up in a contrasting faith. The attitudes and feelings of the two families will add to the conflict here. Both sets of grandparents will be watching, hoping to see the children brought up in the "right" church.

Religious faith of children in Protestant-Catholic marriages. Since the non-Catholic is required to sign a statement that he will let the children be brought up in the Catholic faith, the question of the religious training of the children would seem to be settled. Most young people are honest in their intentions before marriage when they sign the commitments about the instruction of the children, but it is impossible for young unmarried people to project themselves ahead and know how they will feel when they have their children. After they are married and the children arrive, they find that some things begin to matter to them more than they had anticipated. At this time, or later when the children are old enough for the beginning of instruction, the entire question will come up for rethinking, and some agreement will have to be reached. The study of mixed marriages among the parents of college students gives some indication of what the eventual decision was about the religious upbringing of the children in these marriages. There were 305 marriages of mixed Catholic-Protestant backgrounds; however, in 113 marriages one spouse had dropped his faith to follow the faith of the spouse. There were, then, 192 marriages that were mixed in that each spouse maintained his

[5] Ray E. Baber, *Marriage and the Family,* p. 170. New York: McGraw-Hill Book Company, Inc., 1939.

original faith. In these 192 marriages, half of the 392 children had been reared in the Protestant faith. The remainder had been reared in the Catholic faith (45.0) or had no faith (5.0). The most common tendency seems to be that the children, especially the daughters, follow the faith of the mother. Approximately 65 per cent of the boys follow the faith of the mother, while 75 per cent of the girls follow the faith of the mother. It is not surprising that the children tend to follow the faith of the mother since it is usually true that the mother is closer to the children and takes the greater responsibility for religious training in the home.

Parental policy on religious training in Protestant-Catholic marriages. The students who were the products of Protestant-Catholic marriages were asked to describe the policy of their parents on religious instruction. A ranking from most common practice to least common practice revealed the following:

(1) Mother took all responsibility for the religious training. (36 per cent)
(2) Our parents told us about both faiths but let us decide for ourselves when we were old enough. (27 per cent)
(3) The responsibility for religious instruction was equally divided between our parents. (20 per cent)
(4) We took turns going to both the church of my father and my mother. (7 per cent)
(5) Father took all responsibility for the religious training. (4 per cent)
(6) Some of us went with my father to his church and some went with my mother to her church. (3 per cent)

The domination of the mother in the religious training of the children is observable. In 36 per cent of the families, the mother took all responsibility for the religious instruction of the children. In one-fourth of the families, children were told about both faiths and permitted to decide for themselves which to accept.

In general, the data show that the Catholic father makes a

stronger effort to defend his faith than the Protestant father does, in that the Catholic father has more to do with the religious training of the children. The Catholic father's insistence upon having a place in the religious instruction of the children may be one factor explaining the high divorce rate when Catholic men marry Protestant women. You will remember that in marriages of this combination the divorce rate was 20.6 while it was only 6.7 per cent when Protestant men marry Catholic women. Half of the nominally Protestant men who had married Catholic women were non-church-members, and they were willing to let the wife rear the children in the Catholic faith without much conflict.

The Catholic father is more likely to be a church member and to feel that the children should be brought up in his faith. It may be quite a blow to him if his wife later finds that she is not willing to live up to the agreement that she signed before the marriage. Serious conflict seems to result in these mixed marriages unless the father gives up and lets the mother have complete charge of the religious instruction, or unless the mother gives up and lets the father have complete charge. The latter solution would be difficult, since the mother usually is closer to the training of the children than the father is, and it would be more difficult for her to give up or to ignore the religious training of the children.

Another factor explaining the lower divorce rate in Catholic mother-Protestant father unions is the hesitation of the Catholic mother to seek a divorce. Three out of every four divorces in the United States are granted to women. This does not mean that men furnish all the grounds for divorce, but simply that the wife is more likely to be the one who petitions for the divorce. There may be as much difficulty in the Catholic mother-Protestant father unions as in any other combination, but they do not end in divorce because the wife does not believe in divorce. She is more likely to stay in the marriage even if it is very unhappy. On the other hand, if a Catholic father-Protestant mother union is unsatisfactory, the Protestant wife will not show as great hesitancy in asking for a divorce. Consequently, the divorce rates in the two different combinations of Catholic-Protestant mixed marriages are different.

Parental conflict in Protestant-Catholic marriages. Each student was asked to state the degree of difficulty the difference in religious belief had created in the parents' marriage. The ranking was on a five-point scale from no handicap at all to a very great handicap. Approximately a third of the students felt that the Protestant mother-Catholic father combination had been a serious handicap, whereas one-fifth of the students from the opposite combination felt that the difference in religion had been serious. Only 3 per cent of the students from families where both parents were Protestants, and only 4 per cent where both parents were Catholic, stated that religion had been a point of conflict in their parents' marriage. Burgess and Cottrell [6] found no significant difference between the happiness of couples in mixed and non-mixed religious marriages. However, the couples in their study were in the early years of marriage and had not yet faced the problems arising when consideration must be given to the religious education of the children.

Change to faith of spouse. In approximately one Protestant-Catholic marriage in three the couple attempted to resolve their differences over religion by one of the spouses' accepting the faith of the other, usually before marriage. Of the 305 mixed marriages in this study 113 had tried this solution. In 56 of the marriages the Protestant member had changed to the Catholic faith, and in 57 marriages the Catholic member had changed to the Protestant faith. What evidence we have indicates that the marriage has a better chance for success when this solution is attempted. The divorce rate was higher when each spouse held to his own faith. Among the cases in which one spouse changed to the faith of the other, the divorce rate was still high (10.6 per cent). The evidence available indicates that the divorce rate is higher when the Catholic mother changes to

[6] E. W. Burgess and L. S. Cottrell, *Predicting Success or Failure in Marriage*, pp. 87-88. New York: Prentice-Hall, Inc., 1938.

the Protestant faith or when the Protestant father changes to the Catholic faith, and lower when the Protestant mother changes to the Catholic faith or the Catholic father changes to the Protestant faith.

The lower divorce rate among the couples who become of the same faith is due in part to the removal of conflict over the religious training of the children. In these marriages from 90 to 95 per cent of the children followed the religion of the faith adopted by the couple. In only 5 per cent of the cases did the children follow the faith renounced by the one spouse. These findings suggest that when one member gives up his faith at the time of marriage he seems to hold to his bargain, at least to the extent that he does not interfere with the religious instruction of the children.

Summary of findings on mixed Catholic-Protestant marriages. Our investigation of marriages in which couples have tried mixed Catholic-Protestant unions indicates that this type of mixed marriage presents serious difficulties. Many hurdles must be overcome before a successful and happy marriage can be achieved. Although the church tries to help young people avoid trouble and although young people think they have removed causes for friction before they enter marriage, most of the causes making for friction must be faced repeatedly after marriage. Agreements made in good faith before marriage may have to be altered after marriage, but they cannot be altered without conflict. These conflicts arise from the differences in belief concerning the religious instruction of the children, birth control, divorce, and other points.

A Catholic young person may be sincere in agreeing with the Protestant partner before marriage that birth control will be practiced in marriage; but he may find later that his conscience will not permit him to stand by his agreement. A Protestant may agree before marriage that birth control will not be practiced, but after the arrival of a few children he may feel that it is unreasonable for the spouse to expect the agreement to be kept. Acceptance of the theory of the "safe period" may seem before marriage to be a solution to the difference in beliefs over birth control, but when a couple finds the "safe period" to be unreliable, the question of using contraceptives will have to be faced and settled all over again.

In places where there are parochial schools the question arises of whether the children will be sent to the public or to the church school. Often the Protestant member cannot see the value of a church school and objects to spending money for private education when the children could be sent to a public school.

Even if the young people themselves can bridge the gap in religious differences, the families of the two present a further problem. Often the parents cannot understand how the children can marry outside the faith. They may use every possible means to prevent the marriage. If the marriage takes place, the parental opposition can be an important source of in-law friction. An illustrative case follows:

Jane, a Protestant, and John, the only son of devout Catholics, were engaged. John insisted that they be married by a priest because of the feelings of his parents. Jane at first refused to sign the agreement requiring the children to be brought up in the Catholic faith. Two priests refused to marry them, but a third, realizing that they would be married by a Protestant minister otherwise, persuaded Jane to sign the agreement and married them, even though Jane stated that she considered the signing of the agreement a mere formality. It was of course known to Jane that John's mother had used every possible means to try to persuade John not to go ahead with the marriage.

When the first baby was born, the mother-in-law repeatedly suggested making plans for the Catholic baptism of the child, without response from Jane. One day Jane phoned her mother-in-law and invited her to attend the christening of the baby by a Protestant minister. The mother-in-law, shocked and hurt, refused to attend. John took no active part in the controversy, but left all decisions in the matter to Jane.

The marriage has lasted for 12 years and is fairly happy. Jane takes all responsibility for the religious training of the three children, who are being brought up in the Protestant faith. John attends the Catholic church several times a year on special days with his mother. Jane privately tells her friends, "He would never go to the Catholic church at all if I didn't insist on it." Jane and John's mother have as little as possible to do with each other and there is mutual antagonism.

All Jane's resentment seems to be directed toward John's mother and not toward John. But it would not have been so directed if John had made any effort to control the up-bringing of the children. If John himself had had any stronger religious convictions, he could not have adjusted to the complete domination of the family life in this area by his wife. One reason why this marriage was able to survive seems to be the fact that John had been dominated by his mother until his marriage, and the pattern continued after marriage with the wife substituted for the mother. There was little conflict, since the husband could accept the situation and the wife could enjoy her position of dominance.

Jewish-Gentile marriages. The Jewish-Gentile marriage is mixed not only in religion but also in additional aspects of culture. Differences in food habits, holidays, and days of rest are involved. Because of these cultural differences and also because the Jews have strongly urged their people to marry within their group, relatively few Jewish-Gentile marriages take place.

Jews recognize two types of Jewish-Gentile marriages, intermarriage and mixed marriage. Intermarriage is marriage between a converted Gentile and a Jew.[7] Orthodox, conservative, and reformed rabbis will perform marriages of converted Gentiles and Jews; however, this type of marriage is discouraged, since Jews do not feel that Gentiles converted to Judaism are faithful Jews. When the Gentile does not accept Judaism, the marriage is termed a mixed marriage. No orthodox rabbi and few reformed or conservative rabbis would officiate at a mixed marriage.

[7] Solomon B. Freehof, "Report on Mixed Marriages and Intermarriage," *Yearbook*, Vol. 57, Philadelphia: Central Conference of American Rabbis, 1947.

By a margin of only two votes, the Central Conference of American rabbis meeting in Montreal in 1947 defeated a resolution which would have completely forbidden marriage between Jews and unconverted Gentiles.[8] One study of Jewish-Gentile intermarriages in New Haven between 1870 and 1950 shows that approximately 5 per cent of the Jewish marriages were interfaith.[9] Other studies of interfaith marriages in New York, Cincinnati, and Stamford all show a low interfaith marriage rate among the Jews.[10] In interfaith marriages the Jewish man is much more likely to marry outside the faith than the Jewish woman. Baber found in a study of 130 Jewish-Gentile marriages in New York City that Jewish men marry Gentiles about twice as frequently as do Jewish women.[11] Another study of 59 intermarriages revealed that the Jewish partner was male in 40 of the 59 cases.[12] The greater tendency for the Jewish man to marry outside the faith is due to the fact that the young men have greater freedom to mingle with Gentiles and are not so carefully supervised as are the Jewish girls. One student of interfaith marriages points out that the male friends of Jewish girls are very carefully checked, more so than in the case of Gentile girls. Although Jewish boys are also closely guarded, they take advantage of the wider mobility which is a prerogative of their sex. However, the interfaith marriage rate of the Jewish men is low because of parental supervision of dating. "One or two dates with a Gentile girl are sufficient for the relationship to become a topic of gossip in the community. In such cases word usually reaches Jewish parents quite rapidly, and they plead with their wayward sons to confine their interest to Jewish girls." [13]

[8] *Family Life,* 7:9 (September, 1947), 8.

[9] Ruby Jo Reeves Kennedy, "Single or Triple Melting Pot? Intermarriage Trends in New Haven, 1870-1950," *American Journal of Sociology,* 57:1 (July, 1952), p. 56.

[10] Milton L. Barron, "The Incidence of Jewish Intermarriage in Europe and America," *American Sociological Review,* 11:1 (February, 1946), 11-12.

[11] Baber, *op. cit.,* p. 168.

[12] Barron, *op. cit.,* p. 12.

[13] Barron, *op. cit.,* p. 12.

Conflict in Jewish-Gentile marriages. Most of the differences we have discussed in relation to Protestant-Catholic marriages exist in Jewish-Gentile marriages as well. In addition, cultural differences in Jewish-Gentile marriages make adjustment more difficult than in the Protestant-Catholic marriages. Discrimination has forced Jews to emphasize family and group solidarity. The Jewish family is a closely knit in-group into which it is often difficult for an outsider to fit. Family resistance is often

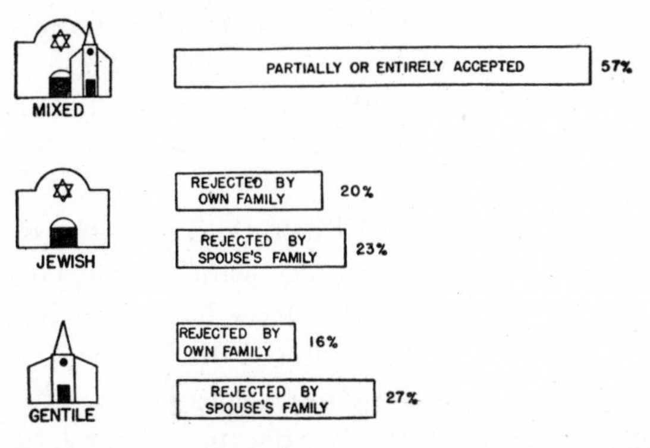

Fig. 30. Family acceptance and rejection in Jewish-Gentile marriages. Young people in love may bridge the gap in a mixed marriage, but it is more difficult for their families to merge their mixed backgrounds. Data from J. S. Slotkin, "Adjustment in Jewish-Gentile Intermarriages," *Social Forces,* Vol. 21, December, 1942, pp. 226-230.

offered to accepting the member from the out-group by both the Gentile and the Jewish families. Slotkin[14] found in his study of 183 Jewish-Gentile intermarriages that 57 per cent of the intermarried people were either partially or entirely accepted by both families, 20 per cent of the Jews were not accepted by their own families, and 23 per cent were not accepted by the family of the spouse, 16 per cent of the Gentiles were not accepted by their own familes, and 27 per cent were not accepted by the family of the spouse. The higher percentage of non-acceptance by the Jewish families indicates stronger

[14] J. S. Slotkin, "Adjustment in Jewish-Gentile Intermarriages," *Social Forces,* Vol. 21 (December, 1942), 226-230.

pressure toward endogamy on the part of the Jewish group.

Baber found that the children of Jewish-Catholic marriages and Jewish-Protestant marriages were brought up in the Jewish faith more frequently than in either the Catholic or the Protestant faith. This finding would seem to indicate that the Jewish parent dominates in the religious training. It means also that in Jewish-Gentile marriages the father more often dominates. Baber found that half the conflicts occurring in these marriages were over religion, and the children were usually involved. Conflict was as frequent in marriages in which the spouses were "indifferent" as in those where the spouses were devout.[15] This finding is contrary to the beliefs of many, who contend that if neither spouse is religious little trouble over religion will develop.

Another factor which stands in the way of successful Jewish-Gentile marriages is the prejudice which some Gentiles hold against Jews. As a people, the Jews have been driven from country to country and have suffered discrimination for centuries. In some sections of the United States today groups are engaged in anti-Jewish campaigns. Because of these attitudes on the part of some Gentiles and because the Jews have tried to preserve their culture, the Jews are treated as a minority group. The Gentile who marries a Jew is conscious of Gentile attitudes and sometimes attempts to avoid being identified with Jews as a group, even though he loves the individual Jew whom he has married. If the family lives in an area where discrimination exists, the Gentile is pained to see his child suffer as a Jew.

A college girl in a midwestern school fell in love with a Jewish boy from New York who was taking part of his aviation training in Illinois. They decided to marry, but the parents of the girl objected. The girl could not understand why her parents opposed the marriage. She was not acquainted with prejudice against Jews. In her town there was only one Jewish family, and they were highly respected. In her college no distinctions were made between Jewish and Gentile students. The

[15] Baber, *op. cit.*, pp. 169-170.

girl and her friend planned that after marriage they would live in the East near the boy's family. An older friend, from whom the girl sought advice, suggested that the marriage be postponed and that the girl go to New York City for a semester and take work toward her degree, meanwhile using the opportunity to become acquainted with the fiancé's family. The plan was agreed upon, and she spent a semester in the eastern school, after which she decided that her parents were right in opposing the marriage. She felt that she could accept the young man's religion and she liked his family, but she found it difficult to adjust to family customs that were quite different from those of her own family. She also concluded that she did not love him enough to endure with him the discrimination that existed in his city. She realized, too, that she would be half-hearted in her acceptance of his life and that she might not be willing to have her children brought up in his faith and subjected to the discrimination which she had observed. She decided not to go ahead with the interfaith marriage.

This young woman did well to analyze carefully before marriage her attitudes and feelings concerning the different backgrounds of herself and her fiancé. This analysis enabled her to recognize that she was not capable of overcoming the difficulties that would be involved in the intended marriage. Some young people in a similar situation may find that to them the difficulties would not be insurmountable. Such persons may well decide, after careful self-analysis, to proceed with an interfaith marriage. However, they should be fully aware that it is easy to underestimate the importance of cultural and religious differences when one is emotionally involved during the courtship period, and that it is hard to be realistic about the future. One tends to put future problems out of mind and avoid facing them before marriage.

Mixed marriages among Protestants. Before leaving the subject of mixed religious marriages, it should be pointed out that marriages between members of different Protestant groups may include almost as many problems as the interfaith marriages we have been discussing. Marriage between a member of one of the conservative Protestant denominations that condemn dancing, motion pictures, smoking, and reading newspapers on Sunday as sinful, and an Episcopalian who knows nothing of such beliefs or considers them remnants of fanatical attitudes of a past generation, could involve as many wide differences as any interfaith marriage. The difference in religious beliefs would enter into many phases of living, just as in other interfaith marriages.

Further, the individual who has a religious orientation to life may find that his is a mixed marriage if he marries one who is not religiously oriented. The spouse who is religiously oriented represents the sacred point of view in contrast to the secular or naturalistic viewpoint.[16] The contrasts in beliefs between the religiously oriented and non-religiously oriented may be as great as the contrasts between Jews and Gentiles or Catholics and Protestants. Our study of mixed and non-mixed religious marriages with a total of 125 couples in which the wife was a church member and the husband was of no religious faith revealed that 16.0 per cent had ended in divorce. If the wife had been Protestant the divorce rate was almost as high (19.0 per cent) as when the Protestant wife had married a Catholic. The high divorce rate in this combination of spouses may result in part from a clash of sacred and secular values. Available information seems to indicate that young people should compare and contrast their religious values and philosophies as well as contrasts in faiths.

Interracial marriages

Biologically, there is no reason why races should not intermarry. Superior people mentally and physically beget superior children, regardless of the color of the skin or the shape of the eyes. However, as long as society not only frowns upon inter-

[16] For a fuller discussion of sacred and secular points of view see Howard Becker and Reuben Hill, eds., *Family Marriage and Parenthood,* pp. 19-40. Boston: D. C. Heath and Company, 1948.

racial marriages but also makes them illegal in some states it is extremely difficult for two people of different races to find happiness in marriage. They can hardly be completely indifferent to the thinking of those about them. Even if the two who marry are able to accept philosophically the fact that both will be subjected to discrimination, not only as members of the minority race but also because of their defiance of the social disapproval of such a marriage as theirs, they will still face serious problems when children come. People who can endure prejudice against themselves may suffer intensely when the prejudice strikes at their children. The children of mixed racial marriages are sometimes subjected to discrimination by both the races represented in the marriages. When the parent from the majority race experiences pain through the children, or suffers because of family attitudes toward the marriage, it is easy for him to begin to blame the spouse. The reaction is much the same in all types of mixed marriages. When the pressure of the opposing backgrounds becomes severe, the tendency is to focus all conflicts around the differences: "It is all because he is a Jew," or "a Protestant," or "a Catholic," or "belongs to that race."

However, the most serious objection to all mixed marriages is their effect upon the children. This is especially true of mixed racial marriages. Parents may possibly change their religion when they see the damaging effects of their differences upon the children. But they cannot change their race. As long as the children live, they will suffer from the social stigma of their parents' marriage. Therefore, although there is no biological excuse for the opposition to interracial marriages, it must be recognized that to cross racial lines in marriage will create problems that are extremely difficult to solve. The hazards to happiness in such a marriage are great.

Internationality marriages

G.I. marriages to girls of other nations face many difficulties which may result in a high divorce rate. Not only do broad cultural and religious differences exist in such marriages, but additional problems arise because the marriages were contracted under abnormal circumstances and the wives in most instances are now living thousands of miles from home. Newspapers frequently carry stories of foreign brides who are returning to their homes because they cannot make all the required adjustments. Most of us have among our personal acquaintances at least one couple who contracted a mixed marriage growing out of wartime travels, so the problems involved are not unfamiliar. Some of the marriages in which there has been little success in making the adjustments will survive because of the unwillingness of the wife to give up and to return home. The case of a mixed marriage from World War I illustrates some of the factors involved:

At the time the case came to our attention the couple had been married for fourteen years. They lived on the plains of western Oklahoma in the famous dustbowl area. Their house was a fairly comfortable four-room farmhouse set in the midst of acres of wheat land. There was no tree on their land; nor were there any in sight in any direction. The husband was a hard-working man of crude appearance. He owned his land, but he was not well off. By careful management he was able to make the income from his wheat farming carry them over from year to year.

The wife was of French parentage. She had never been happy in the marriage and through all the years had not become resigned to the circumstances of their lives. Her reasons for the failure were, "He told me he had a big American ranch, and I pictured beautiful trees and hills like my own France. So I left my family and came with him. This is what he brought me to. At home we had lots of fun and music, and I gave music lessons to the children of the village. But here it is always quiet—he never talks and he never laughs. When I've wanted a piano he says we can't afford it. In my family we could get along without a tractor but not without a piano. My family were so happy for me when I had a chance to marry him, so when I was disappointed, I couldn't write and tell them. It seemed better to stay and try to make the best of it, but I don't know if I did right. He doesn't think I am a good farmer's wife."

Both these people were unhappy in the marriage, but they were in agreement in trying to stay together. The husband felt responsible for the wife's support and care, and she was unwilling to admit defeat publicly. It will be seen that this marriage involved not only a nationality difference but differences in the way of life which presented serious barriers. From a French village to an Oklahoma wheat farm proved too great a step for this wife.

The case above illustrates the fact that many mixed marriages involve more than one type of "mixture." With more differences there are more adjustments required of both members of the couple. In some internationality marriages there is a difference in language, one member having to learn to speak a new language, and a difference in religion, as well as differences in customs and manner of living. These marriages will require unusual understanding and adjustability of both partners if the marriages are to be successful.

Other marriages across nationality lines may not involve such serious differences. If both husband and wife happen to be of the same religion, of approximately the same economic level, and if both are familiar with the same language, the difference in nationality alone need not hinder the success of the marriage. In these, as in all marriages, much depends upon the viewpoint and personality traits of the individuals. If both recognize that adjustments will be required, and marry with the will to build a successful marriage in spite of any problem circumstances that may exist, their chances for happiness are more favorable.

Difference in intelligence

Differences in intelligence, or in economic status, are less serious than some others, but they may still constitute a mixed marriage and involve hazards to happiness for one or both spouses. Terman found that in cases where the husband was far superior to the wife in intelligence the husbands rated low in happiness, although the wives rated high. If the intelligence ratings were reversed, the husband being inferior to the wife, the wife's happiness score was low. Couples with the highest rating for both husband and wife were those in which the husband and the wife were equal in intelligence. (See Figure 31.)

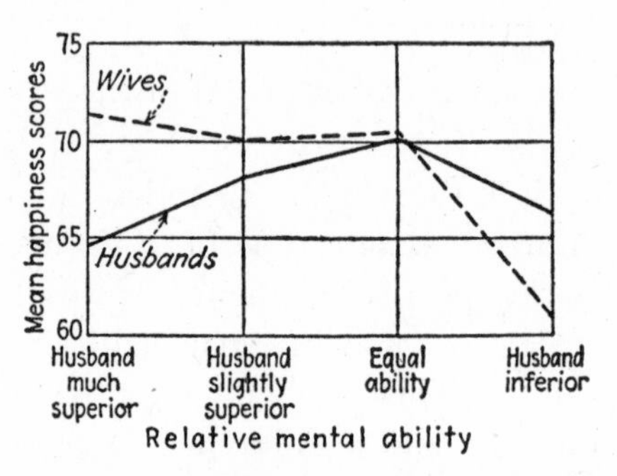

Fig. 31. Curves of mean happiness according to rated mental ability of spouses. *By permission* from *Psychological Factors in Marital Happiness* by L. M. Terman, Copyrighted, 1938, by McGraw-Hill Book Co., Inc., p. 193.

Educational differences

Several studies have been made in an attempt to discover whether educational differences of the spouses affect adjustment in marriage. The majority of these studies show that the same amount of education is slightly favorable to good adjustment in marriage.[17] The general pattern seems to be that if the husband has more education than the wife, he has a lower happiness score. If the wife has more education, she has a lower happiness score than her husband, but the husband's happiness score may be unaffected. These were the findings of the Terman study. Or, as in our study and the study by Hamilton, the husband whose wife has more education than he may be happier in his marriage than the average husband. And so we will have to conclude that although the usual belief is that great disparity in education is undesirable between spouses, research data have yielded little evidence to support that belief. It is probably true that if a person from a family of highly educated people who place a great value upon education mar-

[17] Kirkpatrick, Hamilton, Landis, and Terman.

ried into a family with little or no formal educational background or interest in education, the marriage would involve elements of a mixed marriage. If difference in education also meant a great difference in intelligence, then the educational difference between the spouses might have a greater effect upon marital happiness.

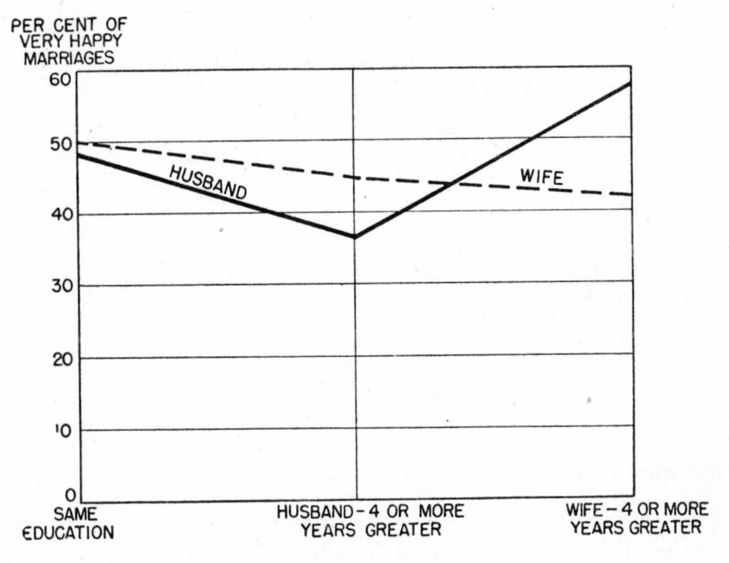

Fig. 32. Educational differences of 409 husbands and 409 wives and self-rated happiness in marriages.

Our analysis of the divorce rate in 3,796 families of college students shows that there seems to be little relationship between the educational difference of the parents and the divorce rate. The divorce rate had been highest in the marriages in which the husband had had four years more education than the wife and the lowest in those in which the wife was a college graduate and the husband had an eighth-grade education. (See Table 9.)

We cite these findings not to suggest that young men ought to try to marry women with more education than they have, but to call attention to the fact that, as is true of many generally accepted beliefs on mate choice and marital happiness, no sound basis exists for the belief that it is desirable for the husband to be the more intelligent or the better-educated partner in a marriage. Many men will not wish to marry wives who have more education than theirs; however, the men who do court and marry women with more education seem to have successful marriages.

TABLE 9

DIVORCE RATES IN 3,796 MARRIAGES BY EDUCATION OF SPOUSES

Education of Spouses	Number of Marriages	Per cent Divorced
Total cases	3,796	6.3
Both grade-school graduates	793	6.4
Both high-school graduates	1,054	6.7
Both college graduates	422	5.7
Husband 4 years more education	646	6.8
Husband 8 years more education	58	5.2
Wife 4 years more education	721	6.1
Wife 8 years more education	102	1.9

Differences in economic status

Differences in economic status may constitute a mixed marriage if they are great, and if the two families have correspondingly great differences in ways of life. Here again the outcome will depend in part upon the two individuals. Some girls who marry into a higher economic level renounce their "poor relations" and live entirely within the circle of the husband's family and friends. If the economic status or "the money" is in the wife's family, problems of adjustment may arise because of the husband's attitude. Traditionally, the American husband expects to support his wife and is expected to do so. Many men rebel at economic domination by the wife. Some men will compensate by aggressive attitudes in other areas. However, research studies have not yet yielded enough reliable data on this type of marriage to warrant definite conclusions.

Physical differences

Physical differences will cause problems only if they loom large in the minds of either one in the marriage. A tall woman who feels embarrassed and conspicuous when dating a man shorter than herself might adjust more happily in a marriage with a man of her own height or taller. A man who feels inferior and conscious of his shortness when with taller girls might better marry a girl of his own height or less. But if a person is not height-conscious, there is no reason why height differences or other differences in physical type need matter.

Age differences

Young people are often concerned about age differences between the husband and wife. Various research studies which have attempted to determine whether age differences affect the happiness of marriage have provided no conclusive evidence. Marriages in which there is as much as ten years' difference in ages seem to have as much chance for happiness as those in which the spouses are the same age.

Terman's study found the happiest wives among those whose husbands were four to ten years younger.[18] However, Terman did not feel that age difference in spouses was important enough to include in a prediction scale. Burgess[19] found no consistent relationship between age differences in the spouses and their marital happiness. The age combinations with the largest percentage of good adjustments were those in which the wife was older than the husband. After analyzing these data, Burgess states, "When we summarize the findings regarding age differences, the popular romantic notion that, for marital happiness, the husband should be somewhat older than the wife, is not substantiated for the group studied."

Our study of 409 marriages of long duration showed no con-

[18] Lewis M. Terman, *Psychological Factors in Marital Happiness,* p. 185. New York: McGraw-Hill Book Company, Inc., 1938.

[19] Burgess and Cottrell, *op. cit.,* pp. 161-164.

sistent relationship between age differences of husband and wife and happiness in marriage. The largest percentage of very happy marriages was among couples in which the husband was from one to eight years older than the wife. However, it is interesting to note that the largest percentage of very happy husbands had married women who were three or more years older than they were.

We have analyzed 1,226 marriages among the parents of college students to see whether any significant relationship existed between age differences of the spouses and the divorce rate. Table 10 gives the results of this study.

TABLE 10

DIVORCE RATES IN 1,226 MARRIAGES BY AGES OF SPOUSES

Age of Spouses	Number of Marriages	Percentage Divorced
Total cases	1,226	6.7
Same age	141	4.2
Husband Older		
1-4 years	684	8.0
5-8 years	195	7.2
9-12 years	66	3.0
13 or more	28	10.7
Wife Older		
1-2 years	75	2.7
3 or more	37	.0

The divorce rate in these marriages had been lowest in marriages in which the wife was older than the husband.

If a woman marries a man ten years older than she, it may mean that she has been conditioned to respect older men or has idolized her own father; she finds greater happiness in marriage to an older man because of such conditioning. Similarly, the man who marries an older woman may marry her because he needs to be mothered and because she wants to mother someone. The marriage may be above average in happiness because it fulfills needs of both. A man of a different make-up would find such mothering intolerable. No set rule can be stated. All types of age combinations can be found that have worked well provided they were suited to the two personalities involved.

The majority of people do marry spouses of approximately the same age, or else the woman marries a man a few years older than she is. But the fact that this is the average does not mean that it is necessarily the desirable standard. Actually, a few reasons exist that suggest it would perhaps be desirable if men more generally married women somewhat older than themselves. Since women's life expectancy is several years greater than men's, women would face fewer years of widowhood if their husbands were younger than they. Further, there is evidence that in our culture women develop their maximum sexual responsiveness somewhat later than men do; consequently a couple in which the wife is in her late twenties and her husband a few years younger at marriage may approach a mutually satisfactory sex adjustment somewhat sooner than in the average marriage in which the wife is younger.

In discussing age differences we have been speaking of differences that would not be great enough to constitute a mixed marriage. When extreme differences in age exist, such as a variation of twenty years or more, the marriage might have less chance for happiness, since that much difference approaches a mixed marriage. The two would represent two different generations with different friends, recreational interests, and life values. Although we have few cases in our study, the divorce rate seems to increase if the husband is thirteen or more years older than the wife.

Summary

A mixed marriage may result from a combination of factors, all of which make for extreme difference. The greater the number of contrasts, the more hurdles will have to be surmounted to achieve happiness in the marriage.

Consideration of all types of mixed marriages forces the conclusion that whether the difference is in race, religion, nationality, or in certain other characteristics and circumstances in the individuals' make-up or background, serious hazards to success may be involved. Further, it seems that the differences in mixed marriages do not usually decrease with the passing of time after marriage. They tend to become magnified in the minds of the couple and their families. To achieve happiness in such marriages, individuals must be mentally and emotionally mature and must possess more than average understanding and tolerance.

Chapter X

ENGAGEMENT

IN THE PAST, a promise to marry constituted a legal contract. If the engagement was broken by one of the parties against the will of the other, the one breaking the engagement could be sued for damages. In many states, breach of promise suits are still allowed in the courts, but a number of states have outlawed such suits. The right to sue for breach of promise is one of the privileges women are giving up in exchange for greater social, political, and economic freedom. In the past, in order to protect the woman, society took a firm position to force the man to go ahead with marriage after his declaration of intention to marry. A woman's future was endangered if she had once been rejected or jilted, for other men might consider her undesirable. Since marriage was the chief career open for women, serious damage was done to the woman whose engagement was broken, especially if the man had monopolized her affections during her most marriageable years. It is now recognized that a broken engagement is not so serious a handicap for a woman, since today women are freer to be active in hunting a husband. A jilted girl now has resources other than sitting by the fireside and suffering with a broken heart.

Formerly it was not unusual for the parents of a girl to approach the man she was dating if he had not proposed within a reasonable time and to ask whether he had "serious intentions." They were realistic in recognizing that it was not fair for the girl to have her time taken up with the attentions of a suitor who did not intend to marry her. Further, parents felt a man should not be too slow in making up his mind. Parental interference of this type is relatively unusual in our day. Parents may worry over the fact that a daughter is wasting her best years on a man who is not a marriage prospect, but they will hardly feel that they can ask him either to declare his intentions or stop seeing the girl.

Average time from first date to engagement

How long does it take young people to become acquainted well enough so that they feel they are ready to become engaged? According to the love stories presented by the movies, it would seem that two people meet, love strikes, and they become engaged, the time required for the procedure being negligible. But in reality people usually take a longer time to become acquainted than is indicated by the movies. The majority do not rush into engagement. We asked over 500 single and married students who had been engaged to state how much time had elapsed between the first date and the engagement. A summary is presented in Table 11. It is of interest to note that nearly half

TABLE 11

AVERAGE LENGTH OF TIME ELAPSED IN 546 COURTSHIPS FROM THE FIRST DATE TO ENGAGEMENT

	Number	Percentage
1-2 weeks	11	2.0
3-4 weeks	15	3.0
1-2 months	50	9.0
3-4 months	70	13.0
5-8 months	105	19.0
9-11 months	39	7.0
1-2 years	142	26.0
3 years up	114	21.0
Total	546	100.0

dated for a year or more before becoming engaged, that 53 per cent were engaged within the first year of dating, and that 27 per cent were engaged within less than five months.

Importance of becoming well acquainted

It is more important than ever before that people become thoroughly acquainted before engagement or marriage. In Chapter I we noted that marriages are no longer held intact by institutional forces, that the stability of a marriage depends upon qualities within the marriage itself. Marriages last if comradeship, cooperation, emotional security, and affectional satisfaction are present. If these elements are not present, there is a good chance that the marriage will be unhappy, whether or not

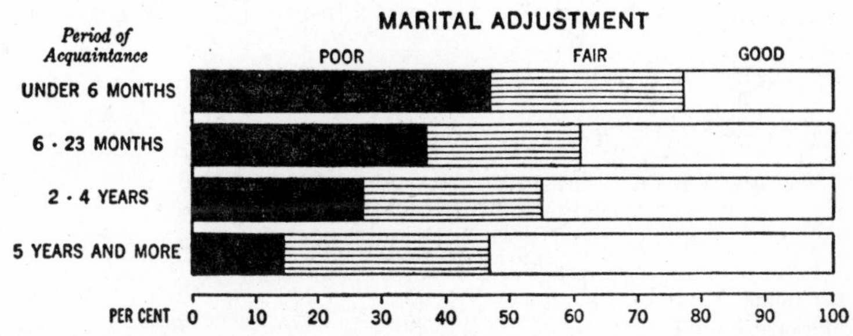

Fig. 33. Duration of acquaintance before marriage and marital adjustment. From E. W. Burgess and L. S. Cottrell, *Predicting Success or Failure in Marriage,* p. 165. New York: Prentice-Hall, Inc., 1939.

it ends in divorce. Couples who are friends for a reasonable length of time, during which they become well acquainted with each other before they enter upon an engagement, have a better chance for happiness. Terman found that husbands were happiest who had been acquainted with their wives for three years or more before marriage. He found that wives were happiest who had been acquainted with their husbands for at least a year before marriage. These findings suggest that a woman may be able to learn as much about a man in one year as he can learn about her in three. Burgess and Cottrell found that the chances for happiness were best if couples had dated each other for three or more years before marriage. All available evidence indicates that the period of time during which a couple associates together in various activities before becoming emotionally involved is important in building a good relationship.

Becoming engaged

With the modern trend toward smaller homes and apartments, courtship customs have changed. Table 12 summarizes the findings of Paul Popenoe concerning the places where 1,181 couples became engaged and whether the engagement ended in marriage. It will be noticed that approximately 50 per cent of the proposals were made either at the girl's home or while riding or driving. One-fifth of the proposals were made in some public place, which may mean that the girl's home did not provide the necessary privacy.

TABLE 12

PLACE OF 1,181 PROPOSALS OF MARRIAGE AND ACTION FOLLOWING THE PROPOSALS[a]

	Rejected	Broken	Marriage	Total	Per cent
At her home	84	15	173	272	23.0
Riding or driving	97	20	176	293	25.0
Vacation, resort, train, or ship	48	12	90	150	13.0
By letter, telegram, or telephone	12	4	47	63	5.0
Private party, dinner, or dance	45	7	71	123	10.0
Street, park, restaurant, or other public place	92	12	138	242	20.0
Miscellaneous	7	2	29	38	4.0
Totals	385(33%)	72(6%)	724(61%)	1,181	100.0

[a] Paul Popenoe, *Modern Marriage*, p. 267. New York: The Macmillan Company, 1940.

It is assumed that the man does the proposing, but there are many cases in which for various reasons the woman proposes. More common than an actual proposal by the woman is for her to interpret the man's remarks about marriage as an indirect proposal and to accept, knowing that he might never have the temerity to make an outright proposal. In Popenoe's study, one-third of the proposals made were rejected, so a man has reason to feel cautious. It is deflating to the manly ego to offer his life to a woman and to have the offer rejected; the more timid the man, the more devastating to his ego will be a refusal. In self-protection, a man may make hints that can be interpreted as proposals and yet allow him to remain always on safe ground. If

Fig. 34. *By permission,* Walter Goldstein and *The Saturday Evening Post.*

his hints are met with a negative response, he may decide to postpone taking the risk of an outright proposal; or he may even decide he did not want marriage with the girl as much as he had thought. If his hints meet with a cordial response, he may then pursue the subject to the point of a proposal. Romantic literature pictures the lover as approaching the surprised and blushing maiden with a moving declaration of love and an eloquent proposal of marriage to which she can respond with a simple yes. That is seldom the picture in real life.

Meaning of rings and pins

The ancient Egyptians used the ring as the symbol of a pledge. This custom has come down to us and is widely followed in present-day engagements. The man gives the girl a ring as a seal upon the agreement. The wearing of a fraternity pin on college campuses is a common custom similar to the wearing of an engagement ring, but it has a slightly different meaning.

Over 700 students at Michigan State College were asked to check this statement: "If a girl wears a boy's fraternity pin at MSC it means they are engaged." A much larger percentage of the girls than of the boys interpreted the wearing of the boy's pin as a sign of engagement. (See Figure 35.) When we asked

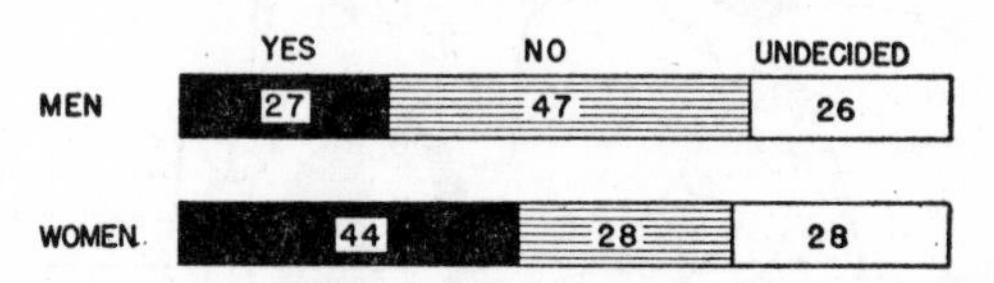

Fig. 35. Percentage of disagreement among men and women students on the statement, "If a woman wears a man's fraternity pin it means that they are engaged."

450 students at the University of California what the wearing of a fraternity pin meant, 63 per cent of the boys and 80 per cent of the girls answered, "engaged to be engaged." Again we notice that the girls seem to take pinning more seriously than the boys do. Thirty-one per cent of the boys said it meant "going steady," while only 12 per cent of the girls thought it had this meaning. Although confusion exists, it seems that a new step in the courtship process is evolving: instead of dating, going steady, engagement, and marriage, the pattern seems to be dating, going steady, being engaged to be engaged, engagement, and marriage. Undoubtedly, on almost all campuses a girl accepts a boy's fraternity pin only when some sort of an "understanding" has been reached. But evidence suggests that these understandings are not considered generally to be quite so binding as an en-

gagement announced and sealed with a ring. For example, some fraternity pins "go the rounds," being worn by several different girls in succession.

The fact that in the polls of student opinion there was such a difference between the meanings the boys and the girls attached to pin-wearing suggests a reason why the understandings indicated by acceptance of the pin are not considered strictly binding. A girl will learn to take "pinning" lightly if she accepts a pin in the belief that it means a promise to marry and later learns that it did not have that meaning for the boy who gave it to her. So, although pinning is a common custom, its meaning varies. The giving of a ring is much more universally accepted as indicating a serious engagement to marry.

Purpose of engagement

When a couple becomes engaged, they usually believe that the matter is settled for all time. However, as they come to know each other better through engagement, they sometimes find that they are not suited for each other and decide to break the engagement. Thus engagements today differ from those in earlier days, when the promise to marry was considered a legal contract which must eventuate in marriage. In those days the engagement was a period specifically for planning the wedding and making the trousseau. In practice, it has now become, in addition, a period of more intimate acquaintance during which both partners may more accurately evaluate marriage desirability. Today we recognize that many promises to marry never should have been made and that it is better to break an engagement than to go into an unhappy marriage which may end in divorce. It is more desirable, however, to delay an engagement until after the two have come to know each other well and have associated together long enough to build up a strong basis of friendship and affection. There is then less likelihood of a broken engagement and the emotional upheaval that may result for one or both.

Permanence of engagements

Quite a large percentage of modern engagements are broken. One study of a thousand engaged couples showed that one-fourth (23.8) of the men and one-third (35.8) of the women had broken one or more previous engagements, and that 14.9 per cent later broke the current engagement.[1] We found that of 143 married students one-third had been engaged at least one time before the engagement which finally resulted in marriage. In studying 307 single students in 1947 who had been or who were engaged, we found that approximately half had already broken at least one engagement. The students in this study were largely men who had been in military service. Women as well as men would probably show a higher incidence of broken

Fig. 36. Many engagements to marry do not end in marriage.

engagements during and after a war. The 1600 students studied in the 11 colleges in 1952 had a much lower broken-engagement record. Twenty-nine per cent of the women and only 14 per cent of the men had broken one or more engagements. Since many more of the 1600 students will no doubt have broken engagements before they eventually marry, it is safe to assume that from one-third to one-half of engagements do not end in mar-

[1] Ernest W. Burgess and Harvey J. Locke, *The Family,* p. 390. New York: American Book Company, 1945.

riage. It is well to keep this in mind as we discuss the engagement period.

Why engagements are broken

The fact that a large percentage of engagements are broken may indicate that young people are becoming engaged sooner than they should; that engagement is not taken so seriously as it was at one time; or that young people are getting better acquainted during the engagement period and are realistic enough to recognize when there is little possibility of the planned marriage being successful.

Table 13 summarizes the reasons given by students who had broken one or more engagements in the 1952 study. The causes of broken engagements as given by the students can be grouped as follows: (1) one or both lost interest, (2) separation, (3) incompatibility, (4) contrasts in family background, (5) influence of family and friends, (6) other factors, such as fear of marriage.

TABLE 13

PERCENTAGES OF 380 STUDENTS IN 11 COLLEGES GIVING SPECIFIC REASONS FOR BROKEN ENGAGEMENTS

Cause of breakup	Men (N–92)	Women (N-288)
Parents	9.0%	11.0%
Friends	1.0	2.0
Mutual loss of interest	13.0	8.0
Partner lost interest	14.0	7.0
I lost interest	18.0	23.0
Separation	20.0	18.0
Contrasts in background	7.0	16.0
Incompatibility	9.0	9.0
Other	9.0	6.0
Total	100.0	100.0

Loss of interest. Almost half the boys and over one-third of the girls said that the reason the engagement was broken was that one or both lost interest. A higher percentage of girls said that they had lost interest and a smaller percentage admit that it was the boy who had lost interest. Kirkpatrick,[2] in his study of broken love affairs among Minnesota students, observed this same tendency. Are girls quicker to perceive that a planned marriage would be unworkable and so "lose interest"? Or are they unwilling to admit that the man in the case lost interest and broke the engagement? Or are today's men students more chivalrous than they get credit for being, allowing a girl to feel that she was the one who lost interest when an engagement goes flat?

Engagements resulting after a short acquaintance are often based upon some superficial attraction which may wear off as the couple becomes better acquainted. Love-at-first-sight engagements are frequently of this type, since they are based upon attraction rather than upon common bonds. They, therefore, may not survive the more careful scrutiny of the engagement period. The element of strangeness which may have represented romance when the couple became engaged wears off during the engagement period and often leaves little to hold the couple together.

Separation. When engaged couples separate to attend different colleges, the engagement has little chance of withstanding the four years of separation. Both are constantly in the company of other attractive young people; they enter into activities common to students and usually become interested in dating someone among the new acquaintances. Thus they gradually drift apart. If an engaged young man goes to college, leaving his high-school fiancée at home, there is a good chance that he will find someone else and will wish to break the engagement. At first he may feel the separation keenly and tend to withdraw from the life about him; but if he is normally gregarious he will be drawn into association with others. Gradually, new interests will take precedence over the old. We have mentioned the high percentage of broken engagements among young people of the war

[2] Clifford Kirkpatrick and Theodore Caplow, "Courtship in a Group of Minnesota Students," *American Journal of Sociology*, 51:1 (September, 1945), 114-125.

generation. The students studied in 1952 gave separation, next to loss of interest, as the most common cause of broken engagements. (See Table 13.)

An important factor causing broken engagements is the rapid emotional maturing of people of the courtship age. The young person who becomes engaged while in high school but who does not plan to be married before finishing college will change and mature greatly during the four years. His conception of a perfect mate will be modified so that the high-school sweetheart may later fail to measure up. The boy who went into the service at 18 will find that the mate he will choose at 23 may bear little resemblance to the girl he would have chosen at 18. Many of the broken engagements are those which were made at an early age when young people were immature; the engagements could not stand the test of more mature judgment. Young people in college not only mature, but their interests and values are changed by college experience.

Incompatibility. During the engagement period the couple usually spends more time together than during the period when their dating was casual. They now have a chance to see each other in more varied real-life situations. With extra time to spend together, they may learn whether they have many interests in common. Sometimes they discover that they have few activities which they can enjoy together and they come to the conclusion that there would be little to make for permanent companionship in their marriage. In such cases they are wise to break the engagement.

As they become more intimately acquainted, each will get a better understanding of the real personality of the other. On occasional dates it is quite easy to be on "good behavior," but when a couple is together constantly during engagement, each has an opportunity to observe the other's accustomed behavior around his family and friends. If a young man sees his fiancée behave rudely and selfishly in her own home, he may for the first time realize that the girl has these personality traits; and the girl whose fiancé has always treated her as if she were a queen may be shocked to see that he shows little thoughtfulness or consideration for his mother and sisters. Habitual behavior has a way of showing itself if given time, and true attitudes on many matters, such as likes and dislikes concerning people and activities, and one's true interests, are likely to come to light if the engagement is long enough. An advantage of longer engagements is that they offer opportunities for a couple to be more realistic about their compatibility or incompatibility.

Cultural contrasts. Many "mixed" engagements do not survive the contrasts in backgrounds. The Catholic boy may become engaged to the Protestant or Jewish girl, but upon becoming more thoroughly acquainted with the beliefs of the girl and the problems involved in a mixed marriage, he may realize that he should not go on with the wedding plans. Engagements are often entered into before the young people have had any opportunity to know each other's family. If it is a mixed engagement of nationality or race, the couple may have thought the difference was of little importance while they were dating; but as they approach the reality of marriage and become better acquainted with the future in-laws, each may find it more and more impossible to accept the cultural background of the other.

Friends and family. Although a modern youth is free to marry whomever he chooses, he is influenced by what others think of his choice. During engagement the friends and families have an opportunity to come to know the prospective husband or wife. Most young people find it hard to go on with marriage if the fiancé(e) is looked upon unfavorably by friends and family. A young woman seems to be sensitive to how the fiancé is "going over" with those who matter to her. If she recognizes that he does not seem to them to be very desirable, it not only wounds her pride but may also cause her to look at his attributes more candidly herself. She may begin to see him as others see him and decide to break the engagement.

Other factors. Fear of marriage is sometimes a factor which causes broken engagements. Some people court and become engaged, but when it comes to marrying they are fearful for various reasons. The spinster may hesitate to give up her job with its economic security to face the uncertainties of marriage; or the bachelor who has been fairly contented in his single state may fear loss of his accustomed independence. Some women who have been conditioned to fear sex experience and child bearing will postpone or avoid marriage even if they do become engaged. People who are controlled by such fears may, themselves, be unaware of their real reasons for stopping short of marriage. The spinster or the bachelor may rationalize concerning economic or personal independence without recognizing the existence of an underlying fear concerning ability to cope with a close relationship such as marriage. And no doubt many women find rational reasons for postponing marriage without recognizing that their conditioned fearful attitudes toward sexual experience and childbirth are influencing their thinking.

After longer acquaintance, a girl may decide that the man she loves could not support her in the manner which she would wish, or a boy may decide that the girl has expensive tastes and that he could not support her. During the financial planning of the engagement, the economic values are more likely to be revealed so that each comes to know how the other thinks. A clash in economic values may cause the couple to decide that the marriage would be unwise.

Sometimes an extreme parental attachment on the part of one partner does not show up until the couple have become thoroughly acquainted during engagement. A girl may admire the way the boy reverences his mother and she may interpret his behavior as evidence that he will treat his wife in the same way. In some cases that would be the correct assumption. However, if the son's devotion is so strong that he can see no reason why, as newly-weds, they should live alone when Mother's home is open to them, the fiancée may recognize the danger signal and postpone marriage until the partner is willing to start married life in a separate place. If the man never reaches that point, the girl will be well out of a situation that might have meant an unhappy marriage. Devotion to parents is right in its place, but successful marriage requires a mature independence.

Some girls go into marriage recognizing that the man is overly attached to his mother and that their lives will always be dominated by the mother. A few can adjust to that situation and make the marriage a success in spite of it. Most girls, however, cannot make the adjustment and be happy. If the boy recognizes his too great dependence upon his mother, then there is some hope that he may eventually become emotionally mature. However, the girl who marries such a man is apt to be disappointed if she allows her happiness to depend upon ending the maternal domination. If she doubts whether she could adjust to the maternal domination, she would do well to break the engagement.

So there are many reasons why couples break their engagements, and most of the reasons are sound. Engagement provides the couple with an opportunity to hesitate on the verge of marriage and to make sure the marriage has a chance for success. With divorce as easy as it is today, it is well that engagements have changed from binding legal agreements to a period of serious courtship in which couples may try to be realistic as they contemplate marriage.

Emotional trends in courtship

Kirkpatrick and Caplow[3] have made some interesting studies of the emotional trends in the courtship experience of college students. They ignored engagement, but asked students to report on their emotional development from the beginning to the end of their love affairs and, in addition, to report on their emotional turmoil after the love affairs had ended. The group consisted of 141 men students reporting 314 love affairs, and 258 women students reporting 582 love affairs. The students were asked to check from eleven prepared graphs the one which most

[3] Clifford Kirkpatrick and Theodore Caplow, "Emotional trends in the courtship experience of college students as expressed by graphs with some observations on methodological implications," *American Sociological Review,* 10.5 (October, 1945), 619-626.

nearly represented the love affair. The eight most common graphic representations of the eleven are shown in Figure 37. In most of these love affairs the emotional development had progressed to a certain point and then had gradually receded (Graphs I-V). Only 15 per cent of the students said their love affairs were of the type which fluctuated violently from one extreme to the other (Graphs VI and VII).

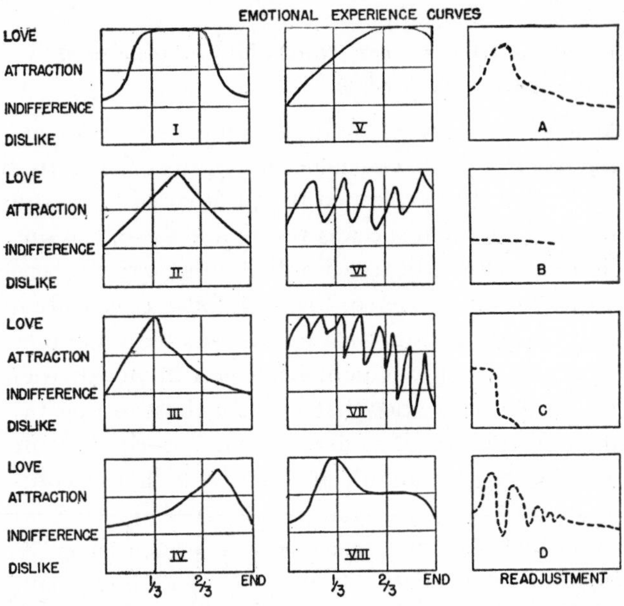

Fig. 37. Emotional trends in the courtship experience of college students as expressed by graphs. Of 400 university men and women students who had 900 love affairs, the largest percentage thought Graph I most nearly represented their emotional trends toward the love object during the love experience.

The students were asked to check one of the four graphs to indicate their emotional feelings during the readjustment period after the love affair had ended. Over half of the students said Graph B represented their feelings. That is, their feelings approached indifference to the former love partner and no serious emotional trauma remained. Fifteen per cent indicated that there was a temporary flare-up of affection for the love partner which soon decreased and became indifference (Graph A). Another 15 per cent went through a period of recurring up-surges in affection for the former love object before tapering off to a state of indifference (Graph D). In 11 per cent of the cases what had been love for the love object turned into dislike (Graph C). In approximately 90 per cent of the terminated love affairs reported in this study, a normal state of adjustment, indifference to the former love object, was achieved.

Time required to get over emotional involvement when engagement is broken

Much has been written and spoken about "broken" hearts resulting from broken engagements. Spinsterhood in the last generation was often explained by the story of how Auntie had her heart broken when she was young and never got over it. Or Uncle Joe had a sweetheart who died and there has never been another girl to replace her in his affections. The study by Kirkpatrick and Caplow dealt with love affairs without reference to whether or not an engagement had been involved; their study indicated, as we have said, that most of those young people recovered from emotional involvements in a normal manner. Our study of broken love affairs, in all of which the couples had been engaged, showed also that people seem to recover from the emotional shock within a reasonable length of time. We asked specifically for the length of time that had been required to reach a normal emotional state after the break.[4] One-third of those responding reported that the emotional trauma lasted less than one month, another third reported that it took from one to six months, and one-third reported that they were not completely "over" it for a year or more. There was little difference between lengths of time required as reported by men and by women. (See Table 14.) These responses show that in two-thirds of the cases the old love was largely forgotten within a short time and there was little carry-over from the affair.

Where more time was required to heal the broken heart,

[4] Unpublished study of 320 formerly engaged students.

peculiar circumstances probably prevented the usual recovery. Some war veterans stated that the circumstances of their service prevented their forgetting the broken engagement as easily as they would have ordinarily. If the engagement was broken by the girl at home while the man was in some isolated region where there were no girls of his own kind, it was natural for him to brood over the affair more than if it had been possible for him to shift his attention to a desirable substitute or to mingle socially with suitable girls.

TABLE 14

LENGTH OF TIME TO GET OVER THE EMOTIONAL INVOLVEMENT OF THE ENGAGEMENT REPORTED BY 320 FORMERLY ENGAGED STUDENTS

Length of time	Men (N-249)	Women (N-71)	Total (N-320)
1-2 weeks	21.0%	24.0%	22.0%
3-4 weeks	12.0	7.0	11.0
1-2 months	17.0	18.0	18.0
3-5 months	19.0	17.0	18.0
6 mos.-12 mos.	4.0	4.0	4.0
13-23 mos.	13.0	21.0	15.0
2 years and over	14.0	9.0	12.0
Total	100.0	100.0	100.0

The young person who is faced with the emotional crisis of a broken love affair may take courage from the fact that most people seem to survive broken love affairs without any permanent ill effects. A study of the graphs presented in connection with Kirkpatrick and Caplow's study (page 191) might enable a person to predict the course of his emotional reactions. When one is in the midst of the emotional turmoil that sometimes accompanies the breaking of a love affair, the experience seems unique. The tendency is to feel that no one else has ever endured quite the same ordeal. It is helpful in such circumstances to realize not only that others have suffered similarly but that the experience tends to follow a pattern.

In the study among students in 11 colleges in 1952 we included a section adapted from Kirkpatrick's study of adjustment reactions to broken love affairs among University of Minnesota students.[5] Table 15 summarizes the responses of over 1,000 of the 1952 students who had broken off serious love affairs. It is interesting that the adjustment reactions are quite universal

TABLE 15

PERCENTAGES OF 1059 STUDENTS FROM 11 COLLEGES GIVING ADJUSTMENT REACTIONS WHEN MOST SERIOUS LOVE AFFAIR ENDED

Reaction thought of or experienced	Men (N-367)	Women (N-692)
Remembered pleasant association	64.0%	66.0%
Got dates with others	59.0	64.0
Daydreamed about partner	30.0	25.0
Preserved keepsakes	11.0	29.0
Avoided meeting him (her)	21.0	22.0
Read over old letters	16.0	21.0
Attempted to meet him (her)	20.0	17.0
Remembered unpleasant association	12.0	21.0
Frequented places of common association	14.0	16.0
Liked or disliked people because of resemblance	11.0	12.0
Daydreamed	8.0	13.0
Avoided places of common association	9.0	11.0
Resolved to get even	2.0	3.0
Imitated mannerisms	0.0	3.0
Thought of suicide	0.5	2.0

and that men and women resort to the same ones with about the same frequency, except that women "preserve keepsakes" and remember unpleasant associations more than men do. You will notice that most of the adjustments are normal and acceptable reactions, although some tend to be neurotic or, if they became extreme, would have to be classed as neurotic. The girl who constantly daydreams about the former lover, refuses to date others, and imagines how unhappy the former lover is with his new girl friend or wife, is developing an unhealthy mental state and may need counsel to reorient her life.

[5] Clifford Kirkpatrick and Theodore Caplow, "Courtship in a Group of Minnesota Students," *The American Journal of Sociology,* 51:114-125. Reprinted in Judson T. Landis and Mary G. Landis, eds., *Readings in Marriage and the Family,* 79-90. New York: Prentice-Hall, Inc., 1952.

However, it is not true that there is always any serious adjustment reaction when love affairs are ended. In the study just quoted, the students were asked what their emotional state was when the most serious love affair was ended. The most common response checked by the students was that they were hurt; almost half gave this answer. However, almost one-third said they were relieved or indifferent. The next most common emotional states were bitterness, anger, or feelings of resentment. Some affairs develop to a point and then die out at about the same rate in both partners, with neither being hurt. However, the above information and also our findings on how long it takes to get over broken engagements point up a common relationship in love affairs: the one-sided involvement. One member of the couple may feel that he is very much in love and wish to continue a relationship while the other has already decided that she is not in love and may be plotting her escape from the affair. When the affair is ended, one is relieved and happy, the other hurt.

The emotional upset of a broken love affair may be compared with a case of measles, in that it follows a definite course. Mothers of children ill with measles sometimes become frantic with worry during the time when the disease is at its worst stage, just before recovery begins. At this point the family doctor will attempt to comfort the mother and the patient by telling them that it is a "typical" case, that there are no complications, and that if the patient is kept comfortable and given reasonable care, nature will bring about recovery. When several children in succession in a family have to be nursed through the measles, the mother learns to ease each child through by giving good care and by encouraging the patient to recognize that the disease is taking its course and will soon be over. Friends and family of the person suffering from a broken love affair have much the same role. They can do little except to try to live peaceably with the emotionally upset individual, meanwhile hoping there will be no "complications" such as a sudden marriage on the rebound or an unhealthy clinging to grief.

It is hard, however, to convince the victim of a broken love affair that his is a "typical" case. A part of the process of attaining maturity is learning by experience that recovery, in the sense of regaining emotional balance, is possible from even the most devastating loss or bereavement. The person who can apply himself to absorbing tasks as soon as possible after emotional loss can hasten such recovery. The students who reported broken love affairs said that "Getting dates with others" was one of their most common adjustments to a broken affair. That is a good adjustment if the dates are an attempt to fill time and to enjoy life by mingling with others, and not an attempt to "show" or get even with the former love. But sometimes people who date others in order to forget a former love allow themselves to fall quickly in love on the rebound. Rebound loves and marriages may result in far more permanent pain than that which they are designed to cure.

Breaking engagements

The question of how to end an engagement when one of the pair has concluded that the marriage cannot work is sometimes a serious one. If both arrive at the conclusion that they are not suited for marriage to each other, little difficulty arises. Young people who are mature in their thinking will recognize that it is much better to break an engagement than to go into a doubtful marriage. They can be thankful if they discover their unsuitability before they marry. Some engagements are broken in immature ways, with a careless disregard for the feelings of the partner, or even with a deliberate attempt to hurt. It is humiliating to both men and women to have their affections suddenly repulsed and to have to face friends and family with the announcement that the fiancé(e) has broken the engagement.

A rather common problem when engagements are broken is that the one most hurt by the break may regress to an immature level of behavior in an attempt to hold the unwilling partner. Threats of violence to himself are common. Sometimes threats are made to "tell" things that might be damaging to the partner,

Fig. 38. "When we break up, Melvin, I'm certainly going to miss your candy."
By permission, Walter Goldstein and *The Saturday Evening Post.*

and pathological individuals may even resort to threats against the life or person of the partner. These are ways of reacting to situations in which the individual feels extremely frustrated. A small child may react to a blocking of his wishes by running away or by telling his mother that he will run away. It is not that he enjoys leaving home, but in his childish way he is attempting to bring sorrow to his mother by harming himself. The immature adult who threatens suicide when a love affair is ended against his will does so because he wishes to force the loved one to worry over him, to fear that he will harm himself, and to feel responsible for his behavior. He hopes it will cause the loved one to decide she loves him too much to risk allowing him to harm himself. The movies have played up stories in which the jilted lover drinks to drown his sorrow until the former sweetheart comes back to him. Then they marry happily.

If one partner threatens violence when the engagement is broken, the one wishing to break the engagement should look upon the threats objectively. In the first place, there is little chance that they will be carried out. The small boy who starts to run away from home to hurt his mother seldom runs more than a block. The making of threats is simply an indication of immaturity and instability and should be recognized as convincing proof of the desirability of breaking the engagement. If the movies pictured life situations rather than romantic fantasy, they would show what happened afterwards in the married life of the girl who weakened and married the man after he proved his love for her by becoming a drunkard. Instead of living happily ever after, she would be spending the rest of her life trying to pacify a husband who resorted to sulking, temper tantrums, or drunkenness whenever things failed to go according to his wishes. Immature patterns of behavior do not change with marriage any more than selfishness is cured by marriage.

We have already mentioned the quick marriage to someone else, which is another form of childish revenge sometimes resorted to by the disappointed lover. The person taking this step is attempting to save face and at the same time to hurt the lost one by demonstrating that she (he) has been quickly forgotten. Marriages for spite, or on the rebound, have little chance for happiness. The innocent mate in the rebound marriage is to be pitied. Courtships in which one or both partners have not had time to get over previous love affairs should not end in engagement or marriage until ample time has elapsed so that both may evaluate their chances for happiness as carefully as if it were the first love affair. They need to be sure that they have had time to let their wounded affections heal and that no spite or "rebound" is involved. Quick marriage after a broken affair usually indicates that the person is seeking an escape from the former love affair and that he may be still emotional over the former love partner.

When an engagement must be broken, it is better if both can recognize that one-sided affectional attachments would result in unhappiness in marriage. Impossible as it may seem at the time, the rejected one will find that there are others whom he can marry, who have all and sometimes more of the desirable traits of the ex-partner. Unfortunate is the young man who thinks that there is only one girl in the world and she will not have him. It is better if one can be philosophical about the whole matter.

Length of engagement

How long should engagements be to result in the best adjustment in marriage? Some people can get thoroughly acquainted during a relatively short period of engagement, whereas others may be engaged for years without having settled many of the questions which should be faced during the engagement period.

In the past, when engagements were for the purpose of planning and preparing for the wedding, short engagements were considered desirable. Since couples are permitted greater freedom in expressing affection during engagement, long engagements mean more possibility that the problem of premarital sexual intercourse will arise. Formerly the logical solution to the problem was to recommend short engagements so that couples could be ushered quickly and safely into marriage.

Research studies show that longer engagements are among the factors predictive of happiness in marriage. A summary of studies dealing with the length of engagement and happiness in marriage is presented in Table 16. It will be noticed that all studies show that short engagements are more likely to be followed by poor adjustment in marriage and that engagements of two years' duration or longer are more likely to be followed by happiness in marriage. Our study of 544 couples found the lowest percentage of very happy marriages among those who had not been engaged at all. Figure 39 summarizes Burgess' study of length of engagement and happiness in marriage.

Locke, in comparing the length of engagements of a matched sample of divorced and happily married couples in Indiana, found short engagements, under one month for men and under

TABLE 16

LENGTH OF ENGAGEMENT AND CHANCES FOR HAPPINESS IN MARRIAGE AS REVEALED BY STUDIES OF MARRIED COUPLES

Adjustment in marriage	Terman[a] 792 couples	Burgess-Cottrell[b] 526 couples	Landis[c] 544 couples
Poor	Under 6 months	No engagement, or under 9 months	No engagement, or under 6 months
Good	6 months-4 years	9 months-23 months	6 months-23 months
Excellent	5 years and up	2 years and up	2 years and up

[a] Terman, *op. cit.*, p. 199.
[b] Burgess and Cottrell, *op. cit.*, p. 168.
[c] Unpublished research.

six months for women, much more prevalent among the divorced, and relatively long engagements, 12 or more months, much more prevalent among the happily married. Divorced

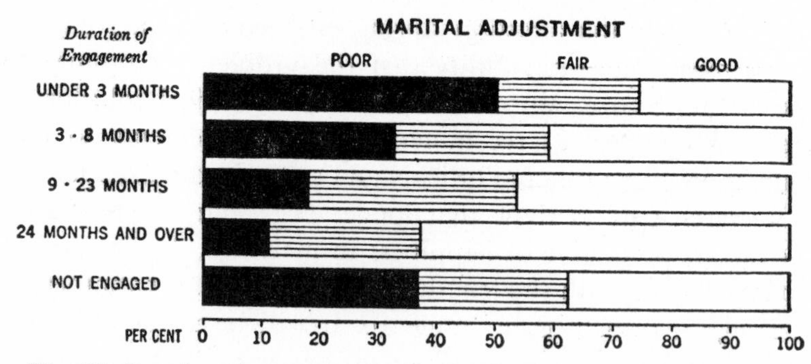

Fig. 39. Duration of engagement and marital adjustment. Long engagements often weed out couples who would not make a go of marriage. Better a broken engagement than a broken marriage. From E. W. Burgess and L. S. Cottrell, *Predicting Success or Failure in Marriage,* p. 168. New York: Prentice-Hall, Inc., 1939.

men and women had been engaged an average of seven months, whereas happily married men were engaged an average of 10 months, and happily married women 12 months.[6]

[6] Harvey J. Locke, *Predicting Adjustment in Marriage,* pp. 93-94. New York: Henry Holt and Company, 1951.

Popenoe estimates that the average engagement is about a year in length, longer in professional classes, and shorter in the skilled and unskilled labor groups. In the 544 student marriages in our study three out of four married within one year after the engagement. Fourteen per cent had not been engaged at all, and only 12 per cent had been engaged for two years or more.

It might be expected that short acquaintances would be followed by long engagements, but the opposite seems to be true. Those who are acquainted the longest before engagement also have the longest engagements.[7] Apparently the personality make-up which causes people to become engaged after a short acquaintance also impels them into an early marriage. The personality type that will take time to court may also take time to approach marriage after the engagement. This willingness to proceed carefully is part of the explanation for the greater success of marriages following longer engagements. People who are able to weather the storms of long engagements are more likely to have the emotional balance helpful in weathering the storms of married life.

Locke found marriages forced by pregnancy very prevalent among his divorced couples. The average length of engagement in these marriages had been approximately three months.[8] Personality make-up may help to explain the greater unhappiness in marriages followed by short engagements. Those who have coitus early in their acquaintanceship and are forced into an early marriage perhaps do not have the general foresight possessed by those who plan more carefully for the future.

Another factor in the success of marriages following longer engagements is, of course, the weeding out of the poorer marital risks. Many of the people who were not engaged or who were engaged for a short time would not have married had they attempted a longer engagement. One study showed that 5 per cent of the applicants for marriage licenses in California failed

[7] Paul Popenoe, *Modern Marriage,* p. 176. New York: The Macmillan Company, 1940.

[8] Locke, *ibid.,* p. 92.

to return to get their licenses at the end of the three-day waiting period.[9] The additional three days were all the time some of those couples needed in order to realize that they did not wish to marry each other.

In summary, available evidence indicates that marriages with no engagement or engagements of less than six months are unwise. How much longer than six months the engagement period should be depends upon how well acquainted the couple have become during the dating and engagement period.

Coitus during engagement

As we have said, one of the problems of a longer engagement is the question of controlling the sex impulse. Engaged couples often ask why such control is desirable since they are to be married soon anyway. We have presented the pros and cons of premarital intercourse in Chapter VIII; we need not repeat them here except to reiterate that premarital intercourse is poor preparation for satisfactory sex relationships in marriage. All the reasons for refraining from coitus during courtship apply with equal force to the period of engagement, since many engagements do not end in marriage and the engagement period is for the purpose of preparing to make a good marriage. Further, an unplanned pregnancy can force an engaged couple into a hasty marriage when one or both may still be uncertain as to the real desirability of the marriage. Popenoe found in his study of elopements that two-thirds of the marriages ended in failure when the elopement was motivated by pregnancy.[10] Some of these marriages were doomed to failure from the start, and the couple would never have married had they not felt an obligation to protect the child. If one partner of the engaged couple, usually the man, is persistent in the determination to indulge in sexual relations, the other partner may well consider whether an

[9] Oliver Butterfield, *Love Problems of Adolescence,* p. 126. New York: Emerson Books, Inc., 1941.

[10] Paul Popenoe, *Modern Marriage,* p. 225. New York: The Macmillan Company, 1940.

exploitative pattern exists in the love affair. Some individuals become engaged with the intention to exploit sexually rather than with a serious intention to marry.

Problems to be discussed during engagement

The engagement provides a couple with the opportunity to give serious thought to some of the problems that they will face in marriage and to consider the respective roles that they will play in the marriage relationship. Since handling of money has been found to be a cause of friction in marriage, they will wish to discuss frankly their attitudes not only on who should hold the purse strings but on how their money should be used. They will be interested to find out how well they agree on how the money should be spent: for life insurance, for a car or a home, for travel, or for education for themselves or their children.

Certainly they should discuss their feelings about the desirability of having children. In our study of student attitudes, a fifth of the students said they would not marry another who did not want children. Many young people would wish to break an engagement with a person who showed a dislike for children. Sixty-three per cent of divorces granted are to people who do not have children. A partial reason is that those who refuse to have children are more likely to be poor matrimonial risks. As discussed in the chapter on courtship, it is not always possible to discover true attitudes on this point before marriage; however, a longer engagement offers better chances for discovering them.

Attitudes toward sex expression and the use of birth control should be compared—especially in marriages of mixed religious faiths. If the couple cannot come to an agreement on the use or non-use of contraceptives, or if their views on the place of sex expression in marriage differ greatly, they are not ready for marriage. If one partner looks upon sex as a wholesome, normal part of marriage while the other is repulsed by the idea of the sex phase of marriage, the couple should recognize the danger of conflict. Such a difference in attitudes means that greater effort must be made if a satisfactory adjustment is to be reached in marriage. If one is persistent in wanting to indulge in coitus during engagement in spite of the reluctance of the other, especially if the reluctance is based on conscientious beliefs or on a desire to reserve complete sexual indulgence until after marriage, a difference in values and in basic attitudes should be recognized. Marriage between these two will not automatically harmonize their differences.

Couples need time to discuss their goals and their standards of what things are worth striving for in life. The woman whose greatest wish is to live in her hometown among people she has always known may not find happiness married to a man who would gladly move from place to place if that seemed desirable in order to be successful in a chosen occupation. And he, in turn, would feel hindered and held down if it became necessary for him to live in one place in order to keep his wife happy. The person who values an active religious life may be disillusioned and unhappy if married to one who gives no thought to religion. Difference in attitudes on the value of an education may create special problems among the present generation of young people. Many young men eligible for veterans' educational benefits would like to attend college to prepare for some specific business or profession. Some of them, however, are married to girls who feel it is more important for the husband to have a job at the present high wage levels so that they can settle down at once and enjoy a higher standard of living than would be possible if the husband became a student. It is impossible for a young couple to weather G.I. student life if the wife is unwilling to make the sacrifices required. If some of these couples had discovered during the engagement how much their views were at variance, they would not have married.

Finding a suitable place to live has been a serious problem facing newly married couples for some years. If one or the other insists upon living in the parental home, the wedding may possibly be postponed until another arrangement can be made. Starting marriage while living with parents is difficult at best.

Either person is justified in asking that the marriage be postponed until a place can be found where they can live alone. Many engaged couples find this problem hard to discuss. The one who will be the resident-in-law hesitates to object too stubbornly for fear of being considered jealous of or aggressive toward the future in-laws.

Confessing the past

At some point in the love affair there comes a time when one may feel that he must confess the past, if there is anything to confess. It is more apt to be the man who has the urge to confess, possibly because he may have more on his conscience. To have the loved one accept the misconduct causes the individual to think that his behavior is not so bad as he had thought it to be. He rises in his own esteem, accordingly. With some people, "confessing all" is a childish way of getting attention. A person may be attempting to impress the loved one with the fact that in his day he has been a very wild fellow. It stems from the same motive as that which, in old-fashioned, religious testimony meetings, prompted the good brother to regale the members with the story of his past sins, his exploits in the realm of wine, women, and song.

What rule should be followed when a young person reaches the place in his courtship where he feels he should tell all? He should ask himself four questions before doing any confessing: (1) Why do I wish to tell? (2) Will our marriage be more happy if I do tell? (3) Will my fiancé(e) be happier if I tell? (4) If I must tell, is the fiancé(e) the best person to hear it?

If the individual will analyze his motives carefully, he may find that his reason for wishing to tell is simply to have the pleasure of exhibiting his past. If he has any selfish motive in his wish to confess the past, he might better control the impulse and keep the secret. In general, only those things should be confessed which would lead to a better adjustment in the marriage, or those which, if found out later, would make for poor adjustment in marriage. If a man has had venereal disease, has illegitimate children, has been married before, or has a prison record, his fiancée should, in most cases, know of these things before marriage. These matters could seriously affect the marriage and their effect might be far more damaging if they were unknown to the spouse until after marriage. Venereal disease can be cured, but the person who marries someone who has had a venereal disease has a right to evidence that a permanent cure has been effected. If telling an event would make the fiancé(e) unhappy without accomplishing any constructive good, the story would be better left untold.

Often over-conscientious individuals are bothered by insignificant incidents in their past which would have nothing to do with future marital happiness. These events can become magnified in the individual's mind and he may feel he must tell the fiancée. Upon hearing it, the fiancée may become worried and attach exaggerated importance to the matter, creating unhappiness for both. If the urge to confess is uncontrollable, one should seek counsel from a qualified person, such as a marriage counselor.

The premarital examination

It is advisable to have a premarital examination from a competent physician during the engagement. Many states now require an examination for venereal disease before a marriage license can be obtained. This law is important in helping to prevent the spread of venereal disease. A premarital examination should provide the following: (1) a complete physical examination, (2) an examination of the female pelvis and genitalia, (3) attention to diseases or defects that might be hereditary, (4) an opportunity to secure reliable contraceptive information if it is desired, (5) a blood test, and (6) a chance to ask questions about sex.

It would be better if a couple could go to a doctor or clinic specializing in giving attention to premarital examinations. People living in parts of the country where special counseling services have been established should take advantage of them. Some counseling services provide a series of tests to determine the chances for success in marriage.

A physical check-up will determine the couple's state of health and will reveal any diseases or defects needing medical attention. The examination of the female genitalia and pelvis will reveal any conditions which might hinder coitus or make conception improbable. If there has been mental disease in either family, the couple will wish to be reassured concerning types of mental difficulty which cannot be passed on through heredity. For couples who do not plan to have children during the first year of marriage, it is important to secure reliable birth-control information. The most generally satisfactory contraceptives necessitate examination by a physician and instruction from him.

Young people usually have questions they would like to ask about sex in marriage. Here the doctor may not be prepared to be of much help. The doctor has been trained in the physical phases of sex functioning; but sex functioning is also psychological and many doctors are not in a position to advise on this important aspect of the subject. However, doctors who have made a study of the psychology of sex and who are interested in this phase of preparation for marriage may be good sources of information.

After the premarital examinations and a talk with the doctor, a couple will find it helpful to read some of the reliable books on the sexual side of marriage as a part of their preparation for marriage. It is well to own one of these books so that it can be read before and after marriage. Much of the information will be more meaningful after marriage.

Planning the wedding

Marriages which are planned and made public have a better chance than those which are secret. Sometimes, when parents are opposed to the marriage, the young people see elopement as their only choice. In a study of 738 elopements Popenoe found that 46 per cent were caused by parental opposition.[11] A smaller percentage of these marriages turned out happily than of marriages that had parental approval. When "economy" was the motive for the elopement, 63 per cent turned out happily; 60 per cent when "avoidance of publicity," 45 per cent

". . . steady now . . . easy . . . almost there . . . courage . . ."

Fig. 40. *By permission,* Ted Key and *The Saturday Evening Post.*

when "parental objection," and 33 per cent when "pregnancy" was the motive. If strong parental opposition exists, the couple should seriously consider whether the reasons for the opposition are valid. If they decide to marry in spite of opposition, they should make every effort to secure the cooperation of the families before the marriage. Often the parents will consent when

[11] Popenoe, *op. cit.,* pp. 222-227.

they see that the young people are determined to marry. If the opposition continues, however, the marriage is handicapped. Family ties of affection are not easily broken, and there is likely to be an emotional reaction either of antagonism toward the parents or unhappiness on the part of the married couple who marry despite opposition. When other marital adjustments have to be made, it becomes easy for the unfavorable parental attitude toward the marriage to enter the situation as an aggravating factor.

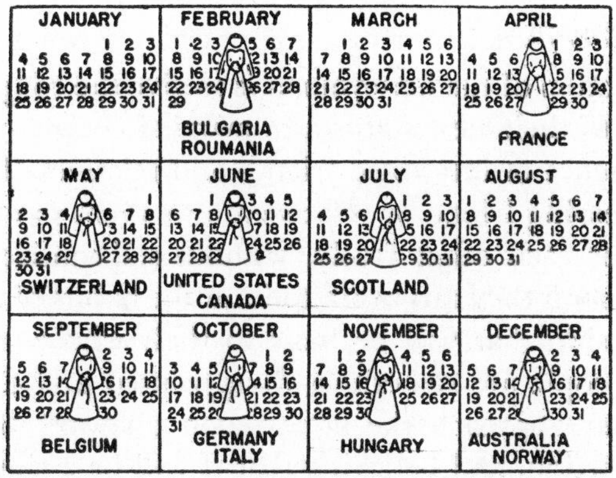

Fig. 41. "Brides' month" varies in different countries of the world. June is "brides' month" for us, but not for the girls in Norway; they prefer December. Adapted from Metropolitan Life Insurance Company, *Statistical Bulletin,* 19:9 (September, 1938), 2.

In studying divorced and happily married couples Locke found parental approval of the prospective mate closely associated with marital happiness and parental disapproval closely associated with marital maladjustment.[12]

Traditionally, the bride plans and pays for the wedding and the groom plans and pays for the honeymoon. In practice, many such customs are not rigidly followed. Frequently the bride and groom together plan both the wedding and the honeymoon. It would seem unwise for any couple to go heavily into debt for the wedding and the honeymoon. Their total bill

[12] *Op. cit.,* p. 118.

for the marriage should be in keeping with the income they will have after they are married.

Some ministers like to cooperate in planning church weddings, and because of their experience they can often give helpful suggestions. Whether the wedding is to be a large and pretentious or small and simple will depend upon the wishes of the pair and their economic level. From the viewpoint of marital success the important thing is that the wedding marks a change in status which should be looked upon as permanent.

The honeymoon

The function of the honeymoon is to give the couple a chance to settle into their new status as a married couple, unhindered by the presence of interested friends and relatives. The absence of any observing friend or relative allows them to express their affection for each other freely, without self-consciousness. On the honeymoon they can begin to form the habits of affectionate companionship that will be basic to their whole married life.

Young people are sometimes disappointed and disillusioned because they approach the honeymoon unaware of its broad, general function, and believing that it will be a time chiefly of perfect sex fulfillment. But sex fulfillment may not be full and complete during the honeymoon. If conditions are ideal, the couple's first attempts at sexual union may be all that they had anticipated. But most couples require time and experience in order to achieve complete and mutually satisfactory sexual response. The honeymoon is the beginning of their sex life as well as of their companionship as a married couple. But it is only the beginning. They may need weeks or months of living together before their sex experience approaches that which they may have thought would come automatically as a part of the honeymoon.

The establishment of a pattern of understanding cooperation and unselfish consideration for each other in all their relationships is more important than complete sexual satisfaction for either one on the honeymoon.

In setting the wedding date, girls usually try to plan so that they will not be menstruating during the honeymoon. It is well to plan that way so that conditions may be as ideal as possible for the beginning of their sex life in marriage. But many girls find that the added strain of the last few days or weeks preceding the wedding may cause menstruation to be delayed until the relaxation that comes with the honeymoon.

If the honeymoon is to serve its function, a few points must be considered when it is planned:

1. Whether the time is to be only a day or two or much longer, the plans should provide for privacy and anonymity. Most newly married couples want only to be Mr. and Mrs.—, inconspicuous in a world of married people. Anonymity may be found in a hotel in the city or a cottage in the country, on a lake or ocean cruise, or hiking in the mountains. The important consideration is that the couple go where no one knows them.

2. The honeymoon should provide freedom from fatigue and nervous tension. Strenuous travel schedules should be avoided. If a couple tries to cover a predetermined amount of territory and to make sure that they miss nothing of educational or cultural value, they may find themselves working so hard at having a wedding trip that the purpose of the honeymoon is defeated.

3. The kind of plans made should depend upon what activities both can enjoy. If they like to see and do the things that are offered by a large city, they may choose to spend their honeymoon in that way. If they are both enthusiastic campers or if they enjoy hiking or fishing, they may plan a honeymoon of that type. The point is that the honeymoon is a time for them to enjoy each other in an environment that allows them to be themselves and to relax in each other's company.

4. The cost of the honeymoon should be kept well within what they can afford so that they will be free from financial pressure or worry.

1. The Marriage Prediction Schedule[10]

Please Read Carefully Before and After Filling Out Schedule.

This schedule is prepared for persons who are seriously considering marriage. Although designed for couples who are engaged or who have a private understanding to be married, it can also be filled out by other persons who would like to know their probability of success in marriage.

The value of the findings of the schedule depends upon your frankness in answering the questions.

The following points should be kept in mind in filling out the schedule:

1. Be sure to answer every question.
2. Do not leave a blank to mean a "no" answer.
3. The word "fiancé(e)" will be used to refer to the person to whom you are engaged.
4. Do not confer with your fiancé(e) on any of these questions.

Part One	1	2	3
1. What is your present state of health: poor health [*a*) chronic -------- *b*) temporary--------]; *c*) average health--------; *d*) healthy--------; *e*) very healthy--------			
2. How would you rate the physical appearance of *your fiancé(e)*? (Check): *u*) very good looking-------; *v*) good looking-------; *x*) fairly good looking--------; *y*) plain looking--------; *z*) very plain looking--------			
3. Your present marital status: *u*) single--------; *v*) widowed --------; *x*) separated--------; *y*) divorced--------			
4. Check total number of years of schooling completed at present time. *a*) Grades 1--2--3--4--5--6--7--8--; *b*) High School 1--2--3--4--; *c*) College 1--2--3--4-- *d*) Graduate of college (check): --------; *e*) Number of years beyond college in graduate work or professional training-------- Training for what profession---------------; for none in particular (check)--------			
5. Present occupation------------------------------------ Work record (check): *u*) regularly employed--------; *v*) worked only during vacations or/and only part time while in school --------; *w*) none because in school or at home--------; *x*) always employed but continually changing jobs--------; *y*) irregularly employed--------; other---------------------- --			
6. Are you a church member? yes--------; no--------. Your activity in church (check): *a*) never attend--------; *b*) attend less than once a month--------; *c*) once or twice per month --------; *d*) three times a month--------; *e*) four times a month --------; other activity in church (state what it is)---------- --			

[10] Reproduced by permission of Ernest W. Burgess, Leonard S. Cottrell, Jr., and Paul Wallin.

1	2	3

7. Did you ever attend Sunday School or other religious school for children and young people?-------- At what age did you stop attending such a school? *a*) never attended--------; *b*) before 10 years old--------; *c*) 11-18 years--------; *d*) 19 and over --------; *e*) still attending--------
8. How many organizations do you belong to or attend regularly such as church club, athletic club, social club, luncheon club (like the Rotary, Kiwanis, Lions), fraternal order, college fraternity, college sorority, civic organization, music society, patriotic organization, Y.W.C.A., Y.M.C.A., Y.M.H.A., C.Y.O.? (check): *a*) none--------; *b*) one--------; *c*) two--------; *d*) three or more------
9. In leisure time activities (check): *u*) We both prefer to stay at home--------; *x*) We both prefer to be "on the go"--------; *y*) I prefer to be on the go and my fiancé(e) to stay at home --------; *z*) I prefer to stay at home and my fiancé(e) to be on the go--------
10. Check what you consider to have been the economic status of your parents during your adolescence: *u*) well-to-do--------; *v*) wealthy-------; *w*) comfortable-------; *x*) meager------; *z*) poor--------
11. Check what you consider to be the social status of your parents in their own community: *j*) one of the leading families--------; *k*) upper class--------; *l*) upper-middle class--------; *m*) middle class--------; *n*) lower-middle class--------; *o*) lower class--------
12. Marital status of your parents (check): *l*) married (both living) --------; *m*) separated--------; *n*) divorced--------; *t*) both dead--------; one dead (specify which one)--------; If parent is dead give *your* age when the death occurred-------- If parents are divorced or separated give your age at time of divorce or separation--------
13. Your appraisal of the happiness of your parents' marriage (check): *i*) very happy--------; *k*) happy--------; *l*) average--------; *m*) unhappy--------; *n*) very unhappy--------
14. Check your attitudes toward your parents on the following scales:
    (1) Your attitude toward your father when you were a *child:* *j*) very strong attachment--------; *k*) considerable attachment--------; *m*) mild attachment--------; *n*) mild hostility--------; *o*) considerable hostility--------; *p*) very strong hostility--------
    (2) Your *present* attitude toward your father: *j*) very strong attachment---------; *k*) considerable attachment---------; *m*) mild attachment---------; *n*) mild hostility---------; *o*) considerable hostility----------; *p*) very strong hostility --------
    (3) Your *present* attitude toward your mother: *j*) very strong attachment--------; *k*) considerable attachment--------; *m*) mild attachment---------; *n*) mild hostility---------; *o*) considerable hostility---------; *p*) very strong hostility --------

1	2	3

(4) Your attitude toward your mother when you were a *child:* *j)* very strong attachment--------; *k)* considerable attachment--------; *m)* mild attachment--------; *n)* mild hostility--------; *o)* considerable hostility--------; *p)* very strong hostility--------

15. Rate the marital happiness of your parents. Write *M* for mother's rating; *F* for father's: *i)* extraordinarily happy--------; *k)* decidedly happy--------; *m)* happy--------; *n)* somewhat happy --------; *o)* average--------; *p)* somewhat unhappy--------; *q)* unhappy--------; *r)* decidedly unhappy--------; *s)* extremely unhappy--------
16. Outside of your family and kin how many separated and divorced people do you know personally? (check): *j)* none--------; *k)* one----------; *m)* two----------; *n)* three----------; *o)* four ---------; *p)* five---------; *q)* six---------; *r)* seven or more --------
17. With how many of the opposite sex, *other than your fiancé(e)* have you gone steadily? (check): *v)* none--------; *w)* one--------; *t)* two--------; *l)* three or more--------
18. Defining friends as something more than mere acquaintances but not necessarily always boon companions, give an estimate of the number of your men friends *before* going steadily with your fiancé(e) (check): *a)* none--------; *b)* few--------; *c)* several ----------; *d)* many---------- In round numbers about how many?----------
19. Estimate the number of your women friends *before* going steadily with your fiancé(e) (check): *a)* none--------; *b)* few--------; *c)* several--------; *d)* many-------- In round numbers how many?----------
20. How many of your present men and women friends are also friends of your fiancé(e)? (check): *u)* all--------; *v)* most of them--------; *x)* a few--------; *y)* none--------
21. Have you ever been engaged before (or had any previous informal understanding that you were to be married)? (check): *u)* never--------; *w)* once--------; *x)* twice--------; *y)* three or more times--------

T

Part Two

1. Do you plan to be married (check): *u)* at church--------; *v)* at home--------; *x)* elsewhere (specify)--------
2. By whom do you plan to be married? *v)* minister--------; *x)* other person (specify)--------
3. Where do you plan to live after marriage? (check): *j)* private house--------; *k)* small apartment building--------; *l)* large apartment building--------; *m)* apartment hotel--------; *n)* hotel--------; *o)* rooming house--------
4. *j)* Have you bought a home?-------- *k)* Are you planning to buy a home?-------- *m)* will you rent a home?--------
5. Population of city or town where you plan to live (check): *i)* open country--------; *j)* 2,500 and under--------; *k)* 2,500 to 10,000--------; *l)* 10,000 to 50,000--------; *m)* 50,000 to 100,000--------; *n)* 100,000 to 500,000--------; *o)* over 500,000 --------; *u)* suburb--------

	1	2	3

6. After marriage do you plan to live (check): *j*) in own home ----------; *n*) with your parents----------; *o*) parents-in-law ----------; *p*) relatives (specify)---------------; *q*) relatives-in-law (specify)-----------------; *r*) other persons (specify) -------------
7. Check *your* attitude toward having children: *v*) desire children very much---------; *x*) mildly desire them---------; *y*) mild objection to them----------; *z*) object very much to having them--------
8. How many children would you like to have? *u*) four or more --------; *v*) three--------; *w*) two--------; *x*) one--------; *y*) none--------
9. Check what you think your fiancé(e)'s attitude is toward having children? *v*) desires children very much--------; *x*) mildly desires them--------; *y*) mild objection to them--------; *z*) objects very much to having them--------
10. Do you think your fiancé(e) is spending a disproportionate amount of present income on (check): *a*) clothes (or other personal ornamentation)--------; *b*) recreation--------; hobbies (specify)-------------------; *c*) food--------; rent--------; *d*) education--------; *e*) do not think so--------
11. What is the attitude of your closest friend or friends to your fiancé(e)? (check): *v*) approve highly--------; *w*) approve with qualification--------; *x*) are resigned--------; *y*) disapprove mildly--------; *z*) disapprove seriously--------
12. Do you smoke? (check): *u*) not at all-------; *w*) rarely-------; *x*) occasionally--------; *y*) often--------
13. Do you drink? (check): *u*) not at all--------; *w*) rarely--------; *x*) occasionally--------; *y*) often--------
14. *u*) Do both your father and mother approve your marriage --------; *y*) do both disapprove--------; *z*) does one disapprove--------: your father--------; your mother--------
15. What is your attitude (check) toward your future father-in-law: *k*) like him very much----------; *l*) like him considerably --------; *m*) like him mildly--------; *n*) mild dislike--------; *o*) considerable dislike--------; *p*) very strong dislike--------; mother-in-law: *k*) like her very much----------; *l*) like her considerably----------; *m*) like her mildly----------; *n*) mild dislike--------; *o*) considerable dislike--------; *p*) very strong dislike--------
16. Was your first information about sex *v*) wholesome--------; *x*) unwholesome-------- Where did you get your first information about sex? *j*) from parent--------; *k*) from wholesome reading----------; *m*) brother----------; sister----------; other relatives---------; *l*) other adult---------; teacher---------; *n*) other children--------; *o*) from pernicious reading--------; other (specify) ------------------ Do you consider your present knowledge of sex adequate for marriage? *v*) Yes----------; *x*) no--------; doubtful--------
17. How long have you been keeping company with your fiancé(e)? (check): *a*) less than 3 months----------; *b*) 3 to 6 months ----------; *c*) 6 to 11 months----------; *d*) 12 to 17 months ----------; *e*) 18 to 23 months----------; *f*) 24 to 35 months ----------; *g*) 36 months or more---------- Enter here exact number of months----------

Question	1	2	3
18. How many months will elapse between your engagement (or time at which you both had a definite understanding that you were to be married) and the date selected for your marriage? (check): *a*) less than 3 months__________; *b*) 3 to 6 months __________; *c*) 6 to 11 months__________; *d*) 12 to 17 months __________; *e*) 18 to 23 months__________; *f*) 24 to 35 months __________; *g*) 36 months or more__________			
	T		

Part Three

Question	1	2	3
1. Do you and your fiancé(e) engage in interests and activities together? (check): *v*) all of them__________; *w*) most of them ________; *x*) some of them________; *y*) a few of them________; *z*) none of them________			
2. Is there any interest vital to you in which your fiancé(e) does not engage? (check): *v*) no________; *z*) yes (specify)__________ ____			
3. Do you confide in your fiancé(e)? (check): *i*) about everything ________; *k*) about most things________; *m*) about some things ________; *n*) about a few things________; *o*) about nothing ________			
4. Does your fiancé(e) confide in you (check): *i*) about everything ________; *k*) about most things________; *m*) about some things _________; *n*) about a few things_________; *o*) about nothing _________			
5. Check the frequency of demonstrations of affection you show your fiancé(e) (kissing, embracing, etc.): *i*) occupies practically all of the time you are alone together________; *j*) very frequent ________; *m*) occasional________; *n*) rare________; *o*) almost never________			
6. Who generally takes the initiative in the demonstration of affection? (check): *u*) mutual_________; *m*) you_________; *x*) your fiancé(e)________			
7. Are you satisfied with the amount of demonstration of affection? (check): *j*) yes_________; no_________; *p*) desire less_________; *q*) desire more__________ Is your fiancé(e) satisfied with the amount of demonstration of affection? (check): *j*) yes_________; no_________; *p*) desires less_________; *q*) desires more_________			
8. State the *present* approximate agreement or disagreement with your fiancé(e) on the items listed on the following page. Please place a check in the proper column opposite every item.			

Check one column for each item below	*j)* Always agree	*k)* Almost always agree	*l)* Occasionally disagree	*m)* Frequently disagree	*n)* Almost always disagree	*o)* Always disagree	*t)* Never discussed	1	2	3
Money matters										
Matters of recreation										
Religious matters										
Demonstrations of affection										
Friends										
Table manners										
Matters of conventionality										
Philosophy of life										
Ways of dealing with your families										
Arrangements for your marriage										
Dates with one another										

9. When disagreements arise between you and your fiancé(e) they usually result in (check): *v)* agreement by mutual give and take --------; *y)* you giving in--------; *z)* your fiancé(e) giving in --------
10. Do you ever wish you had not become engaged? (check): *u)* never--------; *x)* once--------; *y)* occasionally--------; *z)* frequently--------
11. Have you ever contemplated breaking your engagement? (check): *u)* never--------; *x)* once--------; *y)* occasionally--------; *z)* frequently--------
12. Has your steady relationship with your fiancé(e) ever been broken off temporarily? (check): *v)* never--------; *x)* once--------; *y)* twice--------; *z)* three or more times--------
13. How confident are you that your marriage will be a happy one? (check): *v)* very confident--------; *w)* confident--------; *x)* a little uncertain--------; *y)* extremely uncertain--------

T

Part Four

On the opposite page, compare the following personality traits of yourself, your fiancé(e), your father, and your mother. Write F for father, M for mother, S for fiancé(e), and Y for yourself. If either of your parents is dead, rate as remembered. Be sure to rate your father, your mother, your fiancé(e), and yourself *on each trait.* (In scoring, score *yourself* only.)

	Very much so	Considerably	Somewhat	A little	Not at all	1	2	3
Takes responsibility willingly...	*u*......	*v*.......	*w*......	*x*.......	*z*.......			
Dominating................	*a*......	*b*......	*c*.......	*d*.......	*e*.......			
Irritable..................	*a*......	*b*......	*c*.......	*d*.......	*e*.......			
Punctual..................	*u*......	*v*.......	*w*......	*x*.......	*z*.......			
Moody....................	*a*......	*b*......	*c*.......	*d*.......	*e*.......			
Angers easily..............	*a*......	*b*......	*c*.......	*d*.......	*e*.......			
Ambitious.................	*a*......	*b*......	*c*.......	*d*.......	*e*.......			
Jealous...................	*a*......	*b*......	*c*.......	*d*.......	*e*.......			
Sympathetic...............	*u*......	*v*.......	*w*......	*x*.......	*z*.......			
Easygoing.................	*u*......	*v*.......	*w*......	*x*.......	*z*.......			
Selfish....................	*a*......	*b*......	*c*.......	*d*.......	*e*.......			
Stubborn..................	*a*......	*b*......	*c*.......	*d*.......	*e*.......			
Sense of duty..............	*u*......	*v*.......	*w*......	*x*.......	*z*.......			
Sense of humor.............	*u*......	*v*.......	*w*......	*x*.......	*z*.......			
Easily hurt................	*a*......	*b*......	*c*.......	*d*.......	*e*.......			
Self-confident..............	*u*......	*v*.......	*w*......	*x*.......	*z*.......			
Nervous...................	*a*......	*b*......	*c*.......	*d*.......	*e*.......			
Likes belonging to organizations	*u*......	*v*.......	*w*......	*x*.......	*z*.......			
Impractical................	*a*......	*b*......	*c*.......	*d*.......	*e*.......			
Easily depressed............	*a*......	*b*......	*c*.......	*d*.......	*e*.......			
Easily excited..............	*a*......	*b*......	*c*.......	*d*.......	*e*.......			
						T		

Part I----, Part II----, Part III----, Part IV----, Total------

II. Scoring the Marriage Prediction Schedule

The three narrow columns at the right-hand side of each page are for scoring the replies to the questions. The score values assigned are arbitrary in the sense that usually each gradation in reply differs by one point. For example, the following question is scored as follows. Do you and your spouse engage in outside interests together? (check): *j*) all of them, +2; *k*) most of them, +1; *l*) some of them, 0; *m*) few of them, −1; *n*) none of them, −2. Although arbitrary, the score values are in general conformity with the findings of the studies in this field, particularly those of E. W. Burgess and L. S. Cottrell, *Predicting Success or Failure in Marriage;* L. M. Terman, *Psychological Factors in Marital Happiness;* and E. W. Burgess and Paul Wallin, *A Study of 1000 Engaged Couples.*

The letters in italics before each subdivision of the question provide the code for scoring the replies. The code value of each letter is as follows:

a...............	−2	*j*................	+2
b...............	−1	*k*...............	+1
c...............	0	*l*................	0
d...............	+1	*m*...............	−1
e...............	+2	*n*...............	−2
f...............	+2	*o*...............	−3
g...............	+2	*p*...............	−3
h...............	+2	*q*...............	−3
i...............	+3	*r*...............	−3

s	−3	*w*	0
t	0	*x*	−1
u	+2	*y*	−2
v	+1	*z*	−2

The following is the procedure for scoring the replies to the questions:

1. For each question enter in column 1 at the right-hand side of each page the letter in italics which precedes the answer which is checked for the given item.
2. Enter in column 2 all the plus scores and in column 3 all the minus scores corresponding to the appropriate code value for each letter as indicated above.
3. Add the scores in columns 2 and 3, entering them for each part; then transfer them to the appropriate place as indicated on the last page of the Marriage Prediction Schedule.

High scores, those above 60, are favorable for marital adjustment, as indicated by research findings that approximately 75 per cent of persons with these scores in the engagement period are well adjusted in their marriages. Low scores, or those below 20, are much less favorable for happiness in marriage, as shown by the probability that only 25 per cent of persons with these scores will be well adjusted in married life. Intermediate scores, those between 60 and 20, should be regarded at present as nonpredictive since the chances of persons with these scores for marital success may tentatively be considered as about even.

The prediction score of a person and his corresponding matrimonial risk group assignment should be interpreted with extreme caution. The following points should be kept in mind:

1. The prediction does not apply directly to the individual. It states the statistical probabilities of marital success for a group of persons of which the individual is one. If he belongs to the lower risk group, in which 75 per cent of the marriages turn out unhappily, there is no way of telling by this statistical prediction whether he falls in the 25 per cent of the marriages with varying degrees of happiness or in the 75 per cent of unhappy unions.
2. The prediction is an individual's general matrimonial risk irrespective of the particular person to whom he is engaged. The individual's specific matrimonial risk for marriage to a given person is much more valuable but also more complicated and therefore not suited for self-scoring.
3. In the majority of cases the specific matrimonial risk of a couple may be roughly estimated from the two general matrimonial risk groups to which the two persons are assigned. An average of the two scores will generally be close to what may be expected from a specific matrimonial risk group assignment worked out by combining the answers on each question given by the two members of the couple.
4. With the above reservations in mind, a low prediction score should not be taken as indicating lack of suitability for marriage. It should, however, be helpful to the person in stimulating him to secure adequate preparation for marriage, to be more careful in the selection of a marriage partner, and to give attention to the solving of any difficulties in the relation before rather than after marriage.

Chapter XI

LEGAL CONTROL OF MARRIAGE

THE STATE has a stake in every marriage. Its basic interest is in the children who may result from the marriage, but it is also concerned with the rights and responsibilities of the individuals who marry. Both men and women are guaranteed privileges and assume obligations when they enter into a marriage contract. The state exercises control over the making and keeping of marriage contracts through legal requirements and restrictions. Many marriage laws are for the purpose of protecting the children who may be born. The children of legal marriages are legitimate and have clearly defined inheritance rights. The laws attempt to guarantee the children not only legitimacy but also a stable environment for growth. Thus it is necessary to regulate who may marry and to exercise control over the dissolution of marriages which have been made. Further, attempts are made to prevent the marriages of those who would produce biologically unfit children. Legal regulation of marriages is also designed to protect women from sexual exploitation and to guarantee property rights of husbands and wives.

Thus marriage laws, like other laws, are designed to protect the interests of both the individual and society. The individual yields a measure of personal freedom for the good of society and is compensated by guarantees of personal security and social stability.

Problem of regulation

It is almost universally recognized that the state must have laws governing marriages. There is much disagreement, however, as to the kind and extent of regulation which will achieve the desired ends. Although it is generally agreed that it is not desirable for the biologically unfit to be permitted to marry and to reproduce, difference of opinion arises over who are the biologically unfit and how to control their relationships. Some believe they should be prevented from marrying; others maintain that preventing their marrying will not prevent their reproducing, and hold that it is better to legalize their union to give their children legitimacy. Still others advocate permitting the biologically unfit to marry if they first submit to a sterilization operation.

It is agreed that young people should not marry before reaching a mature stage of development, yet there is no agreement on when people are mature enough to marry. Some state laws permit marriages of boys 14 years old if they have parental consent; other states set the age at 18. Girls may be legally married in some states at 12; in others they are not old enough until they reach 16 or 18. Where the age for legal marriage is low, the belief is that a high age requirement would encourage sexual promiscuity. In the states where the age requirement is high, the prevailing attitude of the legislators is that, even though more sexual promiscuity may result among those below the legal age for marriage, a higher age requirement makes for more stable marriages and so is best for the individual and for society.

It is common for states to accept marriages as valid even though they do not conform to legal requirements, provided that no one takes action to have such marriages annulled. Those who have the responsibility for administering the marriage laws differ about how far to go in permitting the individual's romantic impulses to take precedence over the established regulations. The problem is to exercise enough regulation to achieve desired ends but not so much that people will flout the laws, follow their individual desires, and form illegal unions.

Marriage laws are in the hands of the separate states, and in attempting to solve the problem of effective control for the good of society, a great variety of laws have been enacted. The result has been confusion. There are 48 different sets of marriage and divorce regulations, since the states have acted quite independently of each other.

Baber points out that a man, by traveling 15 miles to get into three different states, would be considered a married man in one state, a single man in another, and a bigamist in the third.[1] In a test case in North Carolina, a man had gone outside the state to get a divorce and had then returned to North Carolina to remarry. He was arrested as a bigamist because North Carolina did not recognize his out-of-state divorce. The case was appealed to the Supreme Court, and in a 1942 decision the Court declared that North Carolina must recognize a divorce if legally granted in another state. This decision seemed to clear up some of the confusion. But then another case came up in 1945 in which the Court reversed itself and handed down a decision stating that it was up to each state to decide whether it would accept divorces granted in other states.[2] The Supreme Court reversed itself again in 1948 in a test case originating in Massachusetts. The Massachusetts courts had declared as "no good" divorces obtained in Florida and Nevada. The Supreme Court ruled that the Massachusetts courts had erred and that each state must give full faith and credit to the official acts of other states. Lawmakers are showing an increasing awareness of the complications arising because of the diverse laws, and the present tendency is toward greater uniformity.

We will look at some of the more common regulations concerning marriage. In each case we shall quote one state's law and

[1] Ray E. Baber, *Marriage and the Family,* p. 138. New York: McGraw-Hill Book Company, Inc., 1939.

[2] Sidney E. Goldstein, *Marriage and Family Counseling,* pp. 80-81. McGraw-Hill Book Company, Inc., 1945.

compare or contrast it with the laws of other states. The marriage laws in Michigan, which we shall use for purposes of comparison, are not "model laws." We quote them simply because they include most of the regulations found in other states and because the reader will gain a better understanding of the nature of marriage regulations if specific laws are quoted from a state which has detailed regulations on all phases of marriage relationships. The student who is interested in the specific marriage laws in his home state should read Vernier's *American Family Laws*. This five-volume work, with its supplement, details the marriage regulations in the forty-eight states, Alaska, Hawaii, and Washington, D.C.

Marriage as a civil contract

12691. Marriage, as far as its validity in law is concerned, is a civil contract to which the consent of parties capable in law of contracting, is essential.

Contract: Chastity is not a requisite to validity of a marriage and while marriage is, in a very important sense, a contract, it is also a relation governed by rules of public policy, which apply to no mere private agreements. *Intention is the essential ingredient,* as in every other contract, and, when one of the parties, instead of assenting to the contract, positively dissents from it, there can be no legal or valid marriage, although a ceremony is gone through by the officiating minister or magistrate. A contract of marriage cannot be presumed when such presumption would do violence to facts in the case. This section does not make a ceremony essential to validity, and a common law marriage, when shown, binds the parties.

Marriage is a contract which the legislature, under Constitution V32 may not dissolve, though contracted merely for convenience and with unhappy results.

The law as quoted is typical of the law found in other states in that it specifies that marriage is a civil contract between two individuals. The marriage contract differs from ordinary contracts in that (1) it cannot be rescinded or its fundamental terms changed by agreement between the two parties; (2) it results in a *status;* (3) it merges the legal identity of the parties at common law; (4) the tests of capacity differ from those applied to ordinary contracts (in other words, those who may not bind themselves by ordinary contracts may make a valid marriage).[3] Although a marriage can be entered into easily, it cannot be dissolved by mutual agreement as other civil contracts can be terminated. Society is profoundly interested in the family as an institution, and once the contract is made in marriage, society seeks to see that the contract is not readily dissolved. To get out of his contract a man must go through court procedure.

The important point which makes a marriage contract valid is the consent of the two parties to the agreement. What really marries the couple is the mutual and willing expression of *I do* when they accept each other as husband and wife. The law prescribes a wedding license and someone to officiate, but although both of these may be present, if one partner has been forced into the marriage by the other, no marriage has taken place, since the willing consent was not given by one party to the contract. Coercion or unwillingness on the part of one partner makes the contract void. On the other hand, marriage can take place without either the officiant or the license if the couple willingly agree to live as husband and wife and do so. This is termed common law marriage and is recognized in many states.

Eugenic regulations

12695. No insane person, idiot, or person who has been afflicted with syphilis or gonorrhea and has not been cured of same shall be capable of contracting marriage. No person who has been confined in any public institution or asylum as an epileptic, feeble-minded, imbecile, or insane patient or who has been adjudged insane, feeble-minded, an epileptic, or an imbecile by a court of competent jurisdiction shall be capable of contracting marriage without, before the issuance by the county clerk of the license to marry, filing in the office of the said county clerk a verified certificate from two regularly

[3] Chester G. Vernier, *American Family Laws,* Vol. I, p. 51. Stanford University Press, 1931.

licensed physicians of this state that such person has been completely cured of such insanity, epilepsy, imbecility, or feeble-mindedness and there is no probability that such person will transmit any of such defects or disabilities to the offspring of such marriage.

All states have regulations governing the marriage of those who are mentally ill or those whose minds have not developed to an adult stage. People who are not of sound mind cannot make a legal contract of any type, and since marriage is a contract they are incapable of contracting a marriage. Emphasis on this matter is changing, however, so that now the more generally accepted reason for preventing these marriages is the danger that the mentally defective may have defective children. A survey of inmates of the Alabama State School for the Feeble-minded in 1945 revealed the following: 318 inmates had one feeble-minded parent, 325 had two feeble-minded parents, 87 had an insane, hospitalized parent, 15 had a parent in prison, 136 had alcoholic parents, and 46 had syphilitic parents.[4] Three states have now amended their laws so that feeble-minded persons may marry if they first undergo a sterilization operation. This is a sound step. For the states to have laws preventing the marriage of mental defectives has accomplished little. In the rare cases where the laws preventing mental defectives from marrying are enforced, the end result is that the mental defectives often have illegitimate children instead of marrying and having legitimate children.

Although all states have some mental requirements for marriage, little is done to enforce these laws. The couple may be required to swear that they are not of unsound mind, but how many mental defectives will state that they are of unsound mind when applying for a marriage license? It is safe to assume that their judgment might be biased. Seventeen states also prohibit the marriage of epileptics. Although the Michigan law requires that one who has been confined to a mental institution must have two physicians swear that he has been cured, little

[4] Marian S. Olden, "Present Status of Sterilization Legislation in the United States," *Eugenic News*, March, 1946, 10.

effort is made to enforce this regulation. Only one state, Oregon, has now a law requiring an examination to determine the presence of insanity or epilepsy.[5] There is some doubt as to whether this law can be enforced. Laws prohibiting the marriage of persons with venereal disease were on the statute books for years, but little was done to enforce them. In many states the man had to swear that he did not have a venereal disease. In 1935, Connecticut passed a new type of venereal disease law, often referred to as the eugenic marriage law. Since 1935 a total of 38 states have passed venereal disease laws. These laws require both the man and the woman to have a physical examination for venereal disease sometime before the marriage. The examination is good for a period of from 10 to 40 days, the time limit varying in the different states. If the marriage does not take place within that period, the examination must be repeated. In 29 of the states the test is for syphilis only, but in the other states the test includes all venereal diseases. Under the older health laws the physical examination, if required, was required of the male only. Table 17 gives a late summary of the marriage laws in the various states. Over a period of three years 1.3 per cent of the applicants for marriage licenses in Illinois have been found to have syphilis.[6]

Some have argued against the law requiring a venereal disease test because of the expense for the individuals and the profit possible for the doctors who may charge for the examination. Some states, in order to prevent exorbitant charges, set the fee that can be charged for the examination. North Carolina has a provision in the law making the examination free to those who are not able to pay.

Since the law has been generally accepted as a desirable means of controlling the spread of venereal disease, the examination will probably be made free to all in the not distant future. It

[5] Sidney E. Goldstein, *Marriage and Family Counseling*, p. 109. New York: McGraw-Hill Book Company, Inc., 1945.

[6] Department of Public Health, *Illinois Health Messenger*, p. 106. Springfield, Illinois, September, 1942.

could easily be made a part of the preventive program of the public health service.

There are few other physical prohibitions to marriage, although it would be desirable to have more. Two states, North Carolina and North Dakota, require a certificate from a licensed physician stating that the man and woman desiring to marry are free from tuberculosis in the infectious or advanced stages.

Age for marriage

12690. Every male who shall have attained the full age of 18 years and every female who shall have attained the full age of 16 years shall be capable in law of contracting marriage if otherwise competent.

Age of Consent. Consent is the first requisite in marriage and, in case of persons under ages specified, the capacity to consent is withheld by law. A person under the statutory age cannot be lawfully married.

All states have regulations which prohibit the marriage of young people before a certain age. States usually set two ages at which marriage may take place, one age which is legal if the parents give their consent, and one at which the young people may marry without the consent of the parents. The most common ages for permitting marriage with consent of the parents are 18 for boys and 16 for girls. Twenty states have adopted this standard. According to the Michigan law, a girl cannot legally give consent until the age of 18; the parent or guardian must give consent in writing before a marriage license can be issued.

The most common minimum age at which marriage may take place without the consent of the parents or guardian is 21 for boys and 18 for girls. Approximately three-fifths of the states have adopted those ages. The next most common age is 21 for both men and women.

Idaho, Mississippi, New Jersey, and Washington permit boys of 14 and girls of 12 to marry. Since these states have not passed any laws concerning age for marriage, the common law prevails

TABLE 17*

MARRIAGE LAWS

As of January 1, 1953

State	Minimum Marriage Age Specified in Law[a]		Common Law Marriages Are Valid	Prohibit Marriage of Those with Transmissible Disease in Infectious Stage	Physical Examination and Blood Test for Male and Female			Waiting Period	
	Male	Female			Date of Enactment	([b])	Scope of Laboratory Test	Before Issuance of License	After Issuance of License
Alabama	17	14	★	....	1947	30 da.	([h])	....	....
Arizona	18	16	....	....	....	....	....	....	....
Arkansas	18	16	....	....	....	....	....	3 da.	....
California	18	16	....	....	1939	30 da.	([d])	....	....
Colorado	16	16	★	....	1939	30 da.	([f])	....	....
Connecticut	16	16	....	....	1935	40 da.	([d])	5 da.	....
Delaware	18	16	....	★	1947	30 da.	([d])	....	★[k]
Florida	18	16	★	....	1945	30 da.	([d])	3 da.	....
Georgia	17	14	★	....	1949	30 da.	([d])	5 da.[c]	....
Idaho	14[e]	12[e]	★	....	1943	30 da.	([d])	....	....
Illinois	18	16	....	....	1939	15 da.	([h])	....	....
Indiana	18	16	★	....	1939	30 da.	([d])	....	....
Iowa	16	14	★	....	1941	20 da.	([d])	....	....
Kansas	18	16	★	....	1947	30 da.	([d])	3 da.	....
Kentucky	16	14	....	....	1940	15 da.	([d])	....	....
Louisiana	18	16	....	....	([i])	....	....	....	....
Maine	16	16	★	★	1941	....	([d])	5 da.	....
Maryland	18	16	....	....	....	....	....	2 da.	....
Massachusetts	18	16	....	....	1943	30 da.	([d])	5 da.	....
Michigan	18	16	★	....	1939	30 da.	([h])	5 da.	....

Minnesota	16	15	....	....	....	....	....	5 da.	....
Mississippi	14[e]	12[e]	★	....	....	....	....	....	....
Missouri	15	15	....	....	1943	15 da.	([d])	....	....
Montana	18	16	★	....	1947	20 da.	([d])	....	....
Nebraska	18	16	....	★	1943	30 da.	([d])	....	....
Nevada	18	16	....	....	....	....	....	....	....
New Hampshire	14	13	....	....	1937	30 da.	([d])	5 da.	....
New Jersey	14[e]	12[e]	....	....	1938	30 da.	([d])	3 da.	★
New Mexico	18	16	....	....	....	....	....	....	....
New York	16	14	....	....	1938[g]	30 da.	([d])	3 da.	★
North Carolina	16	16	....	....	1941	30 da.	([d])	....	....
North Dakota	18	15	....	....	1939	30 da.	([d])	....	....
Ohio	18	16	★	....	1941	30 da.	([d])	5 da.	....
Oklahoma	18	15	★	★	1945	30 da.	([d])	....	....
Oregon	18	15	....	....	1937	10 da.	([i])	3 da.	....
Pennsylvania	16	16	★	....	1939	30 da.	([d])	3 da.	....
Rhode Island	18	16	★	....	1938	40 da.	([d])	....	★
South Carolina	18	14	★	....	....	....	....	1 da.	....
South Dakota	18	15	★	....	1939	20 da.	([d])	....	....
Tennessee	16	16	★	....	1939	30 da.	([h])	3 da.	....
Texas	16	14	★	....	1949	15 da.	([d])	....	....
Utah	16	14	....	★	1941	30 da.	([f])	....	....
Vermont	18	16	....	★	1941	30 da.	....	....	★
Virginia	18	16	....	....	1940	30 da.	([d])	....	....
Washington	14[e]	12[e]	....	★	....	....	....	3 da.	....
West Virginia	18	16	....	....	1939	30 da.	([d])	3 da.	....
Wisconsin	18	15	....	....	1939	15 da.	([d])	5 da.	....
Wyoming	18	16	★	....	1943	30 da.	([h])	....	....

[a] With parental consent.
[b] Time allowed between date of examination and issuance of license.
[c] For those under 21 who do not have parental consent.
[d] Syphilis.
[e] Common law marriage age.
[f] Syphilis and other venereal diseases.
[g] Amended in 1939.
[h] Venereal diseases.
[i] Syphilis and gonorrhea.
[j] In 1924 law adopted applying to male only; laboratory test authorized but not required.
[k] 24 hrs., residents; 96 hrs., nonresidents.

★ Information furnished by the Women's Bureau, U.S. Department of Labor. *The Book of the States, 1948-1949*, p. 343. Chicago: The Council of State Governments, 1948. (Corrected to 1953 through letters to states.)

in them. The English common law on age for marriage followed the Roman law, which permitted girls of 12 and boys of 14 to marry. Although these states have not passed laws prohibiting child marriages, they are not, with the exception of Mississippi, the states which have the most child marriages. The census report of 1940 shows that Florida, Arkansas, and Missis-

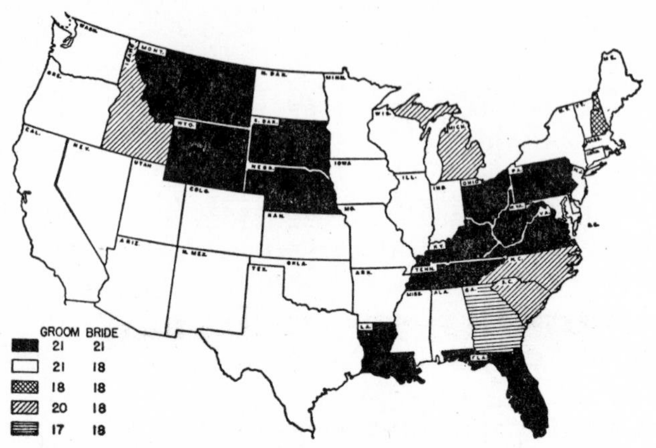

Fig. 42. Legal age for marriage without parental consent.

sippi have the largest percentage of people married at 15 years or younger. Idaho, New Jersey, and Washington rank with the states having the fewest child marriages. Apparently it is not so much the law as the attitude of the people toward child marriage that determines whether children will marry. All states having a large percentage of child marriages are in the southern section of the United States. Child marriages are equally high among white and colored young people in the South.[7] Regardless of what the state law says about age for marriage in northern states, the percentage of child marriages is uniformly low. In 1940 there were 21,000 boys and girls of 14 and 15 years of age in the United States who were or who had been married; 17,000 of these were girls.[8]

[7] U.S. Bureau of Census, *Sixteenth Census of the United States, 1940,* Vol. IV, Parts II-IV.

[8] *Ibid.,* Vol. IV, Part I.

An important reason for discouraging early marriage is that very young people are not emotionally mature enough to use judgment in selecting mates or to be parents. Boys who marry early may not be in a position to support families.

It must be remembered that many child marriages are forced because of pregnancy. In most states judges are given the right to waive the minimum ages for marriage if the girl is pregnant. Many such marriages do not have a chance for success because of a series of reasons in addition to the immaturity of the couple. In some marriages there is great disparity in age, usually the man being a number of years older than the girl. Recently a man of 70 married a girl of 13. The girl believed herself to be in love with the man and her parents willingly gave their consent to the marriage. The law does not attempt to judge the results of marriage contracts. The Michigan law quoted earlier states: "Marriage is a contract which the legislature may not dissolve, though contracted for convenience with unhappy results."

The question arises whether some of the laws make sense. Boys and girls may not vote until the age of 21, yet they may marry several years before this in many states.

Although states prohibit marriages below certain ages, a marriage of people below that age usually stands as valid if it has been consummated. If an interested person takes the case before a court, offers proof of nonage of one or both of the parties, and asks annulment, the court will probably not refuse to annul the marriage. Otherwise it stands.

Marriage between relatives

12692. No man shall marry his mother, grandmother, daughter, granddaughter, stepmother, grandfather's wife, son's wife, grandson's wife, wife's mother, wife's grandmother, wife's daughter, wife's granddaughter, nor his sister, brother's daughter, sister's daughter, father's sister, or mother's sister, or cousin of the first degree. Such marriages are equally prohibited whether parties of parents are legitimate or illegitimate, or of the whole or half blood. This is a public law of which courts are bound to take notice.

12693. No woman shall marry her father, grandfather, son, grandson, stepfather, grandmother's husband, daughter's husband, granddaughter's husband, husband's father, husband's grandfather, husband's son, husband's grandson, nor her brother, brother's son, sister's son, father's brother, mother's brother, or cousin of the first degree.

The Michigan law prohibits marriage of blood relatives or those related by marriage. Some states do not go so far in prohibiting marriage of half-blood relatives, and most states do not go so far in prohibiting marriage because of relationship by marriage. All states prohibit marriages between close blood relatives. Brothers and sisters, fathers and daughters, mothers and sons, grandfathers and granddaughters, grandmothers and grandsons, aunts and nephews, and uncles and nieces, may not marry in any state, with one exception. The State of Rhode Island permits marriage of an uncle and a niece if both are Jewish and if the wedding ceremony is performed by a rabbi. In this matter the State of Rhode Island suspends its own marriage law in order to accommodate itself to the Jewish law which permits the marriage of an uncle and a niece but not of an aunt and a nephew.[9] The next most common prohibition against marriages of consanguinity is that first cousins and brothers and sisters of half blood may not marry. Both prohibitions are found in 29 states. Almost half of the states permit first cousins to marry, and only six states prohibit the marriage of second cousins.[10] Although many states do not permit first cousins to marry, a number of states do recognize the marriages of first cousins if they go to another state to marry and then return to their home state to live. This policy seems inconsistent, but it is commonly followed by states in order to prevent confusion and to guarantee the legitimacy of children born of such marriages.

The strongest objection to marriage of close blood relatives

[9] Sidney E. Goldstein, *Marriage and Family Counseling,* p. 70. New York: McGraw-Hill Book Company, Inc., 1945.

[10] Indiana, Minnesota, Nevada, Ohio, Washington, and Wisconsin.

is the incest taboo. However, there is a biological reason for opposing consanguineous marriage, since relatives are more likely to carry the same hereditary defects in their germ plasm. If marriage takes place between closely related people, defects are more likely to show up in the children, who can inherit the traits from both sides of the family. In animal breeding it is common to "line breed" to build up a particular stock. In line breeding, mothers and sons and fathers and daughters are mated. The principle is that superior stock produces superior stock. In stock breeding, the defective strains have been eliminated so that mating of blood relatives does not present the risk that it does in human mating. In humans it is impossible to eliminate the undesirable strain. If first cousins were of the best hereditary stock, from a biological point of view first-cousin marriage would be desirable.

The incest taboo is carried to an unreasonable and illogical extreme in the laws prohibiting marriage because of affinity. There is no biological reason why in-laws or step-relatives should not marry. It will be noticed that in Michigan the law goes so far as to say a man may not marry his stepmother or his wife's grandmother. It would be unusual for a man to wish to marry his wife's grandmother. However, if he did wish to do so there would seem to be no more valid basis for objection to such a marriage than to his marrying any other grandmother. Only seven other states have all the prohibitions found in the Michigan law.[11] Twenty-six jurisdictions have no regulations at all on marriages of affinity. The most common regulations are those prohibiting the marriages of step-parents to step-children (23 states), parents-in-law to sons- and daughters-in-law (20 states), a man or a woman to grand-daughter-in-law or grandson-in-law (18 states).[12] All these prohibitions, when considered objectively, seem to have no reasonable basis. They are simply based upon misunderstanding of what constitutes blood relationship and upon the general aversion to incest.

[11] Kentucky, Maine, Maryland, Massachusetts, Rhode Island, South Carolina, and Vermont.

[12] Vernier, *op. cit.*, pp. 183-184.

Miscegenetic regulations

12695. All marriages heretofore contracted between white persons and those wholly or in part of African descent are hereby declared valid and effectual in law for all purposes; and the issue of such marriages shall be deemed and taken as legal as to such issue and as to both of the parents.

Interracial marriages are forbidden in 30 states. They were prohibited in Michigan before 1823, but at that time the law was changed to read as quoted above. The intermarriage of Negroes and whites is more likely to be prohibited in the southern states and the intermarriage of whites and Mongolians in the western states. The following states have no regulation concerning miscegenetic marriages: Connecticut, Illinois, Iowa, Kansas, Massachusetts, Michigan, Minnesota, New Hampshire, New Jersey, New Mexico, New York, Pennsylvania, Rhode Island, Vermont, Washington, and Wisconsin.[13]

The following states prohibit marriages of whites with Negroes of one-eighth Negro blood: Florida, Indiana, Mississippi, Missouri, Nebraska, North Dakota, and Texas. Alabama imposes a penalty of from two to seven years for the marriage of a white person to a person of Negro descent.[14]

California's law against interracial marriages was declared unconstitutional in 1948, when a Mexican woman and a Negro man who were refused a marriage license appealed to the courts for a ruling. The court declared the law unconstitutional for several reasons, among them the following: (1) A marriage contract is a fundamental right of free men. (2) Marriage is the right of individuals and not of special groups. (3) Legislative control of marriage must be based on proved peril to the parties involved or to the state. (4) The law discriminates because of race or color. (5) The law is not meeting a definite need. Since both parties applying for the license were Catholic, they declared that their religious freedom was hampered by

[13] Vernier, *op. cit.*, pp. 204-208.
[14] *Ibid.*

the law because they could receive all the sacraments except that of marriage.

Burma[15] reports that in the two and one-half years following the repeal of the California law, Los Angeles County had 445 interracial marriages between whites and members of other races. In three out of four cases the wife was white and the husband Oriental or Negro. He estimates that approximately one-half of one per cent of all marriages are interracial in Los Angeles County.

Although interracial marriages are permitted in many states, few interracial marriages actually take place, because of social pressure. It is recognized that often the parties to a miscegenetic union are ostracized by both racial groups.

Biologically there is no reason why the races should not intermarry, since superior people have superior children regardless of the color of the skin. However, the pressure of social attitudes makes it difficult for these marriages to be happy, and the arrival of children presents additional problems. In some countries interracial marriages have proved and are proving to be the only real solution to the race problem. When no stigma is attached to interracial marriage, then no race problem will exist, since the acceptance of biological fusion represents complete acceptance of a minority group. In the United States so much stigma is still attached to such marriages that those interested in successful and happy marriages cannot but discourage them.

Marriage license

12705. It is necessary for all parties intending to be married to obtain a marriage license from the county clerk of the county in which either the man or the woman resides. If both parties are nonresidents of the state, it shall be necessary to obtain such a license from the county clerk of the county in which the marriage is to be performed.

[15] John H. Burma, "Research Note on the Measurement of Interracial Marriages," *American Journal of Sociology*, 57:6 (May, 1952), 587-589.

All states have adopted the system of requiring a license for marriage in order to keep records of marriages. Although they require licenses, many states, in practice, permit marriage without a license. As we have pointed out earlier, it is not the license that marries the couple, and a majority of states still recognize common law marriage, which takes place without a marriage license. Quakers and some other religious groups are exempted from getting marriage licenses because of their religious beliefs. Georgia, Maryland, and Ohio permit the substitution of the published banns for a license.[16]

A license grants a couple legal permission to be married. However, those qualified to officiate at a marriage may refuse to marry a couple even though a license to wed has been secured. Some ministers are in the habit of questioning couples about their previous marital status and the circumstances of any previous divorce. If a minister concludes that a contemplated marriage has no chance for success, or that for moral reasons the church should not sanction the marriage, he may refuse to perform the marriage ceremony, since the license is permissive and not mandatory.

Waiting period

12708. No license to marry shall be delivered within a period of five days immediately following the date of application therefor. *Provided,* however, that the judge of probate of each county, for good and sufficient cause shown, may, by an order in writing, signed by him, authorize the county clerk to deliver such license immediately following the application therefor.

Two policies are usually followed if a waiting period is required between the time of the application for a license to wed and the marriage. Most states follow the policy of not delivering the license for some time after the application is made, five days being the most common period of waiting. According to the other method, the license is issued at once but is not valid

[16] Vernier, *op. cit.,* p. 60.

for a certain number of days. Forty-three states either require a waiting period or have a venereal disease law, which serves much the same purpose in that it prevents hasty marriages. Illinois once had a law requiring a delay of three days between the application for the license and the issuance of the license, but this law was repealed, since the venereal disease test requirement was held to serve the same purpose. In many states a judge may waive the waiting-period requirement under certain

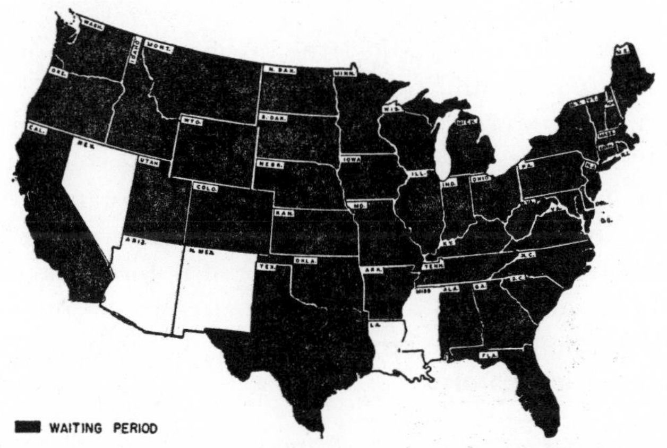

Fig. 43. States in which hasty marriage is impossible because of a required waiting period after application for a marriage license or a requirement for a blood test.

conditions. If the girl is pregnant, if both members of the couple are definitely old enough to know what they are doing, or if other circumstances seem to make the waiting period unnecessary, the judge may use his power to waive.

The waiting-period requirement, like the physical examination for venereal disease, is relatively recent. Most states have passed this requirement within the last 30 years. Maine is the only state which has always required a waiting period or the publishing of banns. The custom of publishing advance notice through the posting of or the reading of the banns started early in the Middle Ages and has continued among Catholics to the present. Publishing of the banns was made mandatory by the

Fourth Lateran Council in 1215. It is now recognized that this old church custom was important in preventing hasty marriages. In the 1920's a series of widely publicized "Gin Marriages" awakened many state legislatures to the need for a waiting period before the issuance of marriage licenses. The law reduces the number of ill-advised marriages. In Los Angeles alone, 1,000 marriage license applicants per year do not bother to return to get the license at the end of the waiting period.[17]

Fig. 44. Known for its easy divorce laws, Nevada also extends a helping hand to couples who wish to be quickly wed. The Gretna Green Chapel, where for fifteen dollars a minister, witnesses, lighted candles, and a license can be purchased as a "package wedding." The justice of the peace in Las Vegas made more money than the President of the United States in 1941. *By permission,* Press Association.

Since all states have not had a waiting-period law, the effectiveness of such a law in any one state has been hampered in the past. Couples wishing to marry could easily cross a state border and be married at once. However, with 44 states now requiring either the waiting period or a venereal disease test,

[17] Paul Popenoe and R. H. Johnson, *Applied Eugenics,* p. 183. New York: The Macmillan Company, 1933.

the problem has been largely solved. It is reasonable to expect that before long some form of a waiting period will be required in all states. Then the last of the "marrying parsons" who have capitalized on interstate marriages will be forced out of business.

Breach of promise

Act 127: All civil causes of action for alienation of affection, criminal conversation, and seduction of any person of the age of 18 years or more, and all causes of action for breach of contract to marry are hereby abolished.

There was a time when it was not uncommon for a girl to sue if a man broke his promise to marry. The engagement was legally binding upon both parties. As late as 1929 a Michigan jury awarded $450,000 damages in a "heart-balm" suit. The change in the way people look upon engagements today is reflected in a change in state laws on breach of promise. The law quoted above was passed in 1935. It clearly states that "heart-balm" suits are forbidden in the future. A number of other states have passed similar laws.[18]

Who is qualified to perform marriages

12696. A marriage may be solemnized by any justice of the peace or judge of probate, in the county in which he was chosen, or judge of a municipal court in the municipality in which he was chosen, and they may be solemnized throughout the state by any minister of the gospel who has been ordained or authorized to solemnize marriages according to the usages of his denomination and who is a pastor of any church or churches in this state, and who shall continue to preach the gospel in this state.

In all states except Maryland, Maine, and West Virginia, marriages may be performed by either the civil or the religious authorities. In these three states the ceremony must be performed by the religious authorities.[19] People usually prefer to

[18] Alabama, California, Colorado, Illinois, Indiana, New Jersey, New York, and Pennsylvania.

[19] Vernier, *op. cit.*, pp. 81-90.

be married by the clergy; three-fourths of all marriages are performed by a minister, priest, or rabbi. Of all the civil authorities qualified to officiate at weddings, the justice of the peace performs most marriages.

In some states the legality of the marriage is doubtful if the officiant is an impostor who is not properly qualified to perform the marriage. However, in other states the legality of the marriage is not affected by the status of the officiant. The important thing is that the couple must be acting in good faith. The Michigan law states:

> **12701.** No marriage solemnized before any person professing to be a Justice of the Peace or a minister of the gospel shall be deemed void. *Provided* the marriage be consummated with a full belief on the part of the persons so married that they have been lawfully joined in marriage.

In 41 states Friends or Quakers and people of any other denomination having any special method of solemnizing marriages are exempted from the law which requires an officiant. Members of these sects are permitted to solemnize their marriages according to the method prescribed by their religion. In the Quaker marriage ceremony the couple marries each other without the aid of an officiant. The marriage is a civil ceremony in which the groom states, "I, John Jones, take thee, Mary Smith, to be my wedded wife, etc." The bride repeats, "I, Mary Smith, take thee, John Jones, to be my wedded husband, promise to obey, etc." After the pledges have been made, all those present sign the wedding certificate and the couple are as thoroughly married as they would be if they had been married by a minister with the use of a marriage license.

Validity of marriage

12696. The general rule of law is that a marriage valid where it is celebrated is valid everywhere; and the converse to this is equally general, that a marriage void where it is celebrated is void everywhere. Whatever the form of the ceremony, if the parties agreed personally to take each other for husband and wife and from that time lived together professedly in that relation, presentation of these facts would be sufficient to show marriage as binding upon the parties, which would subject them and others to legal penalties for disregard of those obligations.

In general, the spirit of the above law on this point exists in other states. That is, if a marriage is void where it is celebrated, it is usually void everywhere. Exceptions occur in a few states that make marriages void if the parties married in order to evade a state law. These states are Illinois, Louisiana, Massachusetts, Vermont, and Wisconsin. Twelve other states have passed laws prohibiting out-of-state marriages to evade the state law, but in most of these states such marriages are not considered void.

As the various state laws now stand, it is easier for each state to recognize the marriage laws existing in other states. Confusion has resulted because some states hesitate to recognize the divorce laws of other states. When people secure out-of-state divorces they may find that if they remarry at home they will be subject to a charge of bigamy. Or, if there is no charge of bigamy, the second marriage may not be recognized as valid in the home state.

Common law marriage

12726. To consummate a common law marriage the parties must personally agree to take each other for husband and wife and live together in that relation.

Common law marriages are still valid in 21 states. These are marriages in which a man and a woman mutually agree that they will live together as husband and wife. No license or marriage officiant is employed. If the validity of the marriage is questioned, the couple must show that they are living as husband and wife. If either is already married, or if other legal reasons make a regular marriage impossible, the couple cannot marry by common law. In the states where common law marriages are valid, they are as binding as other marriages. In these states, a common law marriage must be dissolved through divorce, according to the divorce laws governing all other marriages, before either party may remarry.

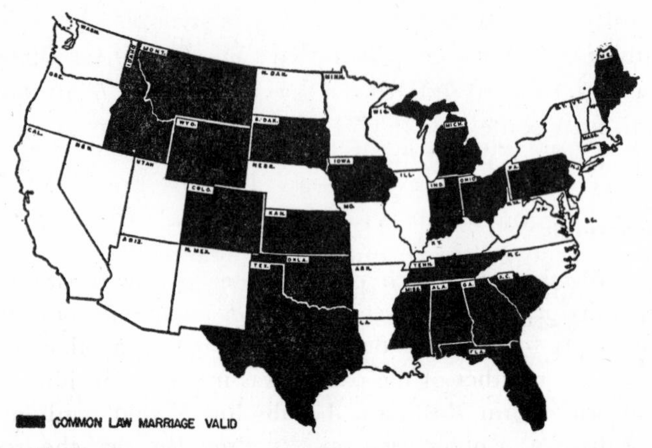

Fig. 45. Twenty-one states recognize common law marriage as valid.

Common law marriages were frequent in Europe during the Middle Ages but were abolished by the Catholic church in the Council of Trent in 1563. England abolished common law marriages in 1753. Common law marriages were suited to the frontier life of early America, since it was often impossible to get a minister when people were ready to marry. Love and death could not always wait on the parson. In many frontier communities people who died were buried with little ceremony and the funeral was held weeks or months later when the circuit rider came around. In the same way, couples pledged themselves as man and wife and began housekeeping, sometimes having a wedding later when the circuit rider appeared. Others dispensed with the wedding, and their pledges and their living together as man and wife were accepted as a marriage.

There is now no good reason for the retention of common law marriages. Only four states, Arizona, Illinois, Missouri, and New York have passed laws declaring common law marriages null and void. Eight other states have laws effective in controlling common law marriages. In the rest of the states, confusion exists. In some states the law is quite clear, but conflicting court decisions have clouded the situation. The American Bar Association, the Commission on Uniform State Laws, and almost all authorities in the field of social reform favor the abolition of common law marriage.[20] Such marriages have been defended by some on the grounds that they protect the legitimacy of children, since some people will always live together as husband and wife without a wedding ceremony.

Void marriages

12723. All marriages which are prohibited by law on account of consanguinity or affinity between parties, or on account of either of them having a former wife or husband living, and all marriages solemnized when either of the parties was insane or an idiot, shall, if solemnized within this state, be absolutely void, without any decree of divorce or other legal process: *Provided,* that the issue of such marriage, except that contracted while either of the parties thereto had a former husband or wife living, shall be deemed legal.

Certain marriages are considered void from the beginning and certain others are voidable. In a void marriage it is not necessary to have the marriage annulled or to take any legal recourse. Although there were mutual consent, a license to wed, and a qualified officiant, no marriage took place, since a legal reason prevented marriage. The Michigan law makes clear what marriages are void. In some states the law is not clear, and an interested person does not know whether a marriage is void or considered voidable.

When relatives marry, the issue is more clear-cut and the marriage can be declared void from the beginning. No provision is made to annul such a marriage in some states. However, three states, Virginia, West Virginia, and Wisconsin, have by statute clearly provided that marriages within prohibited degrees of

[20] Vernier, *op. cit.,* p. 108.

consanguinity shall be void only from the time when they are annulled by a proper judicial proceeding.[21]

One can appreciate the confusion which may arise over marriages of insane or feeble-minded persons. An individual may not be certain that his spouse is feeble-minded or insane until after they have lived together as husband and wife for some time. The judgment of those in love may be inaccurate and the mental ability and stability of the prospective spouse may be overrated. If the marriage has been consummated and the couple have lived together for some time, then the marriage would usually be considered legal until court action had been taken to show that the spouse had been insane or feeble-minded at the time of marriage. Six states have a regulation similar to Michigan's, which makes marriages of feeble-minded and insane people void without legal process of annulment. Twenty-three other states provide that such marriages are voidable only.

It is interesting to note that the language used in the statutes in connection with the mental state of individuals is confusing and unscientific. Terms such as "insanity," "idiot," "feeble-minded," "lunatic," "unsound mind," "imbecile," are used loosely and as though they were interchangeable. The fact is not recognized that there are all degrees of mental incapacity and many varieties of insanity, some curable, some incurable, some acquired, and some hereditary.[22]

Only three states, Nebraska, South Dakota, and New Hampshire, have laws providing that the feeble-minded may marry if one of the partners has been rendered sterile by operation or is otherwise incapable of procreation.[23] Six states permit the marriage of the mentally deficient where the woman is past 45 years of age.

Certain churches have long opposed sterilization laws, and, although some states provide for the sterilization of the mentally defective before marriage, effective pressure has been exerted

[21] Vernier, *op. cit.*, p. 175.
[22] *Ibid.*, p. 190.
[23] *Ibid.* (Supplement), p. 23.

to prevent widespread application of such laws. New Hampshire has a sterilization law, but few sterilizations have been performed there, even though statistical studies have pointed to the need for enforcement of the law in that state. In 1944 a study of the records of the New Hampshire Laconia School for the Feeble-minded revealed that 60 per cent of 211 children of discharged patients were below normal or feeble-minded. Twenty-one of the feeble-minded offspring had already been committed to Laconia at the time of the study.

Bigamous marriages are void in the majority of states. However, a number of states have tried to meet intelligently the situation arising in Enoch Arden marriages. These are marriages in which one spouse has been absent for some time and the other spouse remarries, thinking that the first spouse is dead. Seven states provide that where a former spouse has been absent and unheard of for a certain period of years the second marriage shall be voidable only.[24] A few states provide that the second marriage shall stand after the removal of the impediment. The Louisiana law provides that a spouse is free to remarry after his mate has been gone a certain number of years and he is convinced that his former spouse is dead. The second marriage stands as valid even though "Enoch Arden" returns. Pennsylvania and Tennessee give "Enoch Arden" the right to choose whether or not he wants his former wife back.[25]

Voidable marriages

Some prohibited marriages stand as valid unless reason is shown why the marriage should be declared void. These are voidable marriages and are dissolved through annulment rather than through divorce. Annulment differs from divorce in the following ways: (1) it proceeds upon the basis that no valid marriage ever existed between the parties; (2) property is to be returned to each; (3) usually neither is entitled to further rights of support; and (4) children are considered illegitimate

[24] Vernier, *op. cit.*, p. 216.
[25] *Ibid.*, p. 217.

unless they are protected by some other law. In some states the difference between annulments and divorce is not clear. There are states that make no distinction between the two, so the only ending for an illegal marriage is divorce. The most common grounds recognized for annulling marriages are nonage, insanity or lack of understanding, force or fraud, bigamy, and impotence.

In most states those who marry under age are legally married unless action is taken to have such marriages annulled. One-fourth of all annulments are for nonage. A few years ago a Tennessee girl of nine married a man 22 years old. At that time Tennessee had no statute on age for marriage and the old common law prevailed. At common law, marriages of children under seven years of age were void. Since both the couple and the parents were satisfied with the marriage, nothing could be done to dissolve it. The marriage stood as legal, since the common law provided that marriages of children over seven were voidable but not void. In some states this marriage would not have stood, and the man would probably have been jailed and charges brought against him.

A common reason for having marriages annulled is for force or fraud. The French war bride of a G.I. who had claimed to be the owner of a big plantation in Georgia had the marriage annulled on the grounds of fraud when she found that actually he lived with his parents in a three-room shack on a 20-acre farm. Over one-third of all annulments are for misrepresentations of this type or for fraud due to false promises. Fraud or force may not be the real reason for some of these annulments. Couples must give reasons which are acceptable to the court if they are to get out of a bad marriage, and since fraud is an acceptable reason, that may be the one offered.

One-fourth of annulments are because of bigamy. Although such marriages are usually void from the beginning, it is common to have them annulled through court action. No doubt remains about the marital status of the party once court action has been taken, whereas confusion might arise if no legal action had been taken, especially in states where the law is confusing. Annulment is often necessary in "Enoch Arden" cases also.

In addition, annulment can be secured because of mental incapacity and physical incapacity or impotence. Impotence is not to be confused with sterility, which is inability to reproduce. Impotence is the inability of the male to have sexual intercourse. It is recognized in many states as cause for annulment of marriage. The majority of states recognize mental incapacity as a ground for annulment.

Most annulments come within the first years of married life. Some causes for annulment, such as insanity or impotence, cannot be used if the marriage has been allowed to stand unchallenged for a certain period of time. Approximately one-third of annulments come within the first year of marriage. Annulments account for a small percentage of marriage dissolutions, probably not more than 2 per cent. Most people resort to divorce.

Legitimacy of children of annulled marriages

12750. Upon the dissolution of a marriage on account of non-age, insanity, or idiocy of either party, the issue of the marriage shall be deemed to be in all respects the legitimate issue of the parent who, at the time of the marriage, was capable of contracting.

If a couple were never legally married and they had children during the period when they thought they were married, are their children legitimate or illegitimate? Again there is confusion. Several of the states have passed no regulation on this point and still go according to the common law which held that the children were illegitimate.[26] The most common policy of states that have legislated upon this point is similar to the law quoted above, which declares that children of void or annulled marriages are legitimate. This is the law in 21 states. In some states the children of certain types of illegal marriages are considered illegitimate. Children of incestuous and bigamous

[26] Maryland, Mississippi, North Carolina, Pennsylvania, Tennessee, and Washington.

unions are more likely to be considered illegitimate than the children of other prohibited unions.

The civil position on illegitimacy must not be confused with the religious. The Catholic church considers all marriages of Catholics void that are not performed by the Catholic church. The children of these void marriages are illegitimate in the eyes of the Catholic church.

Legal status of illegitimates

Although many states have made efforts to legitimatize children born of void and annulled marriages, progress has been slow toward an enlightened viewpoint concerning children born out of wedlock. Sexual immorality has been frowned upon, and if the sexually delinquent has become diseased or if pregnancy has resulted, society has had little sympathy. This attitude applied not only to the parent but to the child as well, for the child was stigmatized as illegitimate and made to suffer too. The status of the illegitimate child was such that it was hard for him to live a normal life. It was public knowledge that the child was illegitimate; his birth certificate carried the information and under the law he could not inherit property from his father or from his mother.

Some progress can be seen in present-day thinking on the problem of illegitimate children. We now question whether a child in a democracy should suffer because of his origin. We recognize that there are immoral parents, and the emphasis is correctly being shifted from illegitimate children to illegitimate parents.

Four babies out of every 100 born each year in the United States, or from 120,000 to 135,000 at today's birth rates, are from illegitimate unions. The number of illegitimate births has increased with the increasing birth rate, but the ratio of illegitimate to legitimate births has not changed in several years.[27] To register babies born out of wedlock as illegitimate is

[27] *Vital Statistics of the United States 1949, Part I,* p. 33. Washington, D.C.: Bureau of Census, 1952.

still the practice in most of the states. Throughout life, whenever the birth certificate has to be shown, the illegitimate birth becomes known to others. Birth records are public records kept at the county seat and, as such, are open to public inspection. Some states have revised their laws so that birth certificates showing illegitimacy are recorded only at the state capitol. In this way greater secrecy is maintained. Even this method, however, is small protection, for the illegitimacy still shows up on the birth certificate, which must occasionally be shown.[28]

CERTIFICATION OF BIRTH REGISTRATION

NAME
BIRTH DATE ____ INDEX NO. ____
BIRTH PLACE
SEX ____ FATHER'S RACE ____
DATE FILED ____ DATE ISSUED ____

THIS CERTIFIES THAT THE ABOVE IS A TRUE COPY OF FACTS RECORDED ON THE BIRTH RECORD OF THE PERSON NAMED HEREON

AS FILED AT:

ISSUED BY
TITLE
BY

STATE OF CALIFORNIA

Fig. 46. Copy of a short-form birth certificate. If requested, the short-form may be secured in some states.

Only a few states have changed their laws so that all citizens receive a short form of their birth certificate which lists only essential facts: name, sex, place and date of birth.

Only two states, Arizona and North Dakota, legitimize *all* children and give them equal rights. The Arizona law states:

Every child is the legitimate child of its natural parents and is entitled to support and education as if born in lawful wedlock,

[28] Arizona, Arkansas, California, Colorado, Connecticut, Idaho, Maryland, Massachusetts, New Mexico, Nebraska, New Hampshire, New York, Oklahoma, and Wyoming had eliminated the question of legitimacy from the birth certificate by 1949. *Vital Statistics of the United States 1949, Part I,* p. 33. Washington, D.C.: Bureau of Census, 1952.

except the right to dwelling or a residence with the family of its father, if such father be married. It shall inherit from its natural parents and from their kindred heirs, lineal and collateral, in the same manner as children born in lawful wedlock. This section shall apply to cases where the natural father of any such child is married to one other than the mother of said child, as well as where he is single.

Arizona and North Dakota are realistic in recognizing the rights of all children regardless of their origin. In 44 states the "natural" child does not have the right to inherit from his father.[29] In all but one state, Louisiana, the illegitimate child may inherit from its mother. The most common limitation on inheritance is that although the illegitimate child may inherit from its mother it cannot inherit from her lineal or collateral kindred. The Michigan law represents this point of view. It states, "Every child is heir of his mother, but it [illegitimate child] is not allowed to claim, as representing his mother, any part of the estate of any of her kindred, either lineal or collateral."

Although 46 states have laws which may require that a father support his illegitimate child, it is often difficult to prove paternity.[30] Unless the mother of the child initiates action to prove the paternity of the child, the father need take no responsibility for its support.

Norway has probably the most advanced legislation on illegitimacy. There the state takes the responsibility for establishing paternity and setting the obligation of support. Full inheritance rights from the father and support to the age of 16 from the parent best able to supply that support are guaranteed by the state.[31] If force is necessary in order to collect the payments for the support of the child, the state takes this responsi-

[29] In Arizona, North Dakota, Iowa, and Wisconsin the illegitimate child may inherit from his father.

[30] Texas and Virginia have no legislation applying to the father of an illegitimate child.

[31] Helen I. Clarke, *Social Legislation.* New York: D. Appleton-Century Company, Inc., 1940.

bility, just as it takes the responsibility for protecting the lives or property of other citizens. This guarantee is of fundamental importance. In the United States, when the mother takes the initiative and establishes the paternity and the court orders the father to support the child, little real guarantee of permanent support for the child is made. If the father falls behind in payments or ceases altogether to contribute to the child's support, it is up to the mother to take legal action. In many cases, however, the mother will be unable or unwilling to take such action and the child is the victim.

A Children's Bureau study of illegitimate children born in 1935 showed that 80 per cent of the white fathers and 86 per cent of the Negro fathers had fallen behind in support payments within two years. Almost half of them had failed to pay as much as half of what was due for the child's support.[32]

In Minnesota and North Dakota administrative boards have been created to assist unmarried mothers and their children and to aid in the enforcement of illegitimacy laws.

The amount which a father may be required to pay to support his child is often inadequate and is required for too short a period of time. The amount and time vary from a maximum of $3.00 a month until the child is seven, in Arkansas, to $40.00 a month until the child is 16, in Delaware.[33]

If children born out of wedlock are to have an equal chance with others to become desirable citizens, it would seem that the following policies should be universal:

1. Legitimatize all children and give them equal rights regardless of the circumstances of their birth.
2. Provide birth certificates which do not call for paternity information.
3. Give the state responsibility for establishing paternity.
4. Give the state responsibility for enforcing parental support of all children.

[32] M. C. Elmer, *The Sociology of the Family*, p. 389. New York: Ginn & Company, 1945.

[33] Vernier, *op. cit.*, p. 214.

5. Provide adequate financial support for all children in need.
6. Provide more adequate maternity care for unwed mothers.
7. Create general acceptance of the fact that there are no illegitimate children, only illegitimate parents, and that for the good of society all children must be freed from any stigma attached to their birth.

One registrar of births, in a state that still records "legitimate" or "illegitimate" on each birth certificate, when asked why the state did not change its policy on registering births, responded: "It just is not legal to do what some states are doing in not registering the paternity of children. Their action would not stand up in court at all, and there is danger that the practice will result in many legal tangles." This man was sincere, but his attention was focused entirely upon an outmoded legal viewpoint rather than upon society's obligation to approximately 125,000 children born out of wedlock each year. Considerable evidence indicates that this legalistic way of thinking is giving way to a more socially desirable point of view. Laws need to be adjusted in consideration of their effect upon the welfare of young citizens.

Our analysis of existing marriage laws points to the conclusion that a great many state laws need intelligent revision. Marriage education in colleges and high schools throughout the country should lead to a better understanding of the broad social purposes underlying legal regulation of marriage and, in turn, to revision of marriage and divorce laws so that they may contribute more effectively to the stability of family life.

Chapter XII

ACHIEVING ADJUSTMENT IN MARRIAGE

BEFORE MARRIAGE, people in love have a tendency to emphasize the similarities in their ways of thinking rather than the differences. It is easy for the couple to idealize each other and to impute attitudes which may not be there. Each one oversells himself, and, since both are in a somewhat hypnotic state of euphoria, they fail to learn much about their points of difference during the courtship period. After they have returned from the honeymoon and are launched upon life as a married couple, true personality traits and value systems become more apparent. Gradually the two may recognize that they are not in such close agreement on everything as they may have thought they were during the engagement period. This realization is a normal part of marriage and occurs quite universally in a greater or lesser degree. If the two people are from about the same type of family background, their values may be very similar. If it is a "mixed" marriage, there may be practically no agreement. Married couples become conscious of differences in several well-defined areas in which they have to work out adjustments. As one studies large numbers of marriages which have lasted happily for years, the evidence becomes more and more convincing that successful marriages do not just happen. A conscious recognition of the need for working at building a successful marriage has proved to be the important factor in the success of many marriages, and the failure to recognize the necessity for working at it has resulted in unhappiness in many other marriages.

Adjustment required in all relationships

In most situations involving human relationships elements of conflict are present. Marriage and family living are no different from other human relationships in this respect.

"Of course, *before* we were married he was the life of every party."

Fig. 47. *By permission,* Tom Henderson and *The Saturday Evening Post.*

Whenever two or more individuals attempt to live peaceably and pleasantly together, adjustments must be made. People will have observed this need if they have lived in college dormitories, in sorority or fraternity houses, or in any type of housing where several roommates live together. Living with others under any circumstances requires cooperation, self-discipline, and a willingness to share and to compromise. One person who is selfish and demanding or thoughtless and inconsiderate of the rights of others can create constant friction and unpleasantness. Learning to get along with roommates is in some ways a good preparation for later married life. One learns to be tolerant of the wishes and peculiarities of others and develops the ability to use tact and to avoid controversial issues. Married life requires the same finesse. However, in marriage, people are inclined to take more seriously their differences and to go head-on into controversial issues for the reason that they feel they belong to each other; they cannot go their separate ways and avoid sore points so easily as with a roommate. In addition, the marriage relationship includes the sex element, which plays an important part. It may serve as a strong bond which holds husband and wife together and which aids them in working out points of difference, or it may serve as a focal point of friction, causing them to react more emotionally in all other areas requiring adjustment.

Chief forms of resolved conflict

It is safe to assume that in all marriages differences of opinion and potential conflict situations will exist. That is normal. The success or failure of the marriage will depend upon how these situations are dealt with by the particular couple. The chief areas where adjustment is usually necessary are: spending the family income, sex relations, child training, religion, social activities and recreation, associating with friends, and in-law relationships. How these potential conflict situations are resolved and how soon they are resolved are fundamental to the happiness of the marriage partners.

Conflicts in marriage are commonly resolved in three ways. The most desirable is for mutually satisfactory adjustments to be worked out. Then neither partner is required to make a great sacrifice in giving in to the wishes of the other. Both compromise to a certain extent on an agreement satisfactory to both. Few, if any, couples are in perfect agreement in all areas of living. Through compromise, they may reach an adjustment after a few years that gives them a feeling of confidence and security in the marriage. In the most satisfactory adjustments neither one feels that he has had to make too great a sacrifice in the compromising.

The second type of adjustment may be called accommodation. Accommodation is adjustment to opposing viewpoints or antagonistic characteristics; it may take any one of several forms. It may involve the "renunciation of protest or aggression against undesirable conditions of life and the organization of the character so that protest does not appear and acceptance does. It may come to pass in the end that the unwelcome force is idealized, that one identifies himself with it and takes it into his personality." [1] In husband-wife accommodation, the process of idealization and identification may or may not take place. If it does not, the two may resolve their differences by striking an equilibrium in which each tolerates the behavior of the other with little or no protest. Both may recognize that they have not reached a satisfactory agreement, but their state of accommodation will be such that their differences place very little strain upon the marriage. During the process of accommodation, the couple may discuss issues and attempt to reach mutuality of views. Sociologists speak of cooperation, or collective effort for common ends, as a form of accommodation.[2] And certainly such cooperation is a part of the picture in this type of adjustment in marriage. Differences in viewpoint and reactions to undesirable characteristics may be "tabled," as it were, in the interests of other common goals. The undesirable conditions will continue to exist but will not be allowed to hinder cooperation toward mutually desired ends. The most numerous examples of this form of accommodation are seen among couples who differ seriously on such points as religion or social activities, but who present a united front for the benefit of their children. Since they recognize the value to the children of parental solidarity, they substitute cooperation for conflict.

[1] John Dollard, *Caste and Class in a Southern Town*, p. 225. New Haven: Yale University Press, 1937.

[2] *Ibid.*, Ch. XII.

A third form of adjustment in conflict situations in marriage is a state of hostility. More accurately, this form of adjustment is a failure to arrive at any real adjustment in the conflict areas. Constant quarreling and bickering go on or tension is produced by expressed or unexpressed antagonism. This state of hostility is illustrated by a couple who differ on recreational interests. The husband does not like to dance but is an enthusiastic golf player. The wife continues to try to force her husband to take her to dances. When he refuses, she may retaliate by hiding his golf clubs, going home to mother, or going to dances without him. Or she may appear to have given up her interest in dancing but continue to hold resentful feelings. This resentment may find expression through refusal to participate in other activities which the husband enjoys or refusal to cooperate in sexual intercourse. The husband may retaliate by spending more and more time on recreational interests with others. Thus a couple may settle into a permanent state of antagonism and conflict. It is a most unhappy type of adjustment to differences.

Time required to adjust in marriage

The process of pair adjustment is in the forefront during the early years of every marriage. Although most adjustments are made during this period if the marriage is not to end in divorce, some adjustment will be called for throughout the life of the couple. As they grow older they will encounter new conditions which call for new adjustments. When children are born, when they mature and leave home, when grandparents move in to live with the family, and when death comes, new adjustments will be called for between the husband and the wife. However, these new adjustments are relatively easy if the couple has been able to make satisfactory adjustments in other areas of married living within the first months or years of their marriage. If a good understanding and mature affection exist between them, they will cope with the new developments that come, scarcely recognizing them as potential conflict sources. If areas of chronic conflict have been built up before the new problems arise, adjustments will be difficult.

In our study of the length of time it had taken 409 couples to work out adjustments in marriage, the husbands and wives responded independently of each other, so it was possible to see how well they agreed on their success in making adjustments.[3]

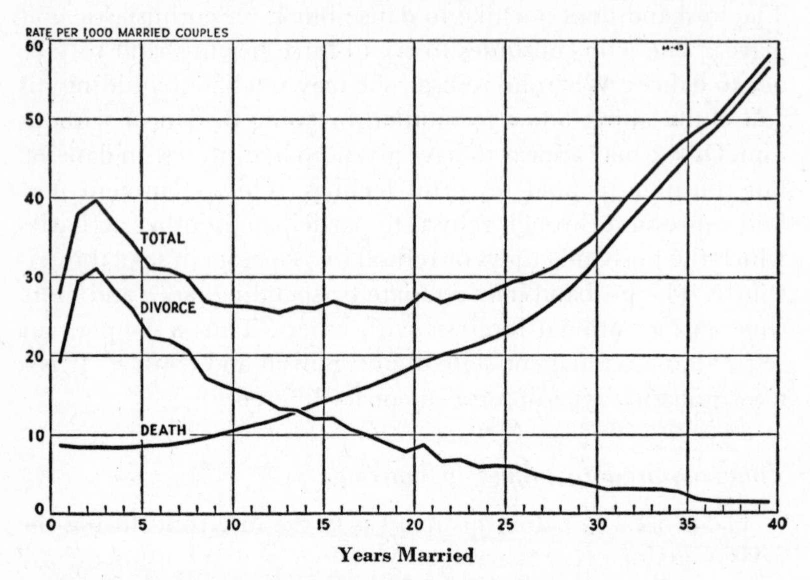

Fig. 48. Marital dissolutions by divorce and death in the first 40 years of marriage, United States, 1947. Marriage failure as measured by divorce reaches a peak in the second and third years of marriage. From *Statistical Bulletin,* Metropolitan Life Insurance Company, 30:11 (November, 1949), 3.

Most couples were in agreement, but about one couple in ten disagreed. In some cases one spouse would state that the couple had been well adjusted from the beginning of the marriage, while the other spouse might say that satisfactory adjustment had taken years or that it had never been made.

Each spouse in the study stated whether he felt the adjustment had been satisfactory from the beginning of the marriage, whether months or years had passed before an adjustment was

[3] Judson T. Landis, "Length of Time Required to Achieve Adjustment in Marriage," *American Sociological Review,* 11:6 (December, 1946), pp. 666-677.

achieved, or whether the couple had never achieved an adjustment. All checked specifically their success or failure and the time required to adjust in each of the following six areas: spending the family income, relationships with in-laws, sex relations, religious life in the home, choosing and associating with friends,

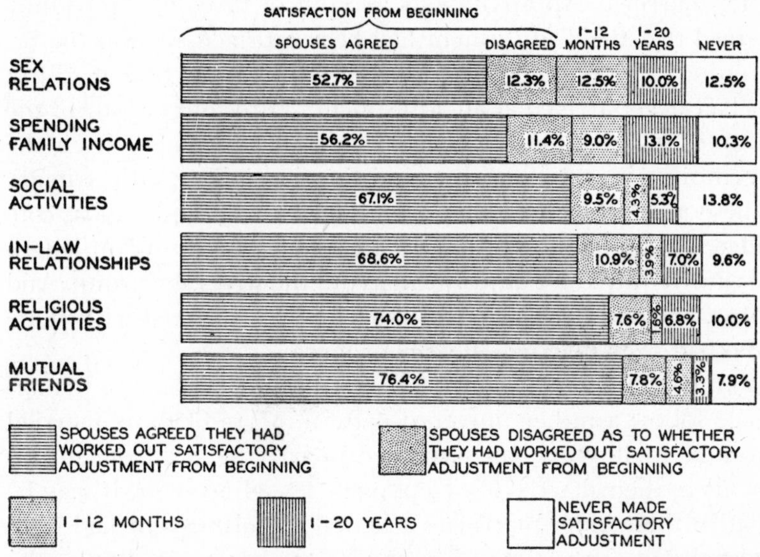

Fig. 49. Percentage of 818 spouses reporting various periods of time required after marriage to achieve adjustment in six areas. People who had been successfully married for an average of 20 years had experienced greater difficulty in adjusting in certain areas. From Judson T. Landis, "Length of Time Required to Achieve Adjustment in Marriage," *American Sociological Review,* 11:6 (December, 1946), 668.

and social activities and recreation. Other minor areas of adjustment could be added to this list, but these are the areas most commonly calling for understanding between marriage partners. Figure 49 summarizes the results of this study of successful marriages.

It will be noticed that more time was required for adjusting in sex relations and in spending the family income than in any other area. Approximately half of the couples agreed that their sex adjustment had been satisfactory from the beginning. The remainder (47 per cent) either disagreed on how long it had taken, agreed that months or years had passed before they made adjustments, or agreed that they had never arrived at a satisfactory adjustment. On spending the family income the picture is about the same. Social activities and recreational interests, and in-law relationships, were equal in time required for adjustment after marriage. Approximately two out of three of the couples agreed that their adjustment had been satisfactory from the beginning; the remaining third had either required time to adjust or had never arrived at an adjustment. Three out of four of the couples in these marriages had made an adjustment from the beginning in religious life and in associating with friends. These areas presented the least difficulty. The husbands, considered as a group, gave the six areas the same rating on length of time required for adjustment as did the wives as a group. And those who had been married under ten years agreed with those who had been married 30 years or more.

Thus the evidence indicates that adjustment problems in marriage follow a rather universal pattern. More of those married from 30 to 40 years had succeeded in arriving at all the adjustments in their marriages except one—sex adjustment. It may be that in these older marriages a better sex adjustment had once existed, but at the time of responding to the questionnaire the couples had reached a period in life requiring a new adjustment. Or it may be that the sex mores of their generation hindered a satisfactory sex adjustment in marriage. If so, it may be literally true that a larger percentage of these long-married couples made poor sex adjustments.

In the following chapters we shall discuss each of the areas in which people must adjust after marriage and analyze the specific factors involved.

State of adjustment in marriage

After the 409 couples in our study recorded how long it had taken them to arrive at adjustments, they stated whether each adjustment was satisfactory to both, satisfactory to one, or unsatisfactory for both. They gave the same information concerning the disciplining of the children. The area in which the fewest had arrived at a mutually satisfactory adjustment was in sex relations; the area in which the most had arrived at a mutually satisfactory adjustment was in associating with friends. The adjustments in the various areas were either states of accommodation or of conflict in from one-third to one-fifth of the marriages. In sex relations over one-third of the couples had either made an adjustment which was a compromise or had continued in conflict in this area. The couples had arrived at mutually satisfactory adjustments in from approximately two-thirds to four-fifths of their relationships in the seven areas. (See Figure 50.)

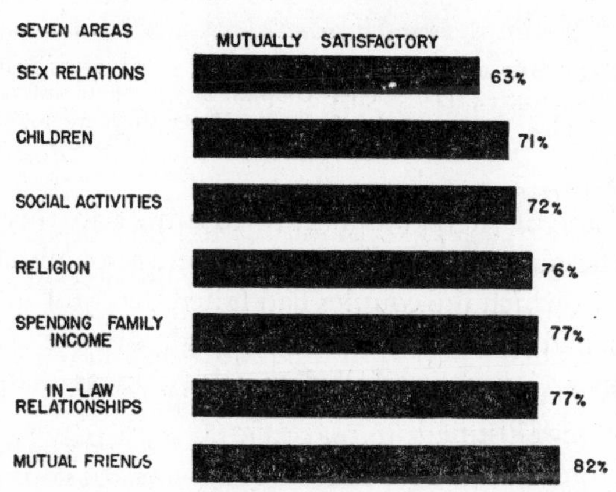

Fig. 50. Percentage of 409 couples agreeing that they had arrived at mutually satisfactory adjustments in seven areas.

Length of time required to adjust and happiness in marriage

Those who find that they are in agreement on all important matters, from the wedding on, are indeed fortunate. The study of the 409 couples showed that a close relationship existed between early adjustment and happiness in marriage. Figure 51 shows the relationship between the happiness of the marriage and the length of time required to make necessary adjustments. Over half of the marriages were rated as very happy if adjustment had been made immediately, whereas only one-fifth were rated very happy if a good adjustment had never been made.

Some couples rated their marriage as very happy, although there was one area in which they had never adjusted. If there was failure to adjust in two areas 77 per cent were average or

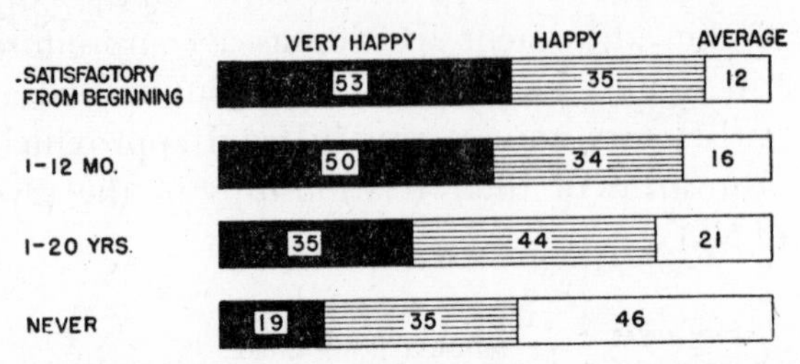

Fig. 51. Composite of time reported to adjust in six areas in marriage and happiness in marriage. The sooner couples merge their interests and find satisfactory working arrangements, the more likely they are to find happiness in marriage.

unhappy, and if there was failure to adjust in three or more areas all the marriages were rated as average or unhappy. Most marriages in which the couples had failed to adjust in more than two areas had been eliminated through divorce. Of the 409 couples only eleven had failed to adjust in as many as three areas.[4] (See Figure 52.)

	VERY HAPPY	HAPPY	AVERAGE -
SPENDING THE INCOME (ONE AREA) 83 CASES	24.1%	22.9%	53.0%
SPENDING THE INCOME & SEX RELATIONS (TWO AREAS) 31 CASES	9.7%	12.9%	77.4%
SPENDING THE INCOME, SEX RELATIONS & SOCIAL ACTIVITIES (THREE AREAS) 11 CASES			100.0%

Fig. 52. Happiness of marriage in which couples had never adjusted in one, two, or three areas. Failure to arrive at satisfactory working arrangements in three or more areas means almost certain failure in marriage; if the marriage survives, it will be average or unhappy.

[4] Judson T. Landis, *op. cit.*, p. 675.

Summary of length of time required to adjust in marriage

Our study of adjustment shows that couples who had been married for some years found it necessary to work out adjustments in several special areas. The earlier the adjustments are made, the more likely is the marriage to be happy; and the fewer the areas in which the couple fails to adjust, the better are the chances for happiness in the marriage.

Tension in modern living and quarreling in marriage

The pace of modern life is such that for almost every individual there are pressures that may produce emotional tension. When a person reacts emotionally to a situation, his glands pour adrenalin into the blood stream, effecting a temporary increase in energy; he thus becomes ready for combat or for self-defense. Our primitive ancestors met conflict situations with physical combat. In modern living many conflict situations cause the glands to prepare us for battle, but civilized society does not accept physical force as an adult way of settling differences between individuals. Children are expected to outgrow fistfighting as they reach adulthood. Only when the dispute is between nations do we regress and resort to violence, thus demonstrating that as nations we have not yet achieved maturity. The adult individual suppresses his impulses toward violent action in times of stress, but he cannot always curb his inner emotional reaction.

Psychologists and psychiatrists tell us that this conflict within the individual is one of the important causes of personality disorganization in modern man. They also tell us that the individual must in some way relieve the tension which is built up within him if he is to preserve his mental health. If he never finds this release from tension, he may break under the burden of inner pressure. Although authorities recognize that "tension-relievers" must be developed, they do not agree on what tension-relievers are acceptable. Some advocate free expression of impulses, not in violent action but by "getting it out of the system" through words. Many of the children of modern parents are brought up according to the "no repression" theory. Their behavior, however, is not always a convincing argument for this theory.

Many adults recognize that it is not practicable to express their emotional reactions freely in most of their relationships outside the family. They exercise self-restraint in their dealings with friends, acquaintances, or business associates because they accept the fact that if they did not, they would soon have few friends and no job. For many people the family serves as a shock absorber, or the place where they relax self-restraint and give expression to the frustrations and tensions which may accumulate in other areas of life. If we could confine ourselves to a consideration only of the need of a specific individual for tension release, we might simply say that to provide a place for such release is a function of the family, or, more specifically, of marriage. We could then suggest that a devoted spouse should welcome the explosive outbursts of the mate as his attempts to make a constructive adjustment to life. The spouse then would feel that in serving as a sparring partner who knew when to retreat and when to meet violence with violence he could fulfill one of his marital functions; he would be enabling the mate to maintain emotional balance. Unfortunately that is not the effect that quarreling usually has in marriage. We cite the case of Sally and Bill, a young married couple:

Bill's work requires him to be in constant contact with other men, many of whom are working under pressure in highly specialized jobs. Bill's immediate superior is a man who is a perfectionist about his work and who has little understanding of human nature. While on the job, Bill works at maintaining harmonious relationships with his co-workers and his superior; this requires serious effort, and sometimes strains his self-control severely. After an especially hard day, Bill, upon arriving at home, finds that Sally has invited the Browns in for waffles and a game of bridge. Bill has no liking for waffles. In his family, waffles were not considered a suitable substitute for a good dinner after a day's work. Moreover, the Browns are a couple he finds hard to tolerate. They have been friends of Sally's since childhood and she can see nothing wrong with them. But to Bill they are just a shallow pair who are not even good bridge players. Their conversation frequently is concerned with occurrences far back in the past before Bill met Sally and these reminiscences irk Bill.

So the stage is set; conditions are perfect for a good marital quarrel. Bill explodes. He gives vent to all the resentments that have been accumulating all day long. He goes further and expresses himself freely concerning the Browns and some of Sally's other friends, past and present. While he is getting things off his chest, he tells what he thinks of any family that would let a daughter grow up thinking that *waffles* were a suitable offering for a hungry man who worked hard to support his wife and family. And since he is on the subject of cooking, he throws in for good measure a few references to the good cooking he was used to before he left Mother's house and married Sally.

According to some theories, Sally, after responding with some uncomplimentary references to Bill's family background, his friends, and his general behavior, would dissolve in tears; they would kiss and make up; and their love would be on a better basis than before because of the progress toward understanding growing out of the quarrel. But is that the way it works in reality? Has enough constructive good been accomplished to compensate for the damage that has been done? One thing has been accomplished that may be considered a step in their adjustment. Sally has decided she will not ask the Browns in any more, because it just is not worth it if it upsets Bill so. She also secretly resolves that if she is going to have to give up her friendship with the Browns she is justified in insisting that Bill drop certain friends of his for whom she has no affection. She will take that up later.

The quarrel has served as a tension-reliever for Bill. But he does not feel any the better for it. He is ashamed of the things he said about Sally's family and he realizes that the comparisons he made between his mother's cooking and Sally's will only widen the rift that is already developing between Sally and her mother-in-law. And worst of all, their four-year-old son, Johnny, had been wakened by the quarrel and had come downstairs crying just after Sally began to cry. When Johnny saw Sally crying he could hardly be comforted. After they got him back to bed Sally remarked with bitterness to Bill that Johnny was getting to be a naughty and unhappy child. She said, "Every time he hears us have a quarrel he is worse for days."

As might be expected, Sally and Bill were developing a quarreling pattern. Their quarrels were becoming more frequent rather than less so. Each quarrel added a few more barbs that rankled. Each left a few smoldering resentments that might break out on another occasion. Although some of their quarrels settled issues, inasmuch as one decided to change his attitude, or both decided to compromise, more of the verbal battles settled nothing at all. They simply added scars. Both Sally and Bill grew more adept at responding with remarks that touched sore points. In the quarrel described above, Sally might easily respond to Bill's disparagement of her family by suggesting that a possible reason for the recent failure of Bill's father in a business venture was his inability to get along with co-workers. This reference would be especially puncturing to Bill's self-confidence and would serve to produce still more tension for him on other occasions when he found the going hard in his own relationships at the office. Thus a vicious circle: more tension, more quarrels, more emotional scars, and Bill and Sally being driven apart in understanding and affection.

In the average marriage the quarrels that could be considered constructive are few. The possible benefits, *i.e.,* release of pent-up emotional tension for one or both and bringing differences into the open in order to resolve them, may be gained by more constructive means. An important consideration is that many marital quarrels do not stem from any real differences that need to be resolved, or from any underlying dissatisfaction with the mate. They do not have as their basis a rational attempt to eliminate differences; therefore they can accomplish little constructive good. Disputes between a married couple are no different from those between friends outside marriage. Few friendships can survive constant or frequent quarrels. Friends learn to curb the impulse to say bitter words in the interest of preserving the friendship. The most happily married couples practice the same rule. They learn to withhold the bitter criticism or the cutting retort in order to avoid unpleasantness and to enjoy greater happiness.

Many couples learn early in marriage that it is better not to discuss problems or to try to make important decisions late in the day when they are physically tired, certainly never when they are hungry.

One couple, both of whom were working outside the home, reported that in the early months of their marriage they found themselves involved in frequent arguments or bickerings. Upon analyzing the situation, they realized that their differences invariably occurred late in the afternoon when both were just home from work and were preparing dinner together. They made it a rule then to have dinner earlier and to refrain from any but the most casual conversation until after they had eaten and had relaxed. That ended the quarreling. They realized that both had been reacting in a childish manner to fatigue and hunger. It is safe to say that most marital quarrels would never occur if the individuals could analyze the real reasons which provoke the quarrels and recognize immature behavior in themselves for what it is.

It is true that some couples who have grown up in homes with a quarreling pattern may carry this pattern over into marriage, accepting it as normal and apparently experiencing no very painful results. An example was one old couple who had lived together and quarreled amicably for 50 years. They seemed to vie with each other to achieve pungency in their verbal attacks. If one scored a particularly cutting hit, the other seemed to accept it almost admiringly, somewhat as a fencer acknowledges the skill of his opponent with "Touché!" When the husband died at 75, the widow was inconsolable and survived him by only a few weeks. Undoubtedly they were completely devoted to each other in spite of their ceaseless quarreling. But such a case is exceptional.

"What do you mean, *we're* incompatible? You're the one who's incompatible."

Fig. 53. *By permission,* Dave Huffine and *The Saturday Evening Post.*

It must be stated also that rather than relieving pent-up emotional tensions, marital quarrels often simply contribute to building up greater tension, as illustrated by the case of Sally and Bill. A feeling of mild antagonism or opposition may become much more intense when emotionally expressed. We are inclined, when faced with opposition, to express things more strongly than we feel them, with the result that our feelings become more intense to back up our words, as it were. Happily married people know that giving frequent expression to their affection for each other seems to build up and to increase their love. Love thrives on expression and response. It is just so with anger, irritation, and criticism. The free and frequent expression of these feelings increases their strength and magnifies the importance of things that might more happily be passed over, overlooked, and forgotten.

Many married couples are unaware of the serious effect that quarreling has upon the children. Research studies have revealed that the quarreling of parents is a source of extreme unhappiness and worry to children who are subjected to it. (Chapter XXI deals with this topic further.) Even if the parents themselves consider the quarreling to be constructive or attach little importance to it, the effect upon the children is not lessened. Couples who know of the ill effect of quarreling upon children may feel that they will get their quarreling over with and their adjustments made before they have any children. But there is a strong possibility that rather than getting the quarreling over with they will establish a habit of meeting problems in that manner, and habits do not change easily. Further, more problems will arise after children come, and there will be less time and nervous energy available for meeting problems constructively.

The family conference

Many couples, recognizing that points of disagreement are bound to arise in their marriage, decide early that they will make it their habit to talk over differences. It is well to agree early that no such conferences will be held when either spouse is under par physically or emotionally. When both are feeling well adjusted with themselves and their marriage, they can discuss differences and be relatively objective because of the more accurate perspective which they will have under these conditions.

Couples find it exceedingly rewarding to work at developing the technique of talking things over frankly, with the acknowledged purpose of understanding each other's viewpoint. In taking this rational approach to marital adjustment they are recognizing that successful marriages do not just happen, but must be built. They are often pleasantly surprised to find that it is possible to reach satisfactory understandings on all important matters without becoming emotionally combative over their differences.

If the family-conference method of resolving differences has been established early in marriage, it can be working well by the time the children are old enough to take part in the family discussions. Children also find conflict-creating situations in the home and need to have an opportunity for expressing their grievances in the democratic family council. In order to present a united front on discipline and child-training, the parents will need to discuss some questions privately. Research shows that having a voice in determining family policy is an important contributing factor to children's happiness and good adjustment in life. Children coming from homes which have used the family-conference method of settling differences are more likely to fit into the community as desirable members than are children brought up in homes with a quarreling pattern.

Wholesome tension-relievers

If at times too much tension has been built up in outside-the-home relationships, it is possible to find tension-relievers other than warring with the spouse. Some mature people have discovered that taking a long walk or ride will do wonders toward helping them to regain perspective. One businessman, who found his security threatened by a change in ownership of the corporation for which he worked, preserved his emotional balance by using his spare time to grub out trees which he did not want in his yard. He learned that an hour or two of working with the spade and mattock helped his emotional balance and enabled him to live peaceably with his wife and family. Some husbands and wives go to a movie or a concert, read a fascinating book, or take a drive in the country when they feel under emotional pressure. Any activity which enables a person to get away from his problem far enough to look at it objectively is an aid to perspective. And perspective is vital to marital happiness.

Resorting to activities rather than to quarreling is not just an "escape." It is constructive, because often when the individual has refrained from quarreling and has turned to other interests in order to relieve tension he realizes that there was no point worth quarreling over from the beginning; he realizes that the difficulty was within himself and could be corrected only by a change in his own attitude.

Often the individual projects the blame for his emotional difficulties upon those who are close to him. A man who is having difficulty holding his job may become critical of his wife and find fault with everything she does. A case illustrating this type of behavior follows:

A college student, whose wife was working in a department store, became extremely critical of his wife's recreational activities and interests. He insisted that she drop the forms of recreation she had been accustomed to enjoying and devote her leisure time to reading books which he brought home to her. She was a highly intelligent girl and read with interest the books on philosophy and psychology her husband recommended; nevertheless she continued to maintain her other leisure-time interests. The husband became more and more critical of her varied interests. He revealed to his friends his fear that her lack of a college education would prevent her from being an intellectual companion to him, and expressed his doubts of the possibility of their permanent happiness. The wife was at a loss to understand the reason for her husband's attitude and was deeply hurt. The real trouble was found to have nothing to do with the wife's interests or intelligence. The husband, a freshman, was having great difficulty making grades which would allow him to remain in school. His emotional tension over his failure was finding expression through worry over his wife's interests and through the focusing of his attention upon her lack of education.

Tremendous trifles

When two people live together as intimately as do husbands and wives, it is natural for them to find that many little things come up to cause irritation. Mannerisms or habits which might pass unnoticed in friends or casual acquaintances often assume importance and provoke extreme annoyance when practiced by one's wife or husband. Carelessness with cigarette ashes, turning down the page corner to mark the place in a book, leaving a ring in the bathtub, being slow to come to the table when meals are called, may become so irritating to the spouse that emotional explosions occur. Baber has called these trivial things which often cause friction in marriage "tremendous trifles." [5]

Why these trifles become so tremendous in marriage is not easy for the outsider to understand, but that they do harass many marriages is certain. The happy couples are those who can preserve a sense of proportion about the relative importance of events. That requires effort, and the effort will be aided by a good sense of humor. A great many things cannot be explained, interpreted, or corrected, but will dissolve into the air if a couple can laugh over them together. A small boy, when taken to task by his mother for some of his annoying ways, said, "I don't know why I do it. Let's just laugh it off." That is often the best solution to annoyances in marriage. Certainly it is a much surer road to peace and happiness than for either spouse to try to change the ways of the other. And as a tension-reliever a hearty laugh is at least as effective as an angry explosion, and it is far more pleasant to hear.

Remodeling the spouse after marriage

Sometimes during the courtship period the members of a couple observe habits and mannerisms in each other which they realize could be annoying in a husband or a wife, but each may pass over such traits with the thought, "He will surely change

[5] Ray E. Baber, *Marriage and the Family*, pp. 250-251. New York: McGraw-Hill Book Company, Inc., 1939.

after we are married." The fact that the future spouse loves so devotedly and is so evidently desirous of making the loved one happy in all possible ways seems conclusive proof that after marriage surely he (or she) will gladly make every effort to change in any small ways the spouse might wish. So when they are married and secure in their love, the wife or the husband may begin tactfully to suggest desirable changes. The result is usually disappointing. One reason why "tremendous trifles" become such a problem is because married people find greater difficulty than they had anticipated when they begin remodeling the mate. Not only is it hard for an adult to change ways which have become part of his personality make-up, but the mate who is "worked on" for his faults suffers ego deflation. He wants to be loved for himself, faults and all, and that is probably one reason he married the person he did. He felt that she knew him well and loved him anyway. If the remodeling program had started before marriage, perhaps no marriage would have taken place.

Certain rare individuals are self-disciplined and mature enough to welcome constructive criticism from the spouse. Such individuals will evaluate criticism objectively and make successful efforts to correct undesirable personality traits in themselves. But for most people contemplating marriage it is much safer and less likely to lead to disappointment if both members proceed on the assumption that the partner will do little changing after marriage. It is better to face the question, "Do I love him (her) enough to tolerate these things as trivial and to refrain from making him (her) uncomfortable by agitating for change?" If the faults loom large and seem very annoying before marriage, there is no reason to believe they will be less irritating after the wedding. No one is without faults. Happy marriages are those between people whose faults are tolerable to each other. Wives have frequently been known to say of someone else's husband, "How can his wife endure that way of his! I couldn't stand it if my husband behaved that way." Yet the wife speaking may have a husband with faults that would seem far worse to the other woman. So it is well to look, not for a faultless mate, but for one who can be loved for his personality traits viewed as a whole and whose faults are those which the one most concerned does not find especially irritating.

Sometimes when spouses have traits or habits which would be moderately irritating to each other they adjust to the annoyances by means of a form of negative adaptation. This adaptation is illustrated by a couple in which the wife may be an inveterate talker, and overzealous in looking after her husband. Friends may wonder how the husband endures her constant directions and suggestions covering every detail of his activities; they may marvel at his self-control. The truth may be that through negative adaptation he has reached the place where he is quite unconscious of her talking; he gives the appearance of listening but in reality is occupied with his own thoughts and hears little of what she says. Her habit causes him little if any annoyance and the marriage may be a happy one.

Courtship patterns carried into marriage

During the courtship period it is natural for a measure of uncertainty to exist. Both partners may need frequent assurances and demonstrations of love. One or the other may occasionally indulge in attempts to keep the other guessing by pretending indifference, or by showing attentions to other members of the opposite sex with the intention of arousing jealousy in the loved one. If the loved one reacts as desired, the little game will be called off until the partner again feels the need for reassurance. Frequent lovers' quarrels followed by affectionate reconciliations often characterize affairs of this type, and each incident leads to new commitments and to a deeper emotional involvement. Although such courtship behavior is not unusual, it is frequently a sign of immaturity in one or in both. An excessive desire to test and to prove the love of the partner is sometimes an indication of inner insecurity and lack of confidence which may cause the immature demands for reassurance to be carried over unhappily into marriage.

Granted that a normal degree of affectional testing may occur during courtship, it is not desirable for this pattern to be carried over into marriage. One of the joys of a good marriage is the calm of emotional security that comes with the knowledge of being wholeheartedly loved. In a happy marriage both partners express and demonstrate their love so that neither one has occasion for doubt. Attempts to test love by pretending indifference or by trying to arouse jealousy after marriage are almost invariably threats to the success of the marriage.

Maturity of married love

It is unfortunate that in so much popular fiction as well as in motion-picture stories the thrills and delights of being in love are presented as associated quite exclusively with the courtship period. All the uncertainties of courtship are offered as exciting and desirable. The depth of happiness achieved in successful marriage is seldom, if ever, pictured. No doubt one reason is that emotional experiences that have depth and permanence are far more difficult to portray. Only great actors or superior writers can hope to do justice to them. The result is that popular misconceptions exist. "He's just an old married man now," or "She's married and settled down," imply that with marriage, romance ends. Some married people go along with such a viewpoint, making frantic efforts to cling to courtship patterns rather than allowing themselves to grow into the normal patterns of marriage. They fear that they may "settle down like other married people" and "take each other for granted." They fail to appreciate the fact that to maintain the level of obsessive emotionalism of the courtship period for an indefinite time could become extremely wearing. They have not yet learned that the security of married love is one of the most satisfying experiences in life. To fight off mature affection and to try to preserve the courtship type of love experience are in the same category as trying to maintain the appearance and behavior of sweet sixteen when one is 35. That is clinging to immaturity because of a failure to appreciate the pleasures of living on a mature level.

Confusion in roles and marriage adjustment

Chapters II and III discussed changes that are taking place in the roles of women and men. The conceptions that individuals hold concerning their own roles in life and their role expectations from their mates significantly affect their marital adjustment. Like many of our other values in life, our feelings about what is "woman's place" or "man's place," and what are the special prerogatives of each sex, are likely to be more emotional than rational. Having absorbed our attitudes from our families and our own life experiences, it is difficult for us to examine them objectively. Therefore, much frustration and antagonism may arise in a marriage in which the two hold differing views. Often neither will be able to define his attitudes clearly or to pin down the true basis of certain antagonisms.

An example of such a case may illustrate the point. John grew up in a family in which the father had been an invalid for many years and the mother had supported the family by running a small business of her own. As the four sons grew up, they worked and helped support themselves, but they always consulted closely with their mother about their affairs and respected her judgment. John married Margaret, who came from a family in which the father was a very successful professional man, with a dynamic and impressive personality. Her family was definitely father-dominated. Margaret's mother happily devoted her full energies to being a good wife and a good mother. She never made decisions without consulting her husband and she relied on his judgment. After some years of marriage, John and Margaret were still struggling with an inability to understand each other or to feel secure in their relationship. No doubt a number of factors entered in, for it is never possible in a failing marriage to isolate one factor and say that it alone is the cause of all the trouble. But in this case it was readily apparent to the marriage counselor whom they consulted that a major point in their lack of adjustment was that each looked for a type of dominance in the other that was lacking. John constantly brought home to Margaret his problems from his job and wanted to talk them over with her and get her ideas and suggestions. This seemed to her a burden, and she tended to get worried and upset over his problems; she felt they were not in her sphere and that she was not capable of helping him. Moreover, his dependence on her for help contributed to a feeling of insecurity and inadequacy in her. She herself wanted to lean on him for far more help than she was able to get. She felt that he should make all decisions concerning money matters and problems related to the children. When he left these things to her, she felt that he was "letting her down" and failing to take the responsibility that she had a right to expect of him as head of the house. Both developed rather serious feelings of inadequacy and insecurity, and discontent with the marriage. Neither fulfilled the role that the other felt was "right."

The opposite situation arises even more frequently. Today the husband is often willing and anxious to be recognized as head of the house but feels that his wife is not willing to accord him his "rightful" prerogatives. Such couples become competitive toward each other and tend to undermine each other's self-confidence by withholding respect and emotional support. Each feels that his or her contribution to the family well-being is undervalued by the other.

At a time like the present, when the roles of men and women are in transition, a great many marriages will involve some differences on this point. And it will continue to be extremely difficult for people to force the mate to fulfill an unwanted role; women especially will no longer allow the husband to define and prescribe their role. Much more adjustability is now required of men than formerly. Flexibility in attitudes about roles is essential for both, and successful marital adjustment will depend in a measure upon the ability of both to throw aside preconceived ideas about dominance and subservience in sex roles. (Chapter III presents a more complete discussion of this topic.)

Success or failure in marriage adjustment

The success or failure of a marriage depends in large measure upon the quality of the material going into the marriage. A wise choice is of fundamental importance, but people are not born to be good husbands and wives; they learn to become good mates through thoughtful, rational, cooperative effort. There is hope even for those who do not make a wise choice. "People who share a cell in the Bastille or are thrown together on an uninhabited island will find some possible ground of compromise if they do not immediately fall to fisticuffs. They will

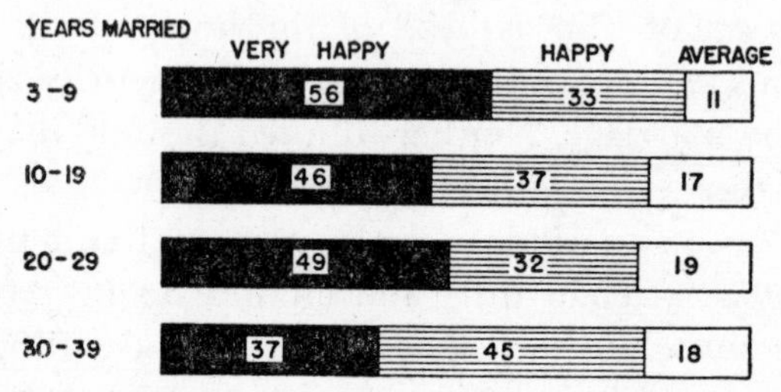

Fig. 54. Duration of marriage and marital happiness. Studies show that couples in the first years of marriage report higher happiness ratings. The above chart is based on 409 marriages. The lower happiness rating of those married from 30 to 39 years may reflect the couples' reaction to life in general as much as their reaction to marriage happiness. They have lived through the "happiest years" in life.

learn each other's ways and humours so as to know where they must go warily and where they may lean their whole weight. The discretion of the first years becomes the settled habit of the last; and so, with wisdom and patience, two lives may grow indissolubly into one." [6]

Most marriages are happy

So much has been written and said about unhappy marriages that sometimes young people may feel that marriage as such is not a happy institution. Happiness is something which is hard

[6] Robert Louis Stevenson, "Essay on Marriage," *Virginibus Puerisque.*

to measure. The several different methods used in research studies of married people all show that the majority of marriages are happy. In some studies the couples have rated their own happiness; in others, friends have rated the happiness of the couple. Other studies have used a combination of factors to determine the happiness of marriages. Studies in which the husband and the wife rated their marital happiness independently of each other show a high measure of agreement between partners. There is also a close relationship between happiness ratings given by the married people themselves and the score rating assigned to them on the basis of other factors by those doing the research or by friends who base their ratings on observation of the marriage.[7] Table 18 gives a summary of four studies which evaluated the marital happiness of couples.

TABLE 18

HAPPINESS RATINGS OF MARRIAGES AS REVEALED BY RESEARCH STUDIES

Happiness Rating	Burgess and Cottrell[a] (N-526)	Terman[b] (N-792)	Lang[c] (N-17533)	Landis[d] (N-409)
Happy or very happy	63.0	85.0	62.0	83.0
Average	14.0	9.0	19.0	16.0
Unhappy or very unhappy	22.0	5.0	20.0	1.0

[a] Burgess and Cottrell, *op. cit.*, p. 34.
[b] Terman, *Psychological Factors in Marital Happiness*, p. 78. New York: McGraw-Hill Book Company, Inc., 1938.
[c] Burgess and Cottrell, *op. cit.*, p. 139.
[d] Landis, *op. cit.*, p. 674.

It will be noticed that from 63 to 85 per cent of the marriages were rated as happy or very happy. The Burgess and Lang studies showed a larger percentage of unhappy marriages be-

[7] See Burgess and Cottrell, *Predicting Success or Failure in Marriage*, pp. 38-44, for a summary of the different methods of measuring happiness in marriage. Our study of 409 marriages agrees with the Burgess study in that approximately 4 per cent of the ratings disagreed by two or more categories. Sixty-three per cent of the couples agreed in their ratings and 31 per cent within one category. Landis, *op. cit.*, p. 678.

cause they included some people who were divorced. The Terman study and our study included only those who were and who had been living together for some time, an average of 11 years in the Terman study and an average of 20 years in our study. In the latter two studies it is recognized that many of the unhappy marriages had been eliminated through divorce.

Terman asked those in his study whether they would marry the same person if they had their lives to live over. Eighty-three per cent of the husbands and 86 per cent of the wives said they would.[8]

Thus the evidence shows that the majority of marriages are happy. This does not mean that marriage doesn't involve some struggle. Actually, it requires more than some people are capable of giving. Such people are unmarriageable; if they do marry they account for a large proportion of the marriage failures. But in the average marriage, couples find the rewards worth the effort and they struggle willingly to make the necessary adjustments. The publicity given to marriage failure rather than marriage success creates the wrong impression. The more desirable emphasis is upon successful marriages and the factors which contribute to their success.

[8] Terman, *op. cit.*, p. 53.

Chapter XIII

SEX ADJUSTMENT IN MARRIAGE

A MUTUALLY SATISFACTORY sex relationship is one of the important factors which contribute to happiness in marriage. However, people contemplating marriage often assume that sex gratification is the basic and all-important factor upon which the success or failure of marriage depends. Such is not the case. Sexual union is but one of a complicated set of relationships and activities which make up the whole interactional pattern of a marriage.

Sex and adjustment in other areas of life

Conflict in other areas sometimes causes the failure of marriages in which the sex phase of life seems to be satisfactory to both partners. Inability to agree on the use of money, for example, with constantly recurring quarrels over finances, may cause a couple to part in spite of sexual compatibility. Friction over in-laws may create such animosity between husband and wife that they will part regardless of what the adjustment may be in their sex life.

Moreover, if conflict exists in other areas of a marriage, it is likely to be reflected in the sex life of the couple. Since sexual union is the most intimately cooperative activity of marriage, the partners have a tendency to come together less frequently if antagonism exists between them. If they are at odds over other matters, one or the other may even show a definite resistance to sexual union, with the result that other conflicts will become intensified.

Conversely, marriages in which the sex adjustment is poor may endure because of the strength of other bonds. Sharing of interests in children, in friends or relatives, in recreation or in work, and in many phases of daily living, all make their contribution to a good marriage. Since all facets of a marriage are closely interrelated, it is often impossible to determine whether a poor sex adjustment is a cause or a result of an unsatisfactory adjustment in a seemingly unrelated phase of life. Similarly, an unsatisfactory and frustrating sex relationship may affect the responses of husbands and wives in other divisions of their lives.

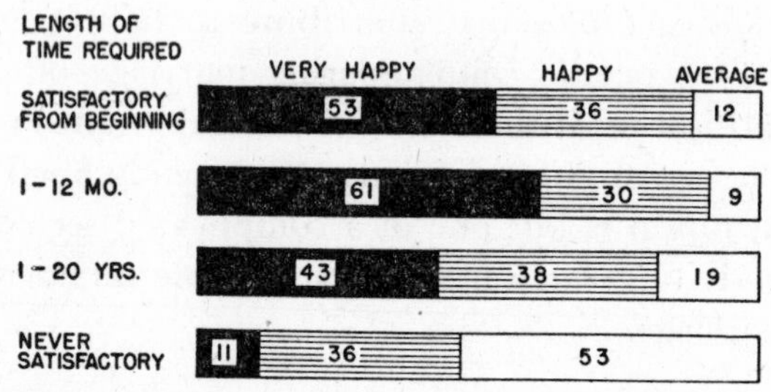

Fig. 55. Length of time required to adjust in sex relations and happiness in marriage (409 couples).

The sex relationship as a measure of marital adjustment

Sex relationships, more often than some of the other phases of marital interaction, seem to be the focal point of tensions, because constantly recurring biological urges force couples to reckon with this part of life. Two people who differ on religion may simply agree to disagree and live together happily; a couple may have widely divergent ideas concerning the use of money, yet if they have enough money so that their differences do not cause financial hardship, they can tolerate their differences and live in peace. But in the area of sex the issue must be faced; for the sex urge is comparable to hunger in that it seeks periodic satisfaction. It also requires cooperation. Differences here cannot be ignored as can some other differences. Therefore, although sex is not an all-important factor in itself, a mutually gratifying sex relationship will serve to facilitate all adjustments, just as conflicts seemingly unrelated to sex will have repercussions in the sex life of the couple.

Although the place of sex in marriage is too often exaggerated, the contribution it makes to successful marriage should not be minimized. Certainly few marriages would take place were it not for sexual attraction between the two who marry; so throughout life the sex attraction can serve to enhance and to color all the couple's association together. Studies among happily married couples all agree that couples who have achieved the highest degree of mutuality in their sex relationships are among the most happily married. The personality traits which each partner takes into marriage will have much to do with the degree of sexual mutuality achieved. People who are cooperative, perceptive of the reactions of others, and considerate of the needs of others are the ones who seek to share gratification rather than having as their goal self-gratification only. Those who are selfish, impatient, unaware of the needs of others, and unwilling to learn from others, will have far less to contribute toward the achievement of a rewarding sex relationship in marriage. These personality factors are of far greater importance in sex adjustment than is simple biological adequacy.

For men and women

In earlier days the belief was generally accepted that sex in marriage was to be enjoyed by men and tolerated by women. It was not recognized that husbands had any obligation toward attempting to achieve mutuality in the sex act. And most women accepted a passive role, with the attitude that coitus was one of their marital duties not intended to involve much pleasure. Evidence of too much pleasure in sex experience was to be avoided by self-respecting wives, since it might be taken as an indication of unladylike tendencies. Many exceedingly happy marriages operated on that basis.

Wives who wholeheartedly accepted their role as passive and who entered marriage with no other expectation may have escaped the conflicts which many women experience today. Young people now generally have accepted the viewpoint that sex expression in marriage should be a mutually gratifying experience. In the conception of woman's role, some have gone so far that they attach too great importance to woman's ability to react vigorously in the early days of marriage. Disillusionment often results at this point with newly married couples. For here a cultural lag exists. Our generation has discarded the belief that woman is the passive, man the active, partner in sex experience, and in theory we subscribe to a belief in mutual sharing of sexual pleasure. But the adverse conditioning of girls in the realm of sex goes on, and the general preparation for marriage which would make mutual sharing a more easily accomplishable fact in marriage has not kept pace with the new attitudes and expectations which young people have concerning marriage.

The crucial period is the first few months or years of a marriage. If too much disillusionment and frustration develops, undesirable patterns may become so set that it will take many years of intelligent effort by one or both partners to remedy the defects in the adjustment pattern. A minority of couples do achieve mutually satisfactory sex adjustments, however, after as long as 10 to 20 years of married life. Therefore, if sex relationships are not what the marriage partners feel they should be, it is worth while to persevere in working to bring about a mutually rewarding relationship. But much conflict in the early years of marriage could be avoided if young people were well prepared before they marry, with scientific knowledge of the differences in the sexes emotionally and physically.

Causes of poor sex adjustment

Research studies show three broad classifications which include most of the causes of poor sex adjustment in marriage. These are (1) problems due to biological or organic factors, (2) problems due primarily to a lack of biological and psychological knowledge, and (3) problems due to social conditioning. Relatively few cases fall within the first classification. In one study of 100 couples, 5 per cent had had difficulty because of organic disturbances.[1]

Most difficulties in sex adjustment are due to causes which fall within the second and third classifications. Both husbands and wives come to marriage with a vast amount of misinformation concerning the role and functioning of sex. Much relearning is necessary. In addition to misinformation on biological and psychological functioning, certain attitudes, more frequently on the part of the wife, are the result of unfortunate conditioning during childhood. Girls have been conditioned to look upon sex with fear, aversion, or shame. This is also true of many boys but is less prevalent than among girls. It is sometimes difficult to distinguish between causes of failure due to lack of knowledge and those due to social conditioning because, in spite of adverse conditioning, many wives would be able to respond and cooperate in building a good sex relationship if the husbands were well enough informed so that they could understand their wives' reactions. Let us consider some of the factors back of the more common problems.

Some factors in the making of a good or a poor sex adjustment

Strangely enough, sex adjustment is sometimes difficult just because those going into marriage believe that the one part of marriage that will pose no problems at all is the sex relationship. Many people reason that since sex is based upon biological drives, all that is necessary for a successful marriage is that one follow one's biological inclinations. People who approach marriage with this attitude are often among the group who experience early disillusionment. If man lived on the animal level, the simple following of biological urges would probably accomplish "mating" as it does with other animals. However, human sexual

[1] E. W. Burgess and L. S. Cottrell, *Predicting Success or Failure in Marriage,* p. 221. New York: Prentice-Hall, Inc., 1938.

intercourse in a civilized society differs as much from animal mating as man's eating of his food according to socially approved rules differs from the animal's unceremonious devouring of his food. Results of research among married people indicate that varying lengths of time are required in order to achieve a good sex adjustment.

Our study of the length of time required after marriage for 409 couples to achieve adjustments revealed that one-eighth of the couples did not make a good initial sex adjustment, but reached a satisfactory adjustment within one year. One-tenth of the couples required an average of six years to work out this adjustment, some of them requiring as long as 20 years. Since the newly married couple plans to live together for the next 40 or 50 years, it is surely worth while to proceed slowly at first rather than to risk endangering a permanently satisfying sex relationship. Because of embarrassment, awkwardness, or the lack of adequate information, the anticipated delights are not always experienced at the first attempts. Another study reveals that the first sex experiences for 925 married women were not pleasant in 50 per cent of the cases.[2] A study of honeymoon experiences by Stanley Brav reveals that approximately half of the women in the study stated that they failed to achieve complete sexual harmony during their honeymoon.[3] These wives listed as their most common problems on the honeymoon "adjusting sexually," and "lack of adequate sex education." However, the same study revealed that three out of four of the wives thought their honeymoon was a complete success. This situation indicates that in many cases the honeymoon was considered a success although sex experiences were not satisfactory.

Handicap of misinformation

In some ways we are still living in a man's world. The woman who is successful in her contacts with men caters to masculine

[2] M. J. Exner, *The Sexual Side of Marriage,* p. 107. New York: W. W. Norton Company, 1932. Quoted from Katherine Davis, *Factors in the Sex Life of Twenty-Two Hundred Women,* New York: Harper & Brothers, 1929.

[3] Stanley R. Brav, "Notes on Honeymoon," *Marriage and Family Living,* 10:3 (August, 1947), 60.

ego either consciously or unconsciously. She does not deflate his ego by showing superior knowledge in the areas that he feels are his specific province. She is especially careful in the sex realm. Many a husband would be offended or chagrined if his bride questioned his knowledge of sex or tried to educate him on the subject. Many men go into marriage with a smattering of information gathered from "bull sessions," from questionable literature, or from premarital experimentation. The man who has had promiscuous premarital experience is inclined to think he knows women and sex and is therefore prepared for marriage. Actually, he has learned little that will help in working out a good sex relationship with his wife; and his confidence that he knows everything is a serious handicap at the outset. His experience before marriage may cause him to be overly critical of his wife's responses, and may prevent his trying to develop techniques which are important in such a permanent relationship as marriage. Regardless of how much more accurate and realistic the wife's information may be, she can do little to help out this type of husband without deflating his ego. Both need to enter marriage, then, with open minds, for much must be learned if a good understanding is to be reached.

Cultural conditioning of sex response

A major complication in sex adjustment in marriage is to be found in the way the subject of sex is handled in our culture. Children are conditioned so that it is often difficult for them to adjust to normal sex experience when they grow up. When they first begin to ask questions about sex, parents try to keep them in ignorance, thus forcing them to seek information from undesirable sources. When children engage in any type of sexual expression or experimentation, they are punished severely. Consequently they conclude that all sex interests are vulgar, shameful, and bad. Girls are usually impressed more than boys with taboos in the area of sex, since much greater social stigma is attached to the girl who deviates from socially acceptable behavior. Many parents solve the practical problem of protecting their daughter by over-impressing her with the dangerous aspects of sex activity. Many young married people have stated that their adjustment would have been easier if they could have been told before marriage about "the beauty of sex relations," that "sex is not sordid" and "not to be feared." [4]

Conditioned responses that have been built up over a period of 20 years preceding marriage will not change with the marriage ceremony or during the honeymoon. Timidity and reluctance to discuss the whole subject of sex make it difficult for couples to cooperate where cooperation is essential for success. Much could be said about the necessity for dropping inhibitions which have been built up during childhood. For most people that is a difficult process. However, an intelligent understanding of themselves and the reasons back of their attitudes will be helpful in overcoming many of the effects of early conditioning. In time, people can be reconditioned so that their responses are normal and satisfying. If constructive sex education became universal, marriage maladjustments would decrease.

Another factor which makes it difficult for women to respond in the early years of marriage is that in general girls have associated pain, or at least unpleasantness, with sex for as long as they can remember. Not only have they been punished for any childish infraction of sex taboos, but they are also conscious of the unpleasant aspects of menstruation, and they have heard tales concerning the pain of childbirth. It is little wonder that the young wife cannot instantly throw off all feelings of resistance toward sexual activity when she enters marriage.

Further, ignorance concerning the facts of physical structure and functioning handicaps many girls. This ignorance is responsible for much of the emotional resistance that some wives experience toward the first experiences in sexual intercourse. Dr. Kavinoky, gynecologist of many years' experience, states:[5]

[4] Student responses in unpublished research at Michigan State College, 1947.

[5] Nadina Kavinoky, M.D., "Premarital Examination," *The Western Journal of Surgery, Obstetrics and Gynecology*, 51 (October, 1943), 412-415.

It is amazing how often the girl is unaware of the fact that there is an opening in the hymen, that "breaking the maiden veil" is unnecessary and that there is a deep vaginal canal. This latter is appreciated with such spontaneous surprise (when the girl is informed of it in the premarital examination) that it is hard for us to realize that vagueness about pelvic anatomy and physiology can be the basis for so many groundless fears.

This discovery of the nature of a vaginal canal, and later a realization of the elasticity of the hymen and of the vaginal canal has a striking effect in the change it causes in the emotional attitude of the young woman. A fearful girl becomes a relaxed, cooperative, and intelligent patient soon after discovering this fact.

The premarital conditioning of the husband has been different from the conditioning of the wife. Men have grown up thinking of sex expression as something to be enjoyed; they have had little reason to be aware of any unpleasant or painful concomitants of sex functioning. If boys are punished for their early experimentations, it is seldom with the zeal that is applied when girls are the offenders. Some parents tend to view boys' infractions of rules on sex behavior as evidence of potential virility, and to be lenient.

If both partners in marriage understand and make allowances for this difference in experience and conditioning, they can more intelligently cooperate toward a satisfactory sex adjustment. Patience is especially necessary on the part of the husband.

Differences in sex response

One thing that has proved most baffling to many husbands is that they find it impossible to understand the reactions of their wives. A young husband who stated that his wife's "sex drive varies with the success of daily affairs" had made a keen observation. The average man finds that he can enjoy sexual gratification regardless of how other phases of the marriage are going. He may be at odds with his wife and critical of nearly everything she does, yet desire coitus. The wife cannot understand this attitude and is often resentful about it. Many wives complain bitterly that husbands show affection only when they are interested in coitus. The woman's viewpoint and feeling is likely to be that coitus is the ultimate expression of a love that includes the whole personality. If personality clashes or antagonisms develop over other things in the daily association, she is much less interested in coitus. The fact that her husband can desire it in spite of other personal factors is to her an indication that his interest in her is only physical and for his own gratification.

The husband can be equally resentful of his wife's attitude. To him it appears that she withholds response from him as a method of revenge or retribution. He naturally interprets her reactions in the light of his own. If he were to withhold response from her, it could be only by a rational and specific effort. What he cannot realize is that her *ability* to respond sexually is often dependent upon her whole general response to his personality. There is probably greater need for an understanding of each other on this point than on any other one thing affecting the happiness of husbands and wives. If a couple can accept the fact that this difference exists, that it is not a peculiarity of their own marriage, but rather a universal difference between men and women in our culture, they can look upon it in a different light. It is often a help to young married couples facing problems to realize that they are not alone; that the problems that loom so large in their marriage have been encountered in greater or lesser degree in almost all the marriages they see about them; and that the happy marriages with which they are acquainted have been achieved not because these conditions did not exist, but because the couples have accepted them realistically and have worked their way through them to a fine and lasting relationship.

Strength of sex drive

Different views are held concerning inherent biological differences between the sex drives of men and women. A great difference in sex desire appears to exist, but it is impossible to say with certainty how much of the difference is due to cultural conditioning and how much is of biological origin.

Many wives at marriage are sexually "unawakened' and time is required for them to learn to achieve full response and satisfaction in coitus. Women experience some measure of sex desire before marriage, but full psychic response through orgasm is experienced before marriage by only a small percentage of women compared to the proportion of young men who at marriage have been experiencing some form of full sex response for some years. Dr. Kinsey has concluded from his research that men reach their peak in sexual drive between 16 and 20, whereas women seem to reach their peak at a much later age.[5a] It takes time, therefore, for the average couple to understand each other and to adjust so that they meet each other's sexual needs. In our study of college students in the 11 colleges in 1952, the married women were asked when they first experienced orgasm. Of significance in our discussion is the fact that 25 per cent of these wives said they had never experienced it, although they had been married an average of three years. In Table 19 we summarize this study and compare our findings with those of similar studies by Terman[6] and Thomason.[7] In approximately half the cases in all three studies, the wives experienced orgasm within the first month of marriage, and one-fourth more within the first year of marriage. The remaining fourth took one or more years, or else they had never experienced it. These studies emphasize the fact that a wide range exists in the ability of wives to respond sexually in early marriage, and that time is required for growth in this area.

[5a] Alfred J. Kinsey, Wardell B. Pomeroy, and Clyde E. Martin, *Sexual Behavior in the Human Male,* pp. 219-223. Philadelphia: W. B. Saunders Company, 1948.

[6] Lewis M. Terman, *Psychological Factors in Marital Happiness,* p. 306. New York: McGraw-Hill Book Company, Inc., 1938.

[7] Bruce Thomason, "The Influence of Marital Sexual Behavior on Total Marital Adjustment," Paper read at National Council on Family Relations, Rutgers University, September, 1952.

The fact that the sex drive in men reaches its peak earlier than in women means that even when the sex drive of the husband is far beyond that of the wife early in marriage they can hope to reach a better balance of approximate equality of drive as they approach their middle thirties. With many couples the sex adjustment is much more satisfying after as much as ten or

TABLE 19

PERCENTAGES OF WIVES IN THREE STUDIES STATING VARIOUS LENGTHS OF TIME BEFORE ORGASM WAS EXPERIENCED IN MARRIAGE

Length of time	Terman (N-792) *Married:* 11 years	Thomason (N-641) 4 years	Landis (N-121) 3 years
Honeymoon to 4 weeks	51.1%	50.0%	48.0%
One month to 1 year	25.7	27.0	22.0
One year or more	16.0	7.0	4.0
Never	7.1	7.0	25.0
No reply	—	9.0	—

more years of marriage. In marriages in which the partners are very unequally matched in sex drive in the early years, both will have to compromise, but they need not conclude that they are permanently handicapped, for time may show that the difference is not so great. Oliver Butterfield states that years of practical experience as a consultant in cases of sexual maladjustment in marriage have convinced him that:

. . . few marriages need fail because of the lack of sexual ability on the part of either husband or wife. Most sexual maladjustment is psychic in nature and is the result either of some unfortunate premarital experience or of ignorant blundering during the early months of marriage. The best proof of this fact is the way in which most cases respond to skilled guidance even after months or years of marital floundering.[8]

[8] Oliver M. Butterfield, *Love Problems of Adolescence,* p. 145. New York: Emerson Books, Inc., 1941.

A great many words have been written about techniques for husbands to employ to arouse their wives to sexual response. Frequently the emphasis has been upon physical manipulation, ignoring the fact that the response of the wife depends upon psychological and emotional elements also. Expression of affection and assurances of love and appreciation are elements of great importance. Some husbands are unaware that the mood of the wife changes with the time of the menstrual cycle. Her ability to be aroused and her reaction to coitus may differ with

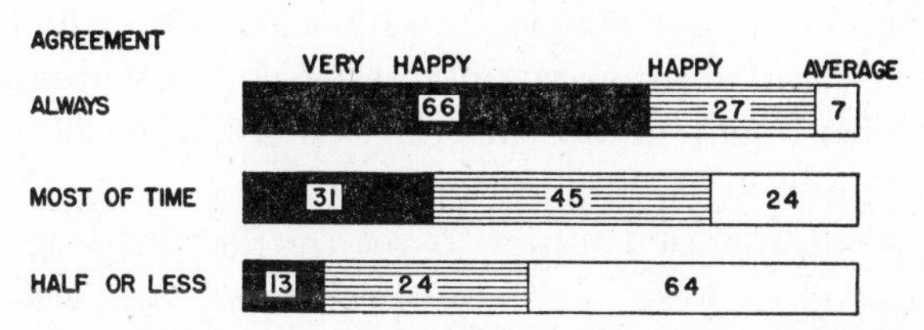

Fig. 56. Agreement in sex expression and marital happiness (544 couples).

each part of the month. Although variations occur in individuals, studies show that with most women the periods of time just before and just after menstruation are periods of greatest sexual response. Terman found that one-half of the women in his study recognized greater desire just before or just after menstruation, about twice as many after as before.[9] Wives who do not have a strong sex drive may enjoy full climactic response only at this time of the month.

Differences in timing and orgasm response

Although there is reason to believe that no biological difference exists in sex drive, still in our culture a significant difference between the manner and duration of reaction in men and women does exist. Men are more easily aroused and can be more quickly satisfied; women are slower to arouse and are capable of response of longer duration.

[9] Terman, *op. cit.*, p. 351.

It is desirable for the wife to receive emotional release through orgasm in sexual intercourse. However, research shows that in a great many very happy marriages the wife seldom or never experiences what is known as full climactic response and yet receives pleasure and satisfaction from the sex relationship. It is not necessary, nor is it possible, for all wives' responses to conform to a typical physical climax. Terman's study of marriage adjustment among the gifted group[10] and their wives found that almost half of the wives who seldom or never experienced orgasm still claimed to derive either complete or fairly complete satisfaction from the sex act. Nevertheless, if the wife expects and desires orgasm and is frequently disappointed, the sex adjustment of the marriage is likely to be adversely affected.

It is important for couples to realize that in general men's sex desire and response are more specific and localized than are women's. Women, in average cases, reach a climax more slowly, their reaction is more diffuse, the emotional reaction is of longer duration and slower to subside. Men's response ends more abruptly with the climax of the sex act. If the partners are aware that these differences exist, the differences need not be a barrier to mutuality. If each focuses his attention upon the needs and responses of the other, complete mutuality can usually be achieved in time. Here the husband has more responsibility than the wife, because his responses are naturally faster than hers. By exercising a measure of control and by studying his wife's reactions, he can make progress toward the desirable goal of a satisfactory sex experience for both. Thus the highest level of emotional and affectional as well as physical union may be achieved.

The successful sex act should result not only in physical release or satisfaction for the husband and for the wife, but in a general sense of well-being for both, in a feeling of security due to psychic as well as physical union.

[10] Lewis M. Terman, "Correlates of Orgasm Adequacy in a Group of 556 Wives," *The Journal of Psychology,* 32 (October, 1951), p. 128.

Other factors

Quite commonly the achievement of a successful sex relationship depends in part upon other factors, such as fatigue of one or both partners. The circumstances under which sex union is attempted must also be suitable. There must be privacy, a confidence that there will be no interruption, and pleasant surroundings. If either feels that haste is necessary because of other obligations or impending interruptions, a mutually gratifying experience will be less likely.

One young couple were having conflict in connection with sex in their marriage. They had prepared for marriage by reading and discussing the best information available on all phases of marital adjustment. Yet after three months they both felt disillusioned. The wife was finding coitus repugnant and the husband remarked bitterly that he felt he had married a frigid woman. An analysis of the facts in their case revealed that their problem was due almost entirely to the circumstances under which they were attempting to live. They were keeping their marriage a secret from their friends and families. Any time they spent together was of necessity clandestine, and in surroundings much different from those desirable for consummation of marriage by bride and groom. Whenever they were together as man and wife they felt the pressure upon them to be careful that their relationship not be discovered. These things weighed more heavily upon the wife than upon the husband, although she had not recognized the connection between them and her inability to respond sexually. After consulting a counselor, the couple announced their marriage and began living together openly with all the inhibiting psychic factors removed. The wife's ability to respond sexually became entirely satisfactory and they reached an adjustment in sex relations.

Frequency of coitus

The question of frequency of coitus often arises with married couples. Some go into marriage hampered with preconceived ideas of what is right and proper. But there can be no set rule. Great variations exist, the range being from nightly or oftener in extreme cases to only two or three times a year at the opposite extreme. The matter is entirely up to the couple concerned and should be determined by their mutual desires, the success of their relationship, the type of lives they lead, and other factors. Most couples in time find the level of frequency most conducive to their happiness and well-being.

Terman found that couples of 20-29 reported a frequency of approximately seven times per month. There was a gradual decrease in the frequency of intercourse until the age of 50-59, when approximately three copulations per month were reported.[11] The same study revealed that for each age group the husbands desired coitus more frequently than the wives did. The fact that husbands usually desire coitus more frequently than wives again reveals the importance of cooperation and willingness to compromise on the part of both partners in marriage.

It is not unusual for husbands to behave unreasonably when their sexual desires are blocked. To wives this behavior may appear to be an immature and undisciplined response to the blocking of desires. In some cases neither husband nor wife will recognize the cause of the husband's behavior; he will simply act generally irritable until the wife loses patience with him and a quarrel results. It is helpful if husbands can analyze their own behavior. Wives can be more sympathetic to husbands' needs if they also understand the causes. Almost all wives are tolerant of the fact that many husbands revert to childish behavior when they are hungry. That is why so many successful homemakers see to it that a comfortable chair, the evening paper, and his slippers are invitingly evident when the man of the house comes home if dinner is not quite ready. And how many times the same wives excuse the explosive be-

[11] Kinsey found a somewhat higher frequency, from approximately 12 times per month for the 20-29 age group to four times per month for the older group. *Op. cit.*, p. 252.

havior of a young son with the explanation, "He is hungry. What he needs is a good dinner."

It is impossible to estimate the proportion of marital difficulties arising because of explosive behavior on the part of husbands who experience blocking of sexual desires. But marriage counselors recognize that in a great many of the cases that come to them for help this is one of the contributing factors. Unfortunately, no simple and effective remedy can be recommended to solve this problem. If both husband and wife recognize that their needs may differ, and if both are willing to compromise, they can eliminate much unpleasantness and build a sex life that is quite satisfactory for both even though they must cope with a considerable difference in the strength of the sex drives. However, even in marriages where the spouses are equally matched there will be times when one spouse is physically or mentally exhausted and not interested in sexual activity while the other may be much interested. Sex adjustments that are perfect at all times are probably relatively rare. The tempo of modern living, success and failure in work, sickness of the spouse or the children, worry and anxiety, all affect the desire and the capacity for sexual enjoyment. For these reasons it must be recognized that a successful sex adjustment is one which provides a satisfying experience for both most of the time but probably not all of the time. We judge success or failure by the emotional factors preliminary to and subsequent to intercourse and by the integration of the sex act with the whole of living.[12]

Anxiety resulting from failure in coitus

Some couples become too anxious to work out a sex adjustment early in marriage and attach too much significance to any early disappointments or failures. Many young wives will not experience full climactic experience in the early weeks of marriage even though they are well informed and their husbands are successful lovers. As we stated earlier in this chapter,

[12] Kavinoky, *op. cit.*

marriage breaks down the physical barrier to coitus but it does not necessarily break down the psychic barrier. Time is required for new conditioned responses to be substituted for old ones. Anxieties generated by early failures sometimes produce a mental state which makes complete sexual response more difficult. Young people who love each other, are companionable, and who have many things in common still have to learn to live together. In their sex adjustment as well as in many other adjustments, time will take care of many of their problems if they are willing to work at building good relationships.

Lack of standardization in sex teachings and attitudes

When any two young people marry, they are almost certain to bring two different, and often contrasting, sets of attitudes toward sex to their marriage. No institutional provision has existed for teaching young people about sex behavior and sex practices. On all other phases of living most people receive some form of constructive teaching from earliest childhood. Families attempt to inculcate in their children proper concepts of social attitudes and behavior. Newspapers and magazines carry discussions of what is desirable in dress, in manners, and in social customs. Public schools accept the obligation for teaching children many of the standards that will help them get along in the world about them. Only in the field of sex behavior and practices is education seriously neglected. Here the teaching is almost entirely negative; it consists chiefly in impressing the child with taboos. And even the taboos are not standardized.

Findings of research on sex behavior in marriage point to the conclusion that no single pattern of normal and proper sex practice in marriage is generally accepted. Rather, a wide range of practices may be looked upon as normal and right, or as improper and wrong, according to the individual's background. This variation in what is considered right, proper, and "normal" in sex relations can make for great misunderstanding, even repulsion and disgust, between two young people who come from families or economic groups with contrasting attitudes toward sex behavior and practice in marriage. What the one spouse accepts as normal the other may feel is abnormal or perverted. Alfred Kinsey states, after an extensive analysis of differing standards at different social levels, that each social level is convinced that its pattern of behavior is the best of all possible patterns and that each level rationalizes its behavior in its own way.[13]

So two young people who find differences in their attitudes toward sex expression in marriage will sometimes encounter difficulty in harmonizing their attitudes. One may be sure his or her standards are best because they are based upon religion or morality or "right." The other may be equally sure that desirable practices can be based only upon what is "normal" biologically. An added difficulty arises because few couples will be able to recognize rationally even that their fundamental attitudes do differ, or to what extent the differences exist. They will simply go into marriage expecting much from sex relations, and if all is not perfect at once or soon, the husband may decide he has a frigid wife, or the wife may decide she has married a selfish and insensitive husband. Or either one may decide that the other is over-sexed or over-aggressive sexually. The couple may not have analyzed the real problem—a fundamental difference over attitudes toward proper and normal sex expression in marriage. The problem need not affect the marriage adversely, however, if both can be tolerant and understanding on differences in levels of "normal" sex expression.

Outside help for problems

Couples who experience difficulties in personal adjustments in marriage are often hesitant to seek outside help. They will readily seek medical help in case of illness, and many will discuss their physical ailments freely among friends and neighbors. But when it comes to working out husband-wife relationships, many couples feel that they must maintain a pretense of perfect harmony and never openly admit that any serious problems

[13] Kinsey, *op. cit.*, Ch. X.

of adjustment have arisen. The attitude of society has supported this viewpoint. Couples have been expected to cover their hostilities and to work out their problems alone. They could perhaps go to their priest or minister with a confession of failure, or go to a lawyer for advice concerning a divorce, but little or no help was available in working out their problems in a constructive way. Little progress was made toward the understanding and cure of mental illness as long as families hid their mentally ill members and tried to keep secret the illness they felt to be a disgrace. An open recognition of any problem is necessary before progress can be made toward a solution.

So, much marriage frustration, unhappiness, and ultimate divorce can be avoided if couples will acknowledge the common marital difficulties and realize that it is no admission of defeat to seek help from an outside authority in solving problems. A shortage exists, however, of people qualified by training, experience, and personality to help married couples who are facing difficulties. Some ministers and doctors have qualified themselves to handle the special problems of marital adjustment, since they realize there are not enough other qualified counselors. But many more specially trained marriage counselors are needed. It seldom is wise to seek help from neighbors, friends, or relatives, for these would be inclined to be prejudiced in favor of one spouse or the other without being able to view the situation objectively.

A trained counselor[14] is in a position to look impartially at the total marriage situation. He may let the couple talk it out, suggest certain readings, or make suggestions according to what he observes as an outsider. In many marriage situations all one spouse needs is a chance to talk about his problems with an unprejudiced outsider. Others need several sessions devoted to self-analysis in order to find the solution to their problems. In

[14] The American Association of Marriage Counselors, Inc., 270 Park Avenue, Room C-701, New York 17, New York, will furnish information on qualified marriage counselors in various parts of the United States. See also Appendix A for more information on marriage counseling facilities.

other cases the counselor may act as a doctor does in diagnosing an illness and then prescribing a specific cure. The trained counselor will decide which method will be of greatest help to an individual couple. As two people live together they will find solutions to many marital problems without the aid of a counselor. Some excellent help is available in reading material.

A number of books treat of the physiology and psychology of sex. Public libraries are becoming increasingly aware of their obligation to provide such books to meet the needs of the public. However, since in many communities these books are still unobtainable from libraries, those interested will have to buy them in order to read them. It is desirable for couples to own helpful books which may be reread when questions arise after marriage. Much of the material dealing with the subject of sex will have greater meaning some time after marriage. Readers are inclined to miss important points which happen to be beyond present experience.

Sex in marriage a positive value

A satisfying sex relationship is one of the positive elements contributing to the well-being of the individual and of the married pair. The couple who find satisfaction together in the sexual relationship are more likely to have well-integrated personalities and to have a home in which children will find happiness. They will also be able to condition their children to look upon sex as one of the normal and desirable satisfactions of living. Just as we appreciate good food and comfortable shelter, a workable philosophy of life, and the security of religion, so we recognize sex fulfillment in marriage as a positive good. Its value consists not only in its function of reproducing the race but also in its constructive force in promoting the happiness of individuals. It can be the most complete form of love expression, contributing to the mental, emotional, and physical balance which is necessary if two people are to have a happy and successful marriage.

Chapter XIV

IN-LAWS AND MARRIAGE ADJUSTMENT

SOME YOUNG PEOPLE go into marriage vaguely aware that they are getting, along with a wife or husband, a new family: a mother-in-law, a father-in-law, brothers- and sisters-in-law, even aunts-, uncles-, and grandparents-in-law. Others marry feeling secure in the belief that marriage is for two alone and blissfully unconscious of all the in-laws that are an inevitable result of the "I do." Those who do realize that one marries a family as well as a mate have a wide variety of attitudes. Some who have been conditioned by years of exposure to mother-in-law jokes marry with a fatalistic attitude that in-law trouble is a part of marriage. A few look forward with pleasure to association with a larger family group. A person who has had no sister or brother may hope to have the lack filled by a brother-in-law or sister-in-law. Whatever the attitudes of those marrying, in-laws will be a factor in marital adjustment.

In-law adjustment a problem of early marriage

Just how important and how serious are in-law relationships as a factor in marriage? Two studies have provided some interesting information concerning the problems involved. When couples who had been married for an average of 20 years were asked to state what had been their most serious problem in achieving happiness in marriage, the women mentioned in-law relationships second, and the men mentioned in-laws third, among six areas. These people had been married long enough to have faced most of the issues which arise in married life. Since none of this group was divorced and 85 per cent classified their marriages as happy or very happy, they would tend to understate rather than to overstate the seriousness of in-law friction as it would exist in a representative cross section of marriages.

The second study asked for the same information from 544 couples who were in the early years of marriage. These couples gave in-law relationships first place in their list of difficult areas. Several things may explain the greater importance given to in-law problems by the younger group. They were in the early years of marriage, when family adjustments were in the process of being made. Some of those experiencing difficulty early in marriage will in the course of time resolve their differences and reach a good understanding with the in-laws, so that if queried on their relationships years hence, they would report the adjustment with in-laws to be excellent. The long-married group includes fewer with in-law difficulties because those who were not able to solve their problems have in some cases ended the marriage by divorce; in other cases the situation has resolved itself through the death of the parents-in-law. The research findings indicate that in-law disagreements are chiefly a problem of the early years of marriage, although some couples settle into a permanent state of friction with the in-laws.

Specific areas of in-law friction

The couples who reported in-laws to be a source of friction in their marriages were asked to specify which in-law relationship was the center of the trouble. Table 20 summarizes their responses. It will be observed that the friction is about equally divided between the mother-in-law and all the other family members combined. In fact, the mother-in-law figures in 60 per cent of the in-law imbroglios, if those cases are counted in which two or more members of the family are involved.

TABLE 20

PERCENTAGES OF 116 HUSBANDS AND 160 WIVES REPORTING VARIOUS IN-LAW RELATIONSHIPS WHICH WERE CAUSING FRICTION IN MARRIAGES

	Husband	Wife	Both
Mother-in-law	42.0%	50.0%	46.7%
Father-in-law	15.0	11.0	12.3
Brother-in-law	3.0	6.0	5.0
Sister-in-law	16.0	13.0	13.8
Two or more of the above	24.0	20.0	22.2

The findings also suggest that in-law friction is a feminine pattern, since mothers-in-law, sisters-in-law, and wives are involved more frequently than are fathers-in-law, brothers-in-law, or husbands. The brother-in-law's contribution to tense in-law relationships is negligible.

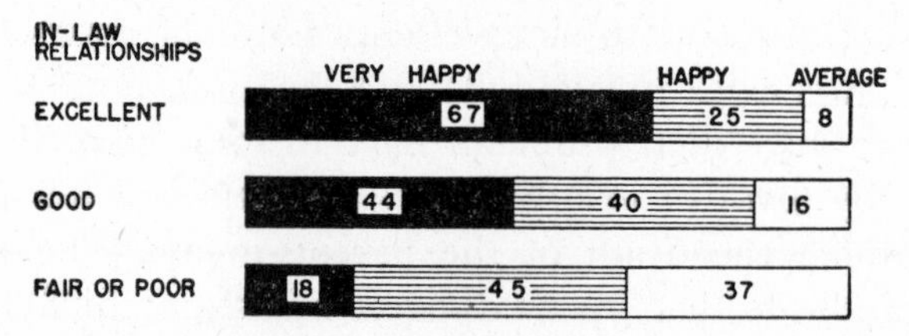

Fig. 57. In-law relationships and self-rated happiness in marriage (544 couples). Excellent adjustment with the in-laws and happiness in marriage go together.

In-law adjustments and happiness in marriage

The study of the 544 marriages revealed a close relationship between happiness in marriage and getting along with the in-laws. Of those couples who had an excellent in-law adjustment, 67 per cent said their marriages were very happy, but if the in-law adjustment was fair or poor, only 18 per cent classified their marriages as very happy. (See Figure 57.) The same relationship was found in our study of the 409 marriages of couples in the parent generation.[1] Further, the longer it took to work out a satisfactory relationship with the in-laws among the parent couples, the more likely the marriage was to be rated as unhappy. Those who had never worked out an adjustment with the in-laws had the largest percentage of average or unhappy marriages. (See Figure 58.)

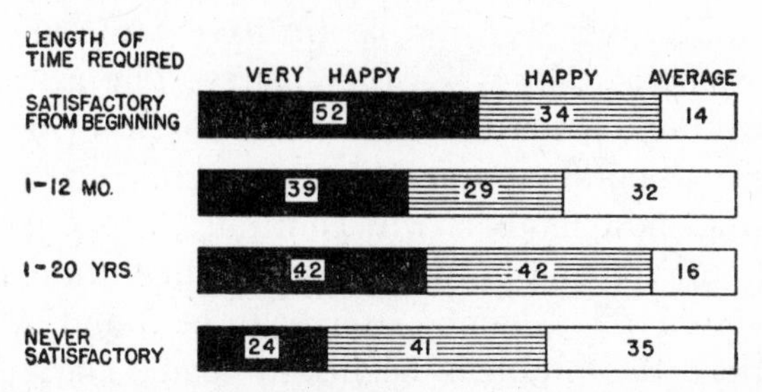

Fig. 58. Percentages of 409 husbands and 409 wives reporting various periods of time required for adjustment in in-law relations and happiness in marriage.

Ability to maintain pleasant and peaceful relationships with in-laws seems to be part of the total personality make-up which is more likely to achieve happiness in marriage. However, the research findings indicate that the whole problem of in-law relationships has not received enough attention in the preparation of young people for marriage.

An analysis of the conflict situation

If we would understand the in-law conflict situation, we must reflect on the family life pattern. For the first 20 years of the child's life his family is a strong "we" group. The mother is wrapped up in the children from the time they are born until they leave home. As small children, they look to her for their every need; to them she represents security. She influences most of their decisions as they grow older and many parents sponsor the idea that "mother always knows best." Although a father

[1] Judson T. Landis, "Length of Time Required to Achieve Adjustment in Marriage," *American Sociological Review,* 11:6 (December, 1946), 666-677.

is in the home, he is usually more occupied with making the family's living and is not so closely associated with the children. He has many interests outside the home, whereas mothers of necessity must center more of their interests in the home and the children. It is normal for children to feel a measure of dependence upon the mother. This is the pattern that the young husband and the young wife take into marriage. Even under the best family guidance, most people have not been completely weaned psychologically when they marry. The marriage takes place today, but a pattern which has been built up over a period of 20 years will not disappear with the wedding ceremony. After the wedding most mothers will continue to give helpful suggestions to the son and in turn the son will continue to counsel with the mother. This same pattern will be found in the wife's family. Here the problem begins in many marriages. Each spouse, while continuing his own accustomed relationships with his family, will feel resentful of the close relationship between the other spouse and his or her family. The offering of parental counsel may seem to the child-in-law to be parental interference, and the fact that the spouse seeks parental advice may be interpreted as an indication that he has more respect and confidence in the parents than in the mate.

A normal situation exists with good intentions on the part of all concerned, yet unless the patterns of a lifetime are altered, in-law friction may develop.

Lack of objectivity in in-law relationships

Both the children and the parents are inclined to lose their objectivity. To the parents, the son-in-law or daughter-in-law may seem to be ungracious and unappreciative, and the son-in-law or daughter-in-law views all parental interest as interference. Some comments made by young people about their parents-in-law are illuminating here. "They try to run our home," "They treat us as children," "They give us too much advice," "—try to help too much," "—try to influence our lives," "—hover over us." These are comments made by the child-in-law about the spouse's parents, not about his own. This same young person may be continuing to seek daily counsel from his own parents with no thought that the spouse might interpret the pattern as parental "interference." Personal conferences with some of the young people who made such comments about their parents-in-law revealed that frequently they were shocked when they realized that the spouse had exactly the same criticism, but directed at *his* parents-in-law.

It seems that many couples find it hard if not impossible to discuss with each other their feelings concerning the in-laws during the early years of marriage. Each fears he will be accused of jealousy. The fact that an element of jealousy is actually present does not make objective discussion any easier. We list some further comments made by daughters-in-law which indicate that an element of jealousy, or at least a competitive attitude toward the parents-in-law, often exists.

"His mother insists on first place with my husband."
"They still think he belongs to them."
"They don't accept my status as daughter-in-law."
"They try to steal my place as his wife and the mother of his child."

It will be readily seen that the young wife would find it difficult to discuss these complaints lucidly and convincingly with her husband. She will find this inability to talk it over with her husband extremely disconcerting, and may seek to relieve her emotional turmoil by talking it over with her own parents or friends, who may lend a more sympathetic ear. This procedure is usually undesirable.

We quoted only comments from daughters-in-law, but sons-in-law find it hard to accept and tolerate close affectional bonds between the wife and her family. Husbands also become emotional over the spouse's continued dependence upon her parents for advice or help.

Parents as a factor in in-law relationships

Some of the parents as well as the children show signs of immaturity in their in-law relationships. Some mothers cling to their children, refuse to let them grow up, and continue to make their decisions for them long after the children should be thinking for themselves. This type of mother has herself never matured to the place where she accepts life as it is. The adult viewpoint is that we have our children and we enjoy them, but as they grow older we encourage them to take on adult ways. This means that they are going to think for themselves, and that they will marry and have families of their own who will be more dear to them than their own parents. The mother who fails to accept this philosophy and who tries to hold the first allegiance of her children will probably have trouble with her children-in-law. On the other hand, some children are late to mature and continue to cling to their parents. The husband or wife married to an immature spouse will have difficulty in adjusting to the in-law situation.

One aspect of mother-in-law trouble centers in regressive tendencies that may show up in people when they are faced with problems. As one looks back, a past level of life may seem easier and simpler than the present situation. In early marriage the inevitable problems to be solved surprise and baffle some people who believed that marriage would end all problems; their urge is to go back home emotionally and sometimes physically. This tendency toward regression appears in sons and daughters after marriage and also in mothers who encourage their married children to come to them with their troubles.

Many mothers experience a crisis in their lives when all the children marry and leave home. Their lives have been full while the children were home and when the last one has gone mothers may feel the emptiness and loss. So the married daughter who runs home to mother may find mother waiting with welcoming arms. Both mother and daughter have regressed, and the young husband understandably feels anger toward his mother-in-law, whom he blames for complicating his life.

Fathers are not so likely to follow the lives of the children, since fathers are not usually so close to them emotionally. The father has his job and is as absorbed in that as he has always been. He may even heave a sigh of relief privately when the last daughter is married, since she has been quite a burden to support during the teen years. It is different with the mother. The loss of the children through marriage and her subsequent loneliness must be taken into consideration when we attempt to understand in-law problems.

The American ideal has been that when young people marry they live alone. In practice, many young people must live with the parents when they marry. If they must live with parents during the first years of marriage, their process of growing up and becoming psychologically weaned from the parents may be delayed. Continuation of the parental-dominance and the child-dependence pattern of the spouse with whose parents they are living is often intolerable for the outsider who has come into the home as husband or wife. The women are more likely to conflict, since the wife is striving to establish herself in her new status and will be quick to resent the mother who continues to hold a dominant place. This type of in-law friction has a much better chance to show itself when the families are living together or near each other.

Because of the common custom of making jokes at the expense of mothers-in-law, many young people go into marriage with a chip on their shoulder, just waiting for the mother-in-law or father-in-law to knock it off. They are looking for any indication of parental interference, and because of the domination-submission pattern which is carried by both young people into the marriage, it is usually easy to find something that can be interpreted as parental interference. Then the battle is on.

In marriages in which the two young people come from contrasting backgrounds, such as different nationalities, religions, economic classes, or social classes, all the usual factors which make for family misunderstandings are present in addition to the contrast in home backgrounds. These contrasts contribute to friction in in-law relationships. In rural parts of America it is hard to convince many farm parents that a city girl can ever make a good wife for their son. It is difficult for farm parents who feel this way to keep from showing their attitude in some way, and the city daughter-in-law is sensitive to this critical attitude on the part of her husband's parents. As one such wife said after 23 years of marriage, "His folks have never really felt I belonged, just because I came from the city. Nothing I did was right."

Sometimes friction develops because the parents are critical of the changes that come over the young people after marriage. It may be that the parents have taught their son to go to church on Sunday; that card playing is wrong; and that dancing is of the devil. If after marriage this son stops going to church on Sunday, or takes up cards and dancing, the parents can come to but one conclusion: it must be that wife of his. The wife may or may not be partly to blame. Young people will do more as they wish after leaving home and when they have established homes of their own. Some may not have been in sympathy with their parents' beliefs but conformed as long as they lived at home. It is to be expected that the thinking of both partners will be modified by marriage. But when parents cannot accept changes, it is hard for them not to offer reproof or counsel, which the child-in-law may resent.

Age at marriage and in-law difficulties

Our study of the 409 parent marriages revealed that the men who married under the age of 20 took longer to adjust with the in-laws than those who married later. Among the 544 couples in the early years of marriage, the wives who married at ages under 20 were having more difficulty with in-laws than were the young husbands. The husbands and wives who married at 24 or over had the best working arrangement with the in-laws. In-law difficulties are much more important as causes of trouble in youthful marriages. Parents may be inclined to interfere more when they feel that the children are not old enough to marry, and the youth and immaturity of the children may cause them on their part to be especially sensitive to parental interference.

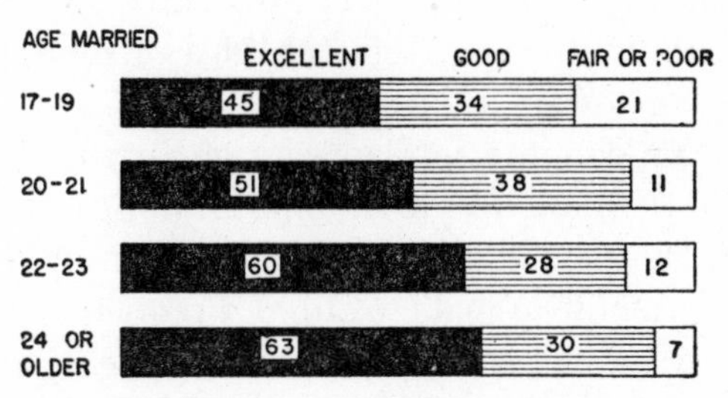

Fig. 59. Age of 544 wives at marriage and in-law adjustment.

Behavior arising from in-law disharmony

So far we have given attention to conflicts between parents-in-law and children-in-law in an attempt to clarify somewhat the background factors of such difficulties. The whole interactional pattern is complicated, for just as the young people fail to understand their parents-in-law, so they are puzzled and frustrated by the reactions of their spouses to the in-law situation. Young husbands complain:

"She takes her mother's advice no matter how bad it is."
"She tells her mother too much about our personal affairs."
"She is too much at their beck and call."

And both husbands and wives complain that the spouse:

"Is tied to their apron strings," "—wants to live near own folks," "—is too worried about them," "—gets homesick," "—agrees with them (though they're ignorant) just to pacify them."

When the partners find it hard to understand these attitudes in each other, they tend to resort to certain types of behavior which are extremely irritating. The husband or wife may (1) behave in an unpleasant manner to the in-laws; (2) behave unpleasantly to the spouse in the presence of the in-laws; or (3) attempt to thwart the mate in in-law relationships by refusing to have anything to do with the in-laws. Such comments as, "He makes the in-laws feel unwanted," "won't talk to them," "argues with them," give an idea of some overt expressions of feeling toward the in-laws.

Few sons- or daughters-in-law engage in this behavior as a conscious effort to offend the in-laws. In most cases the offenses are no more deliberate than the interference by the parents is a deliberate attempt to make trouble. Frequently the offending actions simply mean that the spouse is ill at ease and unsure of himself in the presence of the in-laws. This is also true in many cases when the wife or husband feels critical of the spouse's behavior toward the mate in the presence of the in-laws. Both husbands and wives are often extremely sensitive to the impression that the mate is making upon the in-laws. Since they hope to give the impression that unity and solidarity exist in the marriage, any direct or implied criticism from the partner in the presence of the in-laws is remarkably disturbing.

Again the comments of troubled couples are enlightening. "He embarrasses me in front of them," '—ignores me when we are with them," "—doesn't show any affection when the in-laws are around," "—criticizes me in front of the in-laws," "—doesn't take my side if I differ with the in-laws." All these comments indicate that the child-in-law feels the need of "backing" from his mate around the in-laws. He wants the fact demonstrated that he is loved and respected by the spouse. Many of the things a husband does may provoke no irritation at all when he is alone with his wife, but the same words or actions in the presence of the in-laws will cause the wife to feel that she has lost face and has been repudiated before those whom she especially desires to impress. Husbands react similarly to the face-losing situations.

In-law relationships a "natural" for conflict in marriage

It is of the greatest importance for young people entering marriage to have a realistic understanding of the in-law interactional pattern. Happy in-law relationships can contribute much to the joy of a good marriage, yet because of the nature of normal parent-child relationships before marriage, the in-law relationship is a natural set-up for conflict. It helps for young people to realize that most parents are just as interested in the success of the marriage as are the children, and that the children-in-law have just as many attitudes provocative of conflict as the parents have. If the children-in-law can analyze with a measure of objectivity the motives back of their own behavior, they will find it easier to maintain perspective on the entire in-law relationship.

There is sometimes truth in the old statement that "it takes two good women to make a good husband." If the young wife finds that she resents the implication of the statement, and that it is painful to her to admit that her husband is the fine man she chose to marry at least partly because his mother did such a good job of bringing him up, then she needs to re-examine her own attitudes. She will probably find that she is carrying a chip on her shoulder and looking for mother-in-law trouble. Some mothers-in-law, in the interests of peace, fairly scurry to keep out of the way of belligerent daughters-in-law.

A case of mother-in-law domination

Nevertheless, some mothers-in-law do interfere and make life difficult for their married children.

H. R. lived with his mother until he was forty, at which time he married Helen, who was several years younger. They moved into his home, which the mother continued to dominate. It was the mother who always met him at the door when he returned home in the evening and who sat down to discuss with him the happenings of the day. This had been the pattern of their lives for years and the marriage made no change. He asked his mother's advice in all matters and she was included in all plans. Early in the marriage the couple sometimes went out for an evening of dancing or visiting with friends; but as time passed the mother objected to being left alone, so they gave up these evenings out. At first, friends of the couple came in occasionally, but the mother acted as hostess and entertained the guests with stories of H. R.'s activities and interests, so that soon friends ceased to come. Since the mother planned all meals and directed the housework, the wife found herself in the position of a privileged servant in the home rather than of a wife. Any attempts she made to take over responsibilities or make decisions were taken as affronts by the mother-in-law, who would weep and be forced to go to bed with a headache. If the wife attempted to make any plans with her husband, the mother-in-law's feelings would be hurt. She would assume a martyred attitude and explain to the son that his poor old mother was only in the way, that she was unloved and unwanted by the daughter-in-law, and so on. H. R. would then chide his wife for being inconsiderate of his mother and causing her unhappiness in her own home. Helen's friends and relatives marveled at her endurance and privately predicted that some day soon she would pack up and leave. Her own mother, who lived near by and could observe the situation, once said to a friend, "I don't see how Helen can stand that mother-in-law of hers, but she has never said a word about it to me. She keeps her own counsel."

After a few months Helen accepted a part-time job in a flower and gift shop. She suggested to the mother-in-law that since she had only a little time to help with the work at home she would be glad to take the responsibility for any specific tasks the mother would like for her to do, and that she would do these regularly. That suited the mother-in-law well and she turned certain tasks over to Helen. These Helen did conscientiously and the mother-in-law was kept busy with the rest of the house. Helen centered her interests in her work and made friends with other young women who worked. She resumed the study of music, which she had dropped at her marriage. Since her husband loved music, they began to have musical evenings at home, which the mother-in-law enjoyed since they centered around her son's chief interest. Gradually friends were attracted back to the home. The mother-in-law was delighted to shine in the role of hostess who provided excellent food and served the guests.

Helen acted as accompanist for her husband's singing and mingled with guests almost as another guest. H. R.'s mother had always prided herself upon her success with houseplants, so Helen's work in the flower shop enabled her to take an active interest in this hobby. She brought her mother-in-law unusual plants and then praised and admired the way they flourished under the mother-in-law's care.

In other words, Helen met the whole problem in a constructive manner. She loved her husband and hoped to build a good marriage, so she refused to battle with her mother-in-law, but rather sought to understand her and make friends with her. She cultivated other outside interests for herself rather than brooding over the fact that she was not mistress in her own home.

Her success was impressive. It took time. But by the time there were two small children the home could be called a happy one. The mother-in-law still carried much of the responsibility for running the house, but Helen had her children to care for; she also had many friends, none of whom had ever heard any complaints from her about her mother-in-law. And she had the unquestioned devotion of her husband. A visitor in the home after the marriage had lasted for 15 years noticed that the mother-in-law treated Helen with great respect and affection. She frequently quoted her as authority on almost any subject, "*Helen* does it this way," or "*Helen* says——." Such would never have been the case if Helen had braced herself and battled for her rights rather than being content to work out a solution through compromise, sacrificing some of her preferences for the greater good of a permanently happy marriage.

Few young women would be able to meet the problem as Helen met it. The natural course of action would be for the wife to brace herself for battle and to try to force the husband and the mother-in-law to accord her her rightful place as mistress in the home. In this case that would probably not have worked, and the marriage would not have survived. In other situations, to force the issue might be the best procedure, but in any marriage that is complicated by such an in-law problem the important thing is to maintain perspective and to consider the best way to build a good marriage for all of life.

Living with parents

Young people will find most of their adjustments much easier if they can live alone during the early years of marriage. During times of housing shortages many find it necessary to move in with relatives when they marry. Many such families face realistically the fact that difficulties may arise, and they work out arrangements which keep emotional tensions and frayed nerves at a minimum. Such arrangements require much compromise. The two generations will not agree on how to train the children, the use of money, what is right or wrong

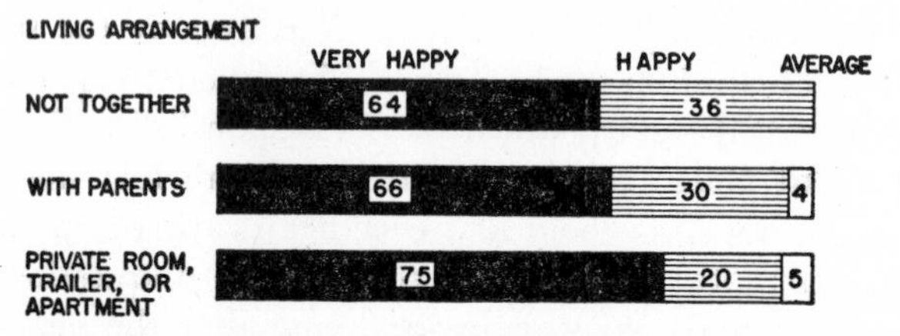

Fig. 60. Living arrangement of 544 couples in the early years of marriage and self-rated happiness. Couples who were forced to live apart were almost as happy in marriage as those who had moved in with their parents. Those who had privacy were happier even if they lived in a single room or a trailer.

conduct, how to cook a good meal, and many other things. Research studies by Burgess and Wallin, and by Locke, found that more in-law trouble is likely to occur in situations when the daughter-in-law must live with the mother-in-law, than in cases in which the son-in-law is living in his wife's parents' home.

When couples live with parents, a complicating factor is the tendency for young people to fail to take full responsibility for their own actions. If things go wrong in the household, if the children are spoiled and tempers are short, there is always a scapegoat handy to blame. It is easy to think that things would be otherwise if only in-laws were not present to complicate life. So the presence of the third person in the home does serve to retard adjustments which need to be made early in marriage.

There is also a tendency for one of the pair to discuss problems with the third person rather than going ahead to work them out with the mate. A wise mother of several children told them all when they married, "If you ever have any trouble in your marriage, don't come to me with it. Send your husband (or wife). I will listen to my child-in-law's side of it, but I don't want to hear any complaints from my own children."

Successful in-law relationships

As we stated early in the chapter, the ability to get along well with the in-laws is one of a number of characteristics which are found in those who have the capacity for meeting adjustment problems constructively. The couples who supplied information on difficulties in this area listed their solutions to the in-law problem. The most successful in their relationships were those who willingly compromised in the interests of harmony, or who made friends with the in-laws and actively liked them. Their comments were of this type:

"Father-in-law is a swell fellow."
"They are easy to get along with."
"We agree on life in general."
and
"I fit in with their ways of doing things."
"Made up my mind to get along."
"Treat them as my own family."
"Respect their views."
"Visit them often but not for very long."
"Am helpful whenever possible."
"Try to be agreeable and friendly to them."
"Ignore things that irritate."
"Realize they have developed their ways over a long period of time so I don't try to change them."
"I try to be sensible about it and not condemn them for faults when I have faults too."

All these comments indicate a positive frame of mind which will avoid or resolve in-law friction. A few couples reported that they had met problems by simply not trying to get along with the in-laws. Most of those who had chosen that solution had managed to live as far as possible away from the in-laws and to see as little of them as possible. Comments made by the couples in the study of older-generation marriages revealed that many of the couples in the older generation had met their problems by this same substitute solution. That is, they avoided any open conflict with in-laws by having nothing to do with them.

In some cases, to have nothing to do with the in-laws may be the only way to avoid friction. The young person whose emotional development has stopped at an immature level may have a better chance to grow up if he is away from his family during the first adjustment period of marriage. Many more tensions would develop for the spouse if they were living near the in-laws during the time that the immature one is "growing up." The too-interested mother may also find interests other than the lives of her children, if the children are not living near her after they marry. So, although putting a wide distance between the married couple and the in-laws is not the most constructive or desirable solution, it sometimes serves to facilitate other adjustments during the early years of some marriages. By thus postponing conflict, some young people may attain a more satisfactory marital adjustment and may also achieve greater maturity in their own personalities, so that after a few years they may be able to live near the in-laws and enjoy a pleasant relationship with them. The better solution, of course, is for the young couple to strive to be mature and generous in their attitudes, because pleasant in-law relationships contribute to happiness in marriage.

Do in-laws break up marriages?

Of themselves, poor in-law relationships probably do not break up many marriages, although divorced people often blame the in-laws for the marriage failure. Usually the failure of the marriage is due rather to a combination of factors. It may appear that the mother-in-law is interfering too much in the marriage, but an objective observer might see also that the son is immature and dependent and very willing to accept the domination of the mother. If the wife is also immature and insecure in her affectional relationship with her husband, she will be more willing to do battle with the mother-in-law.

Outside interference from in-laws is not likely to break up the marriage of a young couple who are working out their adjustments together, who can freely and objectively discuss their families, and who are mature and secure in each other's affection. Couples or individuals who are inadequate in their relationships with others may resort to many different types of behavior in compensating for their own inadequacies. Many of the comments from young people who complain that they have in-law trouble reveal that the trouble lies within the complaining individuals themselves. Such people would have in-law misunderstanding regardless of whom they had married.

In-law relationships during the later years of marriage

Most of our discussion thus far has been of in-law friction in the early years of marriage, for it is then that it is most likely to occur. In-law problems of later marriage are of a different type. After a few years have passed, the many adjustments facing newly married couples have been worked out and the family has become a solid unit. Each partner is more sure of his place in the affections of the spouse and does not need so much reassurance around the in-laws. Most people will have by this time achieved at least a measure of maturity. Some comments by the long-married group suggest the nature of the more common problems of the later years.

"My husband's father lives with us. He has many irritating habits and attitudes which trouble my husband more than they do me."

"My husband's mother tried to be in full charge of all of us until her health failed and she became a helpless invalid."

And from a husband, "My father was compelled to live with us after my mother died and he was irritable and childish, making it hard for my wife."

The problems of the later years grow more from the necessity for caring for old folks who find it hard to fit into the homes of their children. Sometimes the son-in-law or daughter-in-law upon whom the care of the older parent falls feels put upon and believes that some of the other children should carry the load. In such cases friction may develop between the brothers-in-law and sisters-in-law.

Chapter XV

RELIGIOUS ATTITUDES AND FAMILY LIFE

MOST PEOPLE, by the time they reach a marriageable age, have a pattern either of religious orientation or of nonreligious orientation. This orientation is a rather fundamental part of their personality structure. It is not easily changed. Couples approaching marriage need to consider whether they are together in their religious attitudes. Their agreement or disagreement and the extent of their religious or nonreligious orientation will affect the happiness and success of their marriage.

Religious affiliation and marital success

Research studies show that in general the presence of a religious faith is associated with more favorable chances for marital success. Burgess and Cottrell found more favorable adjustment in marriage among those who were regular in their religious observances.[1] Our study of 409 couples showed regular church attendance to be associated with happiness in marriage. In reporting on the happy and the unhappy married men among the group in his study, Terman says, "Unfavorable attitudes toward religion characterize more of the unhappy men. Happily married men are a distinct majority among those . . . who be-

[1] E. W. Burgess and L. S. Cottrell, *Predicting Success or Failure in Marriage,* p. 123. New York: Prentice-Hall, Inc., 1939.

lieve it essential that children have religious instruction."[2]

Terman also found that too strict religious training was almost as bad as none at all.

Studies covering approximately 25,000 marriages showed that there were three times as many marital failures among those with no religious affiliation as among those within given religions. In marriages between persons of different religions, religion is frequently a disruptive factor, yet the failure rate of marriages of mixed religions is generally lower than that among marriages where there is no religion.[2a]

In comparing divorced and happily married couples, Locke found a larger percentage of the happily married couples had had a church wedding, were church members, and were active in Sunday school and church attendance, both before and during marriage. He suggests that being a church member is not only a mark of a conventional person but also of a sociable person, and both characteristics are associated with good marital adjustment.[3]

Religion a part of American life

The United States is called a Christian nation. The implication is, in some sense, that our affairs are conducted according to the principles of Christ's teachings. Whether our national behavior could accurately be called Christian is open to debate; nevertheless it is true that the observances of religion are an integral part of American life. Of the population in the United States as a whole, approximately half of those ten years old and over are members of churches. Religion has an impact upon all our social institutions. Religious concepts make some contribution to the life-philosophy and codes of Americans in all levels of society, whether the individuals are religious or irreligious.

[2] Lewis Terman, *Psychological Factors in Marital Happiness*, p. 164. New York: McGraw-Hill Book Company, Inc., 1939.

[2a] See Figure 29 on p. 154.

[3] Harvey J. Locke, *Predicting Adjustment in Marriage*, pp. 239-241. New York: Henry Holt and Company, 1951.

A family bond

Most churches emphasize the value of religious participation by family groups. In modern life the forces which separate the members of the family and direct their interests into widely divergent channels are more numerous than are the opportunities for participation in any activity as a family unit. Hence it is of value to children to participate with their parents in

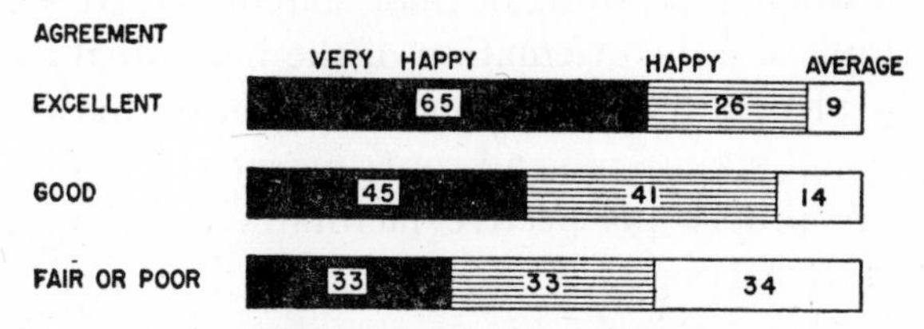

Fig. 61. Agreement on religious expression and happiness in marriage. Agreement on religion was closely associated with happiness in marriage among 544 couples who were in the early years of marriage.

religious worship and in the activities of a church; it aids in building family solidarity. A family religion adds to children's feeling of identification with their parents and so contributes to their sense of security. Family religion also serves as a valuable link between the family and the community. But good as group religious participation by the family is, that alone is not the major value of religion in family living.

Nature of religion

In order to understand the contribution of religion to marriage and family life, let us consider some aspects of the nature of religion. Philosophers and theologians offer many definitions of religion from which we may choose. William James says, "Religion means the feelings, acts, and experiences of individual men so far as they apprehend themselves to stand in relation to whatever they may consider the Divine." [4] John Dewey: "What-

[4] William James, *The Varieties of Religious Experience,* p. 31. New York: Longmans, Green and Company, 1902.

ever introduces a genuine perspective is religious."[5] William Ernest Hocking: "Religion is the habitual reference of life to divine powers."[6] And John Herman Randall: "Religions differ widely but, like art, religions all do the same things for men. They are all man's quest for the divine and his attempt to order life in its light."[7] Randall says further that, "All religions embrace a code for the guidance of living and a set of ideals toward which human life should be directed."

Summarizing the meaning of these statements, we see that all of them emphasize the orientation of the individual to realities outside his physical existence. Such orientation aids people in developing and maintaining a proper perspective on life and its problems. A proper perspective facilitates the adjustment of individuals in marriage.

Religion and adult needs

Few adults are self-sufficient or entirely secure emotionally. It is inevitable that crises arise in life which shake our confidence in material things, even in the permanence of the social environment about us. Change is constant. Political changes, changes in customs and behavior patterns, changes in our manner of life as a result of technological developments, the changes in our closest associations brought about by the death of friends and loved ones—all these things upset our security and we look for something of permanent and unchanging validity to hold to. For many people a religious faith provides the security that enables them to maintain emotional balance in the face of life's vicissitudes. The security which is sought in religion is not dependent upon externals; it is a security of the spirit, based upon values which, for the individual, have an unchanging validity.

[5] John Dewey, *A Common Faith*, p. 24. New Haven: Yale University Press, 1934.

[6] William Ernest Hocking, *Types of Philosophy*, p. 26. New York: Charles Scribner's Sons, 1929.

[7] John Herman Randall, *Preface to Philosophy*, Part IV, "The Meaning of Religion." New York: The Macmillan Company, 1946.

Some people consider religion simply an "escape." Nevertheless it tends to be a sane and constructive escape from the confusion and pressures of modern life.

It is true that many unhappy, poorly adjusted, and intolerant people are fanatically religious. But fanaticism is an attempt to escape from realistic acceptance of the responsibility for living and adjusting among others, and is not comparable to a workable religious faith.

There is a difference between a religious faith that is a commitment of the individual to a way of life, and the verbal acceptance of certain dogma. The person with a positive religious faith is more likely to be a well-integrated personality and hence a better risk as a marriage partner.

Religious philosophy and family living

Certain essentials of a religious philosophy are especially relevant to marriage and family living.

Central in Judeo-Christian teachings is the individual; the emphasis is upon respect for the essential rights of each personality. The religious person will not go into marriage with thought only for his personal needs and satisfactions. A religious faith impels one toward unselfishness and sympathy for the needs of others.

Those who are religious will be slow to judge and censure. They will maintain high standards of conduct for themselves but will be tolerant of the beliefs and behavior of others. Tolerance is not always evident in those who would be classified as religious on the basis of affiliation with a church or with religious activities, but we are considering the attributes of religion as it can affect the lives of individuals in a dynamic way. Many people cling to the outward forms of religion but have not accepted any basic philosophy valid for living. It is just as possible to find a great many people whose religion is an effective aid to their successful life adjustment. These are not intolerant. Whatever their church or creed, they contribute greatly to the happiness and well-being of others in their world.

They respect the views and beliefs of others even though they cannot accept them.

The person with effective religious beliefs will not be a blind adherent to a certain creed or set of dogma, but will be capable of growth under the impact of experiences. This capacity, which we might call the absence of a closed mind, may be seen in the answer given by a religious father to a questioning son. The son, home from school for a vacation, stated that his education was providing him with many enlightening facts

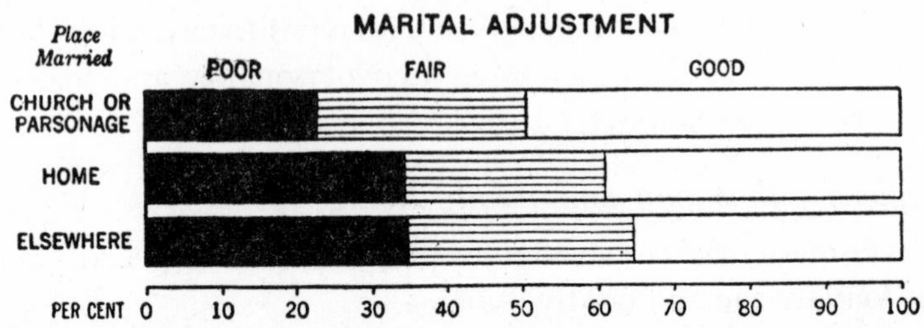

Fig. 62. Relationship of place in which married to marital adjustment. People who were married in a church had happier marriages than those who were not. It does not necessarily follow that if all people were married in churches marriages in general would be happier. People who choose to have church weddings may also have other factors in their backgrounds which make them better "bets" in marriage. E. W. Burgess and L. S. Cottrell, *Predicting Success or Failure in Marriage,* p. 126. New York: Prentice-Hall, Inc., 1939.

which were making him more and more skeptical concerning the values he had been taught as a child. His father answered, "You are right to re-examine your set of values. Our philosophy of life is adequate for living only if it is based on truth. We need never be afraid to seek truth; we need only be careful not to stop short of finding it."

The person who has a faith that "works" in his own life makes a good marriage partner. He will not be ready to do battle over nonessentials, but will rather strive to understand the viewpoint of the other person. He will show a willingness to compromise for harmony. He will respect the personality of the partner, refraining from ridicule or the belittling attitudes that are so devastating to the happiness of a wife or husband. He will build up the self-respect and self-confidence of his partner rather than destroy it. His own inner security will be a source of strength to those about him in the times of crisis that come to every family. He will be able to maintain a perspective on life and its values so that when trouble comes he will not go to pieces but will be able to withstand pressure.

Self-discipline

Another characteristic of religion that gives it relevance to family life is that it demands self-discipline. Religious people do many things because they believe they ought to; they refrain from other things because they believe they ought not to do them. They also act or refrain from acting in certain ways solely out of consideration for the feelings and attitudes of others. The attitude that says, "If the taking of meat offendeth my brother, I will take no meat," [8] is one that will make for peace and harmony in the daily contacts in life.

Self-discipline is a valuable asset for those who would work out happy relationships in marriage. No matter how interesting an unpredictable and undependable person may be as a temporary companion, that type of person is usually difficult to live with as a permanent partner in all the affairs of life. Innumerable occasions arise in family living when the course of life and love is smoother and happier for all if each member can be depended upon to behave as a disciplined individual—to follow the course of action that is for the best interests of all even when it requires a sacrifice of personal preference.

Religion and happiness

Elsewhere we have stated that some people who are unhappy in their marriages would not be happy in any event, married or single. In order to be able to give happiness to others, it is necessary to have the elements of a happy existence within oneself. Religion should contribute to personal happiness. The religious person has confidence in his own destiny, and he believes in the

[8] Corinthians I, 8:13.

permanence of certain universal principles. He is not blindly optimistic, irrationally refusing to recognize the ills that exist in his personal life and in the society about him; but he is realistic in his realization that goodness, beauty, and truth are as inherently a part of nature as are cruelty, sordidness, and ruthlessness.[9] Especially in his attitudes toward others is his lack of pessimism evident. He will give others the benefit of the doubt, assuming that their motives and intentions are as generous as his own. This attitude contributes to his own happiness because he is not tormented by suspicions and distrustful doubts concerning his associates; it also contributes to the happiness of others by helping them to feel valued as individuals.

Religion and parenthood

The person who has the inner security which results from a religious faith does not find it necessary to strike out at others

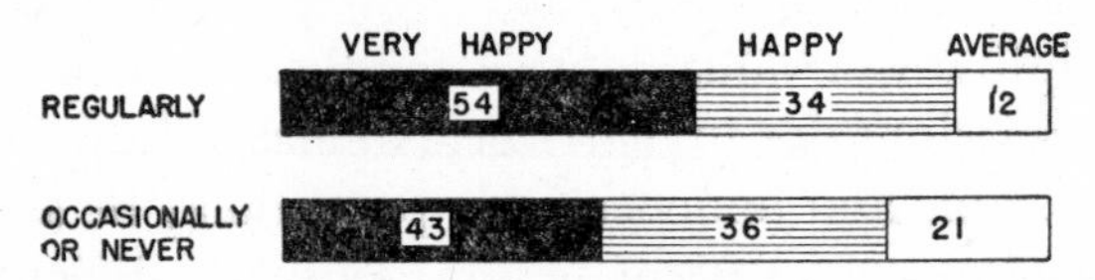

Fig. 63. Church attendance and happiness in marriage. Of 409 couples married successfully for a number of years, those who were regular in their church attendance had higher happiness ratings than those who attended church only occasionally or never.

in the world about him, or to be overly critical, aggressive, or bitter. Consequently, he is far easier to live with. As a parent, he will consider the individuality of each child, not just selfishly as it relates to himself, but in terms of the ultimate possibilities that are within the child. He will seek to understand the child, and to help him develop in his own way toward his highest potentialities. Such a parent will not take the position of demanding instant obedience on the basis of arbitrary parental authority, but will adopt policies designed to help children develop self-control and a positive philosophy of life for them-

[9] Adapted from S. H. Kraines and H. S. Thetford, *Managing Your Mind,* p. 205. New York: The Macmillan Company, 1945.

selves. Ideally, the religious parent will not try to force his beliefs upon his children, but rather will live so effectively that his children will be inclined to give consideration to the values by which he lives.

In summary

The young person contemplating marriage will do well to take stock of his religious attitudes and those of his future mate, remembering that no person is without a religion of some kind. The most irreligious person is nevertheless committed to a set of values. Does this commitment enable him to overcome inner fears and anxieties? Does it direct him toward an understanding of others and a tolerance for the things that matter to them? Does it enable him to face life with equanimity? Or is he seeking security in possessions, in popularity, in dominance over others? Do life's requirements reveal his set of values to be adequate?

Those who desire a good marriage will want to start with every possible advantage in favor of the success of the marriage; the presence of constructive religious attitudes will contribute favorably to chances for success. Religious attitudes are often a key to the general personality pattern of an individual. This explains in part the greater success of marriages between those who have a positive religious belief.

Chapter XVI

FINANCES AND ADJUSTMENT IN MARRIAGE

ALMOST ALL MARRIED COUPLES find it necessary to compromise and adjust in order to arrive at a good understanding on financial matters. Family discord is frequently attributable to a failure to agree on how to spend the money. It will be remembered that the study of the length of time required to adjust in marriage revealed that it had taken the 409 older couples longer to work out problems centering around the spending of the family income than problems in any other area except sex relations. Approximately one couple in five had never satisfactorily agreed on finances, although they had been married an average of 20 years.

Why economic adjustment is difficult

Why should the spending of the money be a problem in marriage? Here it is necessary to look at the values which each partner has brought into the marriage. Our society places emphasis upon money and material possessions, but there is no unanimity concerning what things are worth buying. Since most families do not have enough money for all the things that are desired, they must choose carefully in spending. This necessity for choice is the key to the difficulties which the husband and the wife experience in the early years of marriage. They have come from families in which standards of value differ.

The husband may be from a family where the available money was spent for good clothes, a good car, and frequent entertaining. With this background, his values may center around making a good impression upon neighbors and friends. The wife may come from a family where the chief values were getting an education, saving for the future, or owning a home. During the courtship period the wife may have been charmed and impressed by the husband's free spending to entertain her. They ate at the best places, and she never had to wonder whether there would be a corsage when they were going to a dance. The fact that her family was more conservative in spending money for such things made her enjoy them all the more when provided by her fiancé. However, after marriage this same free spending by the husband may prove to be a source of friction. The wife may be conscious of the limitations of their income and may feel that they should be saving money for a home and for other things that are important according to her set of values. To her the expensive pleasures they enjoyed during the courtship period can now be foregone in order to have money for things she considers of more permanent value. The husband, who has been accustomed to thinking of money as a means of providing pleasure and enjoyment, may not be in sympathy with what he looks upon as a sacrifice of the present for the future. He may find it hard to understand the wife's seeming change of attitude after the marriage, since she appeared to appreciate his free spending during courtship. It would take some time for such a couple to get together on use of the income. Patterns of spending and value systems developed over a period of 20 years will be slow to change. In some marriages the partners will never reach an agreement on the use of money.

During the courtship period a man may be proud of his fiancée because she is always beautifully dressed. He is pleased when his friends admire her appearance. After the wedding he may still wish to be proud of a well-dressed wife but may find that his income is not sufficient to permit his wife to have the kind of clothes she has been accustomed to buying. The wife may feel that clothes are so important that she would gladly cut down on the food bill in order to enlarge the portion of the budget allocated for clothes. However, if the husband happens to be from a family that believed in "setting a good table" he will not take kindly to the idea of saving on food to spend on clothes. The wife will find it hard to understand how he can have "changed" so, for during courtship he seemed so proud of her appearance.

In some families the father takes all responsibility for spending the money, in others the mother; in other families the responsibility is about equally divided between the mother and father. Thus, contrasting family economic systems can be observed. The young man who comes from a family in which the father has taken all responsibility is inclined to feel that he should control the money. The fact that his mother always asked his father for money when she wanted it seemed perfectly normal to him. If this young man should marry a girl from a family where the money had been controlled by the mother or controlled democratically by both parents, there is a good chance that misunderstandings may arise. This wife would feel humiliated if she were forced to ask her husband for money and to account to him for every expenditure. The husband might be unaware of her viewpoint and at a loss to understand why his wife should react emotionally to a seemingly normal financial arrangement. Such a couple faces the problem of harmonizing their ideas concerning the handling of money.

When couples differ greatly on how the money should be used, the feeling of frustrated irritation each may have sometimes affects their behavior in a variety of ways. The husband may become overly critical of the wife's actions in other matters. He may find it easier to be generally critical than to debate with her on the subject of economic values. He may engage in behavior of which she does not approve, such as going out with the "boys" in the evening or drinking "too much." Or he may just become surly, moody, and hard to live with. In many cases he will not have analyzed his own attitudes enough to realize why he behaves as he does.

Growing together on economic values

Young married people often feel that it is a recognition of defeat to admit that they differ widely on economic values. Many couples in the early years of marriage try to keep up the pretense that they are in agreement on everything. In so doing they make no progress toward harmonizing their ideas.

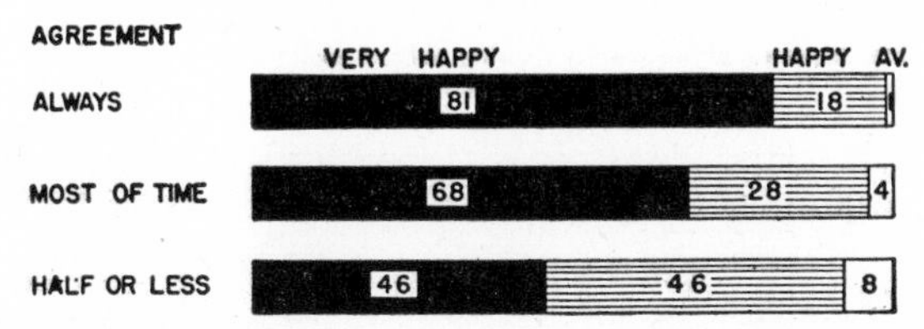

Fig. 64. Agreement on the use of money in early marriage and self-rated happiness in marriage (544 couples).

It is much better for the couple going into marriage to recognize that they will probably differ but to agree that they will discuss differences as they arise in order to arrive at working arrangements as early as possible in marriage. If differences in values are extreme, it will take more time and greater effort on the part of both to reach a compromise. The importance of talking things over in marriage if couples are to avoid emotional explosions cannot be too strongly emphasized. The time to talk things over is when any difference in viewpoint becomes evident *before* the situation reaches the point where either one is ready to do battle. Many men go into marriage with the feeling that women know nothing about finances or that it is a sign of weakness for a man to need his wife's advice on money matters. Most modern women have been brought up to think that their opinions on money are worth while. They feel that they should be consulted when important decisions are to be made in affairs which will affect their lives. Today only a few women are of the old-fashioned type who will gladly allow the man of the family to handle all money and make all decisions. It is more satisfactory for couples to talk matters over and share responsibility for decisions.

Budgeting or financial planning

Since most couples start their marriages on a limited income, they usually have to do some careful planning if the money is to meet all needs. A budget is not primarily a plan to save money; it is a plan to distribute the income in order that the

Degree of self-rated happiness of 409 couples reporting various lengths of time required to make adjustment in spending the family income.

	VERY HAPPY	HAPPY	AVERAGE
SATISFACTORY FROM BEGINNING	54.9%	33.2%	11.9%
1 - 12 MONTHS	46.5%	42.4%	11.1%
1 - 20 YEARS	32.1%	46.2%	21.7%
NEVER SATISFACTORY	24.1%	22.9%	53.0%

Fig. 65. The sooner couples can merge their value systems into one, the greater their chances for happiness in marriage.

family may have the things they consider most essential. The term budget has unfortunate connotations for some people. Many have tried to follow some ideal plan which did not fit their situation. Bigelow[1] states that a budget "is not a classified system of household accounts. It is not a hard-and-fast list of predetermined expenditures, an ironclad arrangement allowing for no variation or flexibility in the use of income. The family budget is a spending plan. It is a tentative estimate of the family's income and the family's expenditures for a realistic list of items. It is a guide to intelligent spending." He goes on to say that the chief thing a budget will do is help the family to get a dollar's worth for each dollar it spends.

[1] Howard F. Bigelow, *Family Finance,* p. 341. Philadelphia: J. B. Lippincott Company. 1936.

Whatever the young couple may call it, they will probably wish to plan their spending so that they will get the most for their money.

Keeping a budget has value in the early years of marriage, for it brings family spending into the open and encourages talking money matters over together. It has been suggested that a young couple work out a financial plan before they marry.[2]

Fig. 66. *By permission,* Joseph Serrano and *Parade Publications.*

This is an excellent plan, for it means that they will discuss their attitudes on the spending of money and discover some of their points of agreement and difference at a time when they can discuss their differences more objectively than might be possible later, after they are married and are faced with baffling financial problems. It should also help them to be more realistic about how they will be able to afford to live after marriage so that there should be less tendency for them to blame each other if they later feel a financial pinch. However, many couples will not be realistic about money before marriage. If they attempt

[2] Howard Becker and Reuben Hill, *Marriage and the Family,* p. 379. Boston: D. C. Heath & Company, 1942.

to discuss the matter and it appears that they differ widely, they will abandon the subject because of a conscious or unconscious wish to believe that they agree on everything. With some couples, one partner may suspect that they are far apart in their views on the use and handling of money but may deliberately avoid discussion of the subject before marriage because of a determination to marry anyway, and a belief that "everything will be all right once we are married."

Budgeting as a source of friction

Family tension is sometimes increased through attempts to follow a budget. A couple may try to follow a theoretically perfect budget plan which may not fit their particular situation. If they cannot make the budget work, it is easy to begin to blame each other for the failure. Conflict may also develop over failure of one spouse or the other to record expenses. Perhaps the husband happens to be the one who believes in keeping a budget, and his method is to keep a record of every cent spent. If his wife is not good at remembering where and for what she spent the money, constant hostility may center around the budget. Such a wife may have no peace because the husband checks up on whether she has recorded her expenditures. A common complaint among young couples is that the spouse will not cooperate in keeping a budget. If following a budget becomes a source of friction, some other financial system should be adopted. Getting more for the family's money through budgeting is good, but if making the budget work can be accomplished only at the cost of peace, it should be abandoned.

Some people who object to keeping records use the system of putting money that is to be used for different purposes in different envelopes. The theory is that when a fund is exhausted the expenditures stop. It is not necessary to point out the complications that may arise with that system also.

The budget should never be thought of as a means for one partner to force the other into line in the spending of money. If this attitude exists, something more fundamental is wrong in the relationships of the couple, and budget-keeping will not correct the difficulty. It will simply serve as a focus for their friction.

If a couple does agree on the method of budgeting which they will follow, neither one should become too concerned if the budget does not balance during a given month. Some couples enjoy managing their money to keep a balanced budget. They record expenses strictly and take pleasure in their success in living within the budget.

Who should hold the purse strings

No set rule can be stated on who should have control of the spending in a family. One husband states, "My wife was a bank bookkeeper before our marriage—she is a grand family treasurer." He had been married for 25 years and was thankful that he had never had to worry about taking care of the family money. In many families it is more practicable for the wife to manage the money because she has better judgment about its use than the husband, or because she has more time to give to the money management. It has been estimated that women do 80 per cent of the spending for the American family. The wife buys the food, clothing, and usually the household furnishings. These constitute the major expenditures for the average family. Since women do most of the spending, there is some logic in the belief that more wives should take over the handling of family finances. One study among young married couples showed that in one-fifth of the couples the wife handled family finances. That system is probably more general among couples who have been married longer.

Many men appreciate having their wives take the responsibility for money management. Couples who have tried this system are usually enthusiastic about it. The wife plans her expenditures carefully when she knows just how much money there is and is responsible for making ends meet. One wife said, "We had constant arguments over money in the early years of our marriage. I was often irritated because my husband would say there wasn't enough money for things I felt we needed. I believed that he just was not in sympathy with what I felt to be 'needs,' and that if he had really wanted the things there would be enough money for them. Finally, we decided to try a different system. He turned over his entire salary to me with the understanding that I would handle it. My problem was to make it stretch to cover our fixed obligations and the other things I wanted too. I no longer felt critical of him for often I found there really wasn't enough money for things I felt were 'needs' and I revised my ideas about where the money should go. I enjoy planning and trying to see how I can make the money stretch. And my husband would never go back to the old system. He says it is wonderful not to have to spend time and thought on managing the money." Of course, such an arrangement is based upon mutual confidence. If the husband spent money carelessly he could upset his wife's financial plans just as she could upset family finances by failure to cooperate if the husband were handling the money.

In many families the responsibility is equally divided. The couple has a joint checking account and both use their judgment in the spending of the money. This system is sometimes hard to carry out smoothly in the early years of marriage. Only after people have lived together for some time and have reached agreement on financial planning and spending will they have enough confidence in each other's judgment so that they can handle the money together easily.

Some men feel they must handle the money in order to preserve their sense of importance and dominance in the family. A young man from a patriarchal type of family may feel that to turn over the money management to his wife would be to abdicate his place as head of the house. Perhaps the least desirable way of handling family finances is for the husband to have complete control. However, in many American families this is still the policy. In some cases it works satisfactorily, for some women prefer that their husbands take this responsibility. Some husbands attempt to use the allowance system as a means of control;

this attempt may indicate that other adjustment failures are present in the marriage. In such marriages the husband may feel that although his wife dominates in many areas of family living he can occasionally have the last word so long as he holds the purse strings. One woman, after 23 years of marriage, said, "I

Fig. 67. *By permission,* Stan Hunt and *The Saturday Evening Post.*

receive a weekly allowance which is sufficient for food only. I receive money for other things only after an argument." This woman's bitter resentment toward her husband extended into other areas of living, but the focal point of their adjustment failures was in their conflicts over family finance.

There are modifications of the three chief plans for managing the family income which have been discussed in this chapter. In some homes the children are given a part in deciding how the income shall be used. This plan is especially desirable in the purchase of items such as a new luxury in the home. However, small children should not be burdened with all the financial decisions faced by the average family. Financial worries are hard enough for adults, and little is to be accomplished by having children feel too much of the burden of financial responsibilities. As children grow older and have more understanding, they should be encouraged to take more part in money management in the home.

The fundamental thing is agreement. If a couple finds that one system does not work satisfactorily for them both, it is well to try another. Success is more probable if people can throw aside preconceived ideas and be adjustable. Money should smooth the path, not serve as a provoker of family battles.

Chapter XVII

GETTING YOUR MONEY'S WORTH

FEW PEOPLE have means that they consider entirely adequate. The family with an income of $3,500 thinks $4,500 would mean luxurious existence, and the family living on $5,000 or $6,000 a year feels the need for $10,000. So it goes. Whatever the actual dollar income, careful management is necessary. A couple can learn much about buying, borrowing, and investing which will help in family financial management.

Buying on a cash basis

Buying all the family needs on a cash basis has some advantages. Buying for cash makes it possible to shop around and buy where quality and prices are most satisfactory. It also encourages taking advantage of seasonal sales, which are often on a cash basis. Perhaps the chief advantage is that the policy of paying cash prevents overbuying. Some young married couples who have started out on the basis of doing much of their buying on credit have learned that it is not difficult to get in so deep that they have a long, hard struggle to get out of debt.

One disadvantage of operating entirely on a cash basis is that no credit ratings are kept on cash customers. If it does become desirable or necessary to use credit, it takes a little longer to establish it. Cash buyers often complain that in many stores they are not treated with the consideration that is accorded to the charge customers.

Charge accounts

The chief advantage of charge accounts is their convenience. It is easy to say "charge and send." Then if articles have been charged and the buyer finds after getting them home that they are not suitable, it is simple and easy to return them and be given credit. With a charge account, the busy housewife can also make use of the shopping service which most large stores provide. She may phone or write a description of the articles she wants and the approximate price she wishes to pay and they will be selected by the shopper and delivered. A third advantage of charge accounts is that a complete record of expenditures comes with the bill at the end of the month. Payment is made in a lump sum and record-keeping is facilitated.

A disadvantage of charge accounts is that sometimes they are too convenient. It becomes too easy to overbuy. One housewife said, "We don't keep any charge accounts because if I have one I buy everything I see that I want as I walk through the store, then we have an awful time paying the bills." That is true in too many cases. If the family finds it impossible to develop sales resistance, it is better not to have any charge accounts.

Of course, all the conveniences offered by the charge account are reflected in the prices paid for goods. The store that charges and delivers and then accepts returned goods courteously after the customer changes her mind has to be paid for these services. Enough general mark-up has to be made to allow for the goods which are sometimes returned after being carelessly handled. The salaries of the "shoppers" who fill mail or phone orders must also come out of prices paid by the customer. Many other costs of service are included in prices paid by both charge and cash customers at the better stores.

One housewife said, "I *use* the services offered by the stores where we have charge accounts. I never take the time to go to the stores where my shopping can just as well be done by phone or mail. I realize that I pay for the service in the price of the goods, but I am willing to pay that much in order to save the time, energy, and carfare it would take for me to go and do the shopping. My sales resistance is not as good as it should be, and when I order by phone or mail, I buy only what are definite needs."

Cash or charge

In making the decision on whether to pay cash or use some charge accounts, the family must consider its own situation. Can they afford to pay for the services offered by a charge account? Do they need these services? If they have no children, or if they have help in the home so that the housewife has plenty of time and energy for shopping, perhaps she will never need to use a shopping service. If they have no help and if they have small children so that she is closely tied to the home, it may be well worth while to use the shopping service. What about the sales resistance of the family? Have they learned to consider before buying, or is it impossible for them to pass up items that make a momentary appeal? The little boy who said, "I saw a honey of a squirt gun. If I still want it next week I am going to buy it," was beginning to develop the sales resistance that is valuable. He had already learned that a good way to make the money stretch is not to buy until we are sure that we really want or need the thing that looks so desirable at the moment. All these things enter into whether the family should buy only for cash or use credit.

Where to buy?

If the buying is to be on a cash basis, the family will find it worth while to consider the stores that do not offer so many services. There is no point in paying for services which one does not intend to use. Various types of chain stores and affiliations of independent stores can offer lower prices because they have the advantages of mass buying and they offer no special services.

Judging goods

When it comes to the actual buying of goods, the family buyer can learn much to her advantage. In buying foods she will do well to read labels carefully and decide for herself which brands and sizes are best to buy. The nationally advertised brands are not necessarily the best buys. It is sometimes confusing to find in the same store several different brands of the same canned vegetable with quite wide variations in price. Many housewives who have been taught that "it pays to buy the best" will automatically choose one of the higher-priced cans. But other factors than quality often have a part in determining price, so that paying higher prices does not insure getting the best. If the shopper is in doubt, it is a good plan for her to buy one of each price level, take them home and open them all to see for herself what the difference is. Housewives who do this often make interesting discoveries. Sometimes the lowest-priced can of food, or the medium-priced one, will prove to be of the best quality. No hard and fast standard of judging can be given in one simple rule. Unfortunately, the grades and standards stamped upon foods are not very enlightening to the buyer. The best thing a housewife can do is to make it a habit to read labels, note weights, observe whether foods are wet-pack or dry-pack, whether sweetened or unsweetened, and then choose as intelligently as possible, always making tests for herself if she is in doubt. She will eventually learn to recognize good buys or poor buys without so much effort.

Many of the same factors apply to the buying of clothing and household materials. A high price does not insure quality. Nor is the cheap item necessarily a bargain. Sometimes it is a total waste of money to buy the cheapest; it would be better to pay more and have a more durable item. But that is not always the case. It is necessary to learn to distinguish the good from the shoddy, rather than to judge the value of an article by its price. The wise buyer will judge for herself and will learn much by experience.

Care of purchased goods

Proper care of clothing and furniture is important as a means of making the money go further. Careful laundering of clothing, dry cleaning when needed, and mending done "in time" will pay well in lengthening the life and adding to the good appearance of clothing. Intelligent care should be taken of various types of woods and materials. Furniture can become increasingly beautiful with proper care, or it can deteriorate until the family is ashamed of it and will want to replace it. Excellent pamphlets are available on the care of furniture and clothing.

When to shop

Grocery stores usually offer the best prices as well as the best selection of articles in their week-end sales. Most of the grocery buying may well be done once a week when advantage can be taken of these better buying opportunities.

Off-season buying pays dividends. Winter clothes can be bought more reasonably during the January sales when merchants are anxious to clear their stocks so they will not have to hold them over. There are some goods that one would not wish to buy in off seasons because of style changes, but a great many things, particularly in children's clothing, can be purchased at these times if foresight is used.

Some goods can be bought *in season* to advantage. This is true of most of the farm products. Family meals may be planned to take advantage of the times when oranges, grapefruit, lettuce, oysters, and other food items are abundant on the market and when the prices are lowest. Canned fruits are often featured in sales during the canning season. If no home canning is done, this season is the time to purchase a supply of canned fruits and vegetables.

Organizations to aid consumers

Some progress has been made in setting up private testing agencies to help consumers. The best known of these are Consumers' Research, Incorporated, in Washington, New Jersey, and Consumers' Union, 17 Union Square W., New York, New York.

The two organizations work similarly. They are independent

of all business organizations, secure their income from sale of books, reports, and reprints, do not accept money or articles to be tested from manufacturers, and buy on the open market the samples to be tested. We quote from CR: "No manufacturer or dealer, as such, makes any contribution, directly or indirectly, to CR's technical or editorial work, or to any of CR's officers or employees, directly or indirectly, nor will any such contribution be accepted if offered. No one pays in money, goods, or services to have any product recommended or any unfavorable comment made, modified, or omitted from the Bulletin of Consumers' Research." [1] CU follows a similar policy.

CU and CR test articles in their laboratories before rating them. They make use also of the findings of noncommercial technical experts in arriving at their conclusions concerning some articles.

Both CU and CR publish monthly and yearly buying guides. These guides give a rating of all types of articles and explain the basis for the rating given each article. Those who are having their first experience in planning family expenditures will learn much from a study of these guides. It is not desirable to follow blindly the recommendations made by these organizations, but their discussions of the various considerations which determine quality are a most helpful contribution to consumer education. One of the chief values of this type of service is that it will stimulate the buyer to study values and to buy intelligently; it will help consumers to develop resistance to advertising which may be highly attractive but not wholly reliable.

Miscellaneous methods for making the money stretch

1. Eat at home as much as possible. It costs more to eat at restaurants.

2. Have a garden in summer. It not only saves money but provides a healthful hobby.

3. Can or preserve by freezing surplus fruits and vegetables in summer months.

[1] *Introduction to Consumers' Research*, p. 7.

4. Take proper care of clothing, household tools, and equipment.

5. Wear suitable clothes for the type of work being done, *i.e.*, washable clothes for gardening or household tasks.

6. Learn to use a screwdriver, hammer, saw, pipe wrench, and paint brush. Cartoonists enjoy depicting the household goods submerged because the man of the house has attempted to fix the plumbing, but people of average intelligence can learn to make a great many of the minor repairs that are required about a home. The saving of money will be worth while, and there is a satisfaction in personal achievement.

7. Learn to do some of the routine work in caring for your car. A few cents' worth of grease, water, and polish, with a little effort, will accomplish what would cost dollars at a garage or filling station.

8. Work at developing the family's own resources in the matter of recreation. A good time need not be gauged by how much it costs.

What about borrowing?

Whatever may be the attitude of the family toward borrowing money, borrowing is sometimes necessary. Unexpected expenses may arise, such as illness or accident, before there has been opportunity to accumulate savings to take care of these things. Some who are accumulating savings toward a home or some other major expenditure prefer to borrow to meet unexpected expenses rather than to dip into accumulated savings. Others will decide to have the new refrigerator, car, or furniture now and will mortgage their future income to do so.

Several sources of credit are open to people who want to borrow. The interest rates that are charged vary greatly from one agency to another. The rates are charged according to the risks involved in the lending. Some agencies specialize in lending money to high-risk classes of people and therefore charge high rates of interest. The problem for the individual consumer is to find the agency that will lend him money at the lowest rate. It is important to shop carefully before buying credit. Because of a lack of information, many people with a good credit rating borrow money from agencies that specialize in lending to people who have a poor credit rating and so pay unnecessarily high interest rates.

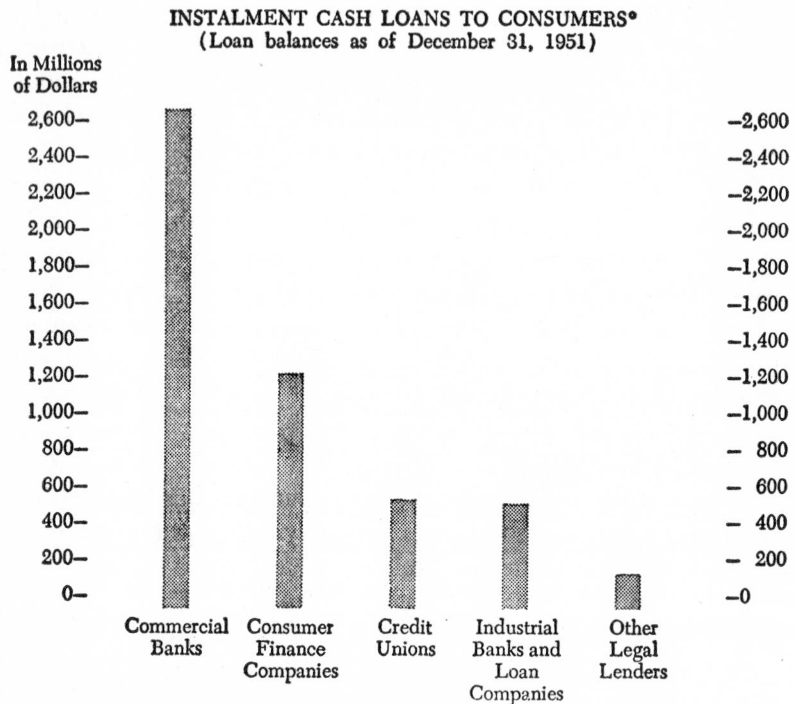

Fig. 68. Wallace P. Mors, "Consumer Credit Facts for You," p. 5. Cleveland: Bureau of Business Research.

Usually it is cheaper to borrow on property rather than on a promise to pay. Tangible evidence of ability to repay is worth more to the lender than the borrower's promise to pay. For this reason agencies that ask the borrower to give collateral can lend money cheaper than those that simply require the borrower's signature. Many people will resist mortgaging the home, car, or furniture to secure a loan, and so will pay unreasonably high rates of interest. Loans that are justifiable and that are not beyond the borrower's ability to repay should be secured as cheaply as possible, even if it does require mortgaging of property. If there is danger that the loan cannot be repaid and that the property might be lost, the borrowing should not be done in the first place. Life insurance policies can also be used as collateral. The insured may borrow from the insurance company or he may deposit his policy with a bank as security for a loan. Figure 68 shows where people borrow money.

Some people are confused about interest rates because they think of all interest rates as being stated on a yearly basis. If the rate of interest is 3 per cent, they assume that means 3 per cent a year. However, it may mean 3 per cent per month. Credit unions may charge 1 per cent per month on the unpaid balance, which is actually 12 per cent per year. The finance company may charge 3 per cent per month on the unpaid balance, which is actually 36 per cent per year. The banks usually charge 6 per cent per year. A young woman who had worked for a finance company for two summers stated in all seriousness that it was cheaper to borrow from the finance company where she worked than at a bank, because the finance company only charged 3½ per cent. When it was explained to her that that was actually 42 per cent per year she was amazed.

Installment buying

A common method used to get goods without having the cash is to buy on the installment plan. The carrying charges one pays for this privilege must be recognized by the buyer as interest. Since the buyer usually is not posting security, except that he does not own the goods until the last payment is made, the carrying charges in terms of interest may be anywhere from 0 to 500 per cent. A great variety of installment plans are offered to the consumer and it is safe to say that few consumers know what interest rates they are paying when they use installment buying. Even those who work in the time payment departments of large stores may have no conception of the rates the customers are paying.

One buyer went to the time payment office of a large mail-order house and stated that he wished to buy a $100.00 radio on time payments. The girl in charge looked on the time payment chart, observed that the carrying charge would be $9.00 with 10 per cent paid down and the remainder paid in 12 equal payments. The total charge would be $100.00 plus $9.00 carrying charge, or a total of $109.00. When the girl was asked what the interest would amount to she said approximately 9 per cent. The buyer expressed doubt and suggested that they figure it together in detail. Their figures showed that if the buyer purchased and paid according to the plan he would be paying not 9 per cent but almost twice that. If the interest had been actually 9 per cent on the *unpaid balance* throughout the transaction, the charge would be not $9.00 but $4.82. The girl protested that something must be wrong with the figures, for she had always been instructed to say that the interest was 9 per cent, and certainly it appeared to be so. However, if a person borrowed $100.00 at a charge of $9.00 and retained the entire amount for one year, he would then be paying interest at 9 per cent. But in a transaction in which more than half of the purchase price would be paid within six months but for which the charge was still $9.00, it will be seen that the interest rate would be almost twice 9 per cent. The following shows the method for figuring interest on such a transaction.

Balance due	*Interest for 1 month at 9%*
$99.00	$0.74
90.75	.68
82.50	.62
74.25	.56
66.00	.50
57.75	.43
49.50	.37
41.25	.31
33.00	.25
24.75	.18
16.50	.12
8.25	.06
Total Interest at 9%	$4.82

Before buying on time, the wise buyer will not only figure the exact rate of interest he will be paying and consider whether he might better "borrow" elsewhere, but he will also read carefully the terms of his contract. What if he cannot make his payments? What does it say about repossession? What about fines for failure to pay? Does the dealer turn the time payment contract over to some other agency? Can a claim be made on goods other than those purchased? Does the purchaser get a rebate on the carrying charge if the total cost is paid before it is due? The buyer should know the answers to these and other questions before he signs a time payment contract.

Families are offered many tempting things through attractive advertising. They may have a fine new kitchen or a beautiful bathroom with 24 months to pay. All they have to do is to decide whether they want the $4.50 per month bathroom, the $10.00 per month kitchen, or the $12.00 to $15.00 per month kitchen or bathroom. What interest rates will they be paying on the total purchase price? Would they be better off to go to a bank and borrow the total price at around 6 per cent or 7 per cent? How are they to find out? Many families who would not mortgage their home to borrow the money at a bank will readily buy on terms that are far more expensive.

Small-loan companies

One of the most highly advertised forms of credit is that offered by small-loan companies. These companies operate under laws enacted to eliminate illegal lenders, but not all states have such laws. The Uniform Small Loan Law was drafted in 1916 by the Russell Sage Foundation after a number of years of research on lending practices. The Foundation has constantly revised its original recommendations in order to keep small-loan laws up to date.

The Uniform Small Loan Law states that those lenders who choose to be licensed under the law may make charges higher than those which are otherwise considered legal, on condition that the lender will submit to rigid regulation and supervision.

The Law permits the charging of 3½ per cent per month on the unpaid balance. Some state laws do not permit an interest rate as high as the Uniform Law permits.

Small-loan companies specialize in lending money to borrowers who have little security. They may require a chattel mortgage and may take wage assignments as security. But usually all they have as security is the borrower's promise to pay. The rates of interest are extremely high because of the risk involved. Too many consumers who could borrow from banks, from their insurance companies, or through credit unions, borrow from small-loan companies at a rate of interest that they cannot afford to pay.

However, the small-loan companies still serve a useful purpose. People without security could not borrow money except through illegal lenders or loan sharks if it were not for the small-loan companies.

A report from Kansas, a state without a small-loan law, shows that one illegal lender had charged rates varying from 192 per cent to 418 per cent per year on his more than 2,000 loans in Topeka.[2] Even in states with small-loan laws, consumers must "shop" among the legal lenders, for a legal rate may still be an exorbitant rate.

Credit unions

Credit unions are permitted by the Federal Credit Union Act to charge interest at the rate of 1 per cent per month on the unpaid balance. Although this rate is higher than the borrower would pay if he could furnish security and borrow at his bank, it is still a much lower rate of interest than he might pay through installment buying or to a small-loan company. Credit unions are formed by groups of interested people who have money to lend, or who wish to borrow relatively small amounts without security.

[2] *Small Loan Laws of the United States,* p. 12. Cleveland: Bureau of Business Research, Western Reserve University, 1952.

Commercial banks

Some commercial banks have set up personal loan departments and, although their interest rates are higher than those charged when the borrower has assets, the rates are usually much lower than would be paid to a small-loan company. Table 21 will tell you at a glance the different rates of interest that are usually charged by different types of lending agencies.

TABLE 21

RATES PER YEAR ON CONSUMERS CREDIT

Financing Agency or Type of Loan	*Common charge*	*Range of charges*
A. Cash Lenders		
Savings Bank Accounts	...	3-6
Building and Loan Ass'n Shares	6	6-12
Insurance Policies	5	3-6
Credit Union	12	6-12
Industrial Banks	15	12-24
Remedial Loan Societies—other loans	18	15-30
pledge loans	24	9-36
Commercial Banks—personal loans	12	8-36
Consumer Finance Companies—under small-loan laws	30	16-42
Pawnshops	36	24-120
Illegal Lenders	260	42-1200
B. Retail Instalment Financing in Five States Having Rate Legislation—12 month contract		
New Cars	12	8-24
Used Cars Under Two Years Old	24	9-31
Used Cars Over Two Years Old	30	9-43
Other Commodities	24	9-34
C. Retail Instalment Financing in States Without Rate Legislation—12 month contract		
New Cars	12	9-120
Used Cars	40	9-275

Chapter XVIII

BUYING LIFE INSURANCE

UNWISE BUYING of insurance often complicates the financial problems of families. The average couple believes that some insurance is necessary, but they find it difficult to know which of the many types would be most suitable to their circumstances. Consequently, many families simply buy insurance from the first salesman who approaches them, and they usually buy whatever type the agent happens to be promoting. It is the purpose of this chapter to present some facts and considerations which may be useful to those who wish to make sure that their insurance dollars serve them well.

Some general considerations

Confusion about life insurance results because people do not have clearly in mind the fact that the chief purpose of life insurance is *protection* and not *investment.*

Some life insurance companies promote the sales of policies which are to be considered by the purchaser as investments along with protection. It will be to the financial advantage of the family of moderate means to disassociate completely their protection needs from their savings or investment program. Protection is simply the provision of an income for the dependents who would be left without support if the breadwinner should die. Insurance which does not include an idea of investment or savings but which does provide the needed protection can be bought cheaply and should be carried by all young husbands and fathers. If it is possible to provide for regular investments at the same time, that may be done also, but it should be done as a separate plan. In our discussions of term insurance and endowment insurance we shall attempt to make clear the reasons why it is to the advantage of the head of the family to have this distinction clearly in mind.

For some reason it is hard for people to look at life insurance as they look at home or car insurance. The average family insures the house for a period of three to five years. If no fire or other disaster occurs, they are thankful, and they do not

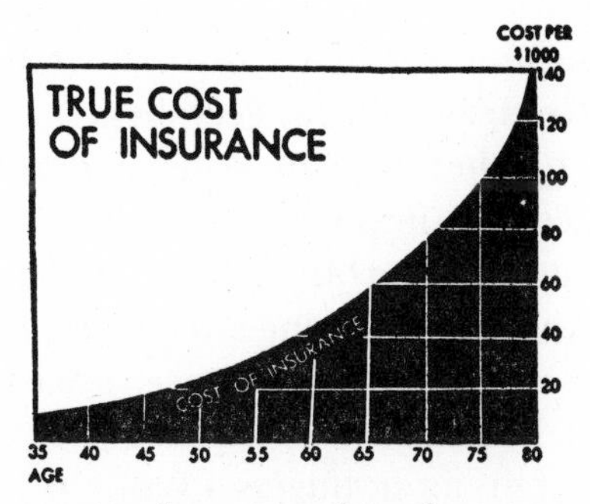

Fig. 69. If insurance premiums were figured on a year to year basis, one would pay a higher premium with each year's increase in age. From Maxwell S. Stewart, *How To Buy Life Insurance,* p. 3. New York: Public Affairs Committee, Inc., 1941.

waste any time on regrets that they had no opportunity to collect on the insurance. They bought protection, which meant that they could leave the house with the confidence that if catastrophe struck they would have the means to secure another home. It is with the same attitude that they insure the car against fire, theft, or collision. They consider the money well spent for *protection* and do not regret that they have had no occasion to collect on the insurance. It is this principle upon which life insurance should be judged.

Classifications of life insurance

Industrial insurance. Life insurance companies issue policies under three classifications: (1) industrial, (2) group, and (3) ordinary.

Industrial policies are sold in small denominations. The average industrial policy was $350 in 1951. Weekly premiums of five, ten, or twenty-five cents are paid to the agent who goes from door to door collecting. This insurance is sometimes referred to as "burial insurance," since the policies are small and are often taken out by low-income groups to cover the cost of burial. Industrial policies should not be confused with insurance plans which cover employees of certain industries. These are forms of group insurance and are distinctly different. The purchaser of industrial insurance gets little protection for his money because of the company's expense in writing small policies and collecting the premiums each week. It costs companies 50 per cent more to collect by this method than through the ordinary method of receiving premium payments.

Weekly premium policyholders are usually given an opportunity to save 10 per cent by mailing the premium directly to the company, but most buyers of this type of policy still prefer to pay the agent each week.

The advantages of industrial insurance are that the policies are small and the premiums can be paid conveniently by people who could not get together the total annual premium at one time. The disadvantages are that the premium rates are high because of the weekly collections, the extra expense of handling many small policies, the high lapse ratio which makes it impossible for the company to write off expenses over a long period, and, since no medical examination is required, the high mortality rates among those insured. It has been estimated that 83 out of every 100 will drop the industrial insurance policy in a period of less than 20 years. In 1951, 12 per cent of all industrial policies in force lapsed or were surrendered; in the depression year of 1932, almost a third of all such policies in force lapsed.[1]

It is unfortunate that low-income families who need to get the most for their money in insurance are forced to buy a type of policy which gives them little protection for the money spent. Although ordinary insurance has been sold in $1,000 policies, people with low incomes may feel they cannot afford the premium for that amount of insurance. Some companies are now issuing ordinary insurance policies in amounts as low as $500, at regular premium rates.

Although industrial insurance is a poor buy, 108,000,000 of the 210,000,000 policies outstanding in 1951 were of this type. This figure represents one-half of all insurance policies but only one-seventh of the face value of insurance policies. The fact that there was such a large number of policies outstanding indicates that many families buying this expensive type of insurance could afford better insurance if they were informed on the subject.

More than a third of all industrial insurance policies are on children under 15 years of age, most of these children under four.[2] The very people who can least afford the security they need have bought insurance that contradicts the soundest principles of life insurance. It should be kept in mind that the chief purpose of insurance is to protect the dependent members of the family in case of misfortune. The Institute of Life Insurance, a national organization of insurance companies, states, "Juvenile insurance should not be considered until the father's life is adequately covered, since obviously his economic value is his family's basic safeguard and should be the primary consideration in setting up his family's life insurance program." [3]

In summary, we can say that a person gets the least insurance protection for his money in buying an industrial insurance

[1] *Life Insurance Fact Book,* p. 40. New York: Institute of Life Insurance, 1952.
[2] *Ibid.,* p. 27.
[3] Marion Stevens Eberly, *Feminine Focus on Life Insurance,* p. 9. New York: Institute of Life Insurance, 1951.

policy. It should never be bought unless it is the only insurance possible for the family.

Group insurance. Group insurance is the term applied to policies which are written to cover a large number of people. It is a relatively new type of insurance but is growing quite rapidly. In 1951, over one-fifth of the face value of insurance was of this type. Usually an institution or industry employing 25 or more people is eligible to have its employees insured under a group plan. Premiums are paid by contributions from the employer, or from both employer and employee.

Group insurance is a good buy for many people. The premiums are low, since the insurance is written on a term basis. Cost of collection is low because: (1) the company pays the premiums in a lump sum, (2) one policy is written to cover the group rather than many, (3) physical examinations are eliminated, and (4) commissions paid for selling the insurance are low.

It might seem that since no physical examination is required the mortality rate would be higher among group policyholders. However, the experience of various companies shows that little difference exists between the mortality rates of group policyholders and ordinary life policyholders, for the reason that many industries and organizations require a physical examination of employees before putting them on the payroll.

Group insurance has the disadvantage that the amount of insurance one can carry is usually limited. The common practice is to permit the insured to carry enough insurance to provide his beneficiaries with about one or two years' income. With group insurance the rate paid by younger employees may be higher than necessary for their age. This disadvantage is usually balanced by the fact that all premiums are fairly low, so that actually the young worker gets cheaper insurance through the group plan than he could buy elsewhere. Older workers profit most through group insurance, since many of them could not buy ordinary insurance, or if they could buy insurance at their ages, the rates would be high.

Group insurance is the cheapest of all forms of private insurance, since it combines the best features of the cheapest ordinary insurance, term insurance, with the advantages of writing insurance by the group method.

Those working in companies which have group insurance should investigate the desirability of availing themselves of the opportunity to take out what insurance they can under the plan.

Ordinary insurance. Ordinary insurance is the most common type of insurance. It is sold by all insurance companies and, in terms of face value of policies, it accounted for two-thirds of all insurance in force in 1951. It is usually sold in amounts of $1,000 or more, although, as we have noted earlier, a few companies now sell policies as small as $500. Premiums are paid monthly, quarterly, semi-annually, or annually, by mail. The phrase "ordinary insurance" is sometimes used to apply only to whole life policies on which premiums are paid annually as long as the policyholder lives. However, the term really covers four basic kinds of policies: (1) term, (2) whole or straight life, (3) limited payment life, and (4) endowment. The term "ordinary insurance" is used to distinguish these policies from industrial or group insurance. We shall discuss briefly these four types of ordinary insurance.

Term insurance. Term insurance is written for a certain specified length of time, one year, five years, or ten years, and the premiums are figured on the probability of the individual's dying during that period. At the end of the period the insurance expires unless renewed. If the insurance is renewed, the premium is slightly higher, since the insured is older and his chances of dying are greater than during the previous period. Term insurance does not combine any saving principle; it is bought for just the reason that car insurance is bought—namely, protection.

Term insurance has several advantages. Next to group insurance the insured gets the most protection for his money, since he is paying solely for protection and he pays only at the rate of his present death risk. This type of insurance makes it possible for the young person with a limited income to provide well for his dependents in case of his death. Those who have debts can carry enough insurance to cover the debts, with a minimum outlay in premiums. The individual who is not certain about his permanent life insurance program may take out a term policy for protection and in the meantime study all policies to determine his life program.

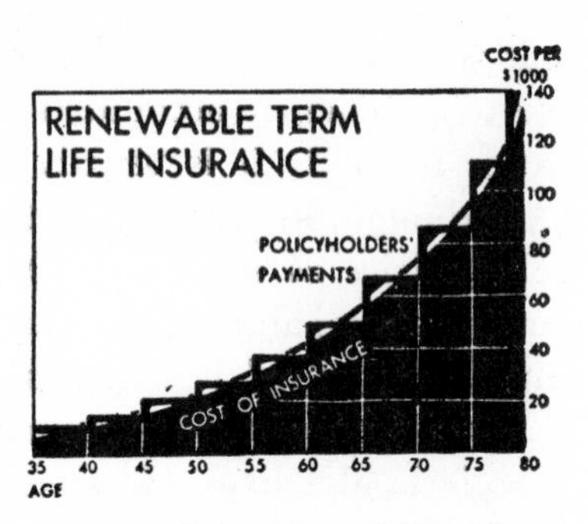

Fig. 70. Premiums on term insurance are figured to cover the chance of death for the present age of the insured. Each renewal calls for higher premiums. Stewart, *op. cit.,* p. 10.

Term policies have the disadvantage of having to be renewed from time to time. As one grows older, the rate becomes higher. This is a disadvantage for those engaged in occupations in which earning power decreases after 50 years of age. Many term policies are non-renewable without a new medical examination; others are non-convertible.

One should give consideration to buying term insurance for immediate protection. During the first 20 years of marriage, when a man may have debts and when his dependency load is greatest, he can buy a maximum amount of protection in the form of term insurance at minimum expense. During that period many married men cannot afford to buy the more expensive insurance policies which combine saving with protection. As the number of dependents decreases and as the man becomes financially able, he can convert his term insurance into some other type of policy if he wishes. If the term insurance is purchased, care must be taken to buy a policy which is renewable without a medical examination and one which is convertible to some other type of insurance. Later in life the family head may wish to convert to an annuity policy to provide funds for old age. When the time comes to convert to another policy, he can either take the new policy at his age when converting or start it at the age at which he took out the term policy. He will pay the premium difference between the cost of a term policy and the new policy. Another good plan is to carry the renewable term policy as long as he has dependents and gradually to drop it as the children leave home. Other investments may be made to finance the old age of the head of the household, or he may purchase annuities.

Whole or straight life policies. Whole life policies are the most common type of ordinary life policies sold. The policyholder pays a fixed sum each year as long as he lives and the insurance company agrees to pay the face value of the policy upon the death of the insured. The policy has been set up to distribute the cost of the protection through the lifetime of the insured, eliminating the necessity for higher and higher premiums as the insured grows older. For a young man the premiums are higher than would be necessary to cover the cost of protection at his age; for an older man they are lower. Although the face value of the policy is not payable until

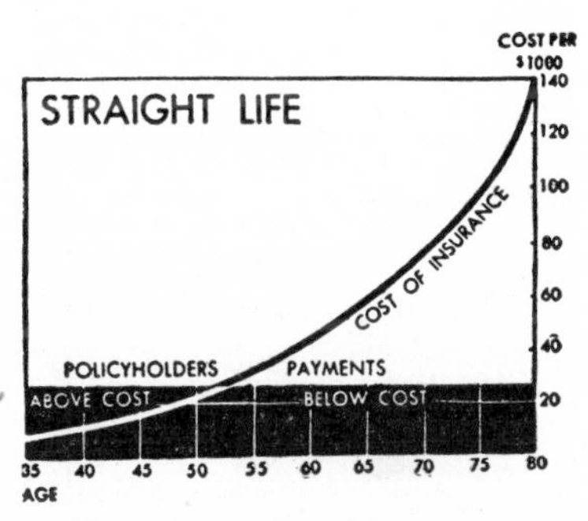

Fig. 71. In straight life policies premium costs are distributed so that a young man pays more than is necessary for protection. As he grows older, however, he will pay less than is necessary for protection. Stewart, *op. cit.*, p. 8.

death, unless the insured lives to be 100, when all whole life policies endow, the insured may at any time withdraw the cash or loan value of the policy. Whole life policies have a cash or loan value chiefly because the younger people in the insured group pay higher premiums than are required by the mortality risk at their age. However, most of the premium is used to pay for protection only.

The chief advantages of this policy are that it distributes the cost over the lifetime of the individual and that it is a permanent plan of insurance for the dependents of the insured. The disadvantage of whole life insurance is that for young people with several dependents it provides less protection for the money. The same amount of money spent on term insurance would provide approximately twice as much protection.

Limited payment policies. All limited payment policies are modifications of the whole life plan. The total cost of the insurance is paid in 10, 20, or 30 years instead of throughout the lifetime of the insured. The advantage is that the insured pays the policy up in a short time and then can forget about it. The great disadvantage of this type of policy is that during the years when the dependency load is greatest the insured is paying large premiums and yet is providing little protection for his dependents during that time. Term or whole life policies would give his family more protection when they need it most.

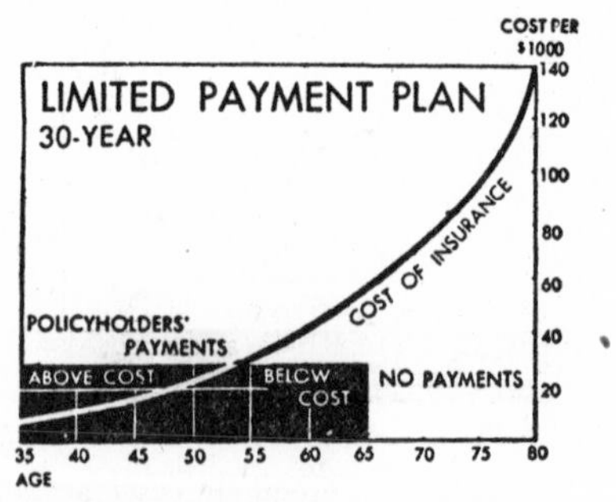

Fig. 72. With limited payment policies premiums are figured so that one pays the total costs of his insurance during his most productive years. Stewart, *op. cit.,* p. 9.

Endowment insurance. Many people buy endowment insurance because they feel that it is one policy in which the insured does not have to die in order to get something out of his insurance. The endowment policy places emphasis upon savings rather than upon protection. Endowment policies are usually sold to run for periods of from 10 to 30 years, with the provision that if the insured dies during the period his beneficiaries will receive the face value of the policy. If the insured outlives the contract, he will be paid the face value. What the company actually does is to take out a decreasing term policy

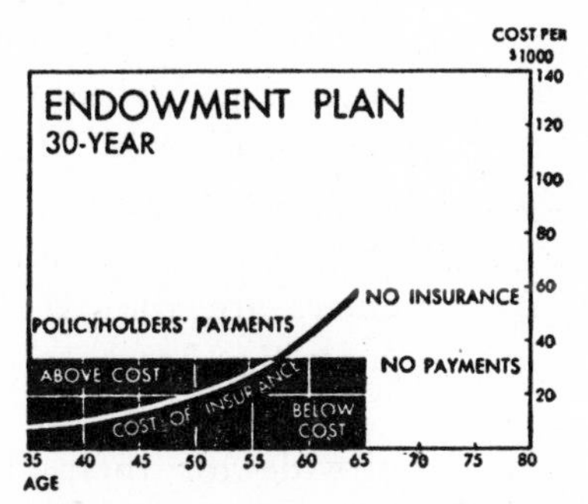

Fig. 73. Endowment insurance calls for high premiums for a limited period. Stewart, *op. cit.*, p. 9.

to cover the life of the insured in case of death. The rest of the money is invested. If the insured does not die, the term policy is canceled, and the insured is paid the face value of the policy.[4]

The person who is thinking of buying endowment insurance and who has confidence in his ability to invest money may wish to consider another plan for his investments. He may wish to take out the term part of the endowment policy but, instead of having the company invest his money, he may wish to do his own investing. If he knows how to invest wisely, his long-time return may be greater than if he had put all his money into the endowment policy.

Most of those who sell insurance feel that the insurance

[4] Some companies write participating endowment policies in which the insured gets the $1,000 face value of the policy plus additional earnings.

company is better qualified to invest money than is the individual. They recognize that insurance is not a profitable investment, but they argue that if people are not forced to save they will not save, and that therefore the compulsive nature of the insurance contract is a benefit. They support their position by pointing out that in the great majority of cases life insurance is the only savings middle- and low-income families have been able to accumulate. There is some validity to their arguments.

However, when reverses come, the masses of low-income people are forced to drop their insurance. We have already noted the lapse rate among industrial policyholders. The lapse rate on ordinary policies in commercial companies was approximately one-third of the new policies written in 1936. In 1951, with economic conditions much different, the lapse rate was very low, only 3.2 per cent. In some years the number of lapsed policies of ordinary insurance exceeds the number matured in the same year.[5] When policies are allowed to lapse, not all money paid in is lost if the policy has been in force for two years or more.

Parents who wish to provide for their children's college education often consider taking out an endowment policy on each child to mature when the child is ready for college. Some insurance companies make a specialty of selling this type of insurance to parents of young children. Authorities on family insurance are agreed that any insurance to provide for the education of a child should be placed upon the one who will be responsible for paying for the education of the child and not upon the child to be educated. If the father should die before the child reaches college age, the mother might find it impossible to keep up the insurance payments on the child, and there would be little guarantee of a college education. The best endowment for the child's education would be some from of good insurance on the father's life together with a program of sys-

[5] David F. Jordan and Edward F. Willett, *Spend Wisely and Grow Rich,* p. 211. New York: Prentice-Hall, Inc., 1945.

tematic saving, so that whether the father lives or dies funds will be provided for the education of the child.

We would emphasize that endowment insurance is largely for the person who wishes to look at insurance as an investment. All other types of insurance will provide more protection for the money. With a $40.00 annual premium, the individual 25 years old can buy approximately $5,000 in protection in 20-year term insurance; $2,000 in whole life insurance; $1,400 in 20-pay life; and $900 in 20-year endowment. It should not be difficult for the man who is interested in protection for his family to decide upon the type of insurance suited to his needs.

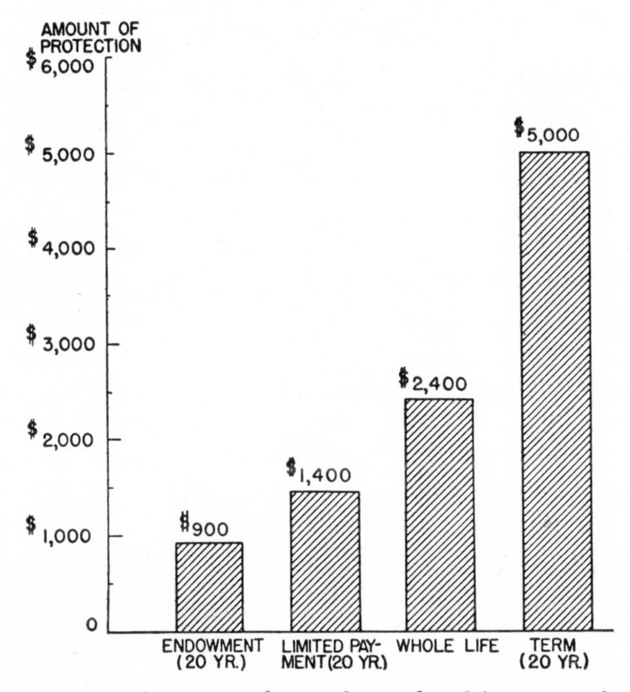

Fig. 74. Amount of protection that can be purchased for an annual premium of $40.00 in different types of ordinary insurance. If one's needs are for a maximum of protection, he should consider the types of policies which emphasize protection.

Costs of insurance

It is almost impossible for the consumer of insurance to compare costs of insurance. The claim is made that competition between companies keeps the cost of insurance about the same in all companies. However, the Temporary National Economic Committee's study of insurance companies showed that the net cost for the same protection varied in different companies from $36.20 to $133.94. Upchurch and Francis[6] found that in two companies the administrative expense was respectively $4.43 and $10.07 per $1,000 of insurance. In the first company 30 per cent of the first year's premium went to pay the first-year commission of the agent selling the insurance, and in the second company 79.2 per cent was used to pay the first-year commission. The cost of insurance varies according to the size and age of the company and its ability to invest funds, to administer the company efficiently, and to keep mortality expenses down through wise selection of insurees. Since the second company mentioned was a new company, it was forced to pay a higher percentage of the first premium in order to secure new business.

The insurance consumer is often dazed when he tries to compare costs. He learns that in a mutual company he will pay a high premium but receive a dividend each year, whereas in a joint-stock company he will pay a low premium and receive no dividend. In the mutual company the insured pays more than necessary and the company simply returns his overpayment in the form of a dividend. The insured should not be misled by dividends; what he really wants to know is the net cost of insurance in different companies. Upchurch and Francis,[7] two economists of the American Institute for Economic Research, have made a careful analysis of the net costs of insurance in many different companies operating in the United States to determine how much costs vary from company to company for

[6] Garland R. Upchurch and Bion H. Francis, *Life Insurance from the Buyer's Point of View,* p. 45. Great Barrington: American Institute for Economic Research, 1949.

[7] *Ibid.,* pp. 66-69.

the same policy. They have taken all factors into consideration in computing the net costs of insurance in the different companies. They state that for the ordinary life policy the 20 year net cost at age 25 for $1,000 protection varies from $105.00 in the least expensive company to $231.64 in the most expensive company. For the 20-payment life policy the 20-year net cost varies from $145.45 in one company to $266.49 in another.

Companies that have a low rate on one policy may not necessarily have the lowest net cost on all their policies.

It is important for the buyer to determine the best buy in the particular policy that he wants.

Buying life insurance

Determining needs. Because of differing needs, it is impossible to lay down universal rules on what insurance each person should buy. In determining his specific needs the individual should take into consideration (1) age, (2) debts, (3) dependents, (4) present earnings, (5) possible future earnings, and, if married, (6) earning ability of his wife.

People in the teens or early twenties without debts or dependents need not be too concerned about taking out insurance. If some temporary protection to cover small debts or funeral expenses is needed, a term policy can be bought for around $8.00 per thousand per year. The future of most young people of this age is still too uncertain to make it advisable for them to take out permanent insurance, especially contracts which feature the saving principle.

As obligations become greater and as dependents increase, serious thought should be given to protecting the dependents and those to whom debts are owed. During the period of early marriage it would seem that the need is for as much protection as can be purchased for a small cost. Term insurance gives the most protection for the smallest yearly premium. If the wife has special training so that it would not be difficult for her to support herself and the children in case of the death of the husband, it may not be necessary to carry as much protection as would be needed in cases where it would be a hardship for the wife to provide for herself and the dependents.

As the man becomes established in his profession, he will wish to consider permanent investments. If he has taken out a ten-year renewable and convertible term insurance policy at age 25, he may, at age 35, wish to convert it to permanent insurance such as a whole life policy. If he can save systematically,

"But what do I get if he lives?"

Fig. 75. *By permission,* Chon Day and *The Saturday Evening Post.*

he may wish to keep his renewable term insurance until he no longer has a high dependency load, then it can be dropped completely since it will have served its purpose. His need then will be for savings or for an annuity for his own support in old age, rather than for protection for his dependents.

Figure 76 shows the consumption unit responsibility of the male family head in the average American family from age 20

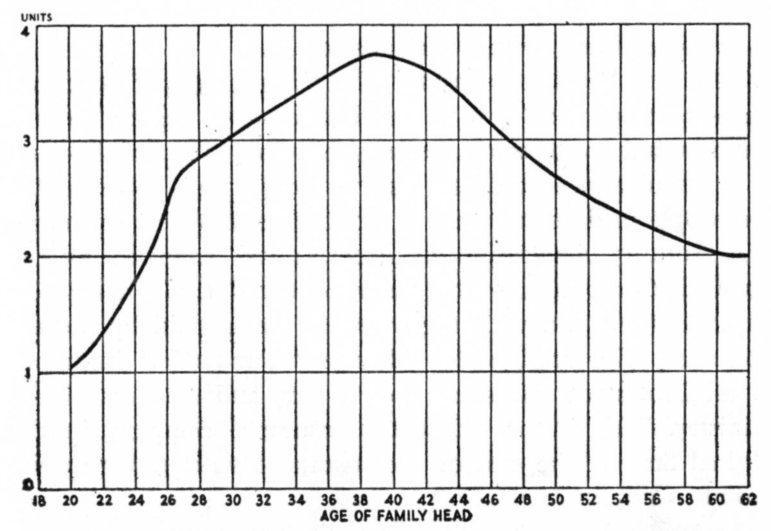

Fig. 76. Consumption units in the average American family according to age of male family head. Insurance purchased should provide maximum protection when the breadwinner has the greatest consumption unit responsibility. From Metropolitan Life Insurance Company, *Statistical Bulletin,* 26:5 (May, 1946), 6.

to age 62. An "adult consumption unit" is the amount spent a year for food, clothing, shelter, medical care, recreation, and other items by an average adult male. At age 20 the average American family head is supporting slightly more than one unit. This responsibility gradually increases until age 39, when a maximum of 3.75 units are being supported. After age 39, the family responsibility gradually decreases as the children take over their own support. In determining insurance needs it is well to plan an insurance program which will take care of the peak family responsibility load in case something should happen to the breadwinner.

Where to buy insurance. After the individual has carefully considered his present needs and future prospects, he is ready to consider where he will buy his insurance. It must be remembered that our discussion is for the masses of people who have limited incomes or who wish to have the most for their money. People with ample funds may spend conspicuously for insurance as for other items, without serious results.

The next step is to consider where the most protection can be bought at lowest cost. If the individual is eligible to take out insurance with some special group, he will probably find it to his advantage to do so. Various group plans are available for people in different lines of work. The Teachers Insurance and Annuity Association of America was endowed by the Carnegie Corporation so that insurance could be sold to teachers without profit and with the overhead being paid by the endowment. The Presbyterian Ministers' Fund offers insurance to all Protestant ministers, their wives, and students of the ministry. This is the oldest life insurance company in the United States. The cost of life insurance written for special groups is usually low.

Savings bank life insurance. To eliminate some of the undesirable features of insurance, especially the high costs of protection, savings bank life insurance has been set up in three states: Massachusetts, New York, and Connecticut. People in those states may purchase life insurance over the counter in savings banks. The immediate situation which brought about the development of savings bank life insurance was a series of scandals involving life insurance companies. Louis D. Brandeis, later Justice of the United States Supreme Court, and other interested citizens, organized and were successful in getting the Massachusetts legislature to pass a bill in 1907 providing for savings bank life insurance. New York passed a similar law in 1938 and Connecticut in 1941. Savings bank insurance is set up especially for low-income people. The growth has been rapid in Massachusetts and New York during recent years.

Savings bank life insurance has many advantages over insurance sold by other insurance companies. Considering the

Graphic Associates for Public Affairs, Committee, Inc.

Fig. 77. From Stewart, *op. cit.*, p. 5.

average length of time a policy stays in force, Massachusetts savings bank insurance costs, on the average, about one-fourth less than ordinary insurance written by the regular companies, and only about one-half as much as industrial insurance. In New York, straight life insurance issued by the savings banks costs approximately 15 per cent less than similar insurance purchased from other companies.[8]

[8] Maxwell S. Stewart, *Buying Your Own Life Insurance,* pp. 13-14. New York: Public Affairs Committee, Inc., 1947.

The Temporary National Economic Committee found that in 1936 the number of industrial policies allowed to lapse amounted to 35 per cent of the new policies written, while the lapse in ordinary insurance amounted to 30 per cent of the new policies. The lapse rate of savings bank life insurance was only 1¼ per cent.[9] The difference in the lapse rate is explained in part by the fact that no high-pressure tactics are used to sell savings bank life insurance. It is purchased by people who have given careful thought to their insurance program and who have purchased the insurance without having to be "sold."

Bills for the establishment of state savings bank insurance plans have been introduced in many states, but only those in Massachusetts, Connecticut, and New York have been passed. Old-line companies and their agents have been strong in their opposition to the extension of savings bank insurance. They feel that savings bank insurance is unfair competition.

The life insurance agent. If a person is not eligible to buy insurance through any group plan, then it is time to seek the agent of a life insurance company. When talking with life insurance agents, it is well to remember several things. In the first place, the agency method of selling insurance has placed emphasis chiefly upon one thing: selling. In the companies with the best standards, agents are carefully selected for their congenial personalities and then are trained to become masters in the art of salesmanship. The agent's success depends upon how much insurance he sells and not upon his objectivity about family finances. Naturally, a successful agent can be expected to push the types of policies that "sell" best.

The American College of Life Underwriters was organized to do something to see that qualified people enter the insurance field. Those who successfully pass the examinations given by this organization are recognized by being designated C.L.U. (Chartered Life Underwriter). In 1951, only 4,000, or 2 per cent of life insurance agents, were C.L.U. men.

[9] *Ibid.*, p. 17.

Some insurance companies have a good training program for agents before they are permitted to sell insurance. Other companies encourage their agents to take in-service courses to qualify them for their work.

An agent may be sincere in recommending a certain policy, but it is up to the buyer to determine for himself what policy will meet his needs. He should not feel that he must buy from the first agent with whom he discusses the matter, any more than he must buy the first house a real estate agent shows or the first car an auto salesman demonstrates. The intelligent buyer will shop for insurance just as he shops for anything else and will recognize that each salesman is going to do his best to sell, for that is how he makes his living. The careful buyer will not buy a policy until he has asked the agent to submit his plan in writing so that it can be studied. Then the buyer will be able to compare the policies of the several companies under consideration and he will also avoid haste in buying. Certainly he should never buy any policy he does not clearly understand. Before buying a policy the buyer should also check up on the standing of the company.

Paying premiums. The buyer will have a choice of paying premiums quarterly, semi-annually, or annually. The privilege of paying quarterly or semi-annually will add to the cost of the policy. On a $10,000 whole life policy the extra charge per year will be from $10.00 to $20.00 more if the buyer pays quarterly.

If one cannot make payments annually, it is much more economical to take out policies for smaller amounts and have them dated so that they come due at different times of the year. There is no extra charge for having more than one identical policy written. Such an arrangement has a further advantage in that if some insurance should have to be dropped, one small unit could be dropped. A few policies written in amounts of $5,000 are cheaper than five $1,000 policies; however, with most policies there is no advantage in buying one large policy rather than several smaller ones.

Conclusion

If there is a limited income it is important that all insurance be placed on the one who supports the family. Usually this is the husband. He could support himself and the children if the wife died, but if he died the wife might find it difficult to manage without his support. It must be kept in mind that we are speaking of the average American family with limited money for insurance; the money must buy the greatest possible amount of protection for dependent members of the family. Families with unlimited means may wish to insure all or none of the family members, since their provisions for security are different.

Chapter XIX

FAMILY PLANNING

FROM THE VIEWPOINT of society, a major function of marriage is reproduction. All societies have found it necessary to regulate the sex behavior of men and women so that offspring will be guaranteed care and protection during the long period of immaturity. There are variations from society to society but whether the recognized type of marriage be monogamy, polygyny, or polyandry, the system attempts to guarantee some measure of family stability for the children. A secondary object of regulation of husband-wife behavior is protection of the personal and material rights of the husband and wife.

Decrease in family size

Although the chief function of the family is to perpetuate the race by producing and nurturing offspring, many present-day married couples, by choice, have no children. This represents an extreme change in attitudes toward marriage. Throughout history, couples who married expected to have children; if no children came, the marriage could be dissolved. Such marriages can still be dissolved in some countries, and in two states in the Union[1] inability to have children is a legal reason for divorce.

It is impossible to know what proportion of sterile marriages are due to biological causes and what proportion are due to

[1] Pennsylvania and Tennessee.

contraception. It is believed that 10 per cent of marriages are sterile from biological causes.

Studies of completed families have shown that for some decades there has been a tendency toward smaller families among those who did have children. Information gained from college students revealed that the grandparent families had an average of five children, the parent families three. However, there are

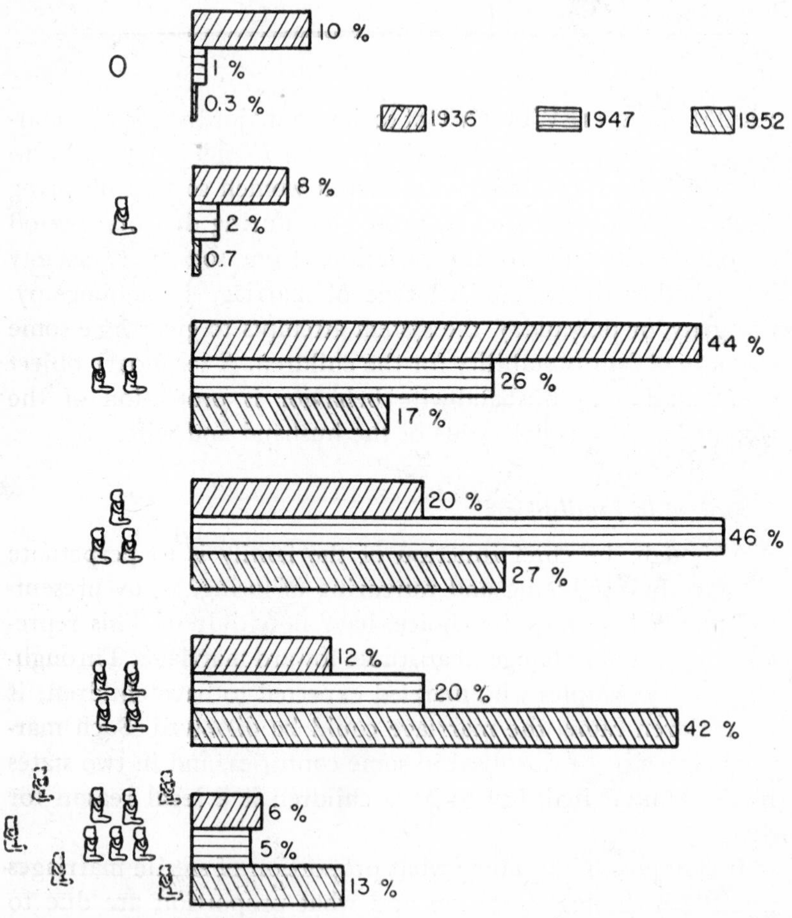

Fig. 78. Size of family considered ideal by young people, 1936, 1947, and 1952. Are family values changing, or is the difference in the number of children desired explained by economic factors?

some indications that this decline in family size will not continue among younger married couples having families. For a number of years we have queried college students concerning the number of children they consider desirable in the ideal family and the number given has gradually increased. Figure 78 compares our most recent study on the number of children desired with a previous study of ours in 1947, and with one by Bell[2] in 1936. It will be noticed that Bell found that over half of the young people thought one or two children constituted the ideal family, whereas of the students queried in 1947 approximately one-fourth named one or two, and only 18 per cent of the students queried in 1952 named this number. The average size of the family considered ideal by the young people in 1936 was 2.3; in 1947, 3.0; in 1952, 4.0. It is possible that the contrast in economic conditions between the depression 'thirties and the prosperity of recent years has caused young people to think differently about the desirable number of children. War and threat of war may also have brought about a shifting of values so that children began to seem more essential to happiness.

Although young people in 1952 stated they wanted large families, each couple will not necessarily have four children when they face the realities of parenthood. In our study of 212 couples who had had their first child, we asked whether they planned to have the same number, more, or fewer children than they had originally hoped to have. About one in five wanted fewer.

The birth rate

The birth rate in the United States decreased steadily for many years, but started increasing after the worst depression years of the 'thirties. It has continued to be high since that time. (See Figure 79.) Whether this is a permanent trend or a temporary increase resulting from prosperity, threat of war, and the increased marriage rate, cannot be stated positively. Some years

[2] Howard M. Bell, *Youth Tell Their Story*. Washington, D.C.: American Council on Education, 1938, 36-38.

ago, advertisements and other pictures featuring family life showed the mother and father and two children, a boy and a girl. Today, however, the typical family is pictured as having three or more children. Publicity has been given to movie stars and other public figures who have large families, and "Cheaper by the Dozen" has become a popular phrase.

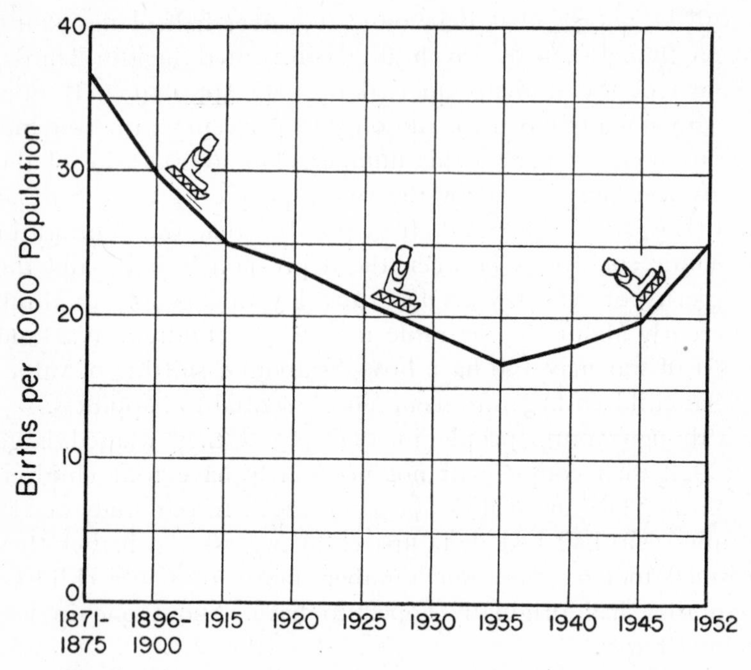

Fig. 79. The crude birth rate in the United States, 1871 to 1952.

Birth rates vary in relation to certain socio-economic factors. In urban areas the birth rate is far lower proportionately than in rural areas. Children remain more of an asset among rural than among urban dwellers. Birth rates are proportionately higher among lower-income groups than among high-income groups in both city and country.

College-educated people have fewer than their proportionate

share of children. However, educated people who live in rural areas have more children than people of equal education living in cities. There is some evidence to indicate that people with more education have been having a larger proportion of the babies in recent years. (See Figure 80.)

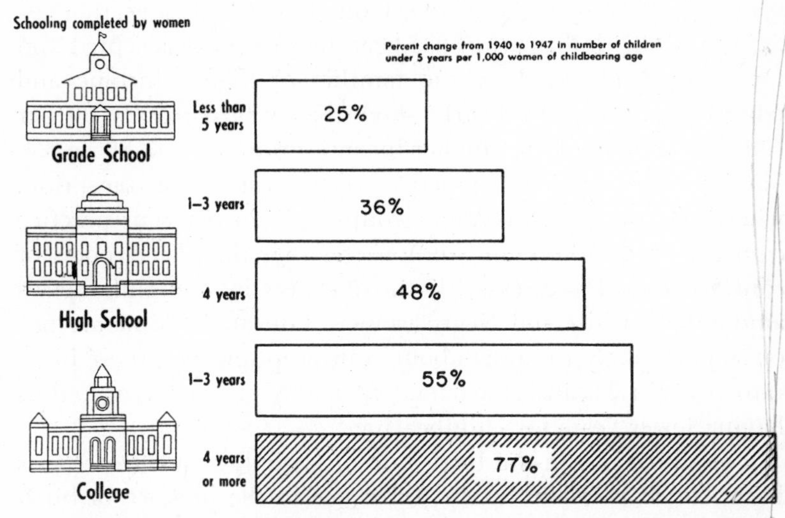

Fig. 80. Increase in the birth rate by years of education, United States, 1940-1947. Although those with less education still have a disproportionate share of the children, the birth rate increased most during the 40's among those with more years of education. Much of this increase was due to a higher marriage rate among the better educated. *A Chart Book, Children and Youth at the Midcentury.* Washington, D.C.: Midcentury Conference on Children and Youth, 1950.

Broad religious classifications differ in number of children born. Studies show that Catholics are most fertile, Protestants next, and Jews least. Mixed marriages of Catholics and Protestants have fewer children than Protestant or Catholic marriages. But within all three religious groups, as in the population in general, those with higher incomes and more education, and those in urban areas, have proportionately fewer children than do the others of their faith.

Contraception

One factor which must be taken into consideration in explaining the difference in the birth rate of different socio-economic groups is the belief in, and the successful use of, contraception. Contraceptive information has been disseminated quite rapidly throughout the United States during the last 30 years. This information has been more readily accepted and more effectively used by the families of higher income and education. Studies by Pearl [3] show that approximately 80 per cent of women of the higher-income groups, aged 20 to 24, having their first baby, practice some form of contraception, whereas of the lowest-income groups only 25 per cent practice contraception. The same study shows that the effectiveness of contraception increases with the increase in economic status among both white and Negro women. Educated people are not only more likely to know about contraception, but their birth rate is lower because they tend to marry at a later age, thus having fewer years for childbearing.

The difference in the birth rate of Catholics and Protestants is explained partially by the difference in the practice of birth control. Although the Catholic clergy had opposed birth control, no official pronouncement was made by the Pope on the subject until 1930. In that year Pope Pius XI made an official pronouncement in which he stated that birth control was "unnatural and intrinsically evil and therefore not to be justified for any reason however grave." The Catholic church does recognize the right to limit the size of the family under certain circumstances by limiting intercourse to the so-called "safe period." However, in 1951 Pope Pius XII warned Catholics against the abuse of this practice.

Catholic couples who follow the teachings of their church on birth control are under pressure to have children and to have

[3] Raymond S. Pearl, *The Natural History of Population,* pp. 234-244. New York: Oxford University Press, 1939. (Data summarizing interviews with 30,000 women during the years 1931 and 1932, after their confinement in urban hospitals.)

them early in marriage. The young couple who find that they are sterile or relatively sterile often feel public disapproval because they know that their Catholic friends will believe that they are practicing contraception. Members of most other faiths do not experience such censorship, whether or not it is justified.

Although Protestants have not taken a united stand on the question of birth control, the Federal Council of Churches of Christ in America, through its Commission on Marriage and the Home, has gone on record as favoring birth control. The Federal Council represents 25 of the largest Protestant denominations. The Council's report expresses recognition of a two-fold function of sex as divinely instituted. We quote from their statement:

> A majority of the committee holds that the careful and restrained use of contraceptives by married people is valid and moral. They take this position because they believe that it is important to provide for the proper spacing of children, the control of the size of the family, and the protection of mothers and children; and because intercourse between the mates, when an expression of their spiritual union and affection, is right in itself. They are of the opinion that abstinence within marriage, except for the few, cannot be relied upon to meet these problems, and under ordinary circumstances is not desirable in itself.[4]

In taking this position, the Council recognizes the dangers involved in a more widespread acceptance of contraception. However, it goes on to state:

> Society faces a new problem of control with each fresh advance of knowledge. If men generally cannot properly use the knowledge they acquire, there is no safety and no guarantee of the future. These members of the committee believe that the undesirable use of contraceptives will not be indulged in by most people, and that if the influence of religion and education is properly developed the progress of knowledge will not outrun the capacity of mankind for

[4] *Moral Aspects of Birth Control,* p. 5. New York: Federal Council of the Churches of Christ in America, Committee on Marriage and the Home, 1938.

self-control. But if the sex impulse and the use of contraceptives are to be kept under moral control, the church and society, including parents, must give greater attention to the education and character building of youth and to the continued education of adult opinion.[5]

Orthodox Jews have not made any official pronouncement on the subject of birth control in modern times. However, the Jewish Orthodox point of view is opposed to birth control. The Talmud states that where the health of the woman is involved it may be practiced within certain specified limitations.[6]

Reformed Jews have taken a favorable attitude toward birth control through the Central Conference of American Rabbis. In 1929, the Central Conference wrote into its social justice program its recognition of "intelligent birth regulation as one of the methods of coping with social problems." Such social problems are those which arise when parents do not have the health, economic resources, or intelligence to guarantee their children a worthy heritage.[7]

The Rabbinical Assembly of America, the Conservative Jewish group, passed a resolution on birth control in 1934:

As rabbis we are deeply concerned with the preservation and extension of the human values inherent in the institution of the monogamous family. Careful study and observation have convinced us that birth control is a valuable method for overcoming some of the obstacles that prevent the proper functioning of the family under present conditions.

Jewish tradition explicitly recognizes the desirability of the use of contraceptives when health of the mother or the children is involved. It is obvious that there is an intimate connection between the economic status of the family and the physical and psychic health of the members. We therefore regard it as legitimate and completely within consonance with the spirit of Jewish tradition to

[5] *Ibid.*, p. 6.

[6] Personal letter from Uri Miller, President, Rabbinical Council of America, December 11, 1947.

[7] Mary A. Cannon, *Outline for a Course in Planned Parenthood.* New York: Planned Parenthood Federation of America, p. 20.

permit the use of contraceptives on economic grounds, as well as where the earning capacity of the family makes the postponement of child-bearing wise and necessary.

Hence we urge the passage of legislation by the Congress of the United States and the State Legislatures to permit the dissemination of contraceptive information by responsible medical agencies. We maintain that proper education in contraception and birth control will not destroy but rather enhance the spiritual values inherent in the family and will make for the advancement of human happiness and welfare.[8]

Although the Catholic church and certain Protestant denominations oppose the use of contraceptives, not all members of these religious groups abide by the teachings of the churches. This situation is evident when we observe the differential birth rate between Catholics with higher incomes and more education and those with lower incomes and less education. Studies of the religious affiliation of clients of birth control clinics reveal that all faiths are well represented.

Legality of contraception

With the change in public opinion on the question of birth-control, there has followed a change in the laws pertaining to the giving of contraceptive information. There has also been a gradual lessening of efforts to enforce existing laws. The Comstock Act, passed in 1873 to prohibit the sending of information on contraception through the mails, was virtually nullified by a decision of the United States Circuit Court of Appeals in 1936. Some states have laws to control the giving and printing of contraceptive information. However, the laws in most states are not enforced. Nineteen states make no mention of the prevention of conception in their statutes; 14 states have statutes which restrict the distribution and dissemination of information regarding the prevention of conception, but expressly exempt medical practice; 13 states have statutes aimed

[8] Personal letter from Ira Eisenstein, Chairman, Social Justice Committee, The Rabbinical Assembly of America, December 26, 1947.

at indiscriminate advertising and distribution of information regarding the prevention of conception, but exempt medical practice by implication or construction; in Massachusetts and Connecticut, state courts have interpreted state laws as prohibiting physicians from advising patients on contraception for any reason whatsoever.[9] In Connecticut the law forbids any person to use a contraceptive.

A change in thinking concerning use of contraceptives is reflected in the establishment of birth-control clinics. The United States Public Health Service has adopted the policy of helping to set up family planning clinics as a part of the public health facilities of the states. A number of states have taken advantage of this assistance and have established such clinics.

Present indications are that dissemination of contraceptive information will be more open in the future. Especially will it be made available to the poorer classes, and to those who in the past could not get reliable information. Since these groups are the ones that have had a high birth rate, greater availability of contraceptive information will tend to depress the birth rate in the future.

Contraception and health

Considerable discussion has developed over the effects of contraception upon the health of those using contraceptive devices. Those opposed to the use of contraceptives have maintained that contraceptives are not only physically injurious but also tend to cause sterility. Those in favor of contraceptives have argued that no harmful results follow their use. Clinical evidence shows that unapproved mechanical and chemical methods may lead to physical injury, but that clinically approved methods do not result in physical injury. Clinicians believe that people who conclude that they have been made sterile through the use of contraception were probably sterile before they started using the control devices. Clinics have found that

[9] *The Legal Status of Contraception*. New York: Planned Parenthood Federation of America, Inc., p. 6.

normal, healthy women of the childbearing age will usually conceive soon after they abandon the use of clinically approved contraceptives.

The psychological effects of the use of contraceptives will depend upon the individual couple. If either spouse feels that it is wrong to limit conception, then the mental state will probably make sex adjustment in marriage difficult. On the other hand, if neither spouse has scruples against birth control, contraception probably makes sex adjustment easier in cases where the wife could not enjoy coitus because of fear of pregnancy. If this fear is removed and if no feeling of moral condemnation exists, then sex adjustment should be easier to achieve.

Effectiveness of contraceptives

Although people have been interested in contraception for centuries, serious research is relatively recent. Papyrus rolls of as early as 1850 B.C. contain formulas to induce abortion, and by the fourth century B.C. measures had been found to prevent conception. It was not until 1937 that the American Medical Association accepted contraception as an integral part of medical practice and education. Since that time, more systematic research has been done to find contraceptives which are harmless, effective, and acceptable. The young couple approaching marriage with no scruples against the use of contraceptives still find it difficult to get the best information on contraceptives. Private companies are manufacturing hundreds of different products and all claim that their products are the best. Some of these devices are not only ineffective but harmful. Doctors are subjected to high-pressure salesmanship through advertising and have no accurate way to judge products. A recent nationwide poll of the medical profession by Dr. Alan F. Guttmacher of the Johns Hopkins Medical School showed that three out of four practicing physicians had received no training in medical school about contraceptives. But the practices of medical schools are changing, and now about two-thirds of them give some training on the theory and clinical aspects of fertility control.

There is little objective research today on the effectiveness of different contraceptives. Much of the so-called research is done by the manufacturers of the products. Few carefully controlled experiments have been set up. It is certain that the effectiveness depends upon many factors, such as proved fertility on the part

Fig. 81. *By permission,* Irwin Caplan and *The Saturday Evening Post.*

of the people using the contraceptive, willingness to follow instructions carefully, and a desire on the part of both to control fertility. If one couple in ten is sterile, they would find any contraceptive effective; a larger percentage of couples are relatively sterile, and they would also find little difficulty in controlling conception. Couples who are highly fertile have the greatest difficulty. To be productive, research would have to be done with this group of people. A study of 212 college couples at Michigan State College[10] who had gone through their first pregnancy, and a similar research among 346 couples by Christensen at Purdue University,[11] showed that only slightly over one-third of the pregnancies were definitely planned. In contrast, one producer of contraceptives claims that its product is 99.4 per cent effective, a claim that is unquestionably an exaggeration. Human error in failing to use a product as directed would result in a certain percentage of failures even if the contraceptive were theoretically perfect. Failure would not usually be so great as among the college couples in the two studies cited above, for they were using assorted contraceptives and were, in general, fertile couples. At least they all had had children.

Couples approaching marriage who have good reasons to postpone their first pregnancy and who wish to plan their families should seek reliable information. The best source of information is the Planned Parenthood Federation of America, which has offices in most large cities. These clinics can be helpful to married couples, whether the problem is the postponement of pregnancy or the inability of sterile or relatively sterile couples to have children.

Abortion as a form of birth control

Abortion is a common form of controlling births in the United States. Abortion is not contraception, since contraception prevents the uniting of the sperm with the egg; abortion destroys the fertilized egg sometime before birth. Abortions are of three types: spontaneous, therapeutic, and criminal. Spontaneous abortions, or miscarriages, are produced by various causes and are more or less accidental or unpreventable. It is

[10] Judson T. Landis, Thomas Poffenberger, and Shirley Poffenberger, "The Effects of First Pregnancy Upon the Sexual Adjustment of 212 Couples," *American Sociological Review,* 15:6 (December, 1950), 767.

[11] Harold T. Christensen and Robert E. Philbrick, "Family Size as a Factor in the Marital Adjustment of College Couples," *American Sociological Review,* 17:3 (June, 1952), 309.

now believed that most spontaneous abortions are nature's way of disposing of imperfect embryos which are not developing properly, whether from defective eggs and sperm or from improper implantation in the wall of the uterus. The belief that miscarriage is due to movements or behavior of the mother is now largely discounted.

Therapeutic or legal abortions are cases in which the pregnancy is interrupted by a qualified doctor in order to protect the health or life of the mother.

Criminal or illegal abortions include all others in which the mother, a doctor, or a midwife interrupts pregnancy.

Many abortions are of the third type, but it is impossible to know how frequently they occur, since they are illegal and no records are kept. It has been estimated that a great many illegal abortions are performed on women who are not pregnant. The menstrual cycle is often upset in unmarried girls who are having coitus. When such girls go to an abortionist, naturally he will not give a pregnancy test since his actions are illegal and solely for criminal financial gain. Even if he suspects that the girl is not pregnant, he can go through the motions of performing an abortion and no one knows the difference. Doctor Rock, of the Harvard Medical School, reports that 40 per cent of the women who came to one clinic thinking they were pregnant found that they were mistaken. He states that if the proportion of non-pregnant women visiting abortionists is as high as at that clinic, a high proportion of illegal abortions are performed each year on women who are not pregnant.[12]

Illegal abortions involve extreme danger for the mother. Since reputable doctors will not perform them, they are usually performed by unqualified doctors, quacks, or devious characters who depend upon such illegal business for a living. The operations are performed under conditions regulated by the necessity for secrecy rather than by surgical standards, with the result that the mortality rate is high. One-third of all maternity

[12] John Rock and David Loth, *Voluntary Parenthood,* p. 156. New York: Random House, 1949.

deaths are the result of abortions. Where death does not result, the effect of the illegal abortion is often either permanent impairment of health, or sterility.

Qualified doctors are permitted to perform therapeutic abortions in certain justifiable cases, such as when the life of the mother depends upon terminating the pregnancy or when demonstrated abnormality in the pregnancy indicates that it could not result successfully in any event. State laws usually stipulate that therapeutic abortions cannot be performed except when advised by a consultation of licensed medical practitioners. This provision not only works toward control of illegal abortions but also serves to protect the reputation of the individual doctor who finds it necessary to perform therapeutic abortions at times to save the lives of mothers. In these cases the danger to the mother's life is decreased, because the operation is performed without secrecy, and under conditions which meet the surgical standards of the medical profession.

The argument is sometimes presented that the high abortion death rate indicates the need for more widespread distribution of contraceptive information. Proponents of this viewpoint believe that since some women will go to any extreme to prevent the birth of unwanted babies it would be better to provide them with contraceptive information so that they would not risk their lives through illegal abortions. Russia tried to solve the abortion problem by legalizing abortion operations. For 16 years, between 1920 and 1936, women could have abortions performed by registered physicians at little or no cost. The Russian abortion rate increased rapidly until it was almost equal to the birth rate. In 1936, the Russian government went back to its former position, making abortion illegal. The reason given for the change in attitude was that scientific observation had demonstrated that it was desirable to prohibit abortions since sterility, invalidism, and psychological shock often resulted. It is possible that the desire for soldiers preceding World War II also had something to do with the change in policy. Sweden, a non-militaristic country, adopted a law in

1938 and amended it in 1942 and in 1946 to permit legal abortion, on the recommendation of the Royal Medical Board in Stockholm, upon certain medical and genetic conditions, or in cases of rape, or under certain social and economic conditions.

The abortion problem in the United States is one which needs to be faced realistically. Whatever the legal status of abortion, more general education on the dangers involved is needed.

Infant mortality

In 1915, one-tenth of all babies died during the first year of life. The infant mortality rate has been rapidly reduced since that time. (See Figure 82.) In 1952 only 29 babies out of 1,000 born died during the first year of life. Usually a high birth rate

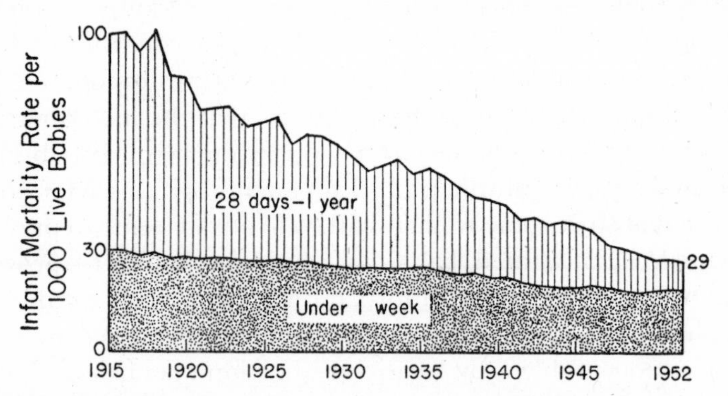

Fig. 82. Decline in the infant mortality rate in the United States, 1915-1952. The first year of life has become much safer. Reducing the mortality rate for the first week of life now presents the greatest challenge.

and a high infant mortality rate go together. To illustrate: in 1949, New Mexico had a crude birth rate of 34.2, compared with 24.0 for the nation, but the infant mortality rate was 65.1 in New Mexico, and 31.3 for the nation. More important than the number of babies born is the chance a baby has of living after it is born.

The infant death rate has fallen for several reasons. The chief reasons are: (1) smaller families, (2) better infant care in the home, (3) more adequate medical care, (4) higher standards of living, (5) advance in medical knowledge, (6) conquest of baby diseases, and (7) better care of premature babies. Studies show that both the infant and maternal death rates increase with the number and frequency of babies born into a home. One reason is that poorer families who lack medical care and proper nutrition are more likely to have many babies, with less time between pregnancies. However, if a mother is in good health and has adequate medical care there is no physical harm in having her children close together.

The distribution of scientific information on baby care to expectant and new mothers is an important advance. In some states every mother is sent an understandable, scientific book on baby care as soon as the birth certificate is registered. The United States Children's Bureau has distributed free books on child care for some years. If a young mother can read, she can get excellent scientific information on how to care for a baby. A further step in progress will be the inclusion in the public-school curriculum of a complete program of education for marriage and parenthood.

During recent years medical care has been taken to many poor people who could not afford such care in the past. This has been accomplished through the provision of free clinics, insurance for low-income families, and free medical care to those on relief.

A higher standard of living has made it possible for families to receive better nutrition, clothing, and housing. Slum-clearance programs and the elimination of undesirable housing have improved living conditions in areas which have had the highest infant mortality rates.

The conquest of certain childhood diseases, such as diphtheria, whooping cough, diarrhea, and measles, has done much to increase the life expectancy of the baby born today. Although the infant mortality rate has already decreased rapidly, it could be much further reduced. It was once thought that a sizable number of infants were defective at birth and that the high death rate during the first year simply weeded out many who were unfit to live. We now know that is not true.

Today over 10,000 babies die before their first birthday. One-third of these are premature babies. With better understanding and care of premature babies, the infant mortality rate can be cut much further. It was once believed by the medical profes-

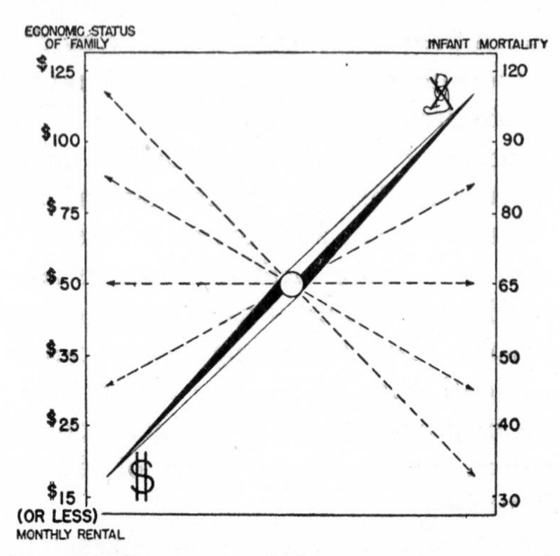

Fig. 83. Infant mortality rates and the economic status of the family as measured by monthly rental paid (Cleveland, Ohio). Adapted from Robert M. Woodbury, "Infant Mortality in the United States," *Annals of the American Academy of Political and Social Science,* Vol. 188, 1936, pp. 94-106. Based on Howard E. Green, *Infant Mortality and Economic Status,* Cleveland Health Council, 1932.

sion that anesthetics given to the mother during labor had little or no effect upon her baby. However, it is now known that anesthetics are dangerous to the life of the newborn baby because they tend to prevent the early attainment of normal blood oxygen saturation after birth.

Premature babies have greatest difficulty in attaining normal blood oxygen saturation. One study showed that of the premature babies dying, half died for this reason. Other research shows that caution should be exercised in the use of analgesic and anesthetic agents which depress the immature respiratory centers of premature infants.[13, 14] The Yale University research on "natural childbirth" shows that one reason for the very low death rate of infants in this program may be due to the minimal amounts of anesthetic agents used with the mothers.[15]

One of the best ways to lower the infant death rate is to make medical care available to the lower-income groups who are not adequately served at the present time. The United States Public Health Department survey of 1935-36 revealed that the death rate among infants of families with incomes of less than $500 was five times as high as the infant death rate in families with incomes of $3,000 or more per year. At that time half the babies born in the United States were born to relief families and families with less than $1,000 income. There are still many families where a baby does not have a chance because of inadequate medical care. These are the same families who lack scientific information on the care and feeding of babies, and who are inadequately housed and fed. All these conditions must be improved if the death rate of infants among the underprivileged is to be lowered to the level of that of the higher-income groups.

Maternal death rate

In 1930, the United States had a maternal death rate higher than that of most other countries in the Western world. Approximately 7 mothers died for each 1,000 live births in 1930, and that maternal death rate had changed very little during the preceding 15 years.

Since 1930, the maternal death rate has decreased rapidly; the death of mothers in childbirth no longer can be considered a

[13] E. S. Taylor, W. C. Scott, and C. D. Govan, "Studies of Blood Oxygen Saturation and Causes of Death in Premature Infants," *American Journal of Obstetrics and Gynecology,* 62:4 (October, 1951), 764-777.

[14] E. Stewart Taylor, Clifton Govan, and William C. Scott, "Oxygen Saturation of the Blood of the Newborn as Affected by Maternal Anesthetic Agents," *American Journal of Obstetrics and Gynecology,* 61:4 (April, 1951), 840-854.

[15] Herbert Thoms and Robert H. Wyatt, "One Thousand Consecutive Deliveries Under a Training for Childbirth Program," *American Journal of Obstetrics and Gynecology,* 61:1 (January, 1951), 205-209.

disgrace to our medical practice. By 1950, the maternal death rate had declined to the place where less than one mother died per 1,000 live births. This death rate is still much higher than is necessary. It has been estimated that one-half of the women who die in childbirth each year could be saved through more complete medical care.[16]

The reduction in the maternal death rate was made possible through several factors. Puerperal septicemia, an infection following childbirth, which in the past was the greatest single cause of maternal deaths, has been greatly reduced through the use of sulfa drugs and penicillin. Other factors contributing

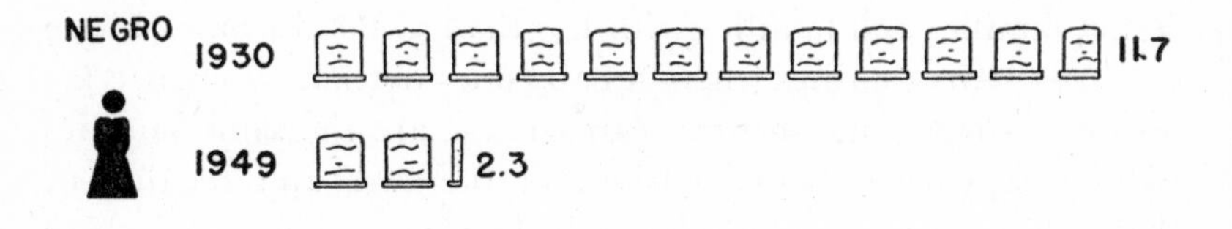

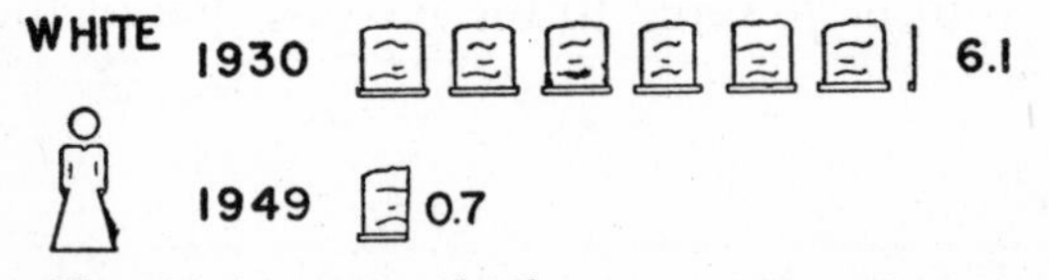

Fig. 84. Maternity death rates, 1930 and 1949, by race, per 1,000 live births. Adapted from *Vital Statistics, Special Reports,* 36:22 (September 10, 1952), 482.

to a lower rate are as follows:[17] standards of obstetrical practice have been raised throughout the country; medical schools have expanded their curriculum, giving special emphasis to obstetrics; hospitals have expanded their facilities for safe care of maternity cases; there has been an expansion of hospital insurance plans; the proportion of hospital deliveries increased from 37 per cent in 1935 to almost 90 per cent in 1952; public

[16] Metropolitan Life Insurance Company, *Statistical Bulletin,* 26:12 (December, 1945), 7.

[17] Metropolitan Life Insurance Company, *Statistical Bulletin,* 28:6 (June, 1947), 6.

health agencies have been greatly expanded; state laws have been passed requiring premarital and prenatal examination for syphilis.

If all these advances in maternal care could be taken to all mothers, childbirth would no longer be a serious cause of death in our country. The difficulty at the present time is that, although childbirth is relatively safe for those with adequate incomes, it is still a hazard for the underprivileged. The maternal death rate varies according to who the mother is and how she is cared for during the prenatal, natal, and postnatal periods.

The death rate of Negro women in childbirth is more than

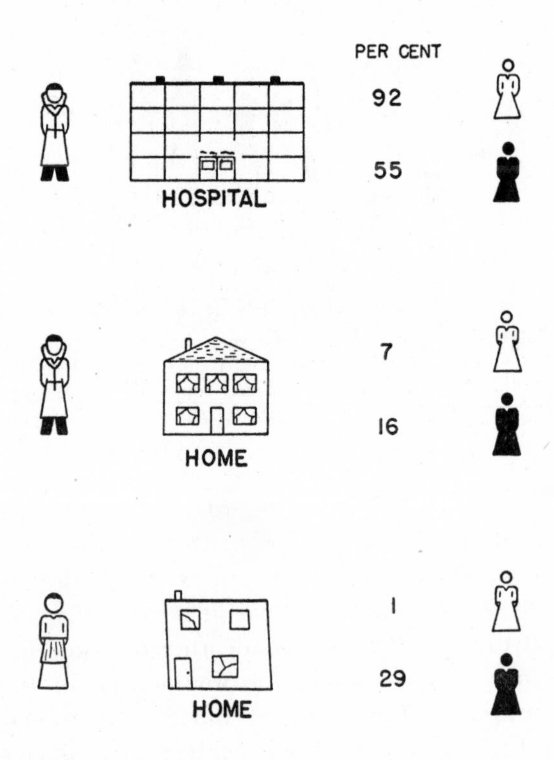

Fig. 85. Percentages of white and non-white mothers attended at birth by a physician in a hospital, a physician at home, and a midwife at home, United States, 1949. Adequate medical care at birth is an important factor in safeguarding the health and life of the mother.

three times as high as it is for white women. Slightly more than two-thirds of non-white women have the services of a physician at birth, whereas almost 99 per cent of white women have the care of a physician. If the family income is low, the maternity death rate is higher. Those who have qualified doctors and whose babies are delivered in approved hospitals have a lower maternal death rate. Many poorer mothers, especially Negro mothers, are attended by midwives when they give birth to their babies. In 1949, 1.4 per cent of the white mothers and 29 per

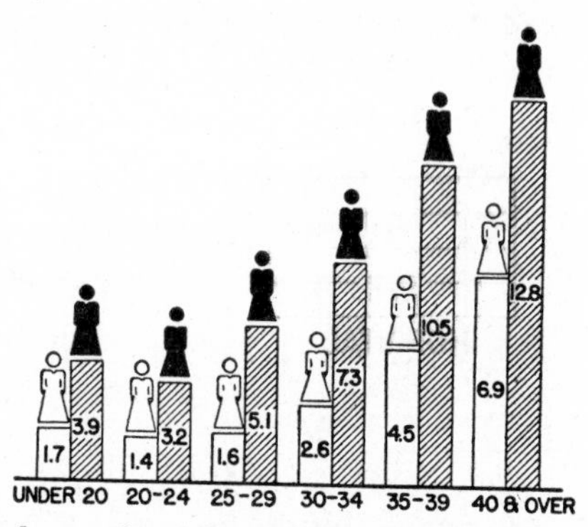

Fig. 86. Maternal mortality by age and race. Age 20-24 is the safest age for women to bear children. At younger or older ages, the maternity death rate increases for both white and Negro mothers. Adapted from Metropolitan Life Insurance Company, *Statistical Bulletin,* 26:12 (December, 1945), 8.

cent of the non-white mothers were attended by midwives.[18]

Maternal deaths vary according to the age of the mother. The most favorable age for giving birth to children is between 20 and 24 years. The maternity death rate increases after those ages, until by the age of 40 and over it is more than four times as high as at the earlier ages. The death rate of mothers under 15 years of age is almost as high as for mothers of 45 years or older.[19] The higher death rate for older mothers may be explained by the greater number of children they have had as

[18] *Vital Statistics Special Report,* July 2, 1951.

[19] Metropolitan Life Insurance Company, *Statistical Bulletin,* 26:12 (December, 1945), 8.

well as by their increasing age. It is difficult to state which is the determining factor in the higher death rate of older mothers. Two studies, one made on 45,514 deliveries at Johns Hopkins Hospital, the other on 250,000 in New York State, arrived at the conclusion that the first birth is more difficult than the second or the third, but equal in difficulty to the fourth. From the fourth to the eighth child, an increasing danger to the mother was revealed. Both studies showed that having a ninth baby was over 300 per cent more dangerous than having the third.[20]

Some eugenic considerations

The question of how many children a couple should have has been discussed pro and con. If parents were to have enough children to replace themselves, each couple producing children would have to bear an average of more than two children, since some will not grow to maturity; some of those that mature will not marry; some who marry will not have children.

The differential birth rate in the United States has alarmed our eugenicists for some years. They have not been alarmed over the decreasing birth rate so much as over the fact that those living in the worst environments are producing a disproportionate share of the future population. They believe that this condition will slowly lead to biological and cultural degeneracy. The eugenicists advocate efforts to cut down the birth rate among the less fit and increase it among the more fit. This is a sound position, but there is confusion about who are the fit. In a society which worships the dollar, the fit are considered to be the ones who have accumulated economic wealth. And yet, ability to accumulate economic goods in a competitive society is not necessarily an indication of fitness for parenthood.

Visher's[21] study of *Who's Who in America,* a listing of individuals who have achieved fame, showed that the children

[20] Alan F. Guttmacher, "Selective Pregnancy," *Human Fertility,* Vol. 6, No. 2 (April, 1941), p. 33.

[21] S. S. Visher, "A Study of the Type of the Place of Birth and of the Occupation of Fathers of Subjects of Sketches in *Who's Who in America,*" *American Journal of Sociology,* Vol. 30, 1925, pp. 551-557.

of clergymen had the best chance to achieve success. Ministers as a group have modest incomes, yet their children, as judged by listings in *Who's Who,* have a very high ratio of achievement when compared with other groups. Listed are 1,400 ministers' children and 600 children of businessmen, for example. Children of other professional groups, such as teachers, lawyers, and doctors, rate second to children of clergymen in achievement. Some years ago, studies by Terman showed that the professional group produced 1,003 per cent of its proportionate quota of gifted children, the public service group produced 137 per cent, the commercial group 128 per cent; but the industrial group produced only 35 per cent of its proportionate quota. Although the professional class seems to be the most qualified, it is producing only three-fourths enough children to reproduce its own numbers.

Positive eugenics

Positive eugenics, the program designed to get the fit to produce more children, has made little headway in the United States. If it were possible to change the life values of the more able people, the birth rate among those who should be having more children might be increased. Marriage education, which emphasizes the importance of successful family life, not only for the happiness of the individual but also as a contribution to the welfare of society, should lead to a wider acceptance of the fact that marriage is not complete without children. Too much emphasis is put upon success in life as gauged by accumulation of economic goods and not enough upon the fact that many of the basic values which contribute to happy life-adjustment stem from successful family life.

Negative eugenics

Negative eugenics, the policy of preventing the unfit from reproducing, has made some progress in the United States. The Supreme Court has declared sterilization laws constitutional and some 30 states have passed such laws. However, little has been done to enforce the laws which provide for the sterilization of idiots, imbeciles, morons, and some types of insane. More than one-third of the 53,538 sterilization operations in the United States have been performed in California.

Birth-control clinics have been established in some areas, with the purpose of allowing regulation of the birth rate among the underprivileged who could not provide for children who might be born.

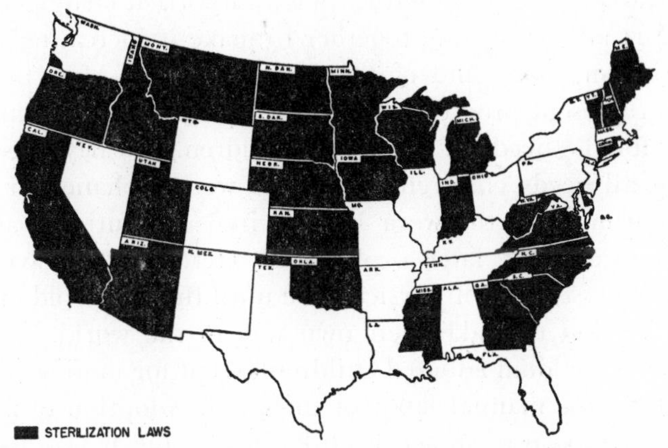

Fig. 87. Twenty-seven states have constitutional sterilization laws.

Euthenics

The realistic view is that the differential birth rate may continue for some time and that not much can be done through sterilization, or through the encouragement of larger families among the better-qualified people. Greater hope would seem to lie in euthenics, working toward a decent environment for all people. The chief differences between the underprivileged and the more privileged are due to cultural advantages and not to biological factors. A social policy would be desirable which would guarantee educational opportunities, adequate medical care, a balanced diet, and adequate housing to all children, regardless of whether their parents are poor, uneducated, or of whatever race. Such provision would aid in correcting disgenic effects of the differential birth rate.

Adoption of children

Many married couples who do not have children born to them, or who have postponed having their children so long that they cannot have more than one or two before the childbearing age is past, wish to adopt children. The number of couples who desire to adopt children is far greater than the number of children available for adoption through authorized channels.

Several factors operate together to make it increasingly difficult for couples to find children for adoption. Most of these factors represent progress in the development of programs providing for the needs of dependent children. In early American history, all needy children, those who were orphaned or those of illegitimate birth, were herded into institutions, at first "alms-houses" and later orphanages. Here they received the minimum essentials of physical care until they were old enough to be released to make their own way in the world. In those days people seldom adopted children except for motives such as a need for the manual labor of the child. Adoption of a child was looked upon as an act of philanthropy and it was assumed that few adopted children would be expected to have the capacity to bring credit to their adoptive parents. In 1909, President Theodore Roosevelt called the first White House Conference to consider the problems of child welfare. Out of that first conference and the three succeeding ones has grown an entirely new understanding of the needs of children, with new programs for providing for them. The Children's Charter which came out of the White House Conference on Child Health and Protection held in 1930 embodies principles which are now setting the standards for the agencies that care for dependent children. Some of the points in the Children's Charter are as follows:

I. For every child, spiritual and moral training to help him stand firm under the pressure of life.

II. For every child, understanding and the guiding of his personality as his most precious right.

III. For every child, a home and that love and security which a home provides; and for that child who must receive foster care, the nearest substitute for his own home.[22]

Progress in the care of dependent children has not been uniform in all states. Many states still lag far behind in their child welfare laws. In all states further progress is needed. Some states still exercise little supervision or regulation of the foster care and adoption of children. However, the principles enunciated in the White House Conferences have had some effect. Child welfare agencies now generally accept the theory that the best place for any child is in his own home, if that is possible. Therefore, more provision is made for aid to mothers. Children are not available to adoptive parents until all possible attempts to help the children's own parents to keep them have failed. When it is not possible for natural parents to keep their children, foster homes are used, under the supervision of social agencies, for as long as there is any hope that the child might eventually be returned to his own parents. When no other arrangement is possible, a child becomes available for adoption.

The application of these principles to the offering of children for adoption has materially decreased the number of children who can be adopted. The wider use of contraceptives and the prevalence of abortion have reduced the number of unwanted children that are born. At the same time, many of the old superstitions and prejudices concerning the inferiority of adopted children have been quite generally discarded. Consequently, with fewer children to adopt, there are many more of the childless couples who would gladly adopt children with no fears concerning the future of the child.

Standards for adoptive parents

However, too much carelessness is still shown in placing children in adoptive homes. Some agencies investigate carefully the

[22] For complete Charter, see Arthur E. Fink, *The Field of Social Work*, pp. 80-81. New York: Henry Holt & Company, Inc., 1942.

financial standing of the adopting parents and their ability to provide for the material needs of the children but make little effort to determine whether the parents are capable of providing the child with the affectional security necessary for his best development. Students of child development place increasingly greater emphasis upon the fundamental importance to the child of love, affection, and the feeling of belonging; they feel that these elements far outweigh the material advantages or disadvantages of a home. But this principle is not always applied in placing children.

Some of the investigators for welfare agencies assume that if a couple are educated, are of the professional class, and have adequate financial means, they are qualified to adopt children. But frequently very unhappy situations arise for both children and parents because couples of this type may be determined to fit the adopted child into a certain mold according to their standards. One of the most essential qualifications of adoptive parents should be their ability to allow the adopted child to be himself and to develop according to his own capacities, free of pressure designed to fit him into some predetermined mold. Many children brought up by their own parents become warped and unhappy adults because of the pressure put upon them by parents who are determined to fulfill their ambitions through the lives of their children. The danger is even greater with adopted children, because the parents may have as one of their primary motives for adoption the desire to see their own specific successes perpetuated in the child.

Agencies should study prospective adoptive parents carefully, with special attention to why they wish to have a child. Is their marriage sterile for reasons beyond their control? Or have they refrained from having children of their own because of selfish or neurotic reasons, only to decide at a late date that they wish to have children by adoption? Have they an "only" child of whose interests they are thinking and may continue to think with more consideration than may be given to the adopted child? How emotionally mature and well balanced are they as individuals? Sometimes the very desperation with which a couple seeks to adopt a child is evidence of a neurotic adjustment to life.

Certainly many adoptive parents are well qualified to be parents, and they do as fine a job with adopted children as they would have done with any children born to them. However, we raise the above points about adoptive parents because too many times the only question asked is about the baby's qualifications. The better qualified placing agencies are more and more concerned about the adoptive parents themselves, for they recognize that babies need protection against being placed with adopted parents whose search for a foster child is an attempt to escape from their own problems and frustrations in life. Adoptive parents, in some ways, need to be supermen and superwomen, for parenthood is always a challenging job and there *are* more difficulties in being a good parent to adopted children. A couple considering adoption should carefully evaluate their own motives for wishing to adopt. Here are several questions that they may well ask themselves before they proceed to adopt a child:

1. *Why* do we wish to adopt a child? Is it because of a genuine love for children or do we look upon a child as a possible source of ego satisfaction for ourselves?
2. Are we thinking of the needs and rights of the child we might adopt or are we looking to him to provide companionship or fulfill other needs for a child we already have?
3. Are we emotionally mature enough so that we will faithfully help a child to grow in his own way toward development of his own abilities, however broad or limited they may be? Or will we seek to make him a reflection of ourselves—projecting onto him our ambitions and interests?
4. Are we capable of carrying through undertakings once begun, or are we likely to make alibis for our mistakes and refuse to accept the responsibility if the child's emotional growth is not satisfactory?
5. Are we capable of making a success of our marriage with or without a child or are we expecting an adopted child to salvage our marriage for us?

6. Do we wish to adopt a child because we are trying to escape from some problem or problems facing us? [23]

People who cannot give satisfactory answers to these questions should not adopt children, for they will be inviting disappointment for themselves and failure for the children. And parents, both adoptive and natural, may well check themselves on these points periodically.

How do adopted children turn out?

In the motives and attitudes of the adoptive parents will be found the answer to much of the successful or unsuccessful adjustment of adopted children to life. People who adopt children through authorized channels, which exercise at least a minimum of care in investigating the physical and mental background and condition of the child before placing it, are taking no more chances on getting an inferior child than they would take if they gave birth to their own children. Few of us check carefully into the hereditary background of our mates before we marry; in almost every combination of parents there is the possibility that undesirable traits will appear in the offspring. With adopted children, parents at least have the protection of a thorough physical and mental examination for the child before it is adopted. They also have in almost all states a required trial period during which the adoption is not final. If valid objections are discovered during the trial period, the child need not be adopted.

Natural parents have no such protection. They must take what nature gives them. Adoptive parents often have the tendency to make alibis when adopted children develop undesirable traits, to blame the trait upon something in the child's hereditary background rather than accepting the responsibility for having made mistakes in handling the child. A case will illustrate this tendency:

[23] For a complete discussion of qualifications for adoptive parents, see Lee M. Brooks and Evelyn C. Brooks, *Adventuring in Adoption,* Ch. III. Chapel Hill: The University of North Carolina Press, 1939.

Mr. and Mrs. A. were professional people in their late thirties in comfortable financial circumstances. They were, in other words, "typical" of those who adopt. They desired a companion for their five-year-old daughter, so they adopted a four-year-old boy. From the beginning the children did not get along well together. Since the parents felt that their daughter needed to learn to play with others, they went ahead with the final adoption.

Whenever the children quarreled, the parents were inclined to see the side of the little girl; having had her from birth, they understood her and made allowances for all her faults. They were careful to apply justice in their dealings with the two children, but the love they felt for the girl was lacking in their attitude toward the boy; consequently, he was often punished for his naughtiness, whereas the little girl could get by without her misdeeds being noticed. When issues between the children had to be decided, it was much easier for the parents to see the viewpoint of the little girl than of the boy, so rulings were seldom in his favor.

The little boy was extremely desirous of affection and often showed an aggressive attitude toward the little girl when the parents were around. He was always punished for this, for he was bigger and stronger than the little girl and the parents feared he would hurt her. They pointed out that the little girl never resorted to such behavior. As time passed, the little boy became accustomed to being always the loser and always in the wrong. He withdrew to himself and avoided playing with his adopted sister or with other children as much as possible. When he did play with other children he was sly in his dealings, taking what he wanted by stealth rather than ever facing an open issue. As he grew older, his adopted parents bewailed the fact that he was untruthful, sly in his dealings, lacking in self-confidence, and lacking in affection for others. At school he was over-aggressive with those younger than he, but was constantly the victim of those his own age, being frequently chased by the other boys.

It was impossible for the parents to see that their own treatment was responsible for the development of the undesirable traits. They had adopted him with thought only for the needs of their daughter, and little thought for the needs of the boy; they had not loved him for himself but had maintained an attitude of comparing him with the other child. Their conception of justice was to judge both children by the same rules, all of which had been made to fit the needs of the other child.

The boy became a very unhappy child and a serious disappointment to the parents. The little girl developed traits of smug self-righteousness. Her assumption that the scales of justice would always be weighted in her favor created later problems for her also.

Legal status of adopted children

Once a child is legally adopted, he is a member of the adopting family just as if he had been born to them. He is entitled to all the rights and subject to all the obligations which would have come with his natural birth into the family. People who would make any reservations in the matter of name or inheritance should not adopt children.

Should a child know that he is adopted?

In the past, it was considered best not to tell a child that he was adopted. This belief was based upon the stigma attached to illegitimacy and the conditions under which adoptions occurred. Adoption was a family skeleton to be kept in the closet.

It is now recognized that the adopted child should be told of his adoption as soon as he is old enough to comprehend what it is about. The truth of the adoption can be treated as matter-of-factly as are the facts of physical birth.

It is now a commonly held view among adoptive parents that the adopted child is a "chosen" child, and many adopted children are told lovely stories about how carefully their parents searched for them and chose them. But like some other good things, this can be carried too far. Some parents, in their zeal to impress the child with the fact that he was wanted and chosen, overdo their emphasis upon the fact of his adoption, and in the end the child may be just as troubled as if they had tried to hide the fact of his adoption from him. In either case, they succeed in impressing the child that he is *different* from other children. To feel that he is different from others is almost always painful for a child. So parents need to be realistic about the matter. They should see that the child knows he is adopted, but should not make a big issue of it. Any questions he asks should be honestly answered, as are his questions about other matters. It is doubtful, however, whether the story of his being chosen should be used as a bedtime story any more often than parents would use the story of his birth as a bedtime story if he had happened to be born to them. More important than how they got him is that they love him now and as he is. It is of the greatest importance that, while an adopted child is still very young, parents build in him a sense of security and a consciousness of their love and respect for him as an individual, because troubled thoughts and doubts are inevitable for adopted children later on when they approach or reach adolescence. Girls especially, as they grow up and become aware of their own potential motherhood, are likely to wonder and think about the mother who gave birth to them. But if a good relationship with the adoptive parents has been built up over the years, the adolescent will adjust to his new awareness of the existing distinction between his adoptive parentage and his physical origin, with less emotional turmoil.

Chapter XX

REPRODUCTION

THROUGHOUT THIS BOOK we have stressed the importance of scientific knowledge as a basis for an understanding of ourselves and our mates, and for satisfactory adjustment in all relationships. Long before the individual reaches the time for marriage he should have a clear understanding of the basic facts of the structure of both male and female reproductive systems; of conception and how it comes about; of menstruation and its relationship to conception; and of the most fundamental facts about pregnancy and childbirth. All phases of sex and reproduction have long been beclouded for many people by superstition and hearsay. In this chapter it is our purpose to present briefly but as clearly as possible the essential facts of the reproductive process. In order to understand physiological functioning it is necessary first to have a clear conception of the anatomical structure of reproductive organs.

Female reproductive system

The female reproductive system consists of external and internal organs. The external are (1) two labia majora, (2) two labia minora, and (3) a clitoris. All these are called collectively the vulva. The labia majora are folds of tissue which form the outer rim or boundary of the vulva. The labia minora are inside, or between, the labia majora and are thinner, elongated folds of mucous membrane. The clitoris is a small organ situated at the point where the upper edges of the labia minora join. It is exclusively an organ of sensation.

The internal organs are (1) the vagina, (2) the uterus, (3) two fallopian tubes, and (4) two ovaries. The vagina is an elastic passageway between the uterus and the vulva, opening into a small space between the labia minora, called the vestibule. The vagina serves as the female organ of copulation, as well as the birth canal. It also is the passageway for the menstrual flow. The vaginal opening is partially closed by a membrane called the hymen. There is much superstition concerning the hymen, not only among primitive people but among modern Americans. Chief among the erroneous beliefs held concerning the hymen is that it is an infallible index to a woman's virginity. Actually its presence, absence, or structure is unreliable as a means for the layman to determine either chastity or unchastity. Variations in size, structure, and thickness of the hymen are great—from membranes that are of such slight development that they are hardly discernible, or that are so loose and dilatable that they survive intercourse and even the birth of a child, to others that are very thick and strong with only a tiny opening into the vagina.

The uterus is a pear-shaped, muscular organ normally about three inches long and two inches wide. It serves as the home of the baby during the period of gestation. Its muscular walls increase in thickness and size during pregnancy and serve as the chief force to expel the child during the birth process. The uterus opens into the vagina through the cervix. The ovaries are the gonads or sex glands of the female. They have two chief functions. They produce the reproductive cells called ova or eggs, and they manufacture hormones which are responsible for the development of female characteristics and for the processes which result in menstruation. The fallopian tubes serve the purpose of conducting the egg cells from the ovaries to the uterus. The meeting of an egg cell with the sperm, and its subsequent fertilization, also usually take place in the larger part of the tube. Each tube is about four inches long; its smaller end opens into the uterus, and its larger end lies closely about the surface of the ovary but not directly connected to it. The end which is in contact with the ovary is made up of numerous fingerlike projections, which are for the purpose of intercepting the egg when released from the ovary, and starting it on its way through the fallopian tubes to the uterus.

Male reproductive system

The male reproductive system consists of the following organs or structures: (1) two testicles or testes, (2) epididymides, (3) two deferent ducts (the testicles, epididymides, and part of the deferent ducts are contained in the (4) scrotum), (5) two seminal vesicles, (6) prostate gland, and (7) the penis.

The testes are the gonads, or sex glands, of the male. Each testicle is about the size of a walnut and they are suspended in the scrotum, a pouch or sac hanging between the thighs just behind the penis. The temperature of the testicles is usually somewhat lower than that of the rest of the body. The lower temperature that is necessary for their functioning is probably the reason they are placed outside the body rather than inside, as are the female gonads (ovaries). The testicles have two chief functions. They secrete the male sex hormone (testosterone) which has much to do with the development of male characteristics such as body build, deep voice, and distribution of body hair. Their second function is to produce the reproductive cells, called spermatozoa or sperm cells. The manufacture of sperm cells begins at puberty and continues for many years. The number of spermatozoa produced decreases with age; in some men their production ceases after middle age. However, cases are on record of men as old as ninety who have fathered offspring.

Convoluted along one side of each testicle is the epididymis, a loosely coiled tube into which the sperm cells are emptied for storage. The epididymis is connected to a tube called the vas deferens which serves to suspend the testicle from the body and also to carry the sperm cells up out of the scrotum toward the seminal vesicle and the prostate gland. After the vas deferens leaves the scrotum, it goes up over the outside of the pubic bone and enters the abdominal wall through a very small opening in the muscles. It is this small opening or muscular ring which sometimes becomes enlarged or ruptured, allowing a portion of the abdominal lining or of the intestine to protrude through the opening, in the condition called unguinal hernia.

After entering the abdominal cavity, the vas deferens goes on to join the seminal vesicle, and then passes through the tissue of the prostate gland to enter the urethra. The seminal vesicles store the sperm cells which are delivered to them, and also secrete a fluid which, with the fluid secreted by the prostate gland, forms the semen, or the material ejaculated in sexual intercourse. During intercourse the seminal vesicles and the prostate gland contract and force their contents out through the urethra. When the glands become full they sometimes empty themselves in what are known as seminal emissions or nocturnal emissions, that is, emission of seminal fluid during sleep. Nocturnal emissions are very common and sometimes quite regular among adolescents or other males who are not having regular sexual intercourse. They are a natural result of glandular activity and are in no way harmful. The penis, through which the urethra makes its way to the exterior, is the male copulatory organ, corresponding to the vagina in the female. It is composed of special tissue, in reality a spongy network of blood vessels which become tense when congested, causing the penis to enlarge, harden, and become erect in position. This condition occurs during sexual excitement and allows intromission of the penis to deposit semen within the vagina.

Conception

Approximately once each month from puberty until the menopause, ovulation takes place in the female reproductive system. That is, an egg is released from the ovary and starts its course to the uterus. When the egg, or ovum, is released, it is swept into the fallopian tube by the fingerlike projections which lie closely about the ovary. If sperm are present, the egg usually meets with the sperm somewhere in its course through the tube and there is fertilized.

During sexual intercourse innumerable spermatozoa are deposited in the vagina near the entrance to the uterus. The sperm cells are extremely motile and begin moving rapidly in all directions, some of them entering the uterus, and traveling on into the tubes. If an egg is encountered, the sperm cell unites with the egg cell and conception has occurred. The fertilized egg continues through the fallopian or uterine tube to the uterus, where it implants itself, and development of the embryo proceeds. If sperm do not appear while the egg is progressing toward the uterus and fertilization does not take place, the egg soon dies and, together with other elements which were involved in its production, is later cast off during the menstruation process.

Menstruation

Throughout the ages, menstruation in women has been the subject of much speculation and superstitious belief on the part of both layman and medical men. Only within the last 85 years has any reliable scientific information been available upon the subject. Even now researches are continuing to add answers to some of the baffling questions which have existed about this function. In general, however, it may be said that menstruation is the result of failure of conception to occur. During the time that the egg is becoming mature and ready to be released from the ovary, elaborate preparations are being made within the uterus to receive a fertilized egg. The exact manner of these preparations and the factors that initiate them are complicated and very interesting. For our purposes, it is sufficient to say that within the ovary are produced hormones which are carried through the blood stream to the uterus, where they cause certain changes to take place. A steadily increasing growth of the mucous membrane lining of the uterus (endometrium) occurs, and also a gradually increasing supply of blood in the endometrium. Another change takes place in the endometrium specifically designed to provide anchorage for the fertilized egg (zygote) if it arrives, to insure that it will not be cast off before it is firmly implanted. All these preparations are completed in time to receive the egg. If no sexual intercourse takes place, or if sperm have been deposited but have failed to make contact with and fertilize the egg, then the egg soon dies and fails to arrive as expected. It has been said that menstruation is evidence of "disappointment on the part of the endometrium at the failure of pregnancy to occur." Since all the preparations for the egg are useless, the uterine lining, which has enlarged and become full of blood, is cast off and makes its way out of the body in what we call menstruation.

Menstruation, therefore, is not an "illness," and normally is not accompanied by pain. In some cases, where pain occurs, medical examination will reveal that abnormal conditions are responsible. In cases where no abnormalities can be found, yet menstruation is accompanied by pain, some authorities believe that the menstrual pain may be of psychic origin. Of course, pain is pain whether it arises from psychic causes or has a purely physiological origin. Some mothers condition their daughters to consider themselves unwell during menstruation, and so help to build attitudes and habits which may contribute to painful or difficult menstrual periods. However, more and more girls look upon menstruation as a normal, if not always pleasant, function related to their femininity. If menstrual periods are regularly accompanied by pain, medical help should be obtained, for such pain is evidence of abnormal functioning, whatever the cause.

The safe period

The rhythm method or "safe period" as recognized by some authorities as a means of conception control, is based upon the principle that conception can take place only at the time when the egg is in the fallopian tubes. If intercourse is limited to other periods of the month, then conception will not occur. This theory is sound but, since many factors remain unknown at the present time, it is of limited effectiveness. For years, Dr. Leo J. Latz, a Catholic doctor of Chicago, has been doing intensive research, attempting to learn enough about the menstrual cycle so that the rhythm method might be an effective means of controlling births.

Research biologists are agreed that conception can take place only when the egg is present, but they do not know when the egg will be expelled from the ovary. In general, it is during the middle of a regular 28-day menstrual cycle. However, not all cycles are regular, and ovulation is believed to take place 14 days before the onset of the next menstruation. This of course means that it is not in the middle of the cycle in a 21-day or a 40-day cycle, or in any other cycle which regularly or temporarily varies from the 28-day cycle. For some years, women have been taught to use a temperature chart to establish the time of ovulation. A sudden rise in body temperature of about three-fifths of a degree in mid-month was thought to indicate ovulation. However, it is now known that the temperature rise indicates the hormonal changes which take place near the time of ovulation.

Research at Sloane Hospital for Women[1] found that the interval between ovulation and temperature rise may vary as much as four days. In some cases evidence seems to show that ovulation may occur at times other than about 14 days preceding the next menstruation. We know that more than one egg can mature at one time, since this occurs when fraternal twins are conceived. It is also possible then that more than one egg may be released at different times in the cycle. Moreover, it is now known that some women do not ovulate during every cycle.

Authorities are not agreed on the length of time the egg lives if it is not fertilized or on the length of time the sperm cells will survive in the uterine cavity. One research authority[2] believes that the spermatozoon retains its capacity to fertilize the egg

[1] C. L. Buxton and E. T. Engle, "Time of Ovulation," *American Journal of Obstetrics and Gynecology*, 60:3 (September, 1950), 539-551.

[2] Edmond J. Farris, *Human Fertility and Problems of the Male*, p. 145. White Plains, New York: The Author's Press, Inc., 1950.

cells no longer than twenty-four hours and that the egg is capable of fertilization no longer than twelve hours.

Sterility

Almost one-sixth of American married women past the childbearing age have borne no children, and the most accurate information available indicates that one married couple in ten is involuntarily sterile. Many more couples are relatively infertile or become so after the birth of one or two children. The problem of sterility is faced by almost 150,000 newly married couples each year. Many young people who marry are concerned only with making sure that they do not have children until they are ready to have them. Some of them are shocked and disappointed to find, when they are at last ready, that because of low fertility or infertility they cannot have children at all.

At one time it was thought that a sterile marriage was always the fault of the wife. This belief existed partly because of a lack of scientific information about reproduction and partly because men preferred to blame their wives rather than entertain any doubts as to their ability to father offspring.

It is now believed that at least a third of the causative factors are to be found in the husband. However, a more accurate description of cause is that in the majority of cases where sterility or relative sterility exists both the husband and the wife show positive signs of sterility.

There are a number of common causes of sterility. Fallopian tubes may have been closed by infection or by injury. Gonorrhea frequently causes the tubes to become sealed so that the egg cannot meet the sperm to permit fertilization. The female genital tract is normally acid, but it may be too acid for the sperm to survive, especially if the sperm are not overly vigorous. Extra secretions from the cervix may prevent the sperm from entering. Some failure in glandular functioning may hinder implantation of the egg after it has been fertilized, so that the fertilized egg cannot remain to grow in the uterus. Since the sex cells are very susceptible to the effects of X-ray and radium, an individual may become temporarily sterile after exposure to them. The sex cells of a particular couple may be incompatible and destroy each other. This condition is called genetic incompatibility. The general health, mental or physical, of one or both may be such that it is impossible or unlikely that conception will occur. Age is also a factor, younger women being much more likely to conceive than older women. Some cases of sterility are due to the failure of the couple to have intercourse during the time of the month during which the egg is present in the tube and available for fertilization. Recent research indicates that normally fertile women will produce a normal egg cell in slightly over 8 out of 10 menstrual cycles, whereas women of subfertility ovulate normally in less than half of the menstrual cycles. Some wives in this second group who were tested regularly in every cycle for more than a year ovulated normally only three or four times in that period of time.[3]

In many men, spermatozoa are not produced in sufficient quantity or of vigorous enough quality, and the result is lowered fertility.

Since any or all of these factors may play a part, fertility may be seen to be relative. A couple may be infertile temporarily, or they may have a low fertility so that they are unlikely to have many children but still may have one or two.

Progress is being made in studies of infertility; conception now occurs in from one-fourth to one-third of the couples who go to infertility specialists for help. The Planned Parenthood Federation has found, in a study of over 8,000 couples who came for aid, that 23 per cent achieved pregnancies. Probably the greatest aid in effecting pregnancy is in helping subfertile couples to determine the exact time of ovulation. One detailed study of 240 infertile couples by Dr. Frank revealed that 26 per cent of the wives became pregnant largely as a result of having determined the exact time of ovulation.[4] There are doubtless many couples who are fertile for only a few hours of the month,

[3] *Ibid.*, p. 191.

[4] Richard Frank, "A Clinical Study of 240 Infertile Couples," *American Journal of Obstetrics and Gynecology*, 60:3 (September, 1950), 645-654.

and the newer methods to determine time of ovulation are important in effecting conception with these couples. It is also believed that men who have a low sperm count become more fertile if there are longer intervals between coitus.

It has often been observed that some couples who adopt a child soon have a child born to them. Some doctors have recommended adoption of an infant as one method to overcome sterility. Doctors Rock and Hanson, in a detailed study of 202 adoptive couples, found that 8 per cent of the wives had become pregnant soon after the adoptions. However, they conclude that this is no proof that the adoption had anything to do with the pregnancies that followed. These researchers point out that spontaneous cures of infertility without adoption can be expected in 10 per cent of cases.[5]

Tests for pregnancy

Although it is usually impossible for a doctor to determine with certainty the presence of pregnancy during the first two months, tests have been devised which are almost 100 per cent accurate if administrated properly. The best known of these tests, the Friedman and the Ascheim-Zondek, work on the same principle. After conception takes place, a new hormone is secreted and excreted in the urine. If the urine is injected into a virgin female animal, it will cause the genital tract to mature and ovulation to take place within from one to four days. The Friedman test uses rabbits; the Ascheim-Zondek uses mice or rats; and a more recent test uses frogs. One advantage of the frog test is that ovulation takes place in from 6 to 18 hours. Consequently, this test will show the existence of pregnancy almost at once.

Presumptive signs

Only those women whose commitments make it necessary for them to know at once usually go to the trouble and expense of having a test for pregnancy. Most women wait until other evi-

[5] Frederick M. Hanson and John Rock, "Effects of Adoption On Fertility," *American Journal of Obstetrics and Gynecology*, 59:2 (February, 1950), 311-319.

dence indicates whether or not they are pregnant. Signs which are not based upon biological tests or the doctor's diagnosis after an examination are said to be presumptive. In the early months of pregnancy the following are presumptive signs of pregnancy: (1) skipping of menstrual period, (2) nausea or "morning sickness," (3) increased frequency of urination, and (4) increasing tenderness of the breasts. None of these by itself is conclusive, since each may be due to some other cause. A combination of these signs, however, could be considered fairly conclusive. In some cases of pregnancy, menstruation continues for one or two periods, although the flow may be light.

Conversely, failure to menstruate may be due to worry, nervous tension, or climatic changes as well as to pregnancy. Although more than half of pregnant women report nausea or morning sickness, some women have had nausea when they thought they were pregnant but actually were not; upon discovery that they were not pregnant the nausea disappeared. Nevertheless, in our study of 212 couples who had gone through their first pregnancy we found many cases in which the wife began to have nausea before she suspected that she was pregnant.[6] Those findings suggest that the nausea of early pregnancy may have a basis in metabolic changes or in changes in glandular balances which occur with conception. However, no one of the presumptive signs alone may be taken as conclusive evidence of pregnancy, for most of them can occur at other times and for other reasons.

Positive signs of pregnancy

By the third month, the doctor's examination will usually be accurate in determining whether pregnancy exists. By this time there will be an enlargement of and a softening of the cervix. The fetal heart beat can be heard during the fourth or fifth month, and the mother can "feel life," or the movement of the fetus.

[6] Shirley Poffenberger, Thomas Poffenberger, and Judson T. Landis, "Intent Toward Conception and the Pregnancy Experience," *American Sociological Review*, 17:5 (October, 1952), 616-620.

Boy or girl?

Since parenthood begins with conception, couples find themselves in the position of having a child some months before they know its sex. They usually are curious on this point, but so far there is no reliable way of knowing before birth what the sex of the child is. Superstition and "folk" explanations are common. Some of these say that if it is a boy it will be carried high, will kick the mother's right side, will cause the mother to prefer sour foods, will cause more nausea, or will be more active; and that a girl will cause the opposite effects. Guttmacher[7] points out that all these beliefs are without foundation. Some doctors make predictions as to what the baby will be just as they bet on the horses. One doctor had a policy he felt worked to everyone's satisfaction. When a couple asked his opinion as to whether their child was to be a boy or a girl, he took pains to find out which was their preference. Then if they preferred a girl he would predict a boy. If it turned out to be a boy, his reputation as a prognosticator was established. If, however, it was a girl, the couple would be so happy at getting exactly what they wanted that their reaction would be: "The doctor happened to be wrong this time, but how glad we are that he missed," and their feeling of appreciation toward him for helping them get their wish would be favorable anyway. His comment was: "By my system you can't lose."

Sex determination

The sex of the baby is determined at the time the sperm enters the egg, and nothing can be done to change the sex after that. All eggs are alike, but there are two types of sperm cells: one with an X chromosome and one without the X chromosome; the one without the X chromosome is designated as Y. If the egg is fertilized by a sperm having an X chromosome, the baby is a girl; if fertilized by a sperm with a Y chromosome, a

[7] Researchers continue to seek ways to tell the sex of an infant before birth, such as saliva tests. Such tests are still inconclusive.

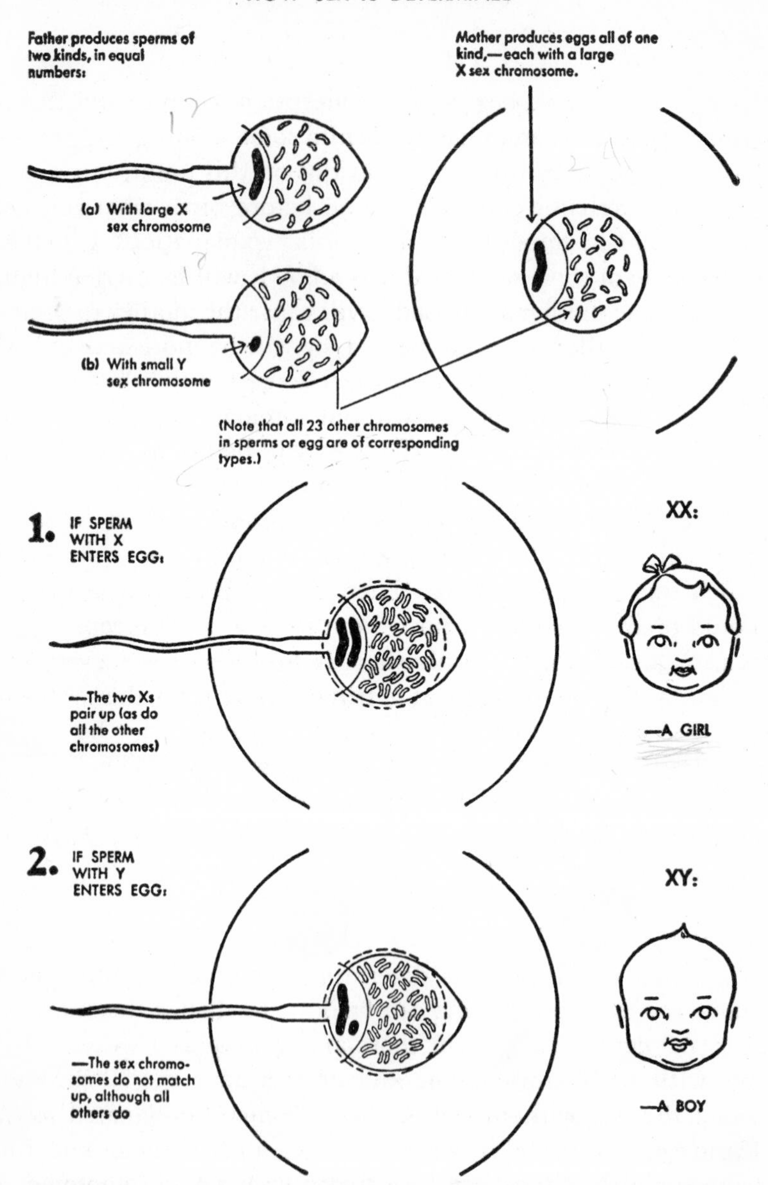

Fig. 88. *By permission,* Amram Scheinfeld, *Women and Men,* p. 12. New York: Harcourt, Brace and Company, 1943.

boy. Scheinfeld [8] has worked out a simple chart which explains the process by which sex is determined. (See Figure 88.) Since it is all chance whether an X or Y sperm will fertilize an egg, it might be expected that an equal number of boys and girls would be born. However, the sex ratio at birth is 105.5 boys to 100 girls, and at conception, it has been estimated to be between 120 and 150 boys to 100 girls. Several theories have been advanced to explain why more Y sperm cells than X reach their mark. Some of these theories are that the Y sperm cells are able to move faster or that the acidity of the female genital tract is more fatal to X sperm.

Twins and triplets

Many gaps still exist in our knowledge of the causes of multiple births. In identical twins the egg seems to divide into two individuals at a very early stage of cell division. (Siamese twins develop if the egg does not completely divide.) Identical twins then are developed from a single egg and a single sperm and usually grow with one placenta. The only fairly accurate way to determine whether twins are identical is for the doctor to make an examination of the membrane at birth. Twins that are not identical grow when two eggs are fertilized at the same time. The reason why this variation from the normal should occur is not known, but in some cases two or more eggs are released from the ovary at the time of ovulation and all may be fertilized, producing a multiple birth. These are no more alike than other brothers and sisters who are produced by single births. Fraternal twins may be of either sex, whereas identical twins are always of the same sex, since they are the result of an egg fertilized by a single sperm, either X or Y. (See Figure 89.)

Other multiple births, such as triplets, quadruplets, and quintuplets, may be identical, fraternal, or a combination of the two. The Dionne quintuplets are thought to be the result of one

[8] Amram Scheinfeld, *You and Heredity,* p. 40. Philadelphia: J. B. Lippincott Company, 1939.

fertilized egg which divided and produced five individuals. Division into two would have produced identical twins.

Evidence indicates that twinning runs in families, but just why or how has not been established. The fact that one mother

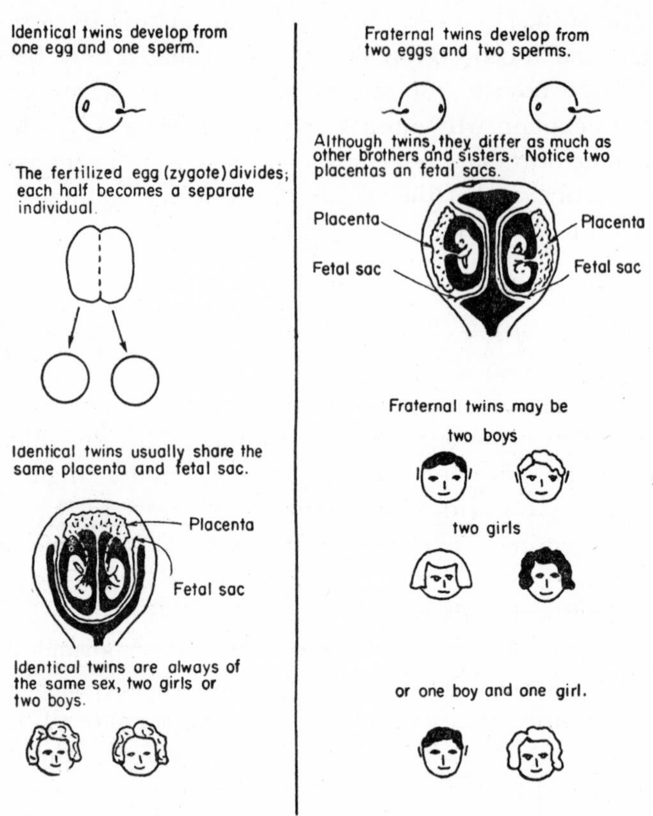

Fig. 89. How multiple births develop.

may have a number of multiple births seems to indicate that in some women the ovaries tend to bring to maturity and release more than one egg at each ovulation. Twins occur once in 92 births, triplets once in 9,000, and quadruplets once in 500,000.[9] Multiple births occur much more frequently among Negro

[9] Metropolitan Life Insurance Company, *Statistical Bulletin,* 27:3 (March 1946), 9.

mothers than among white mothers. The incidence of twins is 25 per cent higher, triplets 74 per cent higher, and quadruplets 600 per cent higher among Negro mothers.[10]

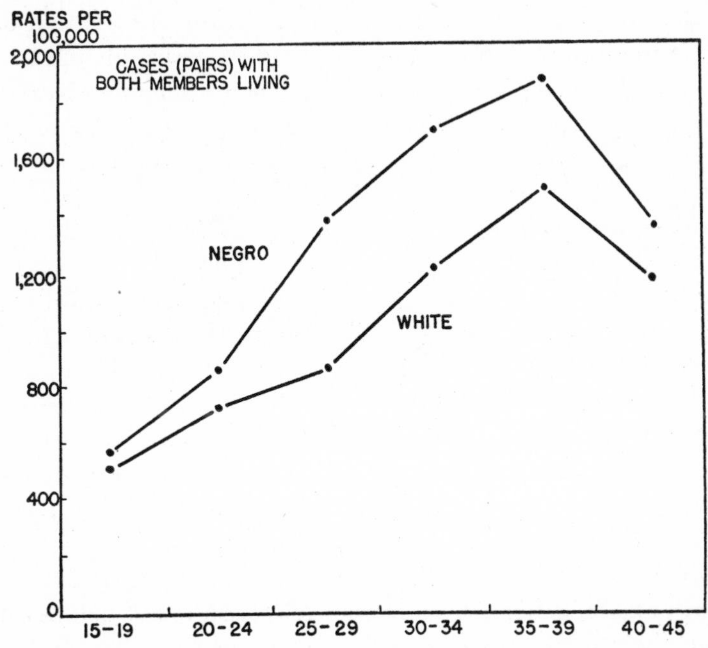

Fig. 90. Rates of twin cases per 100,000 total cases of birth, by race, age of mother, and number born alive with both members living, United States, 1944. "Twinning" increases with the age of the mother up to the age of 40. The same principle holds for other higher multiple births. U.S. Bureau of Census, *Vital Statistics Special Reports,* 25:18 (July, 1947), 346.

Pregnancy

As soon as pregnancy is suspected, the couple faces the problem of finding a doctor whom they can trust. The problem is relatively simple for those who have lived in the same community or city for many years. They will already have a family doctor who will either take the case or suggest an obstetrician. The problem is more complicated for the couple newly located and without a family doctor. But in modern-day America a great

[10] *Ibid.,* p. 10.

many young couples are beginning married life far from their families and the places where they have grown up. To such couples the choice of a doctor may present a serious problem. It is essential that they find a doctor whom they believe to be competent to handle any complications that might arise. Otherwise, worries and doubts may disturb their peace of mind unnecessarily during the pregnancy. In many communities the couple may inquire at a hospital and secure a list of the doctors in the area who take obstetrical cases. Most hospitals will not make any specific recommendations. The most satisfactory procedure is to consult the latest edition of the *Directory of Medical Specialists*. This directory may be found in public libraries. The directory lists specialists in obstetrics and gynecology who have been certified by the American Board of Obstetrics and Gynecology.

If more than one qualified obstetrician is available, the prospective parents may then consult one or two and make a choice. A well-qualified obstetrician will be glad to talk with them in a frank manner before taking the case. He will take a little time to get acquainted with them. He will also tell them what his fees are, whether or not he has a preference as to hospitals, and he will answer other questions they may wish to ask before they make their final choice of a doctor. Some young prospective parents are too timid here. The better-qualified doctors recognize the importance of rapport between the obstetrician and his patients and will welcome this preliminary consultation. Once a doctor has been chosen, his decisions should be followed in all matters concerning the pregnancy and birth.

Early in the pregnancy the doctor will give the expectant mother a thorough physical examination to determine the condition of her general health. He will be interested in her health background, including the obstetrical history of her mother and sisters. He will check blood pressure and make tests for venereal disease. He will also take the pelvic measurements to be sure there is sufficient room for the baby to be born normally. Throughout the pregnancy he will keep a close check on all conditions and developments so that if any abnormal complication is likely to arise at the time of the birth he will be able to anticipate it and be prepared to cope with it. All these things are an important part of the services of the obstetrician.

Throughout the early months of pregnancy most women continue their usual activities, including nearly all forms of outdoor exercise. Women no longer go into seclusion and have to be referred to in whispers as being in a "delicate condition," as was once the custom during pregnancy. Attitudes toward pregnancy today indicate a more general enlightenment toward the facts of life as well as a change in social customs.

Psychology of pregnancy

Pregnancy is accompanied by a number of physical changes, some of which are readily apparent. The one of which both husband and wife are usually most conscious is the wife's gaining weight and her change in figure. With the physical changes, there are also emotional and psychological effects which sometimes cause difficulty in the adjustment of the couple. If the child was desired by both and the pregnancy resulted after it had been planned for, difficulties are less likely to arise, for both enter the experience with a feeling of sharing and mutual responsibility. They feel that, although it is the wife's part to go through the physical processes of pregnancy and birth, the whole undertaking is as vitally important to the husband as to the wife. Such couples often find the months preceding the birth of their child to be some of the happiest in their lives. Even in these cases it sometimes comes as a shock to them to find that the wife may have lost all sexual desire early in the pregnancy. This often occurs. Occasionally a woman becomes aware of an increase in sexual desire during pregnancy, but research shows that many women report that although they feel excellent physically and are conscious of great affection for their husbands they seem incapable of their usual sexual response.

If the couple did not desire a child and if conception occurred without their having planned for it, they sometimes experience more problems of adjustment, although some of these may arise regardless of whether the child was desired or not. Some wives consider pregnancy as an illness and demand all the privileges of a semi-invalid. Other wives may be resentful of the loss of their figure and complain bitterly or react emotionally, blaming the husband for all the inconveniences of pregnancy. Some couples have their first difficulties in sex adjustment at this time.

In the study of 212 pregnancies previously quoted,[11] information was secured on the change in sex desire of husbands and wives during the first pregnancy. Half the wives and three out of four of the husbands said they saw no change in sex desire during the first trimester, but that the desire of both decreased rapidly through the next two trimesters. More than one-fourth of the wives noticed a marked decrease in sex desire with the onset of pregnancy, and less than one in five noticed an increase in sex desire with pregnancy. We do not know why this change in sex desire takes place, but since the pattern of the husband is similar to that of the wife it appears that there must be a strong psychological basis for it. However, in some cases the wife's sudden loss of interest in sex comes as a shock to a husband. Unable to appreciate that it is only a temporary condition, he may lose his perspective and decide that the marriage is headed for the rocks. He may show his frustration by becoming critical of his wife or acting irritable. His wife is in no mood to take such behavior, since she feels she is the one who is carrying the family burdens at the moment. Thus sometimes tensions and unhappiness result which might have been avoided if both had a better understanding of pregnancy and could have kept a proper perspective of the situation.

The wife is only occasionally an invalid and usually can live normally and happily during these months. Our study of pregnancy showed that over half of the wives noticed no change in their health, one-third said their health was better, and only

[11] Judson T. Landis, Thomas Poffenberger, and Shirley Poffenberger, "The Effects of First Pregnancy Upon the Sexual Adjustment of Two Hundred Twelve Couples," *American Sociological Review,* 15:6 (December, 1950), 767-772.

one in ten said her health was poorer during pregnancy. Of course, it is worth while for the husband to show all possible consideration and patience during this time.[12]

In most of the adjustments during pregnancy, it is logical that the husband should be the one who is willing to compromise and sacrifice his personal desires. Our research among the young couples indicated that the husbands did identify closely with their wives; the wives found their husbands more helpful, thoughtful, and affectionate than ever before. However, if the husbands noticed any change in the dispositions of their wives, it was that some wives were harder to live with than before pregnancy.[13] This is not surprising, for a wife may need more than the usual assurance of affection if she is to keep her feeling of poise and self-confidence during pregnancy.

Few wives will feel very kindly toward a husband who shows any embarrassment or unwillingness to be seen with her when her pregnancy is apparent. And any husbandly remarks about the clothes she must wear when pregnant will not be taken lightly by the average wife. Fortunately, nature seems to offer compensation in that many women have an unusual feeling of well-being during pregnancy: their complexions are better; and in general their appearance, with the exception of their figures, improves during pregnancy. One study of pregnancy found that the majority of husbands rated their wives as attractive or more than usually attractive to them physically during pregnancy.[14]

Within about six weeks after the birth of the baby, sex desire returns to about the same level as before conception took place and normal sexual relations can usually be reestablished. Of course, a baby in the house means extra work and loss of sleep, factors which may have an effect upon the sex life of new parents.

[12, 13] *Ibid.*

[14] Leland Stott, Research Report on Pregnancy Study at Merrill-Palmer School, Annual Meeting National Council on Family Relations, Rutgers University, September 1, 1952.

Maternal impressions

Some prospective parents worry over the possibility that their child may be "marked" or abnormal in some way. Since hospital records show that only one baby in 200 is born with any kind of a blemish, the individual mother's chances of having a normal baby are about 199 to 1. Among the exceptions are included babies with only minor and unimportant blemishes, so that in reality the individual chances of having a normal baby are greater than 199 to 1. Old wives' tales abound with examples of infants who are born with various types of marks or deformities that were presumably caused by some experience of the mother during the months of pregnancy. A child is born with a red birthmark, and the mother in trying to explain it remembers that during the prenatal period she was frightened by a fire, or a red car. She concludes that the scare caused the child to be marked. But the facts of fetal development from conception to birth discount any possibility of truth in such stories. No nervous connection exists between mother and child. The incidents that are supposed to "mark" the child usually occur during the months when the pregnancy is well advanced, at which time the baby is completely formed. So anything the mother might see or experience during that time could not affect the child even if there were a nervous connection.

In the past, mothers were urged to cultivate in themselves traits they desired in their child in the belief that they could impress such traits upon the unborn child. Such self-discipline by the mother was doubtless all to the good, although it could not affect the unborn child. Its value lay in the fact that the self-cultivation might have desirable effects upon the mother herself, who was to be the most important factor in the child's environment during his most impressionable years after birth. The expectant mother who spent her time going to concerts, reading the lives of great musicians, and letting her mind dwell upon music, concluded later that her behavior during pregnancy had a great influence in causing her child to become a master musician. In reality, the behavior of the mother during pregnancy had no influence upon her unborn child. However, the mother who tries to influence her child before birth will continue to project her ambitions upon the child after birth. This type of conditioning may be important in shaping the interests of the child.

Fetal development

After fertilization, the egg immediately begins the process of division and growth and continues through the tube where it met the sperm. It is believed that it takes about three days

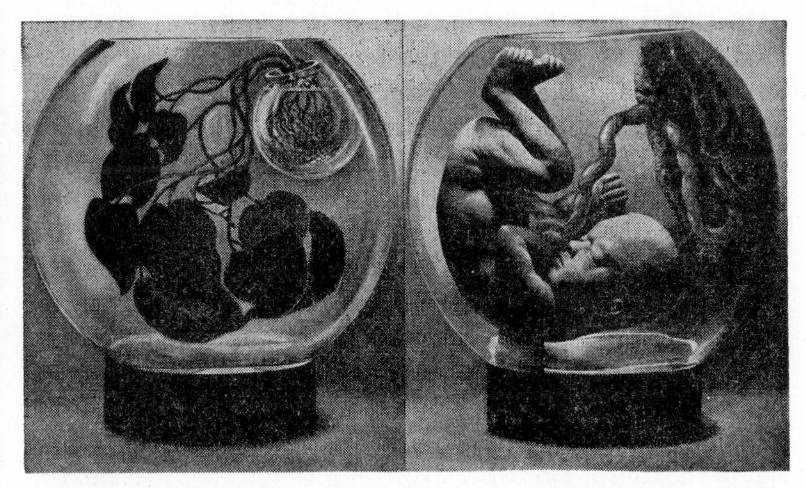

Fig. 91. The baby grows like a plant. *By permission,* Dickinson-Belskie, *Birth Atlas.* New York: Maternity Center Association, 1943.

for the fertilized egg to reach the uterus. Once there, it appears to rest for several more days. During this time, however, a process is taking place by which a part of the ovum is preparing to continue its development into a new individual, and another layer of cells is preparing for its special function of securing nourishment for the fetus during the months of its growth in the uterus. This second layer of cells forms the placenta, which becomes a flat, broad structure attached to the side of the uterus. It has numerous villi which penetrate the uterine lining and through osmotic action secure nutritive substances from the mother's blood. Waste products of the developing fetus are also given off by the same process to be carried away by the mother's blood. All nutritive substances and waste products pass through a membrane by absorption. The placenta is connected to the umbilicus of the fetus by means of a cord containing the blood vessels that carry the nourishment and waste products back and forth. After the placenta has formed and established itself, membranes develop which arise from the margin of the placenta and surround the fetus. This membranous sac fills with a watery fluid in which the fetus lives until almost time for birth. This fluid is called the amniotic fluid and serves to protect the fetus from outside shocks, as well as to keep the temperature constant. This sac of fluid breaks sometime during the birth process. Whether it breaks early or late has nothing to do with the ease or difficulty of the birth.

The length of time required from conception to birth is about 266 to 270 days, or roughly nine calendar months.[15] Doctors usually figure that the birth is due 280 days from the beginning of the last menstruation. However, since conception in average cases takes place approximately 14 days after the last menstruation, 266 days is a more accurate figure. During this time, the embryo develops in size and complexity. By the end of the fourth week it is about ¼ inch long and is composed of a body and small buds that will later be the arms, legs, eyes, ears, and nose. By the end of the sixteenth week the fetus is approximately five inches long and quite well developed; the sex organs, which until this time have appeared much the same for both sexes, have now differentiated, so the sex of the fetus is evident. During the first two months the new individual is called an embryo, after that and until birth, a fetus. From this time on the fetus grows in length and in weight, most of the weight increase coming during the later weeks of the prenatal

[15] H. L. Stewart, "Duration of Pregnancy and Postmaturity," *Journal of the American Medical Association,* 148 (March, 1952), 1079-1093.

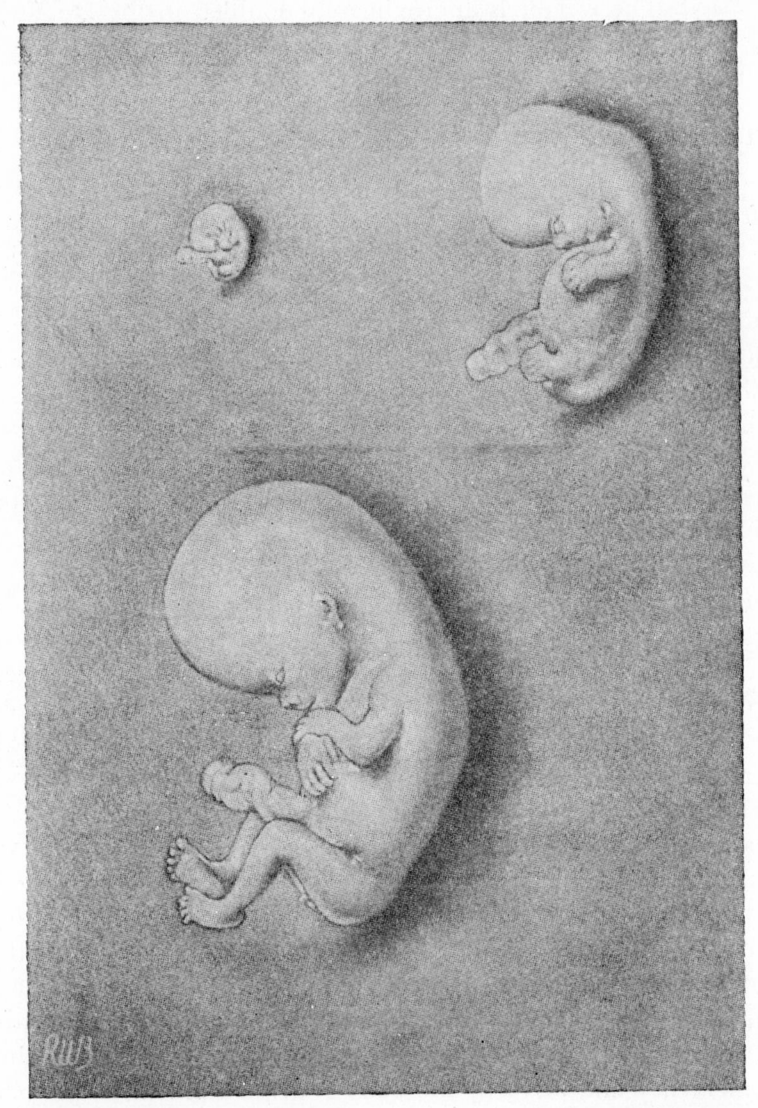

Fig. 92. Actual size of the fetus at one, two, and three months. *By permission,* Nicholson J. Eastman, *Expectant Motherhood,* p. 30. Boston: Little, Brown and Company, 1940.

period. The weight is approximately doubled in the last four weeks before birth. Figure 92 gives the actual size of the fetus at one, two, and three months.

The Rh blood factors

During the early part of pregnancy, when the doctor tests for venereal disease he may also make a test for the Rh factor in the blood of the mother. This factor was first discovered in the blood of Rhesus monkeys, in 1940. Like many other new discoveries, its importance in childbearing has been exaggerated in the minds of many people. At first it was even proposed that tests for this factor should be required before marriage and that people with incompatible blood should not marry. Now the Rh blood factors are better understood and can be coped with in childbearing. About 85 per cent of white persons have the Rh factor in their blood and are called Rh positive, and 15 per cent do not have such a factor and are called Rh negative. The Rh negative mother who conceives by a Rh positive father in some cases has a Rh positive child. In such a case if any minute amount of the baby's blood elements get into the mother's circulation—an occurrence that is extremely rare no matter what the blood types are—the mother's blood stream builds up antibodies against the incompatible blood elements. The presence of these antibodies in the mother's blood will not affect, usually, first or second pregnancies; it may cause jaundice and anemia in later babies. It is estimated that in cases of couples with the father Rh positive and the mother Rh negative only one in 300 pregnancies is actually affected by the wrong combination. Where periodic tests during pregnancy show that the mother's blood is building up the antibodies to the point of danger, doctors now prepare for the emergency and at birth the baby is given transfusions which gradually replace the blood with which the child was born. Thus most of even the small percentage of babies that would be affected by the incompatibility of their parents' blood can be saved. Prospective parents do much needless worrying if they know they happen to have the "wrong combination" of blood. Typical is the mother of four healthy children, all born before tests for the Rh factor were being made, who found during her fifth pregnancy that she was Rh negative and her husband Rh positive. She worried all through her pregnancy and, although this child also was healthy and unaffected, she was afraid to attempt another pregnancy. She would probably have been afraid to have any children after the first one had she known about the Rh factor at that time.

Birth

After approximately 40 weeks of growth, the fetus is ready to be born. Authorities differ as to just what forces initiate the birth process. Some theorize that it is due to hormone action similar to that which initiates the shedding of the uterine lining in the process of menstruation when pregnancy has not occurred. Whatever the force that starts it, the birth process begins in due time and proceeds through three definite stages, which result in release of the child from the mother's body.

In the first stage, the cervix undergoes changes and dilates until it is large enough to permit the baby to pass through. In the second stage, the baby is expelled from the uterus and passes through the cervix and the vagina to be born. The third stage is the expelling from the uterus of the placenta, known as the "after-birth." As soon as the birth process is over, the tissues of the mother begin to return to their former state. The uterus goes through a series of contractions and gradually returns to approximately its original size and shape. This process usually takes about six weeks.

There are many conflicting opinions among both medical men and other interested authorities concerning the pain accompanying the birth process, or labor. Many modern mothers say that the process of giving birth to their children was little different from menstruation in the pain involved; that they experienced a series of cramping sensations that could hardly

Fig. 93. Before labor: thick pelvic floor, cervix closed, uterus relaxed. *Figures 93, 94, 95, 96, and 97 are reproduced by permission from* Dickinson-Belskie, *Birth Atlas.* New York: Maternity Center Association, 1943.

Fig. 94. Labor: uterus contracting, cervix dilating, bag of water below head.

be called pain. Other modern mothers beg for anesthetics almost from the onset of labor and consider the pain to be severe. Many doctors are quite free in giving anesthetics to mothers in labor, and most doctors give an anesthetic at least during the last moments when the baby is being born.

There has been a cycle in the use of anesthetics. From the viewpoint that they should be used little or not at all, there was a swing to the other extreme. All kinds and types of anesthetics were used and much was said about achieving "painless births" through new types of anesthesia. The medical profession is now swinging back to a more conservative stand. Some doctors have taken the position that the pain that goes with the birth process is due to the fact that in our culture birth is generally accepted to be a process involving severe pain, so that most mothers go into labor in a state of great tenseness because of their fear of pain and of the unknown.

Progress is being made now toward a better understanding on the part of both doctors and laymen of the true facts about the birth process. Formerly the idea was accepted that it was the *doctor* who "delivered" the baby, the implication being that the mother was simply present and probably quite thoroughly anesthetized while the doctor engineered the birth process. Now more emphasis is given to the fact that if nature takes its course the mother, not the doctor, gives birth to the baby.

More mothers now realize that during the first stage of labor it is best to relax and rest, for this stage will proceed more smoothly and quickly if the mother is not tense. In this first stage the cervix gradually opens to allow the baby to begin to pass through into the birth canal. The muscles of the uterus automatically contract as the cervix opening enlarges, and the mother experiences sensations similar to the cramping sensations that sometimes accompany menstruation. A relaxed attitude of mind and body is of greatest importance at this stage.

After the first stage of labor is over, the mother is taken into the delivery room for the second stage, or the actual birth of

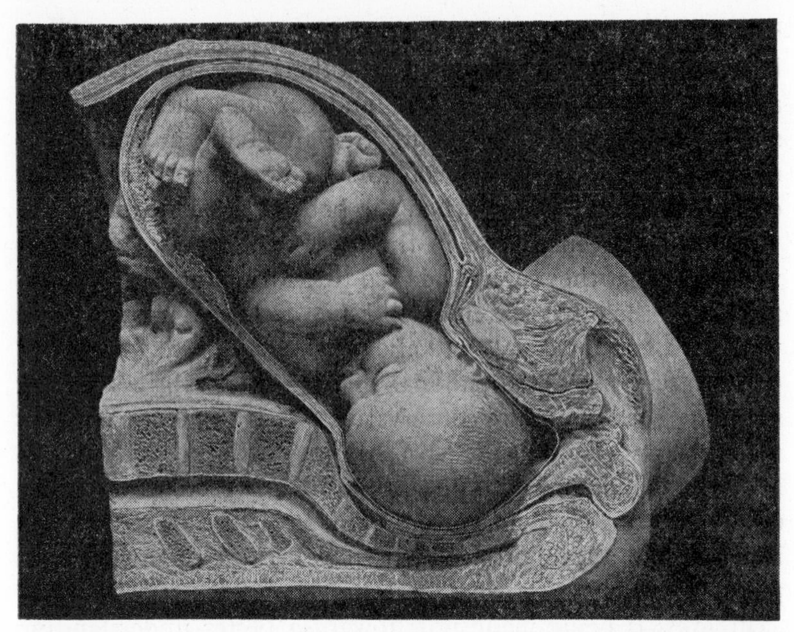

Fig. 95. Full dilation: head deep in birth canal, pull of uterine contractions draws cervix up.

Fig. 96. Head turns upward, pelvic floor slips back over face.

the baby. It is in this stage that the mother "labors" to help give birth to her baby. This stage is much shorter than the first. One obstetrician says of this stage, "It is certainly work, just as playing a game of football or running a footrace is work. How much of it is 'pain' is a matter of viewpoint or definition, and that differs with different women." Certainly the facial expressions of many athletes in action could be interpreted as expressions indicating pain, but few of them would call their

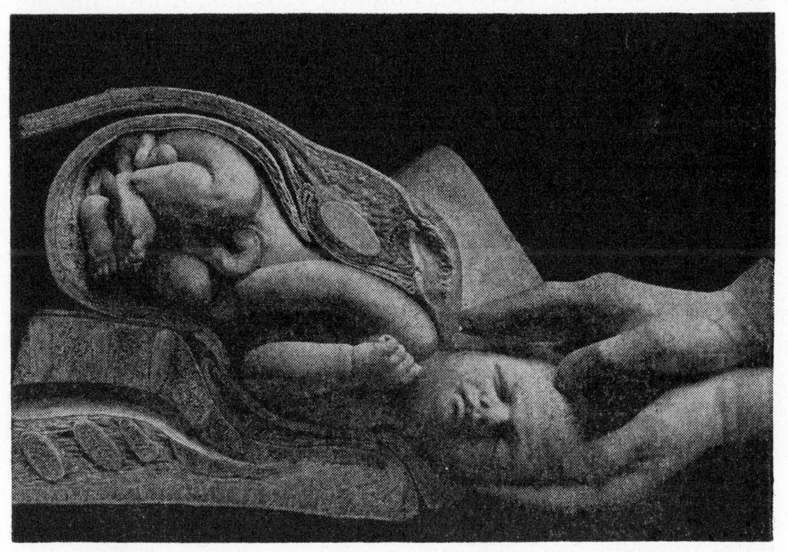

Fig. 97. Birth of the shoulders, turning to fit passage.

sensations pain. So it is with mothers during childbirth. Many of them insist that they be given no anesthetic because they want to be fully conscious, for they look upon giving birth to a child as an achievement which they accomplish at least in part by their own efforts. This viewpoint among mothers is increasing because of the work of certain doctors who are known as advocates of "natural childbirth." These doctors believe that if mothers are thoroughly informed about what actually takes place in the birth process, if they are familiar with how the birth of the baby is to be handled—including some knowledge of hospital conditions and routines—and if they have confidence that the doctor will be standing by ready for any emergency, they will go into the birth process free of tension and able to give birth naturally to the child with little need or desire for anesthetics.

Support is given to these views by research studies which are being carried out at certain medical schools. A study was made of 1,000 consecutive deliveries in the Yale University Service of the Grace-New Haven Community Hospital. All the mothers took part in the Training for Childbirth Program, which gave both physical and psychological preparation. Doctors Thoms and Wyatt say of the program, "The educational aspects of our program consist of four talks given to prospective parents, and four exercise classes given by a nurse. . . . Following the fourth class, which is given in the third trimester of pregnancy, the women visit the obstetrical division of the hospital, meet members of the personnel, see the labor and delivery rooms, and learn how the delivery tables and anesthesia apparatus operate. The patient in labor is in a room by herself; during this period she may have her husband with her if she wishes. The patient is kept informed of her progress and during active labor is not left alone. Attention is focused upon her needs and what she is trying to accomplish. Any therapy or instruction is in the hands of a nurse or a physician. Activity and busyness on the part of those attending her are kept to a minimum." [16]

Of the 1,000 consecutive births reported in the Yale study, the average length of total labor, whether the birth was of a first baby or not, was 10.3 hours; only 8 babies out of 1,000 died.

Helen Heardman studied the duration of labor among 1,000 women who were having their first baby; 500 of the mothers had gone through the "natural childbirth" training program and a control group of 500 had had no special training. The average length of labor was approximately six hours shorter

[16] Herbert Thoms and Robert H. Wyatt, "One Thousand Consecutive Deliveries Under a Training for Childbirth Program," *American Journal of Obstetrics and Gynecology,* 61:1 (January, 1951), 205-209.

for the 500 who had gone through the training program, and there was a much larger percentage of normal deliveries in this group.[17]

Many doctors now consider it routine to conduct classes or to have an assistant conduct classes for expectant mothers. Training similar to that described in the Yale program is usually given. One obstetrician has prepared a series of films showing normal labor and childbirth, and these films are used at the conclusion of the training programs.[18]

The education of young people should emphasize the normality of the birth process and of the launching of a new individual into life. In the past too much emphasis was given to possible pain and risk. Parents have sometimes tried to inspire gratitude in their children by repeated references to the sacrifices and suffering that were necessary to bring the children into the world. Gratitude is never inspired by such tactics, and the picture given by such references is not accurate. For the truth is that to have children and to give them a good start in life, physically and emotionally, is one of the unparalleled experiences that come to human beings.

Rooming-in

It is becoming recognized that certain things can be done from the very moment of birth to give children a good start emotionally. The earliest experiences an individual has with his mother are believed to be the basis for his later human relationships and to influence his total personality. Many hospitals are now following a plan designed to give children a better start in life emotionally than they were given in the past. This is called the rooming-in plan. In the Yale University program described above, "rooming-in" is an important part of the plan in the hospital. According to the rooming-in plan, the babies are not kept in a central nursery but remain in the

[17] Herbert Thoms, *Training for Childbirth*. New York: McGraw-Hill Book Company, Inc., 1950, p. 76.

[18] Earle M. Marsh, "Labor and Childbirth." San Francisco: Medical Films, Inc.

rooms with their mothers. Mothers are encouraged to do as much as they want to in caring for their newborn babies. Mothers get confidence in caring for their babies while in the hospital under direction of a nurse, and they learn from one another, since several may be in one unit of rooms. Breast-feeding is encouraged. More mothers seem to be able to nurse their babies when the babies are with them and when the mother and baby are able to work out their own schedule than when the baby is fed only at stated intervals according to hospital schedules.[19]

New mothers may be more enthusiastic about rooming-in than mothers with several children. The latter may look forward to a vacation when they go to the hospital. Some hospitals are constructing rooms that allow the mother to have her baby with her and still turn it over to the care of nurses when she wants to be free to rest. But even mothers of several children are likely to prefer to have their babies with them because they want to know that their babies are comfortable at all times. Under the system in which babies are all kept in a central nursery, mothers often can hear babies crying and each one may worry over whether it is her baby that needs attention.

Hospitals and doctors using the rooming-in plan believe that a close relationship between mother and baby is important during the first days and weeks of the baby's life and that better mental and emotional health will result for both mothers and babies.

[19] Thaddeus L. Montgomery, Robert E. Steward, and Pauline Shenk, "Observations on the Rooming-in Program in Ward and Private Service," *American Journal of Obstetrics and Gynecology,* 57:1 (January, 1949), 176-186.

Chapter XXI

WHEN CHILDREN COME

MOST PEOPLE WHO MARRY hope to have children eventually. But since a great many modern young couples marry before they feel that they are ready to start their family, they plan to wait a few years before having the first child.

Readiness for parenthood

Some of the reasons for postponing parenthood are financial. Young people sometimes feel that in fairness to themselves and to their children they should be out of debt, should have a home, and should be established economically before they have children. Standards of what constitutes the required economic condition differ. Many couples who postpone having children for economic reasons learn that their standards change; they raise their level of living to keep pace with increased income, so that after a few years of marriage they do not feel any more able to afford children than at the beginning. Society's experience has proved that, although financial stability is not to be minimized as a factor in successful family life, it is one of the more minor considerations in determining whether a couple is ready for parenthood. Some couples who have achieved the happiest and most successful family life with their children would never have had children at all if they had waited to have the first baby until they could afford the luxury of a family.

Far more important than financial stability is the emotional maturity of the parents. Available evidence suggests that happier marriages result and that children get off to a better start in life if couples have time to make the early marital adjustments before the coming of the first child. Since the time required for reaching a good marital adjustment varies, some couples are ready to have children within a year after marriage, whereas others will still be occupied with growing up emotionally themselves several years after marriage.

Do children prevent divorce?

Because the divorce rate is much higher among childless couples than among those with children, some authorities have suggested that the sooner children arrive in the home, the better. It is true that 60 per cent of the divorcing couples have no children. But does it follow that if these couples had had children they would not have divorced? Nearly half of all divorces are secured within the first six years of marriage. Many of the frictions which result in divorce start within the first months of marriage, although the couple may not resort to divorce until months or years later. Some of the divorcing couples do not have children because they conclude early that the marriage is doomed to failure. Or they may not have the will to work at making a success of the marriage, and in the same measure they would not be willing to make the sacrifices that parenthood requires. Couples who are successful in their marital adjustments in general usually go ahead with having a family. That they do not end up in the divorce court is not because they had children, but rather because they worked at making a good marriage.

Some people are emotionally and temperamentally unsuited to be parents for the same reasons that they cannot adjust happily in the married state. An emotionally unstable spouse can wreck a marriage whether children are present or not. If there are children, the complications are greater. Fortunately, then, for the children that might be born, a selectivity seems to operate so that the majority of those who divorce have no children. Adverse conditioning for many phases of married living may account not only for the lack of desire for children but also for other characteristics which go with an inability to make a success of marriage. The presence of children will not transform maladjusted individuals into happy husbands and wives.

Time interval between marriage and the arrival of children

After making a study of 944 graduates of Cornell University, Anderson concluded that the average interval between marriage and first births for college graduates who had completed their families was between 31 and 33 months, or from 2.5 to 2.9 years. The findings indicate that 20 per cent have their first child in the first year of marriage, 32-38 per cent in their second year, and about 29 per cent after the third year of married life.[1] These students were graduated in the classes of 1919-1921; the time interval between marriage and the first child might be different today. In 1940, 364 Cornell students were queried on the preferred interval between marriage and parenthood. Of these students 11 per cent wanted a child during the first year of marriage, 58 per cent during the second, and 25 per cent during the third year.[2] The number of students expressing a desire to have children during the first year was smaller than the number of previous graduates who actually had had children in the first year. But more of the 1940 students expressed a desire to have children during the first two years than there were former graduates who had actually had children during the first two years of marriage.

Many of these people did not wish to have a child during the first year because "We need a year to become adjusted to each other and to continue our good times together." They felt that they did not wish to be tied down to the responsibilities of parenthood too early in marriage.

Since fertility decreases with age, the danger exists that some

[1] W. A. Anderson, "The Spacing of Births in the Families of University Graduates," *American Journal of Sociology*, 53:1 (July, 1947), 23-26.

[2] Lemo D. Rockwood and Mary E. N. Ford, *Youth, Marriage, and Parenthood*, p. 145. New York: John Wiley & Sons, Inc., 1945.

couples will not be able to have any children if they postpone the first pregnancy too long. This is especially true of couples who have a low fertility or are older than average when they marry. It is usually not advisable to postpone having children if the couple are mature and have achieved good adjustments in their marriage.

Why have children?

Basically, the purpose of human reproduction is to perpetuate the species. But few people feel a personal responsibility for the perpetuation of the species. More people desire children because of a wish to have a stake in the future. They may feel a conscious desire to keep a grasp on youth and life through the lives of their children, or they may feel an undefined urge toward self-perpetuation. People may desire children also because of their belief that children are necessary to a complete and happy home life. Then, of course, a great many couples have children simply because nature takes its course. They marry with the expectation that it will be so; they give little thought to whether or not they actively wish to have children, and they welcome the children that come.

Whatever the reason back of the desire for children, it is true that having children does give married people not only a stake in the future but an interest in the present. Matters which we may shrug away as of no concern to us suddenly take on importance after we become parents. Studies of college students show that almost all of them hope to have children eventually. The majority in the study in 11 colleges in 1952 said also that they would hesitate to marry a person who did not want children.

Children and happiness of parents

Do children contribute to the happiness of marriage? Several attempts have been made to determine the relationship between happiness in marriage and the size of the family. Terman, Hamilton, and Bernard found no significant differences between the happiness scores of childless and non-childless husbands and wives. In the study by Mowrer and Mowrer, and in our study of 409 couples, the evidence indicated that the chances for happiness decreased as the number of children increased. However, in our study the number of unhappy adjustments also

Fig. 98. "I'm up! I'm up! Call 'em off!" *By permission,* Harry Mace and *The Saturday Evening Post.*

decreased as the number of children increased. In other words, those without children tended toward the extremes in their adjustments, being either very happy or very unhappy, while those with children approached an average in happiness.

Several difficulties are involved in trying to determine the effects of children upon the happiness of a marriage. Of importance is the duration of the marriages studied. Studies of people who are in the early months or the first year of marriage may show a high percentage of happy marriages, most of which will be childless, but in these marriages of short duration the childlessness is not significant. In marriages of short duration, the partners are likely to rate the marriage as very happy simply because they are still in the honeymoon stage. Even if they suspect that their marriage is less happy than they had anticipated, they are not so likely to admit it as are couples who have been married longer. With couples who have been married for longer periods of time, the fact of desiring or not desiring children may be of greater importance than the actual presence or absence of children. If the coming of undesired children forces a couple to give up the type of life they had planned, or if unwanted children come to a couple who are already unhappy in marriage, the coming of the children may increase the adjustment problems. Burgess and Cottrell found that couples who had no children but desired them, and couples who had one or more children because they desired them, were the happiest in marriage.[3] It seems that for a couple to be in agreement in desiring children is an indication of good marital adjustment. Consequently, whether or not they are successful in having children, they are among the happier couples. Burgess found that those who had no children because they did not want them, and those who had children in spite of their contrary intentions, were among the less happy.[4] Reed, in a careful study of 1,444 Indianapolis couples, found "an increase in marital adjustment with increasing success in controlling fertility according to the desires of the couples." [5]

Need for training for parenthood

Just as it has been the traditionally accepted belief that human beings are prepared for marriage by instinct, so quite

[3] E. W. Burgess and L. S. Cottrell, *Predicting Success or Failure in Marriage*, p. 260. New York: Prentice-Hall, Inc., 1939.

[4] *Ibid.*, p. 260.

[5] Robert B. Reed, "Social and Psychological Factors Affecting Fertility, Part VII," p. 423. New York: Milbank Memorial Fund, 1948.

universally young people feel qualified to rear children, with no special training for the task. Baber reports that among students he has queried concerning their confidence in their ability to rear children properly, only 4 per cent were doubtful of their ability, 68 per cent were "reasonably confident," and 28 per cent were "sure" of their ability. He comments that it is a

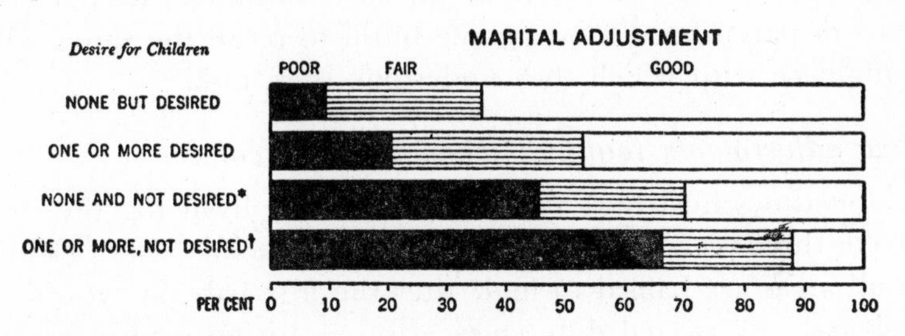

* Not desired by husband or wife, or both.
† Not desired by husband or wife, or both.

Fig. 99. Desire for children and marital adjustment. People who do not desire children are poor marital risks. Children may serve as a bond to hold husband and wife together or the coming of unwanted children may serve as an added handicap to marital adjustment. From E. W. Burgess and L. S. Cottrell, *Predicting Success or Failure in Marriage,* p. 260. New York: Prentice-Hall, Inc., 1939.

"paradox of human nature that people falter before simple tasks but attack difficult ones with all the assurance of ignorance; they are fearful and hesitant over the simple process of learning to drive a car yet cocksure that they can handle the infinitely more complicated mechanism of their children." [6]

In this generation commendable progress is being made toward better preparation for marriage, but need exists for the education of young people for parenthood. One college graduate says of her education, "I could chatter about the minor English poets of the sixteenth century. I knew all about the love life of the earthworm . . . but pregnancy amazed me. Babies scared me, and my knowledge of finance was limited to what-shall-I-do-until-my-allowance-comes." She goes on to state that

[6] Ray E. Baber, *Marriage and the Family,* p. 295. New York: McGraw-Hill Book Company, Inc., 1939.

her class spent six weeks cutting up pickled frogs; they studied the amoeba, the crayfish, and the earthworm. She concludes, "The majority of us could have done with far less concentration on lowly creatures and far more information on pregnancy, childbirth and parental responsibilities."[7] Educational systems have failed to provide training for parenthood, and young people have not felt the need for such training. After a few years of parenthood most people blush to recall the smug self-confidence with which they undertook their task.

New adjustments required when children come

Sometimes husbands and wives who have lived together for two or three years and have worked out satisfactory relationships in all areas are baffled to find, after the first baby arrives, that new and unexpected differences arise, requiring readjustments in their relationships. The arrival of the first baby is one of the first major occasions calling for readjustments.

This period would be easier if young parents were able to be objective about the social-psychological-interactional changes which take place in husband-wife relationships when the first baby arrives. A state of accommodation has previously been reached in the adjustment of the couple. That is, they have in the first two or three years of associating together arrived at working arrangements in their personal relationships which are fairly satisfactory and quite clearly understood by both. The arrival of the third person in the home upsets the status quo and again the couple must achieve a satisfactory working arrangement. The new interaction pattern involves different roles for each. The husband has been used to his wife's playing the part of a devoted wife who centered her attention chiefly upon him. Or she may have been the career wife who helped support the home. Now he must adjust to her as the mother who gives much of her time to the baby, or as the ex-career wife who now may show inexperience and helplessness as the mother of his

[7] Marion Walker Alcaro, "Colleges Don't Make Sense," *Women's Day,* May, 1946, p. 64.

Fig. 100. "I changed my mind—I want a red bike instead of a blue one." *By permission,* Roy L. Fox and *The Saturday Evening Post.*

child. Similar readjustments will be necessary for the wife. Gradually a new interaction pattern will be established, which, however, will never become static. Changes will occur as the child matures, and as other children come into the family.

Rearing of the children a marital problem

Our study of 409 marriages of parents of college students revealed that the care and disciplining of the children had ranked next to sex among those problems on which couples had failed to reach satisfactory adjustments. In the study of marriages of younger couples, disagreements over child training ranked next to trouble with in-laws and economic difficulties as focal points of friction. The explanation is understandable. When two young people enter marriage, each comes with a vast array of "old wives' tales," superstition, hearsay, and very little scientific information. After the arrival of the first baby, the differences in their attitudes, produced by different family backgrounds, will become evident.

In our study of young parents who were students in college, an attempt was made to learn just what points were the causes of friction in the care of the children. Since most of the children involved were under three years of age, the picture is one of early parenthood.

The most common cause of tension was the feeling on the part of one parent that the other "pampers and spoils" the baby. This complaint was made more often by the young father. It seems to him that the wife always gives in to the child, and that she does not use enough disciplinary measures. The wives often complained that the husbands were strict or harsh with the child. The wife is critical because the husband demands too much obedience from a small child, frightens the child by scolding, or shows irritation with the child over trivial things. Both parents are inclined to react emotionally to their differences over training the child. Neither can appreciate the way the other believes.

Another common cause of friction is that they do not agree on methods of training. One may believe in "reasoning" with the child, and the other may believe in requiring instant obedience. One may believe in a rigid schedule, and the other may not. The wife may feel the husband is not applying any principles of psychology to situations; and the husband may complain that the wife shows affection for the child whom she has just spanked. On all these points there is a conflict in the "folk" methods which the young people have taken into their marriage.

Couples who read together some of the more sensible books on child training are sometimes able to compromise and agree on methods recommended by an outside expert. However, some will not change their ideas. One parent may feel he has lost face if he finds his theories are not supported in the literature, and he may decide to stick to his "folk" methods regardless of the consequences. That is evidence of immaturity.

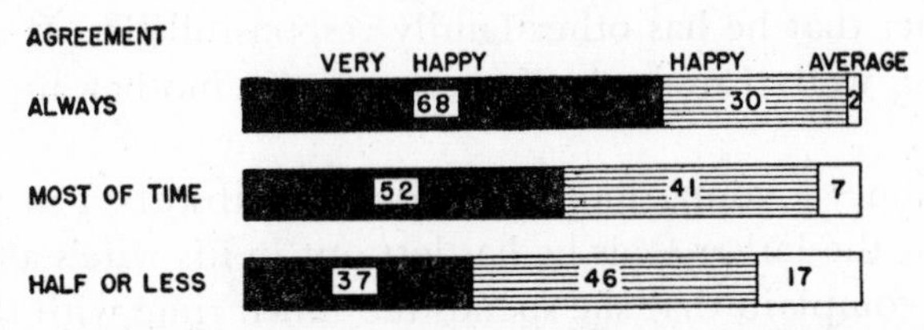

Fig. 101. Agreement on child training and marriage happiness (544 couples). Young parents who see eye to eye on the training and disciplining of their children will find greater harmony in their marriage relations.

A common complaint among the younger couples as well as among the parent generation was that one spouse would countermand orders given by the other. That habit is always irritating and usually proves to be good for trouble in marriage. If the wife tells Johnny to stop throwing the ball against the house and the husband tells Johnny to go ahead, it won't hurt anything, several undesirable effects have been achieved. The wife feels defeated not only because the ball continues to hit the house, but because her authority has been undermined by the husband. Johnny has learned that it is possible to pit one parent against the other in order to do as he pleases. And the husband, besides incurring his wife's displeasure, has also weakened his own future authority with his son.

If discipline is to be effective, the parents must present a united front to the children. It is almost impossible for one parent to do anything with the children if the other is issuing different orders. Not only does such variance cause failure with the children, but it creates increasing marital tension between the husband and wife. Parents will differ, but successful parents will discuss these differences and reach compromises when the children are not present.

A common complaint among wives is that husbands do not take enough responsibility in training and caring for the children. Many husbands go into marriage with the attitude that training the children is the responsibility of the wife and that the husband's duty is to support the family. Too often the father becomes absorbed in his work and is almost unconscious of the fact that he has other family responsibilities. If children are to be well reared, the father and the mother must work together.

Sometimes a young mother becomes so absorbed in the new baby that the father feels he has lost out in his wife's affections. He may complain that she spends too much time with the child and that she is too anxious about minor details of the child's life. He may criticize the wife and all her methods in training and disciplining the child, because he feels that he has to take second place in her affections. Such behavior on the part of a husband is evidence of immaturity but is, nevertheless, common. If the young father could analyze his feelings and identify them for what they are, he would be taking a long step toward solving the problem. Objectivity concerning one's own actions is not easy, but it can be achieved by emotionally mature people.

What is a happy home?

We have been considering the coming of children in relation to the happiness of parents. But what of the children? One hundred and fifty university students made free lists of the specific home circumstances which brought greatest happiness to them when they were between the ages of 5 and 12. The 15 factors listed most frequently by them were then arranged in a list for a second group of 200 students to check. The results are shown in Table 22.

It is interesting that happiness of the parents rated highest. For the parents to be happily married seems to be of fundamental importance to the happiness of the children. Other studies have shown that the happiness of the parents not only contributes to the happiness of the children in the home but also conditions them for successful family living in their own homes later.

TABLE 22

STUDENT RANKING OF 15 SPECIFIC HOME CIRCUMSTANCES WHICH BROUGHT GREATEST HAPPINESS TO THEM BETWEEN THE AGES OF 5 AND 12[a]

1. Happiness of parents
2. Parental expression of love for me
3. Sense of the family's interest in me
4. Sense of parents' trust
5. Mother a good cook
6. Companionship with parents
7. Family unity and fellowship
8. Meals always on time and house always clean
9. Family able to provide adequate financial means
10. Pride in accomplishments of family
11. Pleasure in doing things together as a family
12. Parents' approval of friends
13. Religion in the home
14. Family cooperation
15. Feeling that I had a responsible part in our family

[a] Unpublished research by Judson T. Landis.

Second to happiness of parents, the students named items that emphasize the importance to the children of overt expressions of parental love for them. In many homes the parents take it for granted that their parental care and their efforts to provide for all the needs of the children will be recognized by the children as evidence of parental love. It may not be so. Children must be reassured that they are loved through open expression of affection. Parental care is something which they accept as part of their background, and many young children will make no connection between that and parents' love for them. The desire for emotional security is strong in children and they need reassurance and evidence that they are loved.

It is interesting to note that young people gave adequate finances ninth place in the list. It seems to be true that a sense of being loved and trusted, and a feeling that one is a companion with his parents is more important to the development of the child than being showered with numerous or expensive possessions. Some parents mistakenly think that they have taken care of their children's needs simply because they have given them the material things which money can buy. But nothing can be substituted for parental happiness, love, and companionship in the life of the young child.

The same students were asked to list specific factors which caused greatest unhappiness in their lives as children. Illness and death ranked first as a major cause of unhappiness for children. It is understandable that serious illness or death usually represents a family crisis which threatens or destroys the security of the children. The students ranked a quarreling pattern in the home second to illness and death as a source of unhappiness. Quarrels between parents caused greatest unhappiness but quarrels between siblings also rated high. Not very much can be done to keep children from worrying about illness and death, but families can do something about quarreling. Parents who

TABLE 23

STUDENT RANKING OF SPECIFIC HOME CIRCUMSTANCES WHICH BROUGHT GREATEST UNHAPPINESS TO THEM BETWEEN THE AGES OF 5 AND 12

1. Death and illness in the family
2. Parents' quarreling
3. Conflict with parents' views
4. Quarreling of brothers and sisters
5. Inability of parents to see my point of view
6. Loneliness
7. Misunderstanding in the family
8. Parents' unhappiness
9. Quarreling with parents
10. Feeling of being misunderstood
11. Being compared with other children
12. Parents nagged me
13. Lack of companionship with parents
14. Afraid parents would separate
15. Father hard to get along with
16. Lack of association with those my own age
17. Lack of adequate finances

quarrel easily without considering their quarrels to be serious would be shocked to learn the extent of emotional tension created for children by parental quarreling.

Table 23 includes the most frequently mentioned home circumstances making for the unhappiness of children.

Another source of unhappiness for children has to do with conflicts between parents' and children's point of view. A measure of conflict on this score will be inevitable in parent-child relationships. Sometimes parents do know best even though they may find it impossible to make clear to the child the reasons for their attitudes. Again, parents may make arbitrary rulings with a total lack of understanding of the young person's point of view. Some present-day parents attempt to solve the problem of conflict by relaxing all efforts at control or guidance and escaping into an attitude of "If you won't bother me I won't bother you." This is hardly a constructive solution. It is an attempt to evade responsibility. Successful parents accept their responsibility for guiding their children. They try to avoid making arbitrary rulings and they work for understanding and agreement with their children about what is desirable or undesirable behavior.

Situations causing anxieties in children

If parents are happy together and if little or no quarreling occurs in the home, the children are usually happy and well adjusted. However, even children from happy homes have certain fears and worries which are rather universal. If the home is happy, these childhood troubles are not permanently serious. If the home is not happy, and if the child lacks the inner confidence that comes with family solidarity, the childhood problems assume greater importance.

A common worry in childhood has to do with physical appearance. A third of all the college students queried mentioned this item in their free list. Why are children so acutely conscious of physical characteristics that they suffer over their real or imagined defects? Almost always the reason can be found to go back to thoughtless remarks and comments made within the family circle while the child is small. A parent or relative may remark that Junior has inherited those ears from the other side of the family. Junior may be a handsome, attractive child, but that has nothing to do with his reaction to comments on his ears. He begins to feel that his ears are big and conspicuous. When Sister begins to grow tall in early adolescence before her boy cousins have started their adolescent growth, the parents and relatives remark over and over, "How tall she is! I believe she is going to be taller than the others." And Sister begins to slouch over and try to make herself inconspicuous. Or while she is still a toddler, mother and aunts remark, "It is too bad her hair is straight." After she hears that a few times, she feels that her hair is a serious handicap to her looks. Since any deviation in the shape of a child's jaw and the regularity of his teeth occasions comment in the family, innumerable children and young adults go about with the feeling that they have horribly prominent teeth.

A child's actual appearance seems to have little to do with whether or not he worries over how he looks. Some children do have features or defects that might be expected to be handicaps, yet, if the matter has been handled right in the family, the child may be entirely unconscious of the characteristic so that it handicaps him not at all. Unattractive features can be a handicap only if the child feels conscious of them and considers them as handicaps.

One of the finest gifts the family can give to a child is a feeling within himself that he is a credit to the family; that they like him and are proud of him. Whether he happens to be tall or short, fat or slim, curly-haired or straight-haired, with big ears or small, should be supremely unimportant as far as family love is concerned.

Other childhood troubles have to do with situations in which the child feels that he has "lost face" before others. If he is punished before others, if his parents discuss him and his traits in the presence of others, or if he is forced to dress or act in ways that are noticeably different from those about him, he will feel that he has lost face. Table 24 gives a more complete listing of home circumstances causing anxiety in children.

TABLE 24

STUDENT RANKING OF SPECIFIC CIRCUMSTANCES WHICH CAUSED ANXIETY DURING CHILDHOOD[a]

(*Physical features*)	(*Losing face before others*)
1. Afraid I would always be homely	1. Had to wear long stockings or underwear
2. Crooked teeth	2. Scoldings before other children
3. Awkwardness	3. Had to perform for others
4. Too fat or too slim	4. Parents made me apologize for things
5. Wearing glasses	5. Parents bragged about me
6. Complexion	6. Didn't dress as other children did or had to wear hand-me-down clothes
7. Unattractive hair	7. Teasing
8. Not growing any taller	8. Being left out of things
	9. Couldn't do things others did
	10. Mother always let everyone know I was the baby
(*Conditioned fears*)	(*Desire for security*)
1. Darkness	1. That our house would burn
2. Lightning and thunder	2. That my father would die
3. Animals, snakes, bugs, etc.	3. That my mother would die
4. Being left alone	4. That my brothers or sisters would die
5. Fires	5. That I would die
6. Deep water	6. That I was adopted
7. Being locked in closet	7. That my parents would separate
8. Old empty houses	8. Being kidnaped
9. Fear of not getting to heaven	9. That the world would come to an end
10. Fear of going to hell	
11. Fear of being punished by God	
12. Ghosts	

[a] Unpublished research by Judson T. Landis. Three hundred and fifty college students listed the specific factors which caused great anxiety in their lives when they were between the ages of 5 and 12. These common fears and worries have been classified under four headings in the above table. In each grouping the listings are from those mentioned most frequently to least frequently. Some of these fears are quite universally conditioned in small children, others reflect a child's feelings of insecurity in the home, and still others are natural reactions to "losing face" before one's friends.

Those approaching marriage and parenthood should give some thought to these many things that affect the happiness and sense of well-being of children in the home. The happiness of the children is important not only to the happiness of the parents but because of the influence it will have upon the future marriages of the children.

Chapter XXII

BRINGING UP CHILDREN

IN THIS CHAPTER we shall discuss certain basic traits and characteristics that parents can help their children develop if the parents are able to take the long view of their children's growing up. Parents need to be able to look far beyond the immediate problem that may seem so baffling and decide whether it has any significance in determining what kind of a man or woman this child will eventually be. They need to see in today's fascinating and frustrating two-year-old the prophecy of tomorrow's twenty-year-old. While they are busy coping with specific details of child rearing,[1] they can also have clearly in mind what the fundamental values are, and can try to maintain perspective concerning the personality development of their children.

Trends in child care practices

For some years authorities on infant care have laid much stress upon such matters as breast-feeding, toilet-training, and methods of weaning, as important factors in the development of the basic personality pattern of the child. Many young mothers today feel that if they cannot breast-feed their babies they may be handicapping the child's development of feelings of security. Parents of half-grown children who are aware of the current emphasis upon the superiority of self-demand sched-

[1] *The Pocketbook of Baby and Child Care,* by Benjamin Spock, offers an excellent guide for parents in dealing with many details of child training.

ules in infant-feeding over rigid feeding schedules often are regretful and discouraged because they recall that when their children were infants they conscientiously adhered to rigid schedules. In the 1930's the "good" mother put her child on a three- or four-hour feeding schedule and allowed nothing to interfere with it. She let the baby "cry it out" if he attempted to upset the schedule. She weaned him from the breast or bottle to a cup as early as possible, and she felt that his toilet-training must begin while he was but a few months old and be completed by a set time. Now, mothers are advised to do the opposite, to let nature take its course in the development of the child lest they create tensions, fears, and frustrations in him that will handicap his personality throughout life.

After investigating some 644 articles written between 1890 and 1949 on the subject of child care, Clark Vincent found that most of the 1890 articles suggested that the mother "loosely schedule," most of the writing in 1920 advocated that she "tightly schedule" and let the child "cry it out," and most in 1948 urged that she permit the child to "self-regulate." [2] In this period of about 60 years there was a swing of the pendulum from one extreme to the other on many matters of infant care.

Today the emphasis is upon the relationship between details of the infant's physical care and his psychological and emotional growth. William H. Sewell has attempted to test the importance of that relationship through a study of the personalities of a group of children and through an examination of the methods that were used in their care as infants. He found few significant relationships between infant-care practices and later personality. He reports, "Such practices as breast feeding, gradual weaning, demand schedule, and easy and late induction to bowel and bladder training . . . were almost barren in terms of relation to personality adjustment as measured in this study." [3]

However, Sewell's findings should not be interpreted as mean-

[2] Clark E. Vincent, "Trends in Infant Care Ideas," *Child Development*, 22 (September, 1951), 199-209.

[3] William H. Sewell, "Infant Training and the Personality of the Child," *The American Journal of Sociology*, 58:2 (September, 1952), 150-159.

ing that it does not matter what methods are used in the early months of a child's life. They suggest, rather, that certain more general factors may be of more fundamental importance in personality development. In the years when infant-care practices were characterized by rigidity, just as in the years when the opposite methods were considered best, a great many children still managed to develop well-adjusted and basically secure personalities. That fact alone suggests that successful parenthood goes far beyond following specific "right" or "wrong" methods of infant care.

Basic principles in child-care practices

Basic in determining the personality of the child is the *quality of the total relationships* between parent and child. This is something which defies examination in a study, even in such an excellent one as that conducted by Sewell. To illustrate: A mother may nurse her baby because of a strong sense of duty, although she may reject the child emotionally and actually may have little understanding of its total needs. Another mother may not be able to nurse her baby, but she may show greater warmth and affection for the child than the resentful, nursing mother. When it was popular to put the baby on a schedule and let him "cry it out," there were still a great many babies whose total emotional relationships with their mothers led to their feeling loved and secure. These babies adjusted to the rigid schedules without emotional damage. Parents of young children need help in getting perspective on such matters.

Certainly today's emphasis upon a close relationship between mother and baby from the earliest days of a child's life is good. We have discussed the rooming-in plan in another chapter. Other sound practices are less rigid feeding schedules, and more flexibility in toilet-training and in some matters of discipline. However, no amount of doing certain things right in infant care will ever take the place of that more intangible and more important thing, really wanting the child, understanding him as an individual, and making him feel loved and secure.

Children may have all their physical needs satisfied from the time they are born until they reach adulthood and yet turn out to be unhappy, maladjusted people, simply because their emotional needs were never met in the parent-child interactional pattern. Moreover, a few mistakes in method will not ruin a child if the total parent-child relationship is sound and healthy. We do not accept the theory that a child's personality is absolutely set at a very young age and that early mistakes in method made by parents are inevitably disastrous to young personalities. Children are amazingly tough, both physically and emotionally; parents who, through lack of experience, knowledge, or understanding, make mistakes with their children when the children are young can overcome their mistakes as they themselves mature and gain insight into their children's development.

Parental perspective

From the long-time view, what traits need to be cultivated if the child is to be a well-rounded and happily adjusted individual? What do we want for our child? Do we look upon him with a fair degree of objectivity as a separate personality apart from ourselves, or are we subjective in our attitudes toward him and his needs?

As we stated in the preceding chapter, the first and probably the most important advantage that can be given to children is a background of happily married parents. The couple who can apply self-discipline and objectivity to their own marital relationships in working out happy adjustments will find no insurmountable difficulties in bringing up their children. They will be able to interpret childish behavior in the light of whether an act is a natural, though perhaps annoying, expression of childish nature, or whether it indicates development of an undesirable tendency that has bearing upon the adult personality into which the child will grow.

Some parents will punish a child for getting his clothes dirty at play, for breaking a dish when he is trying to help, or for making too much noise in crowded living quarters; but these same parents may overlook the fact that the child lies easily and frequently, not just because of his pleasure in fantasy, but

"I don't expect you to make her beautiful. Just concentrate on making her look like a girl!"

Fig. 102. *By permission,* Frank Owen and *Collier's.*

because lying enables him to avoid facing unpleasant situations. The same parents who will punish a child for trivial acts that are temporarily annoying to themselves may take no notice of the fact that the child is destructive of property belonging to others or is cruel and unkind in his relationships with other children. Such parents have no perspective upon the development of their child; they are unaware of the relative importance of events, or of the traits which need to be developed if a child is to be happy and well adjusted in childhood, and if he is to achieve successful maturity.[4] Many of the desirable traits are interrelated and can hardly be assigned places of greater or less importance. They tend to be found together as a personality pattern or to be generally lacking in poorly adjusted and unhappy children.

Initiative and self-reliance

The development of these traits begins early, when the child first shows an interest in doing things for himself. He should be encouraged in his attempts to dress himself, feed himself, and so forth. It is often here that parents fail, for it is much easier when time is limited and tasks are many to take over and do for the child rather than to let him muddle through at his own pace.

Many parents, with their first child, fail to realize at how early an age a child's urge toward independence may appear. The mother of a nine-month-old baby was struggling through dinner time with the baby in his highchair. Each time she offered him food in a spoon, he swung at her hand and frequently succeeded in knocking either the spoon or the food to the floor. She said, "I don't know why he's so naughty lately. I have a terrible time feeding him." The observer said, "Why don't you just let him go it alone? He may be swinging at the spoon because he'd like to get hold of it and feed himself instead of having you thrust the food at him." The mother protested that the baby was far too young to feed himself, but she decided to give him a chance. She began setting his food before him with a spoon beside it and going about her other work. Of course he tried the handle of the spoon, and his fingers, and

[4] For an analysis of traditional concepts of parenthood contrasted with developmental concepts, see Evelyn Millis Duvall, "Conceptions of Parenthood," *The American Journal of Sociology,* 52:3 (November, 1946), 193-203.

various other methods of getting his food to his mouth, but in a very short time he was feeding himself with certainly no worse spillage than had been occurring when his mother had been trying to feed him. And his great satisfaction in being able to do for himself independently was easily apparent in the enthusiasm with which he welcomed mealtimes. How better can a young child be spending his time and energy than in learning even by hit and miss to do for himself? If parents can curb their impatience and allow the child to go ahead and learn for himself with a minimum of help or interference, they will be allowing him to make progress toward achieving self-reliance.

As the child grows a little older, he often wants to take part in his parents' activities, to "help" with whatever work he sees them doing. If Dad is pounding with a hammer, the small child wants to pound too. His efforts are not always helpful, especially if Dad's pounding is a hurried attempt to fix something in the apartment that the mother of the family has been requesting for many weeks past. A too frequent result of the child's efforts to help is, "Come get this child out of my hair if you want me to fix anything."

Small children who follow their mothers around wanting to "help" meet the same kind of rebuff too often. One young mother was washing the kitchen floor when in came her three-year-old son with a small pan of water and a clean towel from the bathroom. He put down his pan of water with a big splash on the part of the kitchen floor that she had just nicely finished cleaning, and began scrubbing the floor with great swishing of the towel and splashing of water. Thinking only of the work to be done over, his mother descended upon him angrily, snatching the pan and towel away from him with a "No, no, naughty boy to get the clean floor all wet again," which sent him crying from the kitchen.

There are undoubtedly too many such incidents as this in the background of older children whose mothers complain bitterly, "He never shows any initiative or willingness to take his share of responsibility." The wise parents will from the earliest years respect and encourage evidences of initiative in the child, even if his attempts to help are not always helpful. It is a matter of perspective. Which is of more permanent importance, getting the housework or repair work done exactly according to schedule or helping a little boy to feel that he is needed by his parents and useful to them, that his ideas and help can make a contribution to the running of the home? It it not reasonable to squelch childish evidences of initiative because "he is too little" up to a certain age, and then to assume that "now he is old enough" and expect him suddenly to show initiative. Growth is not that simple.

The same principle applies to the making of decisions. No one certain day or particular age marks the point at which a child becomes old enough to think for himself. It would be easier for parents if that were the case. Parents must decide frequently in individual situations, "Is this a situation that calls for guidance and direction? Is it a decision that is so entirely beyond the child's experience that it should automatically be decided for him? Is it one of the many cases which in itself is not so important, the important thing being that the child should make the decision for himself?"

Some children seem to shrink from making their own decisions and depend upon parents too much. These children need to be encouraged toward independence. Here again objectivity on the part of the parent is important. Sometimes parents, especially mothers, become so wrapped up in the lives of their children that they are too much occupied with making all the child's decisions for him. The wise mother will realize that it is better for the child to make his own decisions in so far as it is possible, because the time is not far ahead when he will have to make his own choices. He will need confidence in his own judgment if he is to take his place with others in the outside world. If a child shrinks from making his own decisions, he can be helped gradually without being made to feel that he is pushed away or that his interests are not important to the parents.

The handling of money

In considering the making of decisions, the subject of the use of money arises. The whole subject of money and its use is one that may be used constructively to aid in the development of the child.

The parents themselves need first to evaluate their own attitudes toward money. There are a great many variations in the matter of what families consider it worth while to spend money for. Some place the value entirely upon material things, a car, furniture, the "newest" items available. Many parents frown on the expenditure of money for books; others will buy books even if it means wearing shabby clothes and using worn furniture. Some consider it an extravagance to spend money for travel or vacations; others will cut down on some of the "necessities" of life in order to have money for travel. Some families consider music lessons one of the necessities; others would call them a luxury item.

These varying attitudes have little relation to whether a family is rich or poor. But it is readily seen that a child's conception of values in life will be influenced by these family attitudes toward money. Further, his conception of his own responsibility in the family will be influenced by his own experience with money. Many families give the child an allowance weekly or monthly. This allowance is handled in various ways. The amount will depend on what the child is expected to do with it. Two cases might be mentioned that illustrate the two extremes in handling the allowance.

In one family, the four children, from eight years old up, received allowances sufficient to take care of all their needs. They were expected to work out a yearly budget, including their clothing, recreation, books, and all expenses except food and shelter. The father spent many hours with them assisting them with their budgets. In the other family the two children, ten and twelve years old, received allowances of 50 cents a week. The allowance was paid to them every Saturday morning and the procedure was always the same. They collected their allowances and rode their bicycles to town in time to be waiting when the dime stores opened. A half-hour later their money was gone. Sometimes they had a small toy or gadget worth carrying home and sometimes they found nothing that could hold their interest even long enough to get all the way home with it. The rest of the week, if they saw something they wanted or needed, they "begged mother" for it and she either bought it for them, gave them the money for it, or an argument followed in which the mother usually came off second best. This mother once said, "We have closets full of the junk the children have bought. I have sometimes wanted to give some of it away when the Christmas toy drives have come along, but the children won't let me. They never use any of it, but after all it does belong to them; they have bought it."

These cases represent two extremes. There is some question as to whether young children should be expected to take so much responsibility as the children in the first case. One wonders if the question of money and its handling might not assume too great importance in their lives. Many adults shrink from struggling with a budget, and it would be an unusual child who would enjoy coping with the problem as part of his regular responsibility. In the second case, the logical outcome of the policy would be that the children would develop no responsibility at all in the matter of money. The comments of their mother would indicate that they were being encouraged to think of money only as a means of gratifying any passing wish they might have, with the result that they were developing permanently selfish attitudes. The solution would seem to lie somewhere in between.

Parents may help the child to develop foresight and self-control in the use of his money, and yet allow him a great deal of freedom to make his own decisions. Progress was being made with the following two children. One seven-year-old boy starting to town with his mother said thoughtfully, "I think I will leave my money at home today so I can just enjoy looking at all the things." And an eleven-year-old said, "I like the looks of that trick-puzzle but I don't believe I'll buy it today. I'm not sure yet whether I want it enough to spend the price for it." This child was saving all he could of his allowance each week toward a fund for his summer camp, several months away. Many cases could be cited to show how experiences in the handling of money and attitudes concerning use of money are important in establishing not only a child's standards of value, but also his code of ethics.

Possessions

Another point that it is well for parents to have settled early in their own minds is the matter of possessions. Is the fact that a friend or neighbor has a certain thing a good reason why we must have it too? Children will have the same attitudes here as their parents. We have all observed the parents who struggle to provide their children with all the things that are demanded because "all the others have it." Sometimes a whole family goes without actual needs in order that one particularly demanding child may keep up with associates.

A mother of a fourteen-year-old was worrying about the future for her child who was entering high school. She said, "All the other children in this school are from families who can afford so much more than we can. I dread the high-school years for my daughter. She can't possibly be happy unless she can have all that the others have, and I don't know how we can ever manage to give her so much." If that had always been the mother's attitude, it was probably too late, but it would seem that much earlier in her childhood the girl should have been helped to develop resources within herself so that her entire happiness would not be dependent upon a certain few possessions.

Parents share their philosophy with their children whether they intend to or not. It is possible for even a young child to understand and accept the idea that we don't need to have just what others have in all cases. "Perhaps they wish to spend their money for that, while we prefer other things that we enjoy more," or "Perhaps we have not as much money to spend as they have, and we spend our money for the things that we think are most important to us." So parents may help even very young children to formulate concepts of relative values.

Consideration for others

The happiest married couples are those in which both partners are able to look at the other person's viewpoint and are not self-centered in relationships with others. The habit of consideration for others usually was developed in these happily married individuals long before they married. It begins in early childhood and is so important to the happiness of the individual and those about him throughout life that it is worth while for parents to work at helping their children to develop attitudes of consideration for others. The very young child can understand that sometimes it is necessary to play quietly because Daddy is tired and needs to rest; and that we do not run and play across the line in our neighbor's yard because our feet might trample flowers that she has worked hard to raise. It is important for a child to begin early to be conscious of the rights and interests of others.

A mother whose small son was crying and fretting while she was hurrying to get his dinner ready for him said, "I know you are hungry and tired and feel cross, but your crying makes it hard for me to think what I'm trying to fix for your dinner, so you must either stop crying or go into the other room and close the door so I may work without hearing you." In the long run this mother's policy should bring results, for the child will be made conscious of the needs of others as well as of his own. Many modern mothers, in their desire to be good mothers, regularly tolerate inconsiderate behavior on the part of their growing children. Their fear of inhibiting or suppressing the child is so great that they have lost all sense of proportion. They are not doing the child a kindness to allow him to develop such a selfish, demanding attitude toward life that he is considered a nuisance by others who come into contact with him. He will be a far happier individual if he is required to think of the wishes and feelings of others in a reasonable measure.

Parents sometimes reach the place where they fear to make any requirements at all of a self-centered child. The rule becomes "Anything for peace," but peace does not result. The fortunate children are those who have brothers and sisters whose interests also have to be considered, and whose parents have continued to be persons as well as parents. The presence of other children in the family forces the parents to require some sharing and some "taking turns." Johnny may be selfish and overbearing toward the neighbor's child without any effect upon his

"We've always encouraged Junior to take part in the conversation!"

Fig. 103. *By permission,* Jeff Keate and *Collier's.*

parents' complacency, but when he shows the same traits in his actions toward their own newest offspring, it is a jolt which usually causes them to go into action to change Johnny's ways.

There was a mother of ten children who, when asked why she had so many children, answered, "We always have to have another one to keep the last one from being spoiled." But that solution cannot be continued indefinitely. A time comes when parents must face the problem realistically and work at encouraging desirable attitudes toward the needs and rights of others.

Sense of humor

Another trait that is of great importance in a child's personality is a sense of humor. If the parents are people who have the ability to laugh together over their own as well as others' actions, the matter will usually be quite well taken care of. Such a sense of humor is a great aid toward keeping a perspective. If they can laugh with the child, never at him, from the time he is little, they will not need to worry about his sense of humor. With parents who are naturally intense and serious-minded or who are especially sensitive and fearful themselves of being laughed at, the problem is greater. But even these can cultivate cheerfulness in themselves and see that there is laughter in their home. The importance of laughter was well expressed by a little child whose parents had been going through a period of unusual strain. He said unexpectedly at dinner one day, "What's the matter with us all? We haven't had a good laugh for a week!" As the remark indicates, this family was a closely knit group who were in the habit of enjoying life together. For them to have passed a whole week without having had a "good laugh" together was occasion for comment.

Family companionship

Many of the goals parents hope to achieve with their children will be easier to attain if the family associates together as people who like each other and enjoy doing things together. This requires a specific effort in the modern home. Formerly, so many activities centered in the home that family unity and fellowship were the pattern more frequently than now. The pressure is now upon all members of the family to participate in activities which are specialized for age and sex. Consequently, members of the family seldom participate in the same groups outside the home. Although many of the organized activities for children and adults are excellent in purpose, they leave little time for family life unless people are intelligent in determining where to draw the line in their participation.

There is no substitute for family companionship as a source of happiness and security for the child. To small children it is not important what the activity is, or how much time is occupied with it, just so it is one in which all participate and one which can be depended upon to have its regular place in the daily or weekly routine. Children gain great pleasure from looking forward to pleasant family activities which they know will take place without fail. The knowledge that the parents will not let them down by allowing unimportant outside interests to displace the family activities is important to a child's sense of security. Very worth while are even such small things as listening to certain radio programs together on one evening a week.

Some parents who established the precedent of spending Sunday evenings together when the children were little have found to their surprise that even when their children are adolescent and have many interests outside the home they prefer to save Sunday evenings to spend with the family. Often the children bring their friends so that the circle is enlarged; such an arrangement adds to the pleasure of family activities as the children grow older. Invariably children from families who have little or no family life as such are anxious to be welcomed into the activities of other families who do things together. It is not always easy or convenient for parents to be consistent about spending time pleasantly with their children, but parents who make it a practice find that it pays well.

Evaluating ourselves as parents

When it comes to evaluating our success as parents it is important that we look at the whole child. First of all, is he happy? Is he developing resources within himself so that he is not too dependent upon outside circumstances for contentment? Does he have a feeling that others like him and value him? Is he dependable? Is he self-reliant, with confidence in himself and his ability to cope with life as it comes? A part of his self-confidence is a recognition of his personal responsibility for his own acts. Can he accept the consequences of his own acts without offering alibis, or blaming other people or circumstances? If his parents are people who do their best but are not afraid to say, "I was wrong," he will appreciate the fact that although his parents are not infallible they are able to work things out in spite of mistakes. This realization will help him to have the same attitude toward himself.

In order to be able to help a child develop desirable traits, parents need to be sure of their own attitudes toward the child. They must love him for himself, the individual that he is now, not as a reflection of their own personalities. Objectivity does not come naturally to parents. It must be cultivated. When it is achieved, one's role as a parent is more easily understood. There must be warmth of love so that from the cradle all the way along the child has the security that comes with a consciousness that he is loved and valued. But this parental love must not be so overwhelming and smothering that it stands as a wall between the child and the realities of the world about him. It is literally true that parents cannot fight their children's battles for them. The most pitiful spectacle is the family in which the parents are trying to do so. The unhappy child spends his time running to the shelter of mother's or father's arms and the frustrated parents are frequently involved in difficulties with other parents and children.

What then is the parental role? It is to help the child grow in his own way toward fulfillment of his own potentialities. Fundamentally, it is to contribute to his physical, mental, and emotional growth so that in due time he will be prepared to stand alone as a mature individual.

Chapter XXIII

SEX EDUCATION

THE BEST SEX EDUCATION consists not just in the giving of information about sex; more fundamentally, it is the shaping of proper attitudes and the incorporation of these attitudes in the personality of the child. Frances Strain, in referring to the "love stream" of life, includes in the concept all affection from earliest childhood to its most complete expression in the love of husband and wife.[1] The guidance of the "love stream" constitutes sex education. The process of shaping the attitudes of the child toward himself and the world about him in regard to his sexual nature starts in infancy and does not stop until the individual has found a good adjustment within his own marriage.

Sex education in the past

There was no planned program of sex education in the past. The subject of sex was taboo. Parents believed that children should be kept in ignorance of the "facts of life." When children first asked questions about babies and reproduction, they were told that they were too young to know, shushed out of the house by a disturbed parent, or punished for asking such questions. Slightly more enlightened parents attempted to answer by saying that doctors brought babies, or that mother went to the hospital to get the baby. When the child approached adolescence, parents usually felt the boy or girl should be told some-

[1] Frances B. Strain, *New Patterns in Sex Teaching,* pp. 5-23. New York: Appleton-Century-Crofts, Inc., 1951.

thing further. So the father would take the son aside for a "facts of life" conference, and the mother would have a similar session with the daughter.

We now know that the old system was often damaging to the emotional development of the child, and was at best useless. Parents who were evasive or showed an emotional reaction of shock or anger when children asked questions created the beginnings of wrong emotional responses in their children. Those who answered with stories about the stork took a step toward loss of the child's confidence. In most cases the child was not long in finding out that the parent had lied to him and from then on he would seek his information from more reliable sources. If the child lost face before his playmates when he first learned that his story about the stork was incorrect, it was natural for him to feel resentful toward his parents for having misled him. Most children did not remain in ignorance about sex under the old plan. Parents deluded themselves into thinking that by withholding information they preserved innocence. Faegre[2] found in her study on this subject that even before 1930 the average child in the sixth grade had sex information from as many as six different sources. The sex information and misinformation which children picked up were not so harmful as the emotional responses which developed because of the type of information they gathered. The conditions under which they sometimes learned about sex and the mental images that were created caused some children to develop extremely undesirable attitudes. Many were conditioned so that they could not think of sex in marriage as being natural or wholesome.

The "facts of life" conference which came as adolescence approached was sometimes harmful and in any event accomplished little in a constructive way. In the first place, it was presumptuous for parents to think that they could tell their children the "facts" in one session of fifteen minutes or a half hour. Sex is a complicated affair, certainly more involved than the function-

[2] Marion L. Faegre and John E. Anderson, *Child Care and Training*, p. 203. Minneapolis: The University of Minnesota Press, 1947.

ing of a radio, and fathers would not attempt to explain all the facts about radio to their sons in one easy lesson. In the second place, fathers are naive to think that they can tell their half-grown sons very much about the simpler facts of sex.

Conclusions based upon personal interviews with 291 pre-adolescent and early adolescent boys are enlightening here.[3] All had a considerable amount of sex information before they were 10. By age 14, nearly all had a fair idea of the process of human reproduction. Over 95 per cent at the age of 14 knew about the origin of babies, masturbation, intercourse, and prostitution. Over 86 per cent at 14 knew about contraception. Half at this age knew about venereal diseases. Ninety per cent of these boys had gotten their first information from companions. Parents had had little part in the giving of sex information.

This study was made among middle-class and upper-middle-class boys in an American city. Percentages might differ among boys from other backgrounds. Nevertheless, the conclusions should be illuminating, perhaps disillusioning, to parents who have believed that children can be kept in ignorance about sex until the parent chooses to tell.

Need for sex education

The realistic viewpoint is to recognize that the question is not whether children should or should not learn about sex. The choice is between their having misinformation from unwholesome sources or receiving scientific sex information from their parents or other qualified adults. Of course, some parents have themselves been so conditioned that it would be impossible for them to talk to their children about sex. Also, if parents are maladjusted in their sex life in marriage it might be better if they did not attempt to teach their children about sex. Their teaching could do more harm than good. Some of these parents may try to give their children the right answers, but may con-

[3] Glenn V. Ramsey, "The Sex Information of Younger Boys," *American Journal of Orthopsychiatry*, 13:2 (April, 1943), 347-352.

vey the wrong impressions by the things left unsaid, or by their embarrassment, avoidance, or apparently emotional reaction to the questions.

In general, however, most parents should give sex information as they give any other information. Studies of marital adjustment point to the fact that the children who have had sex facts presented to them in an open and frank manner by their parents have a better chance for happiness in marriage. The fact that from one-fourth to one-half of couples in the past, as pointed out in our chapter on sex adjustment in marriage, failed to arrive at satisfactory adjustments in sex relations in their marriages, may be explained in many cases by the way the sex instruction of the child was handled in his early years. Misinformation, sordid interpretations, embarrassment, and punishments often shaped the emotional development and attitudes of the child so that it was impossible for him to adjust normally in the sex relationship in marriage. Many personality maladjustments, marital failures, and much delinquency can be traced directly or indirectly to the parents' failure to give children proper sex education.

A planned program of sex education

Just as society has provision for training young people to make a living, so it should offer a well-organized program to help the child to understand his sexual-emotional nature and to train him for successful family living. We would not think we were fulfilling our obligations satisfactorily if we took time out to give children one lecture on honesty and let them shift for themselves after that. The teaching of honesty starts in the earliest years of the child's life in the home and is continued as long as the home functions. The child also learns precepts of honesty in the school and church. A similar program is needed as aid to sexual and emotional adjustment. We must accept the development of normal sexual attitudes as a part of a well-rounded educational program.

Sex education in the home

When is a child old enough to be told facts about sex? Authorities are agreed that a child is old enough to be told about sex when he is old enough to ask questions. We do not ask when a child is old enough to have an answer to his questions about why the grass is green. One of the greatest errors in approaching the subject of sex is that it has been considered as a separate compartment of life. Scientists point out that the human being reacts as a total organism. Children ask questions about sex along with other questions and all their questions are a normal part of development.

By the time a child is three years old he is asking questions about everything, "How do birds fly?" "What makes apples red?" "Where do babies come from?" and so on. In the mind of the child these questions are all of the same type. He is curious about all that he sees about him. Sex has no more emotional connotation for a little child than eating or growing or the other interesting things in his world. Wise parents will try to be as objective as the child is and give accurate answers to questions. Too many parents, because of their own conditioning about sex, and partly because they consider sex a separate compartment of their lives, become confused and do not know what to do when the young child asks, "Where did I come from?" Some parents who do not understand the development of the young child may think that their child is abnormal when at three years he starts asking questions about the origin of babies. Others, who plan to answer the child's questions, find themselves unprepared to do so because they had believed that these questions would not come for some years yet.

The most common question asked by the pre-school child has to do with the origin of babies. When the child first asks this question a satisfactory answer is usually simply that the baby grew in his mother's body. The parent may hesitate to give the answer, thinking it will shock the child. However, there is nothing shocking about it to the child, and his next question may be on some subject far removed, such as why the sky is blue, or why water is wet. He will not remember where he came from after being told once any more than he will remember why the sky is blue. He may come back three weeks later and again want to know where babies come from. When children first start asking questions, biologically complete answers are not

Fig. 104. "Dr. Jones brings good ones—do your folks take offen him?" *By permission,* Mrs. Crawford Young and *The Saturday Evening Post.*

needed any more than a complete explanation is needed of the functioning of the internal combustion engine the first time the child asks what makes the car go. As the child gets older, he will ask more specific questions which call for more detailed answers. "How does the baby get out?" The child may be told that there is a special place in the mother where the baby grows until it is ready to come out into the world through the passageway that is provided for it. This explanation or a similar one will satisfy the young child. As he gets older, of course, or whenever he asks specific questions that show he is ready for specific information, he should be given a more complete answer and the proper terms should be used for various parts of the reproductive system.

The most difficult question for parents to answer is the one about what part the father plays in getting a baby started. Relatively few children ask this question. One study made of the questions asked by 2,000 children in 1,000 homes showed that only 5 per cent of the questions had to do with the father's part in reproduction.[4] A parent may hope that his child will not be one of the few who ask the difficult question. We must remember, however, that the child, not being sexually mature, does not have the same feelings that the adult has. When an exceptional child asks this specific question it is wise to answer it accurately. He may be reminded that mothers and fathers are different physically and that the father is constructed with a special organ with which to unite his cells with the mother's to start the new baby. This is not hard for a child to understand and is in no way shocking to him if the facts are given in a casual, straightforward manner at the time when the question has arisen in his mind. Children are quick to notice if a parent suddenly reacts emotionally to questions in one certain field. At this point begin some of the undesirable attitudes toward sex which may hamper development of healthy attitudes.

During the pre-adolescent years, from 8 to 10, the function of menstruation should be explained to girls. This explanation may be made in a constructive way with emphasis upon the fact that menstruation means growing up. Too many mothers emphasize the pain and discomfort of menstruation, and encourage girls to feel that being a girl is a handicap.

Between the ages of 10 and 13 the boy should have explained to him the physical as well as the emotional changes which are about to take place. He should know about seminal emissions so that he will not worry when these first begin to occur. Excel-

[4] Katherine W. Hattendorf, "A Study of the Questions of Young Children Concerning Sex," *Journal of Social Psychology*, Vol. 3, February, 1932, pp. 37-65.

lent books have been written on the subject of maturing and if these are kept in the home library they will be read by children who are ready for them. These books often accomplish more than can be accomplished by the parents, especially if the parent has failed to handle the sex education of the child properly during the early years. If a parent realizes that his own conditioning makes it hard for him to discuss sex objectively with his child, he may find it well worth while to purchase some of the best books and have them in the home as casually as other books and magazines. Certainly such books should not be presented as "special" literature. Most children will read and find answers for themselves.

Fig. 105. "Can't you just tell them the facts of life without all these visual aids?" *By permission,* Lafe Locke and *Family Circle.*

Birds, bees, and flowers

Some parents have attempted to solve the problem of giving sex information by telling children about reproduction in flowers and bees in the hope that the child will figure out the rest for himself. But that hope has little foundation. Such explanations may cause the child to conclude that he grew from a bee or a bird's egg. Seeds to him are cherry or orange seeds and every time he swallows a cherry seed he may wonder if he will have a baby. The reproduction of the flower is hard for some college students to understand, and certainly the pre-school or grade-school youngster should not be expected to understand it and to make any connection between flower reproduction and human reproduction.

The parent must remember that if the child asks where he came from that is what he wishes to know. If he wants to know about the origin of bees or flowers, he will ask that also. It is necessary to answer only what has been asked. When a child asks what makes the car run he is not interested in the history of the automobile from the first gas engine down to the present, nor what makes steam engines, electric engines, diesel engines, and sail boats run; he wants to know what makes the family car run. When he gets into high school he will learn more about the physics of propulsion. There is no need to go into it at the time of the first question. The same is true in sex education. The child needs to be told only what he asks, but he should have that in a direct and honest manner.

Vocabulary to use

One reason many parents have difficulty in carrying out the sex instruction of children as they approach the adolescent period is that the parents have no language they can use in discussing sex with their children. They have used a baby language for bodily functions and parts of the body. As the child grew older he has learned to say "hand" and not "patty," "feet" and not "tootsies"; but he has not been given the right names for his sex organs or bodily eliminations. The more common thing is for the parent to use "wee-wee" or "toy-toy" when the child is small and never follow through with the scientific terms. In fact, many parents themselves do not use the scientific language; all they know is the street language they learned as children. Since they would feel ridiculous using this language with their children, after the children have passed the baby stage, there is actually an area in which parents and children cannot converse without feeling embarrassed. They have not the proper vocabulary. If terms such as bowel movement, urinate, penis, vulva, nipple, are used from the very first with children, they will accept them just as readily as they accept feet and hands and the family will have a language that is understood by all and accepted without embarrassment.

Student views on sex education

The importance of establishing confidence between the parent and the child cannot be overemphasized. This is one reason why it is important that the parents be prepared to answer their children's questions when they are first asked. Two thousand college students were asked this question, "At what age should children be given their first sex information?" The complete responses to this question are given in Table 25. It will be

TABLE 25

PERCENTAGES OF 2,000 STUDENTS STATING SPECIFIC AGES AT WHICH THEY THOUGHT CHILDREN SHOULD BE GIVEN FIRST SEX INFORMATION

At what age	Men	Women	Both
When children inquire	44.0%	62.0%	48.0%
Pre-school	3.0	3.0	3.0
6-8 years	5.0	6.0	5.0
9-11 years	11.0	10.0	11.0
12-14 years	30.0	19.0	28.0
15-17 years	7.0	0.0	5.0

noticed that 44 per cent of the young people stated that the first information should be given between the ages of 9 and 17 years. The response is interesting for two reasons. First, it represents a high carry-over of the old idea that children should be kept in ignorance about sex until they approach the adolescent age. Second, it suggests that if these young people do not give their children any sex information until they are of adolescent age, they will probably not give their children any sex information at all. In most cases by that time they will have established a pattern which will make it impossible for them to talk frankly with their children. Moreover, their children will already have found sources for their sex information before the parents get ready to do anything about it.

The source of *most* sex information for 1,600 students is shown in Table 26. It will be noticed that "other children" was

TABLE 26

PERCENTAGES OF 1,600 STUDENTS IN 11 COLLEGES IN 1952 STATING SPECIFIC SOURCES FOR MOST OF THEIR SEX INFORMATION

Source of information	Men (N-585)	Women (N-1010)
Mother	10.8%	37.5%
Father	9.3	2.1
Siblings	5.4	5.8
Other children	42.8	24.9
School classes	5.0	7.0
Reading	19.0	17.5
Other or had no information	7.7	5.2
Totals	100.0	100.0

the most common source of information for men and the second most common source of information for women.

Information given by parents

In the study of the 1,600 students, each student was asked to specify the type of sex and reproduction information he had received from parents. Table 27 shows the percentages of students stating the different types of information their parents had given them. The results suggest that a majority of parents believe that telling the girl about menstruation and boys and girls where babies come from constitutes adequate sex and reproduction education. Less than one-third of the children said they received any other type of information from their parents. We recognize that it is difficult for many parents to go beyond this elementary stage. But, since one great worry of the parents

TABLE 27

PERCENTAGES OF 1,600 STUDENTS FROM 11 COLLEGES STATING SPECIFIC SEX AND REPRODUCTION INFORMATION GIVEN BY PARENTS

Information given	Men (N-585)	Women (N-1010)
Where babies come from	58.0%	72.0%
Menstruation	23.0	90.0
Venereal disease	31.0	32.0
Difficulty of controlling sexual emotions	21.0	35.0
Coitus (sexual intercourse)	25.0	32.0
Masturbation	22.0	16.0
Sex perversions	14.0	19.0
Pleasure of sexual relations	10.0	21.0
Nocturnal emissions	21.0	13.0
Contraceptives	12.0	17.0
Orgasm	10.0	8.0
No information given	31.0	7.0

of teen-age young people is that the young people will not be able to control their sex emotions during dating years, it would seem that the pleasure of sex experience and the consequent difficulty of controlling the sexual impulses should be discussed with sons and daughters. Because of their own emotional reactions, most parents cannot or do not discuss this phase of sex, yet they worry about their children's ability to cope with strong sex urges that are new to them in adolescence and for which they are not prepared.

Few parents had discussed with their children the subject of sex deviate behavior. It is understandable that many parents would avoid this subject, hoping the child need never know anything about it. But that is not a realistic point of view. Information we obtained from 700 students in an urban university revealed that over one-third of the men and women had encountered some type of adult sex deviate behavior at some time during their childhood or youth. The types of behavior encountered covered a wide range; the most common were encounters with exhibitionists by girls and homosexual approaches having been made to boys. In recent years, wide publicity has been given to the problem of sex deviates in our society. Whether or not such individuals are more numerous than in other generations, parents are faced with the question of either ignoring the subject or trying to prepare the child to cope with any eventuality. The goal of parents should be first of all to try to help the child to develop normal and healthy attitudes concerning sex; that will constitute a most important form of protection. But just as children are permitted to know that there are dishonest or unkind people in the world, and that part of growing up is learning to cope with whatever kinds of people one encounters, so they ought to know that there are also people with unhealthy and warped attitudes about sex, and they should know how to cope with encounters with these people also. All frightening or "scare" talk should be avoided, for that can contribute as much or more to unwholesome attitudes in the child as an encounter with some types of deviates might do. In fact, the evidence seems to show that much of the trauma following a child's experience with the more common types of deviates is caused by the handling of the matter after it has happened. The shock and horror of parents and adults are more frightening in many cases than the experience itself was.

Sex experimentation

If children know about sex, will they be likely to experiment because of this knowledge? Some parents fear that they will. It seems doubtful that the children would experiment any more than at present and there is reason to believe they would experiment less. Much of the present experimentation arises out of curiosity. If children's natural curiosity has been satisfied, they will have less reason to experiment. The Child Study Association expresses the belief that children who are given information about sex are less likely to experiment than those who are not given information.[5]

[5] Child Study Association of America, *Parents' Questions,* p. 130. New York: Harper & Brothers, 1947.

In the study of the 1,600 college students in 1952, the factor of chastity was related to childhood sources of sex information. A larger percentage of those who had maintained socially accepted standards of behavior had gained their sex information from parents or from school classes, and they were more likely to have had most of the information in Table 27 given to them by their parents. Those who reported having had premarital sexual experience were more likely to have had no information from parents and to have learned about sex facts from brothers

Attitude of Children Toward Sex

Amount of sex information given by parents	Desirable	Undesirable	Neutral	Mixed feelings
None	48	22	15	15
1–3 items	63	18	8	11
4–6 items	86	6	2	6
7–11 items	92	3		4

Fig. 106. Relationship between children's attitudes toward sex and the amount of sex information given by parents. Attitudes were rated according to responses of 1,600 students to a check list of items such as "Sex is dirty and vulgar," "Sex is for mutual husband and wife enjoyment," etc. See Table 27 for parent information ideas.

or sisters or from other children. The research supports the belief that if parents do give their children rather complete sex information it will not lead to undesirable sex experimentation.

There are variables, however, which affect the sexual behavior of the child other than whether he has or has not received accurate sex information. A large and intensive study of teen-age people in San Francisco who were promiscuous in their sexual behavior revealed that their promiscuity was an indication of other serious problems within their lives, and that the promiscuity was an attempt to find a solution to inner conflicts.[6]

[6] Benno Safier, *et al., A Psychiatric Approach to the Treatment of Promiscuity,* pp. 77-78. New York: American Social Hygiene Association, 1949.

Many of the girls had been rejected by their parents, and felt unloved and unwanted; their promiscuity was a striving for a satisfaction of their love needs.

Some problems

Let us assume that young parents have a scientific attitude about sex education. They feel confident that they have been giving the right answers in the proper manner all the way along. Some problems may arise, nevertheless. For the whole area of sex is one that is complicated by many attitudes subject to outside influences. Children may become involved with other children in activities that are not socially acceptable, such as undressing at play, exercising the functions of elimination in public, masturbation, or attempts at sex experimentation. It is important for the parent to maintain his objectivity and to handle the situations in such a way that he does not do more harm than good. He should remember *why* he is trying to prevent some actions: that it is because of social unacceptability and not because in itself there is any thing bad or shocking in the child's act. In the matter of children undressing each other, it may be simply one child's attempt to see for himself how many kinds of people there are. He has seen himself and his sister and his father and mother, four kinds of bodies. How is he to know whether there may be several other variations unless he investigates? It may help to prevent such actions if the parent tells the child early when he asks about his own body, "You are a boy, all boys' bodies are alike, just as all girls' are alike."

It is true that sometimes intelligent parents who have given their children all the advantages of proper sex information will be appalled to learn that their children are attempting sex experimentation with their playmates. This is a strain on any parent's self-control, for they are immediately aware of the dangers involved: not only may the family lose face with the neighbors, but such activity by the children only a few short years hence could result in disaster, such as pregnancy for the girls involved and loss of reputation for the boys. With these things in mind, a parent's natural reaction is to take whatever extreme measures seem necessary to put an instant and permanent stop to such activities.

Many undesirable activities may be forestalled if the parent is alert. It is well to recognize that undesirable sex activities do take place, and not only in other people's families. The parent who takes the attitude that "My child wouldn't" is on unsound ground. That applies to all phases of childish behavior. The wise parent will be realistic in his attitude and will see that wholesome activities are provided.

In the matter of sex experimentation, prevention is much the easiest solution. If, however, the experimentation has already started, then it is well to meet the situation positively. It can be made clear to children that sexual union is for people who are married and ready and able to bring children into the world and take care of them; that if sexual union occurs before that time it may have a disastrously unhappy effect on one's whole life; therefore it is not permitted. Children who do have an understanding of the elementary facts of sex and reproduction will readily understand these things. Such teaching on the part of parents, together with attention to what goes on in the children's play, can take care of the problem of sex experimentation without adversely conditioning the children concerning sex.

Sometimes children who have been freely told the facts of birth and reproduction create neighborhood friction by telling the neighbors' children things their parents consider them too young to know. Actually, the talking about sex that children almost inevitably will do, whether or not their parents approve, will not do any harm, especially if the children are well adjusted children who have been armed with accurate information by their parents. But parents who are worried about what other parents are going to think may usually prevent difficulty by handling the matter honestly with their children.

In one family where the facts of life had been quite frankly faced from the children's infancy, the mother told her children,

"We think all these things are an interesting part of life and worth talking about sometimes. But not all families have the same ideas about what can be talked about and what can't. Some people would be shocked if we talked to them about how babies are started and how they are born, so let's try not to offend people who may feel that way." That her children understood and accepted this difference in views was shown by the fact that her six-year-old son said one day, after coming home from a neighbor's, "Johnny's mother is one of the people who think a lot of ordinary things are hush-subjects. She made us go outside to play when she gave their baby her bath."

The parent's first responsibility is to pursue a course which is for the best interests of his children, whether or not the neighbors approve. However, it is usually possible to spare the neighbors and still give the proper direction to the child's sexual attitudes.

Most parents are confronted with the problem of masturbation among their children, since most children masturbate at some time during the process of maturing. The problem may arise when the child is six months old, six years old, or not until sixteen years; children differ greatly. Because of social attitudes toward masturbation the parent can hardly ignore it. At one time parents quite universally punished their children for masturbation, believing that the habit would cause feeblemindedness, insanity, softening of the brain, stunted growth, and other horrible things.

Even today some people hold such opinions. But careful students of child development now recognize that the physical and mental effects of masturbation are not harmful in normal children. Emotional damage does result, however, if the child is severely censured and made to feel guilty and fearful about the habit.

Although masturbation as it occurs as an accompaniment of certain phases of development is not in itself harmful, it is true that it creates problems which baffle many parents. Parents are conscious of how others who deal with the child will react when they discover the habit. The child may be severely censured or ostracized by others, with serious emotional damage to him.

In general, the best way to cope with the problem is to meet it constructively. Parents need to make sure that the child is provided with interests and activities that fill his time adequately. They must see that he has the security that comes with knowing that he is valued and loved. Excessive masturbation may be an indication that the child has problems in other areas of his life which need to be cleared up. In normal children the habit will cease to be a problem once other interests and activities fill the child's life and once he becomes adjusted to the social world about him.

Family life education

Many community leaders feel that schools as well as parents have a responsibility in the sex education of children. A poll of the opinion of parents in Los Angeles found 97 per cent approving sex education in the senior high school, 95 per cent in the junior high school, and 75 per cent in the elementary schools.[7]

Purdue University's regular poll of a representative sample of high-school students in all parts of the United States found that over 80 per cent of high-school students thought the school should give sex instruction.[8] A similar poll of adults in New Jersey showed the same percentage in favor of such teachings. Parents with children in school when the study was made were more in favor of such teaching and felt the teaching should come to children at an earlier age than those parents who did not have children in school.[9]

A special film, "Human Growth," was produced for use in the sex education program in the Oregon schools. This film has now been previewed and evaluated by over a quarter of a million adults in all sections of the United States. Over 95 per cent

[7] *Family Life,* 8:3 (March, 1948), 5.
[8] *The Purdue Opinion Poll for Young People,* 7:5 (April, 1948), 23.
[9] *Journal of Social Hygiene,* 37:2 (February, 1951).

TABLE 28

TEACHERS' AND MENTAL HYGIENISTS' RATINGS OF THE RELATIVE SERIOUSNESS OF 35 COMMON BEHAVIOR PROBLEMS OF CHILDREN[a]

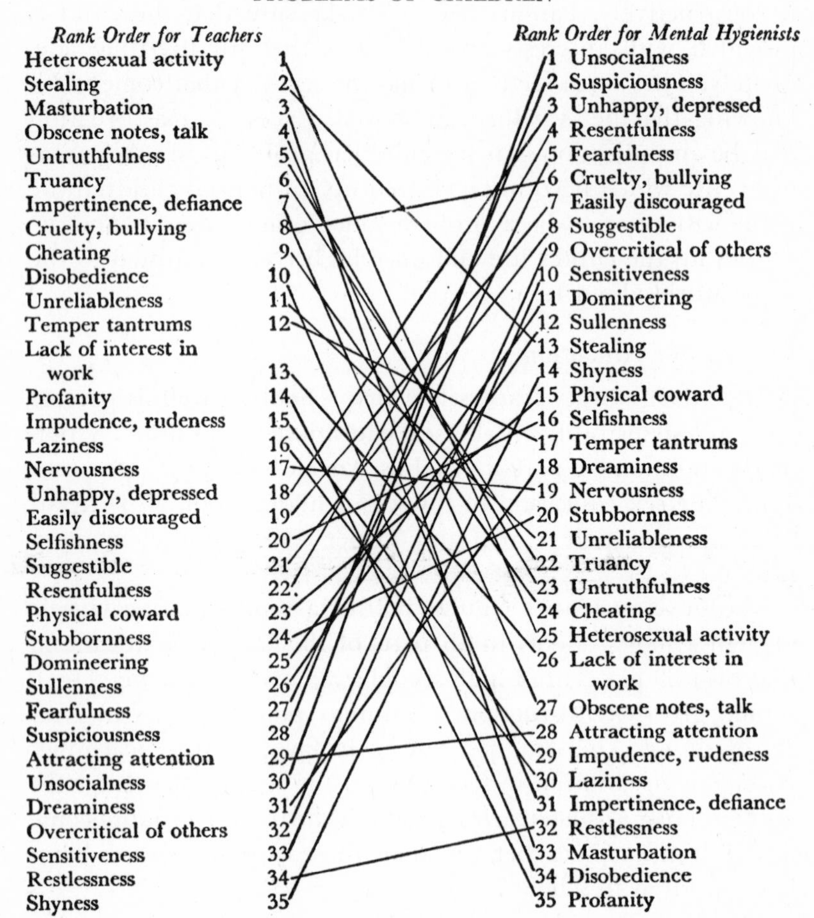

Rank Order for Teachers			*Rank Order for Mental Hygienists*
Heterosexual activity	1	1	Unsocialness
Stealing	2	2	Suspiciousness
Masturbation	3	3	Unhappy, depressed
Obscene notes, talk	4	4	Resentfulness
Untruthfulness	5	5	Fearfulness
Truancy	6	6	Cruelty, bullying
Impertinence, defiance	7	7	Easily discouraged
Cruelty, bullying	8	8	Suggestible
Cheating	9	9	Overcritical of others
Disobedience	10	10	Sensitiveness
Unreliableness	11	11	Domineering
Temper tantrums	12	12	Sullenness
Lack of interest in work	13	13	Stealing
Profanity	14	14	Shyness
Impudence, rudeness	15	15	Physical coward
Laziness	16	16	Selfishness
Nervousness	17	17	Temper tantrums
Unhappy, depressed	18	18	Dreaminess
Easily discouraged	19	19	Nervousness
Selfishness	20	20	Stubbornness
Suggestible	21	21	Unreliableness
Resentfulness	22	22	Truancy
Physical coward	23	23	Untruthfulness
Stubbornness	24	24	Cheating
Domineering	25	25	Heterosexual activity
Sullenness	26	26	Lack of interest in work
Fearfulness	27	27	Obscene notes, talk
Suspiciousness	28	28	Attracting attention
Attracting attention	29	29	Impudence, rudeness
Unsocialness	30	30	Laziness
Dreaminess	31	31	Impertinence, defiance
Overcritical of others	32	32	Restlessness
Sensitiveness	33	33	Masturbation
Restlessness	34	34	Disobedience
Shyness	35	35	Profanity

Teachers and parents may be too close to children to be able to judge the seriousness of their behavior in terms of long-time effects. Could it be that the mental hygienists' rating of these 35 behavior problems is more nearly correct?

[a] Adapted from E. K. Wickman, *Children's Behavior and Teachers' Attitudes.* New York: Commonwealth Fund, Division of Publications, 1928.

of the parents say that they would want their child to see this film on reproduction. The film was made for use in junior high schools, but it is now recognized that a film of this type should be shown to children before they reach puberty, for earlier there is less embarrassment, the film is more readily accepted, and the younger children need the information most.

At present, programs of family life education, including sex education, are developing in schools throughout the country. The right kind of educational plan seeks to help young people become prepared for successful family living in all its aspects, neither overemphasizing nor neglecting the sex phase. Ideally, the subject of sexual growth and development and functioning should receive as faithful attention from educators as does every other aspect of the development of youth into mature and responsible adults. There is no more excuse for biology courses' dealing at length with the structure and functioning of the circulatory, digestive, and nervous systems, and then skipping lightly over the reproductive system or ignoring it, than there would be for courses in literature to eliminate inclusion of all poetry or prose that refers directly or indirectly to love, in fear of putting ideas into young people's heads.

Nevertheless, many people who advocate the frank approach to sex take the position that removal of all old-fashioned taboos concerning sex, and the free giving of sex information, will solve all problems. They fail to recognize that certain standards exist because society has found them to be for the well-being of the individual and society. A recognition by the individual of his responsibility to society is more essential now than in the days when all facts concerning sex were shrouded with taboos and behavior was regulated by inhibitions.

Just as it is necessary to give children positive teaching in the matter of honesty, truthfulness, or personal cleanliness, so it is an obligation of parents to work at developing in children and young people a sense of personal responsibility. Many modern parents enthusiastically give their children sex information and then fail to follow through with any attempt to develop attributes that would make the children responsible members of society. A program of positive sexuality is needed which will take into account the whole individual and all his relationships.

Appendix A

MARRIAGE COUNSELING AGENCIES

The American Association of Marriage Counselors, Inc., is a professional organization of people qualified by training and experience to do marriage counseling. Membership in the association is limited to those who are able to pass an examination administered by the national membership committee. Since it is difficult for the individual in need of marriage counseling to know who the qualified marriage counselors are in a community, we suggest that those in need of counseling write the American Association of Marriage Counselors, Inc., 270 Park Avenue—Room C-701, New York 17, New York, for a list of qualified marriage counselors in any particular area.

We quote the standards of the organization below so that the individual may assess its purpose and the quality of its membership:

> Marriage counseling is here regarded as a specialized field of family counseling which centers largely on the inter-personal relationship between husband and wife. It involves many disciplines and is inter-professional in character. Those who wish to enter this field however, whether physician, clergyman, psychiatrist or social worker, require a common body of scientific knowledge, techniques and qualifications.
>
> *1. Academic Training*
>
> a. Every marriage counselor shall have a graduate or professional degree from an approved institution as a minimum qualification. This degree shall be in one of the following fields:

Education	Psychology
Home Economics	Religion
Law	Social Anthropology
Medicine	Social Work
Nursing	Sociology

b. Whatever the field of major emphasis, there shall be included accredited training in:

Psychology of personality development and interpersonal relations.
Elements of psychiatry.
Human biology, including the fundamentals of sex anatomy, physiology, and genetics.
Sociology of marriage and the family.
Legal aspects of marriage and the family.
Counseling techniques.

2. *Professional Experience and Qualifications*

a. To be eligible for full membership one must have recognized professional training and at least five years' experience in clinical marriage counseling, in accordance with accepted ethical standards. (Two years' clinical marriage counseling for associate membership.)
b. A candidate's qualifications shall include:
   1. Diagnostic skill in differentiating between the superficial and the deeper level types of maladjustment, and the ability to recognize when the latter type requires referral to other specialists.
   2. A scientific attitude toward individual variation and deviation, especially in the field of human sex behavior, and the ability to discuss sexual problems objectively.

3. *Personal Qualifications*

a. The candidate shall possess personal and professional integrity in accordance with accepted ethical standards.
b. The candidate shall have an attitude of interest, warmth, and kindness toward people, combined with a high degree of integration and emotional maturity.
c. The personal experience of marriage and parenthood is a decided asset.

Appendix B

SELECTED READINGS ON MARRIAGE AND FAMILY RELATIONS

The list of annotated books is grouped to make it easier for the reader to find the ones to fit his particular needs. The books are presented under the following headings:

Preparation for Parenthood
- Getting ready to be parents
- Child care and training

Sex Education of Children
- References for teachers and parents
- Readings for grade school children
- Readings for junior high school children

Preparation for Marriage and Family Living
- Textbooks for high-school classes
- Textbooks for college classes
- General books for older youth

Preparation for Marriage Adjustment
- For engaged and married couples

Preparation for Leadership in Family Life Education
- Textbooks for college courses in the sociology of the family
- Books for adult education leaders, ministers, and counselors
- Research reports on family life

PREPARATION FOR PARENTHOOD

Getting Ready To Be Parents

EASTMAN, Nicholson J., *Expectant Motherhood.* Boston: Little, Brown and Company, Revised 1950. 198 pp.

A scientific treatment of the prenatal period by a professor of obstetrics at The Johns Hopkins University and Obstetrician-in-Chief to The Johns Hopkins Hospital.

FARRIS, Edmond J., *Human Fertility and Problems of the Male.* White Plains: The Author's Press, Inc., 1950.

Reports on laboratory research largely on human male, but also on female, to determine real causes of infertility.

GOODRICH, Frederick W., *Natural Childbirth.* New York: Prentice-Hall, Inc., 1950. 176 pp.

A Manual containing information on natural childbirth, diet, exercise, relaxation, and the labor experience. For expectant parents.

HEARDMAN, Helen, *Natural Childbirth.* Baltimore: The Williams & Wilkins Company, 1949. 128 pp.

A manual describing methods used to prepare mothers for natural childbirth. Includes illustrated instructions for exercises designed to aid in the relaxation necessary for uncomplicated childbirth.

LOCKRIDGE, Frances, *Adopting a Child.* New York: Greenberg, Publisher, 1947. 216 pp.

Answers given on where and how to obtain a child for adoption. Appendix gives adoptive agencies in each state.

PORTNOY, Louis, and Jules SALTMAN, *Fertility in Marriage.* New York: Farrar, Straus and Company, 1950. 250 pp.

A guide for childless couples. Discusses methods being tried to help overcome sterility.

READ, Grantley Dick, *Childbirth Without Fear.* New York: Harper & Brothers, 1944. 259 pp.

The thesis of this book is that by doing away with fear through knowledge and understanding of childbirth, birth will be the natural, comparatively painless function nature intended it to be.

THOMS, Herbert, and Lawrence ROTH, *Understanding Natural Childbirth.* New York: McGraw-Hill Book Company, Inc., 1950. 112 pp.

Describes natural childbirth program at Yale University.

Child Care and Training

ALDRICH, C. Anderson, and Mary M. ALDRICH, *Babies Are Human Beings.* New York: The Macmillan Company, 1938. 128 pp.

Good on the development behavior of babies. Outlines practical suggestions for managing the infant. Not as light reading as some of the books on the subject, but valuable for parents who will read it.

BACMEISTER, Rhoda W., *Your Child and Other People.* Boston: Little, Brown and Company, 1950. 299 pp.

A guidebook to the social life of children from one to eight.

BRO, Margueritte Harmon, *When Children Ask.* Chicago: Willett, Clark and Company, 1940. 268 pp.

Deals with ways of answering children's questions on many subjects. Puzzled parents will find help here.

BUNDESEN, Herman N., *The Baby Manual.* New York: Simon & Schuster, Inc., 1944. 590 pp.

A practical and complete manual on the physical care of infants.

Child Study Association of America, *Parents' Questions* (revised edition). New York: Harper & Brothers, 1947. 256 pp.

Suggestions for dealing with specific problems. An excellent guide toward understanding and dealing wisely with children.

FAEGRE, Marion L., and John E. ANDERSON, *Child Care and Training.* Minneapolis: The University of Minnesota Press, 1947. 310 pp.

Provides a basis for intelligent child guidance by analyzing physical, mental, and emotional growth from infancy through adolescence. An excellent book.

GESELL, Arnold, and Frances L. ILG, *Infant and Child in the Culture of Today.* New York: Harper & Brothers, 1943. 399 pp.

A reliable treatment of techniques for child guidance.

GRUENBERG, Sidonie Matsner, *We the Parents.* New York: Harper & Brothers, 1939. 296 pp.

Considers parent relationships with growing children. Includes such subjects as discipline in the home; the child's handling of money; meeting the challenge of movies and the radio; explaining the facts of birth, death, marriage, and divorce; and many other topics.

RIBBLE, Margaret A., *The Rights of Infants.* New York: Columbia University Press, 1943. 118 pp.

Stresses the importance of mothering. Cites cases to show the effects on infants of a lack of mothering. Good reading for young mothers or for others caring for infants, but may cause an over-anxiety on the part of some young mothers concerning the emotional development of the infant.

SHULTZ, Gladys Denny, and Lee Forrest HILL, *Your Baby, The Complete Baby Book for Mothers and Fathers.* New York: Doubleday and Company, Inc., 1948. 278 pp.

SPOCK, Benjamin, *The Common Sense Book of Baby and Child Care.* New York: Duell, Sloan and Pearce, Inc., 1946. 527 pp.

A manual on all phases of the physical and emotional development of the infant and young child. A good book for mothers to own.

———, *The Pocketbook of Baby and Child Care.* New York: Pocket Books, Inc., 1946. 520 pp.

(Pocketbook printing of *The Common Sense Book of Baby and Child Care.*)

STRECKER, Edward A., *Their Mothers' Sons.* Philadelphia: J. B. Lippincott Company, 1946. 220 pp.

A psychiatrist analyzes the factors in parent-child relationships that contribute to the development of emotional maturity in children. Based upon his observation of great numbers of young men at induction centers in wartime.

TENNEY, H. Kent, *Let's Talk About Your Baby.* Minneapolis: The University of Minnesota Press, Revised 1947. 115 pp.

A guide for young mothers. Written in a refreshing style.

U.S. DEPARTMENT OF LABOR, *Your Child from One to Six.* Children's Bureau Publication 30 (revised). Superintendent of Documents, Washington, D.C. (Latest edition)

Examines both the physical and emotional development of the child. Much improved over the earlier editions in that it gives greater emphasis to the relationships involved in living together in a family.

WOLF, Anna W. M., *The Parents' Manual.* New York: Simon & Schuster, Inc., Revised 1951. 331 pp.

Handles the emotional development of the child and his relationships with others.

SEX EDUCATION OF CHILDREN

References for Teachers and Parents

BECK, Lester R., *Human Growth.* New York: Harcourt, Brace & Company, 1949. 124 pp.

Book to be used with the film "Human Growth."

BIBBY, Cyril, *Sex Education. A Guide for Parents, Teachers, and Youth Leaders.* New York: Emerson Books, Inc., 1946. 311 pp.

American edition of an English book that discusses many phases of sex education, especially as it might be developed in the schools. Questions of children and youth with suggested answers.

GILBERT, Margaret Shea, *Biography of the Unborn.* Baltimore: The Williams & Wilkins Company, Revised 1943. 132 pp.

This is the story of the development of a human individual from the moment of conception through birth.

HYMES, James L., *How To Tell Your Child About Sex.* New York: Public Affairs Committee, 1949. Pamphlet No. 149.

KIRKENDALL, Lester A., *Sex Education as Human Relations.* New York: Inor Publishing Company, Inc., 1950. 351 pp.

Excellent background information on the basic principles of sex education. Description of programs, methods, and materials.

STRAIN, Frances Bruce, *New Patterns in Sex Teachings.* New York: Appleton-Century-Crofts, Inc., Revised 1951. 262 pp.

Classifies most of the questions children ask about sex and suggests answers. This is still among the best of the books in this field. Recommended for the family library.

———, *Sex Guidance in Family Life Education.* New York: The Macmillan Company, 1942. 340 pp.

For parents, teachers, and community leaders interested in organizing a program of sex education in the public schools. Outlines a program of sex education from the first grade through the high school. Includes much of the good information given in *New Patterns in Sex Teachings.*

———, *The Normal Sex Interests of Children.* New York: Appleton-Century-Crofts, Inc., 1948. 210 pp.

Considers the developing sex nature of children from birth to adolescence.

Readings for Grade-School Children

DE SCHWEINITZ, Karl, *Growing Up.* New York: The Macmillan Company, 1935. 95 pp.

Explains clearly how we come alive, are born, and grow up. Similar to *The Wonder of Life,* but written in more simple terms.

LEVINE, Milton I., and Jean H. SELIGMANN, *The Wonder of Life, How We Are Born and How We Grow Up.* New York: Simon and Schuster, Inc., 1940. 114 pp.

Contains an unusually good approach to and treatment of the sex facts that children should know. Will be read with interest and understanding by young children if it is available in the home.

STRAIN, Frances Bruce, *Being Born, a Book of Facts for Boys and Girls.* New York: Appleton-Century-Crofts, Inc., 1936. 144 pp.

Suited to somewhat older children than the books by de Schweinitz, and Levine and Seligmann.

Readings for Junior-High-School Children

BERRY, Mary, *Manners Made Easy.* New York: McGraw-Hill Book Company, Inc., 1949. 327 pp.

Discusses behavior for all types of social occasions. Supplementary text for junior and senior high-school classes.

BIBBY, Cyril, *How Life Is Handed On*. New York: Emerson Books, Inc., 1947. 159 pp.

A description of reproduction, courtship, and family life in animals with some attention given to human reproduction. Interestingly written and illustrated.

CRAWFORD, John E., and Luther WOODWARD, *Better Ways of Growing Up*. Philadelphia: The Muhlenberg Press, 1948. 270 pp.

Excellent in treatment of personal, social, and life adjustment problems of teen-agers.

DICKERSON, Roy E., *Growing Into Manhood*. New York: Association Press, 1933. 100 pp.

A discussion of maturing sexually and its meaning. Deals with desirable habits of eating, sleeping, exercising, etc., for growing boys.

FEDDER, Ruth, *A Girl Grows Up*. New York: McGraw-Hill Book Company, Inc., Revised 1949, 271 pp.

Designed to help the adolescent girl understand the problems that face her day by day as she grows into maturity. Stresses the problems of physical and emotional maturity rather than the sexual phase.

KELIHER, Alice V., *Life and Growth*. New York: Appleton-Century-Crofts, Inc., 1938. 245 pp.

Explains social usages for high-school students and then treats physical and sexual development.

KIRKENDALL, Lester A., and Ruth F. OSBORNE, *Dating Days*. Chicago: Science Research Associates, 1949.

Discusses common problems of boy-girl relationships during early teens.

McKOWN, Harry C., *A Boy Grows Up*. New York: McGraw-Hill Book Company, Inc., Revised 1949. 333 pp.

Considers relationships of junior high-school boys with the family and outside groups and gives lists of social usages to follow on all occasions.

NOVIKOFF, Alex, *From Head to Foot*. New York: International Publishers Co., Inc., 1946. 96 pp.

Interestingly written book showing clearly how the body functions. Unusually well illustrated.

STRAIN, Frances Bruce, *Teen Days*. New York: Appleton-Century-Crofts, Inc., 1946. 183 pp.

Bridges the gap between the two books, *Being Born* and *Love at the Threshold*.

WELSHIMER, Helen, *Questions Girls Ask*. New York: E. P. Dutton and Co., Inc., 1939. 128 pp.

Seeks to answer the questions teen-age girls have about dating and courtship behavior.

PREPARATION FOR MARRIAGE AND FAMILY LIVING

Textbooks for High-School Classes

DUVALL, Evelyn Millis, *Family Living*. New York: The Macmillan Company, 1950. 410 pp.

LANDIS, Judson T., and Mary G. LANDIS, *Personal Adjustment, Marriage and Family Living*. New York: Prentice-Hall, Inc., 1950. 400 pp.

LANDIS, Paul H., *Your Marriage and Family Living*. New York: McGraw-Hill Book Company, Inc., 1946. 373 pp.

MOORE, Bernice M., and Dorothy M. LEAHY, *You and Your Family*. Boston: D. C. Heath and Company, 1948. 440 pp.

Textbooks for College Classes

BOWMAN, Henry A., *Marriage for Moderns*. New York: McGraw-Hill Book Company, Inc., revised, 1948. 544 pp.

CHRISTENSEN, Harold T., *Marriage Analysis*. New York: The Ronald Press Company, 1950. 510 pp.

DUVALL, Evelyn Millis, and Reuben HILL, *When You Marry*. Boston: D. C. Heath and Company, Revised 1953.

HARPER, Robert A., *Marriage*. New York: Appleton-Century-Crofts, Inc., 1949. 308 pp.

KOOS, Earl Lomon, *Marriage*. New York: Henry Holt and Company, Inc., 1953. 441 pp.

LANDIS, Judson T., and Mary G. LANDIS, *Building a Successful Marriage*. New York: Prentice-Hall, Inc. Revised, 1953.

———, *Youth and Marriage, A Student Manual*. New York: Prentice-Hall, Inc., 1951.

Keyed to be used with any of the above textbooks.

General Books for Older Youth

DICKERSON, Roy E., *So Youth May Know*. New York: Association Press, 1948. 259 pp.

Deals with sexual maturity in boys and the problems associated with it.

DUVALL, Evelyn Millis, *Facts of Life and Love*. New York: Association Press, 1950. 360 pp.

Rather complete discussion of the problems of teen agers, interestingly written.

FOSTER, Robert G., *Marriage and Family Relationships*. New York: The Macmillan Company, Revised 1950. 544 pp.

KIRKENDALL, Lester, *Understanding Sex*. Chicago: Science Research Associates, 1947. 48 pp.

This is an outstanding pamphlet which presents sex facts for the 14 to 16 year old in understandable language.

LLOYD-JONES, Esther, and Ruth FEDDER, *Coming of Age*. New York: McGraw-Hill Book Company, Inc., 1941. 280 pp.

Presents good material on personality development, family relationships, vocational planning, and getting an education.

SCHEINFELD, Amram, *The New You and Heredity*. Philadelphia: J. B. Lippincott Company, revised 1950. 616 pp.

Presents scientific information about heredity in a style that will hold the interest of the layman.

———, *Women and Men*. New York: Harcourt, Brace & Co., Inc., 1943. 453 pp.

An interesting discussion of the differences between the sexes.

SHULTZ, Gladys Denny, *Letters to Jane*. Philadelphia: J. B. Lippincott Company, 1948. 224 pp.

A mother writes a series of letters to her daughter and her college friends answering their many questions about love and sex.

STRAIN, Frances Bruce, *Love at the Threshold*. New York: Appleton-Century-Crofts, Inc., 1942. 349 pp.

Presents material on dating, romance, and marriage. Addressed to young men and women as they approach the age for marriage.

PREPARATION FOR MARRIAGE ADJUSTMENT

For Engaged and Married Couples

BENTLEY, Marguerite, *Wedding Etiquette*. Philadelphia: John C. Winston Company, 1947. 383 pp.

Offers complete information on weddings. Includes the wedding requirements of the different religious faiths.

BUTTERFIELD, Oliver M., *Sex Life in Marriage.* New York: Emerson Books, Inc., 1937. 192 pp.

A manual for people about to be married or those who are married, but who want a good book on sex expression in marriage. This is one of the best books written on sex in marriage.

———, *Marriage and Sexual Harmony.* New York: Emerson Books, Inc., 1938. 96 pp.

Booklet giving much of the information in the above book by the same author.

CASTALLO, Mario A., and Cecelia L. SCHULTZ, *Woman's Inside Story.* New York: The Macmillan Company, 1948. 203 pp.

Similar to the book listed in this section by Novak.

EXNER, M. J., *The Sexual Side of Marriage.* New York: W. W. Norton & Company, Inc., 1932. 127 pp.

Treats both the physical and psychological phases of sex in marriage in a frank and scientific manner.

FISHBEIN, Morris, and Ernest W. BURGESS, *Successful Marriage.* Garden City: Doubleday & Company, Inc., 1947. 547 pp.

Symposium by 38 authorities.

GROVES, Ernest R., Gladys Hoagland GROVES, and Catherine GROVES, *Sex Fulfillment in Marriage.* New York: Emerson Books, Inc., Revised 1943. 308 pp.

Reviews frankly and clearly the scientific knowledge about marital relations.

HAMBLEN, E. C., *Facts About the Change of Life.* Springfield: Charles S. Thomas, 1949. 86 pp.

This book dispels superstitions and false ideas based upon folklore concerning the menopause.

LANDIS, Judson T., and Mary G. LANDIS, *The Marriage Handbook.* New York: Prentice-Hall, Inc. Revised 1953.

Analyzes the factors that make for successful courtship, marriage, and family living. Includes recent research on courtship and marriage adjustment. Illustrated. (Edition of *Building a Successful Marriage* for the lay reader.)

NOVAK, Emil, *The Woman Asks the Doctor.* Baltimore: The Williams & Wilkins Company, 1944. 130 pp.

An authoritative discussion of special problems of women presented in a clear, understandable style.

POPENOE, Paul, *Marriage Is What You Make It.* New York: The Macmillan Company, 1950. 221 pp.

Largely a collection of articles which have appeared in popular magazines.

STONE, Hannah, and Abraham STONE, *A Marriage Manual.* New York: Simon & Schuster, Inc., Revised 1952.

A practical guide to sex in marriage. Probably the best on this subject.

PREPARATION FOR LEADERSHIP IN FAMILY LIFE EDUCATION

Textbooks for College Courses in the Sociology of the Family

BABER, Ray E., *Marriage and the Family.* New York: McGraw-Hill Book Company, Inc., 1939. 656 pp.

BECKER, Howard, and Reuben HILL, editors, *Family, Marriage, and Parenthood.* Boston: D. C. Heath and Company, 1948. 829 pp.

BURGESS, Ernest, and Harvey J. LOCKE, *The Family.* New York: American Book Company, 1945. 800 pp.

CAVAN, Ruth Shonle, *The American Family.* New York: Thomas Y. Crowell Company, 1953. 658 pp.

FOLSOM, Joseph K., *The Family and Democratic Society.* New York: John Wiley & Sons, 1943. 755 pp.

GROVES, Ernest R., and Gladys Hoagland GROVES, *The Contemporary American Family.* Philadelphia: J. B. Lippincott Company, 1947. 838 pp.

LANDIS, Judson T., and Mary G. LANDIS, *Readings in Marriage and the Family.* New York: Prentice-Hall, Inc., 1952. 460 pp.

NIMKOFF, Meyer F., *Marriage and the Family.* Boston: Houghton Mifflin Company, 1947. 767 pp.

TRUXAL, Andrew G., and Francis E. MERRILL, *The Family in American Culture.* New York: Prentice-Hall, Inc., 1947. 780 pp.

WALLER, Willard, *The Family* (Revised by Reuben Hill). New York: The Dryden Press, Inc., 1951. 637 pp.

Books for Adult Education Leaders, Ministers, Teachers and Counselors

CUBER, John F., *Marriage Counseling Practice.* New York: Appleton-Century-Crofts, Inc., 1948. 175 pp.

Reviews present practice in marriage counseling and presents an evaluation of procedures.

DAVIS, Allison W., and Robert J. HAVIHURST, *Father of the Man*. Boston: Houghton Mifflin Company, 1948. 245 pp.

A study of the development of personality of children.

DYER, Dorothy T., *The Family Today, A Guide for Leaders*. Minneapolis: The University of Minnesota Press, 1950.

Contains a series of planned units for giving family life education in the school, community, church, YW or YMCA. Leaders will find valuable help in it.

ENGLISH, O. Spurgeon, and Gerald H. J. PEARSON, *Emotional Problems of Living*. New York: W. W. Norton & Company, Inc., 1945. 438 pp.

An excellent book that examines the sources of neurotic behavior for the purpose of giving practical help toward maintaining emotional balance at all ages.

LANDIS, Paul H., *Adolescence and Youth*. New York: McGraw-Hill Book Company, Inc. Revised, 1952. 482 pp.

Stresses the social and psychological experiences of youth. Special attention is given to the moral, marital, and the economic maturity of youth.

LEVY, John, and Ruth MUNROE, *The Happy Family*. New York: Alfred A. Knopf, Inc., 1938. 320 pp.

Examines background factors that influence the happiness of marriages and of families. Gives attention to the emotional development of the individual and how this development affects his marriage success.

MUDD, Emily H., *The Practice of Marriage Counseling*. New York: The Association Press, 1951. 336 pp.

A survey of marriage counseling in the United States. Emphasis upon marriage counseling practice at Marriage Council of Philadelphia.

UPCHURCH, Garland R., and E. C. HARWOOD, *Life Insurance from the Buyer's Point of View*. Great Barrington: American Institute for Economic Research. Revised each year.

An unbiased explanation of life insurance in terms understandable by the average lay reader.

Research Reports on Family Life

BOSSARD, James H. S., and Eleanor S. BOLL, *Ritual in Family Living*. Philadelphia: University of Pennsylvania Press, 1950. 228 pp.

A study of ritual as a phase of American family behavior.

BURGESS, Ernest W., and Leonard S. COTTRELL, *Predicting Success or Failure in Marriage*. New York: Prentice-Hall, Inc., 1939. 472 pp. (Out of print.)

A study of 526 Illinois couples during the first six years of marriage.

BURGESS, Ernest W., and Paul WALLIN, *Engagement and Marriage*. Chicago: J. B. Lippincott Company, 1953.

A detailed study of the adjustments of 505 couples during engagement and again approximately three years after marriage.

HILL, Reuben, *Families Under Stress*. New York: Harper & Brothers, 1949. 443 pp.

A study of the adjustment of 135 Iowa families to the crisis of war separation and reunion.

KOOS, E. L., *Families in Trouble*. New York: King's Crown Press, 1946.

The adjustments of 48 middle-class families to a series of troubles.

HOLLIS, Florence, *Women in Marital Conflict*. New York: Family Service Association of America, 1949. 236 pp.

An analysis of 105 families who came for counseling; their problems, basic causes of marital difficulties, and effectiveness of treatment.

LOCKE, Harvey J., *Predicting Adjustment in Marriage*. New York: Henry Holt and Company, 1951. 407 pp.

A comparison of a divorced and a happily married group.

TERMAN, Lewis M., *Psychological Factors in Marital Happiness*. New York: McGraw-Hill Book Company, Inc., 1938. 474 pp. (Out of print.)

Research report on the factors associated with the marital adjustment of 792 couples.

WALLER, Willard, *The Old Love and The New*. New York: Horace Liveright, 1930. 344 pp. (Out of print.)

Appendix C

REVIEW QUESTIONS, SUGGESTED READINGS, SPECIAL PROBLEMS AND ACTIVITIES, SOCIO-DRAMAS

CHAPTER I: *Successful Marriage*

Review Questions

1. What is meant by saying that the attitudes which a young couple hold toward the marriage relationship will have more to do with their happiness in marriage than the intensity of their love at the time of the wedding?

2. What is a successful marriage?

3. In marriage one gives up some of his personal freedom. What does one gain in exchange?

4. What is meant by the statement that those who can build a good marriage are contributing a positive good to the world about them?

5. Successful marriages run in families. Why?

6. How does one's attitude toward the permanence of marriage affect his chances for a successful marriage?

7. Have you known couples who entered marriage with the attitude of Ruth and Tom?

8. "Many marriages which formerly would have been successful now end in divorce." Explain.

9. Is divorce necessarily a solution to serious difficulties in marriage?

10. Could it be that we have oversold the idea that marriage opens the gate to complete happiness?

11. Name several social changes which have affected the stability of the American family.

12. In what ways are the sexes less dependent upon each other today than they were 100 years ago?

13. Contast urban and rural living as they affect family relationships and stability.

14. Why is the affectional function of the family more important today than ever before?

15. Why has there been a rapid development of marriage courses in colleges during recent years?

Suggested Readings

Baber, Ray E., *Marriage and the Family.* New York: McGraw-Hill Book Company, Inc., 1939. Ch. I, "The Family in Transition."

Becker, Howard, and Reuben Hill, eds., *Family, Marriage, and Parenthood.* Boston: D. C. Heath and Company, 1948. Ch. XXVI, "Plans for Strengthening Family Life."

Burgess, Ernest, and Harvey J. Locke, *The Family.* New York: American Book Company, 1945. Ch. XVI, "The American Family in Transition."

Burgess, Ernest R., and Paul Wallin, *Engagement and Marriage.* Chicago: J. B. Lippincott Company, 1953. Chs. I and II, "Marriage in Transition," and "The Study of Modern Marriage."

Cavan Ruth Shonle, *The American Family.* New York: Thomas Y. Crowell Company, 1953. Ch. I, "Issues in the American Family at the Mid-Century."

Christensen, Harold T., *Marriage Analysis.* New York: The Ronald Press Company, 1950. Ch. II, "Society and Successful Marriage."

Landis, Judson T., and Mary G. Landis, eds., *Readings in Marriage and the Family.* New York: Prentice-Hall, Inc., 1952. Part I, Reading 1, "The Contemporary American Family as an Anthropologist Sees It," Margaret Mead; Reading 2, "Cultural Configurations in the American Family," John Sirjamaki; Reading 3, "The Changing Functions of the Family," William F. Ogburn; Reading 4, "The Family in a Changing Society," Ernest W. Burgess; Reading 5, "The Changing Family," Paul H. Landis.

Nimkoff, Meyer F., *Marriage and the Family.* Boston: Houghton Mifflin Company, 1948. Ch. IV, "Modern American Family."

CHAPTER II: *Role Concepts and Sex Differences*

Review Questions

1. Why do some women's groups oppose legislation designed to give women complete equality with men?

2. What do you understand by the statement that the sexes are not equal or unequal to each other but have a complementary relationship?

3. Which is the "weaker" sex as measured by morbidity and mortality? Cite statistics which support your answer.

4. What are reasons for the greater life expectancy of women?

5. What are some of the observable differences in muscular strength and coordination of pre-school boys and girls? Are these differences due entirely to cultural conditioning?

6. How does the rate of growth differ in boys and girls?

7. What do tests show about the mental differences of boys and girls?

8. Give some of the findings of the Yale Clinic of Child Development. Do these findings show that boys or girls are superior?

9. What did Terman find in his study of the achievements of gifted children?

10. Give some factors which would help explain the greater achievement of the male in our society.

11. Why do girls show a lag in intellectual development during later adolescence?

12. Is there a biological basis for the so-called double standard in morals? Explain.

Suggested Readings

Gesell, Arnold, and Frances L. Ilg, *The Child from Five to Ten.* New York: Harper & Brothers, 1946.

Scheinfeld, Amram, *Women and Men.* New York: Harcourt, Brace & Company, Inc., 1943. A scientific discussion of the differences between the sexes.

CHAPTER III: *Changing Sex Roles*

Review Questions

1. Interpret the statement that husbands and wives had "fixed roles" in the past?

2. What social changes have brought about the transition in husband-wife roles?

3. Are young men and women in agreement on what is the best role for women today?

4. What attitudes on the part of society and on the part of husbands sometimes cause wives to become discontented with the traditional role of wife-and-mother?

5. Do you think a girl could be happy playing the subservient role during courtship and yet not be happy playing that role after she is married?

6. What inconsistencies did Kirkpatrick find in men and women in his study of roles?

7. Under what conditions are the egos of both husbands and wives threatened in modern marriage?

Special Problems and Activities

1. Write a case history of a family you know in which confusion and unhappiness have arisen because of the wife's uncertainty as to her role in life.

2. Write a case history of a family you know in which there has been a perfect adjustment in the family although the wife has had a career outside the home. In both cases bring out reasons for the failure or the success.

3. Debate: Resolved: That married women with children should not be permitted to work outside the home.

Socio-Drama

Write and act a skit which illustrates the confusion in women's roles today. You might have one scene showing the women in the neighborhood gathered for tea and talking over their attitudes on women's roles. Another in which a group of husbands discuss their common problems. And a third, a family scene which illustrates the problems resulting in the home because of the confusion of the wife concerning roles.

Film

Who's Boss. Competition in marriage resulting from the confusion in husband-wife roles is the theme of this picture. Illustrates many of the factors discussed in the chapter, "Changing Sex Roles." McGraw-Hill Book Company, Inc. 20 minutes, sound. Can be had through most rental services.

Suggested Readings

Baber, Ray E., *Marriage and the Family.* New York: McGraw-Hill Book Company, Inc., 1939. Ch. XII, "The New Status of Women," and Ch. XIII, "Some Social Implications of Women's New Activities."

Bowman, Henry, *Marriage for Moderns.* New York: McGraw-Hill Book Company, Inc., 1948. Ch. IV, "Marriage Versus Careers."

Burgess, Ernest R., and Harvey J. Locke, *The Family.* New York: American Book Company, 1945. Ch. IX, "Expectations and Roles."

Christensen, Harold T., *Marriage Analysis.* New York: The Ronald Press Company, 1950. Ch. IV, "Men and Women."

Gruenberg, Sidonie M., and Hilda Sidney Kretch, *The Many Lives of Modern Woman.* Garden City: Doubleday & Company, Inc., 1952.

Koos, Earl Lomon, *Marriage.* New York: Henry Holt and Company, 1953. Ch. XII, "Roles in Marriage."

Landis, Judson T., and Mary G. Landis, eds., *Readings in Marriage and the Family.* New York: Prentice-Hall, Inc., 1952. Part XIII, Reading 1, "Cultural Contradictions in Sex Roles," Mirra Komarovsky; Reading 2, "Cultural Contradictions in Sex Roles: A Repeat Study," Paul Wallin; Reading 3, "Inconsistency in Marriage roles," Clifford Kirkpatrick; Reading 4, "Problems of the Modern Homemaker-Mother," Della Cyrus.

Nimkoff, Meyer F., *Marriage and the Family.* Boston: Houghton Mifflin Company, 1947. Ch. IV, "Modern American Family."

CHAPTER IV: *Why People Marry or Do Not Marry*

Review Questions

1. Do people marry at an earlier or later age today than they did 60 years ago? Give some reasons for this change.

2. Trace the development of the affectional needs of the individual as he progresses from infancy to maturity.

3. Define love as it exists between unrelated members of the opposite sex. How does it differ from love for parents?

4. Why do many young people as well as married adults believe in "love at first sight"?

5. Does sex attraction play a part in the initial stages of most courtships?

6. Cite forces other than love which drive people toward marriage.

7. "Social expectancy" is important in causing people to marry. Explain.

8. What are some of the personality needs fulfilled in marriage?

9. Explain the statement, "Our marriage market scraps the older women."

10. It takes greater effort to find an eligible mate in the city than in the country. Why?

11. Is the sex ratio on your campus favorable to the men or to the women?

12. What are some common reasons for failure to hold the interest of the opposite sex?

13. How does emotional dependence contribute to failure to marry?

14. Explain why married men seem to live longer than single men.

15. What do you understand by the "mating gradient"?

16. Should all people marry? Discuss.

17. What program might be undertaken to assure more eligible husbands?

Special Problems and Activities

1. From different sources find as many definitions of love as you can and bring them to class. For a beginning see Burgess and Locke, *The Family,* Chapter XII.

2. Make a study of ten love stories in current magazines. In how many of the stories is it "love at first sight"?

3. Write a short case history of a marriage you have observed which was motivated largely by one of the following: social status, money, escape.

4. From magazines or newspapers clip advertisements of matrimonial agencies and bring them to class. You might write a letter to an agency to gather additional information to present to the class.

Socio-Drama

Write a short play which brings out most of the reasons why people do or do not marry. Have members of the class present the play.

(It often adds to the interest of the socio-drama if members of the audience interrupt to demonstrate how the actors should act the part, i.e., if the girl demonstrating how women pursue men is not doing it properly, a girl from the floor takes her place and offers another interpretation.)

Film

Feelings of Hostility. Portrayal of how disappointment crises enter the life of a girl, their improper handling by the mother, and the girl's inability to establish a love relationship with the other sex in maturity. Gives insight into why some do not marry. National Film Board of Canada. 30 minutes, sound. Distributed by McGraw-Hill Book Company, Inc.

Suggested Readings

Becker, Howard, and Reuben Hill, eds., *Marriage Family and Parenthood*. Boston: D. C. Heath and Company, 1948. Ch. VII, "Steps in Love and Courtship."

Bowman, Henry A., *Marriage for Moderns*. New York: McGraw-Hill Book Company, Inc., 1948. Ch. II, "The Reasons for Marriage," and Ch. III, "The Permanently Unmarried."

Burgess, Ernest W., and Harvey J. Locke, *The Family*. New York: American Book Company, 1945. Ch. XII, "Love and Courtship."

Christensen, Harold T., *Marriage Analysis*. New York: The Ronald Press Company, 1950. Ch. VII, "Learning to Love."

Duvall, Evelyn Millis, and Reuben Hill, *When You Marry*. Boston: D. C. Heath & Company, Revised 1953. Ch. I, "What You Bring to Marriage," and Ch. II, "Love Enough To Marry On."

Folsom, Joseph K., *The Family and Democratic Society*. New York: John Wiley & Sons, Inc., 1943. Ch. XI, "Love as Experience and Relationship."

Koos, Earl Lomon, *Marriage*. New York: Henry Holt and Company, 1953. Ch. XIX, "What if You Don't Marry?"

Landis, Judson T., and Mary G. Landis, eds., *Readings in Marriage and the Family*. New York: Prentice-Hall, Inc., 1952. Part II, Reading 1, "The Family Cycle," Reading 2, "Statistical Perspective on Marriage," Kingsley Davis; Reading 3, "Mate Selection," Paul Popenoe. Part IV, Reading 4, "Cupid Is My Business," Clara Lane; Reading 5, "The Family and Romantic Love," Andrew G. Truxal and Francis E. Merrill.

Waller, Willard, *The Family* (Revised by Reuben Hill). New York: The Dryden Press, 1951. Ch. VI, "The Sentiment of Love."

CHAPTER V: *The Courtship Period*

Review Questions

1. Distinguish between dating and courtship. Why is it hard to separate the two?

2. What is the function of dating and of courtship?

3. Why do young people often settle down to "going steady"? Do you feel that all the reasons given in the text for steady dating are applicable in your community?

4. How does premature steady dating defeat the purpose of the courtship period?

5. What are the real reasons for discouraging petting? Why are parents concerned about the freedom of petting among young people?

6. Whose responsibility is it to control petting? Is it necessary for a girl to pet in order to be popular?

7. From a selfish viewpoint, why should one minimize petting situations during the courtship period?

8. What do you understand by exploitation in courtship? What are some common patterns of exploitation?

9. What are the characteristics of the men and women in college who rate as dates? Are they the same on your campus?

10. Why should one refrain from dating only those who rate?

11. What practice should one follow if he wishes to meet many date prospects?

12. What are some of the common places where couples first meet?

13. Define the term "assortative mating." What are some factors which help explain its operation?

14. What did Bossard's study of residential propinquity and mate selection reveal?

15. Has there been a great change in student attitudes on mate selection during past years?

16. What student attitudes on mate selection are an expression of our democratic ideals?

17. Why do men and women feel that the man should be older and have more education than the wife?

18. What evidence might indicate that it would be better for women to desire husbands who were younger than they?

19. In what respects do the attitudes of parents differ from the attitudes of their children on mate selection?

Special Problems and Activities

1. Mimeograph the questions from Table 3 for class use. Have members of the class check their responses to the questions. Summarize and compare the class responses with those of the other three student generations.

2. Write a few paragraphs describing the rating and dating pattern on your campus. You might make a survey of 25 men and 25 women to find what the most desired traits are in a date. Compare or contrast these with qualities which are desirable in a mate.

Film

Choosing Your Marriage Partner. A young man is trying to decide which of two girls to marry. He is advised to consider maturity, family background, harmony of personalities, and so forth. Coronet Instructional Films. 15 minutes, sound.

Suggested Readings

Baber, Ray E., *Marriage and Family Living.* New York: McGraw-Hill Book Company, Inc., 1939. Ch. VI, "Mate Selection and Courtship," Ch. IV, "Early American Family Life." (Material on colonial courtship behavior.)

Becker, Howard, and Reuben Hill, eds., *Family, Marriage, and Parenthood.* Boston: D. C. Heath and Company, 1948. Ch. VIII, "How Mates Are Sorted."

Cavan, Ruth Shonle, *The American Family.* New York: Thomas Y. Crowell Company, 1953. Ch. XII, "Social Relationships Preparatory to Marriage."

Koos, Earl Lomon, *Marriage.* New York: Henry Holt and Company, 1953. Chs. V and VI, "Dating," and "Courtship."

Landis, Judson T., and Mary G. Landis, eds., *Readings in Marriage and the Family.* New York: Prentice-Hall, Inc., 1952. Part III, Reading 1, "Courtship Practices and Contemporary Social Change in America," Niles Carpenter; Reading 2, "Changing Courtship Customs," John F. Cuber; Reading 3, "Some Changes in Courtship Behavior in Three Generations of Ohio Women," Marvin

R. Koller; Reading 4, "The Rating and Dating Complex," Willard Waller; Reading 5, "Dating Theories and Student Responses," Samuel H. Lowrie; Reading 6, "Courtship in a Group of Minnesota Students," Clifford Kirkpatrick and Theodore Caplow. Part IV, Reading 1, "Cultural Factors in Mate Selection," August B. Hollingshead; Reading 2, "Homogamy in Social Characteristics," Ernest W. Burgess and Paul Wallin.

Nimkoff, Meyer, *Marriage and the Family*. Boston: Houghton Mifflin Company, 1947. Ch. XII, "Courtship."

Waller, Willard, *The Family* (Revised by Reuben Hill). New York: The Dryden Press, 1951. Ch. VIII, "The Social Context of Courtship," Ch. IX, "Bargaining and Exploitative Attitudes," and Ch. X, "Courtship as an Interactive Process."

CHAPTER VI: *Marriageability*

Review Questions

1. How much change in the personality traits of a spouse can you expect after marriage? Why is it hard to admit personality faults?

2. Is it possible to make a list of personality traits for all people to follow in mate selection? Explain.

3. What were some of the personality traits which Terman found to be characteristic of happily married men and women? Of unhappily married men and women?

4. Why is it difficult to evaluate personality traits during the courtship process?

5. What does Terman's study of husband-wife grievances reveal about personality traits?

6. Cite personality traits which successfully married people felt made for good adjustment in their marriages.

7. Why does "talking things over" seem to be an important pattern in modern marriage?

8. What family background factors seem to be important in predicting success or failure in marriage? Do research studies agree upon this subject?

9. Does an unsatisfactory family background mean failure in marriage? Explain.

10. What do research studies show about education and marital happiness?

11. Is there a close relationship between the amount of income and happiness in marriage? Health and happiness?

12. What is revealed by analyses of age at marriage by occupation, education, and residence?

13. Cite evidence from research studies which indicates that youthful marriage is not wise.

14. Cite factors other than age which may explain the greater failure in youthful marriages.

15. What emotional characteristics are probably more characteristic of those who marry early?

16. Name some criteria of emotional maturity.

Special Problems and Activities

1. Make a list of ten personality traits which you find it hard to tolerate in others. Now make a self-analysis and try to determine why it is that you cannot tolerate these traits in others.

2. Make an analysis of your own emotional maturity. Then prepare two lists, one giving the ways in which you are quite mature and the other ways in which you are still immature.

3. Debate the question of deferred *vs.* youthful marriages.

Socio-Dramas

1. Try writing and acting a skit which brings out the personality traits making for happiness or unhappiness in marriage.

2. Try another skit which brings out the most common grievances of husbands and wives.

3. Dramatize the advantages and disadvantages of college marriages by means of a family scene in barracks, apartment, or trailer.

Films

Choosing for Happiness. Two college girls consider different men dated as possible mates for themselves. All fail to meet the needs of Eve because she herself is probably unmarriageable at her present stage of maturity. McGraw-Hill Book Company, Inc. 20 minutes, sound.

It Takes All Kinds. Demonstrates different types of personalities through reactions to frustration. Gives insight into personalities which might or might not meet one's personality needs in marriage. McGraw-Hill Book Company, Inc. 20 minutes, sound.

Suggested Readings

Baber, Ray E., *Marriage and the Family.* New York: McGraw-Hill Book Company, Inc., 1939. Ch. VII, "Mate Selection and Courtship."

Becker, Howard, and Reuben Hill, eds., *Family, Marriage, and Parenthood.* Boston: D. C. Heath and Company, 1948. Ch. VI, "Producing Marriagable Personalities."

Burgess, Ernest W., and Harvey J. Locke, *The Family.* New York: American Book Company, 1945. Ch. XIII, "Mate Selection."

Burgess, Ernest W., and Paul Wallin, *Engagement and Marriage.* Chicago: J. B. Lippincott Company, 1953. Ch. XIX, "Adaptability."

Christensen, Harold, *Marriage Analysis.* New York: The Ronald Press Company, 1950. Ch. VIII, "Choosing a Mate."

Landis, Judson T., and Mary G. Landis, eds., *Readings in Marriage and the Family.* New York: Prentice-Hall, Inc., 1952. Part IV, "The Influence of Parent-Images upon Marital Choice," Anselm Strauss.

CHAPTER VII: *Marriages under Special Circumstances*

Review Questions

1. What changes have encouraged an increase in marriages among college students?

2. Give some of the advantages and disadvantages of college marriages.

3. Why would some couples hesitate to marry in college if they had it to do over again?

4. Give several special problems which couples should consider if they plan to marry while in college.

5. What are some of the chief ways in which marriages involving separation differ from other marriages?

6. Why would one expect a higher divorce rate in marriages made during a war or military separation?

7. Comment on the following statement, "Yes, he has been married before, but that is no concern of mine. He was not to blame and I am marrying him as he is today."

8. How do second marriages differ from first marriages?

9. Why would one expect a higher divorce rate in second marriages?

Suggested Readings

Cavan, Ruth Shonle, *The American Family*. New York: Thomas Y. Crowell Company, 1953. Ch. XIX, "Adjustment to External Crises" (pp. 546-569).

Duvall, Evelyn M., and Reuben Hill, *When You Marry*. Boston: D. C. Heath and Company, Revised 1953. Ch. XXI, "Families in an Uneasy World."

Koos, Earl Lomon, *Marriage*. New York: Henry Holt and Company, 1953. Ch. XX, "Marriage and War."

Landis, Judson T., "On The Campus," *Survey Midmonthly*, 84:1 (January, 1948), 17-19.

Landis, Judson T., and Mary G. Landis, eds., *Readings in Marriage and the Family*. New York: Prentice-Hall, Inc., 1952. Part VII, Reading 2, "Separation and Marital Adjustment," Margaret Mead; Reading 3, "Separation and Adjustment—A Case," John F. Cuber; Reading 9, "Adjustment of the Divorced in Later Marriages," Harvey J. Locke and William Klausner.

Riemer, Svend, "Married Students Are Good Students," *Marriage and Family Living*, 9:1 (February, 1947), 11-12.

CHAPTER VIII: *Premarital Sexual Relations*

Review Questions

1. What do college students give as the approved sex standard before marriage? Do student generations change in their attitudes on sex standards?

2. Does economic and social status seem to affect one's attitudes toward premarital sex experience? Explain.

3. What effect does sexual experimentation before marriage seem to have upon happiness in marriage?

4. Explain why premarital sex relations cannot tell a couple whether they are well mated sexually.

5. What is meant by saying that the psychic is as important as the physical in sex expression? What bearing does this have upon premarital coitus?

6. Discuss some of the problems involved in premarital pregnancies from the point of view of society, the woman, the man, and the child.

7. Is control of the sex urge during the later teens a handicap to adjustment in marriage? Explain.

8. What point of view is desirable for the individual in determining his premarital behavior?

Suggested Readings

Bowman, Henry A., *Marriage for Moderns.* New York: McGraw-Hill Book Company, Inc., 1948. Ch. VIII, "Courtship and Engagement."

Burgess, Ernest W., and Paul Wallin, *Engagement and Marriage.* Chicago: J. B. Lippincott Company, 1953. Chs. XI and XII, "Sex and Engagement," and "Assessing Premarital Intercourse."

Christensen, Harold T., *Marriage Analysis.* New York: The Ronald Press Company, 1950. Ch. V, "Sexual Perspective."

Duvall, Evelyn Millis, and Reuben Hill, *When You Marry.* Boston: D. C. Heath and Company, 1953. Ch. VII, "Does Morality Make Sense?"

Landis, Judson T., and Mary G. Landis, eds., *Readings in Marriage and the Family.* New York: Prentice-Hall, Inc., 1952. Part XIV, Reading 1, "Sexual Behavior, What Is Acceptable?," George P. Murdock, Luther E. Woodward, and Frederick DeWolfe Bolman; Reading 2, "Sound Attitudes Toward Sex," Lester A. Kirkendall; Reading 3, "Penicillin Is Not Enough."

CHAPTER IX: *Mixed Marriages*

Review Questions

1. Define mixed marriage. How do the adjustment problems of mixed marriages differ from adjustment problems in other marriages?

2. Compare and contrast Protestant and Catholic attitudes toward mixed marriages.

3. What differences in belief make Protestant-Catholic marriages mixed marriages?

4. What are some of the factors explaining the higher divorce rate in mixed marriages?

5. In what faith are children reared in Catholic-Protestant marriages? How is this explained if agreement has been made before marriage that the children will be reared in the Catholic faith?

6. What seems to be the most common parental policy on religious instruction?

7. Give some of the reasons for the higher divorce rate in Catholic father-Protestant mother marriages.

8. What agreements made before marriage are often renegotiated after marriage?

9. What is the position of the three large Jewish groups toward mixed marriage? Toward intermarriage?

10. Cite factors which make for conflict in Jewish-Gentile marriages.

11. Are there other types of mixed religious marriages? What are some of the most serious problems of a mixed religious marriage?

12. Do differences in intelligence or education between spouses make for unhappiness in marriage? High divorce?

13. How might differences in economic background affect marriage adjustment?

14. What do research studies show in regard to differences in age of spouses and happiness in marriage?

Special Problems and Activities

1. Write a short history of a mixed marriage with which you are acquainted.

2. Have a rabbi, a priest, and a minister present their views on mixed marriages to the class.

3. In order to break down religious, nationality, and racial prejudice there should be a biological fusing of different groups; or we might say that for the good of society one should make a mixed marriage. Is it possible to harmonize this point of view with what has been said about mixed marriages in this chapter?

Socio-Drama

Write a series of short skits picturing the problems found in different types of mixed marriages discussed in this chapter. Have a different couple act each skit.

Film

This Charming Couple. Focus is on the unreality of romantic love as well as on a type of couple combination which approaches a mixed marriage. McGraw-Hill Book Company, Inc. 20 minutes, sound.

Suggested Readings

Bowman, Henry A., *Marriage for Moderns.* New York: McGraw-Hill Book Company, Inc., 1948. Ch. VII, "Choosing a Mate—Mixed Marriages."

Cavan, Ruth Shonle, *The American Family*. New York: Thomas Y. Crowell Company, 1953. Ch. X, "Cross-Cultural Marriages."

Family Life Bureau, *The Family Today: A Catholic Appraisal*. Washington, D.C.: National Catholic Welfare Conference, 1944. "Mixed Marriages," pp. 107-115.

Landis, Judson T., and Mary G. Landis, eds., *Readings in Marriage and the Family*. New York: Prentice-Hall, Inc., 1952. Part VIII, Reading 1, "Marriages of Mixed and Non-Mixed Religious Faith," Judson T. Landis; Reading 2, "A Study of 48 Interracial Marriages," Ray E. Baber.

CHAPTER X: *Engagement*

Review Questions

1. What relationship is there between length of acquaintance and happiness in marriage?

2. Does the wearing of a fraternity pin at your school mean engagement? Are you certain?

3. What is the purpose of the engagement period today? How does this differ from the past?

4. How permanent are engagements today?

5. What are common reasons for breaking engagements?

6. What are some of the most common trends in courtship as represented by graphs?

7. Does the research on broken engagements lend encouragement to those suffering with a broken heart? Discuss. Apply this same principle to other emotional crises.

8. What are some common reactions to the frustration which comes with the breaking of an engagement?

9. What should the attitude of the wounded partner be when an engagement is broken?

10. Why are long engagements predictive of success in marriage?

11. Cite some subjects which should be discussed during the engagement period.

12. Give reasons for or against confessing the past.

13. What questions should a person ask himself before confessing his past?

14. Give the chief reasons for a premarital examination.

15. Are elopement marriages as happy as conventional marriages? Why?

16. What pointers should one remember in planning the wedding and the honeymoon?

Special Problems and Activities

1. As a class, make a survey of student opinion on exchanging fraternity pins on your campus to determine what students think it means. Summarize and report to the class.

2. Let each student consult two other students who have broken an engagement to find just why the engagements were broken. Summarize the class findings.

3. Study several movies to see what pattern of behavior is depicted when the hero or heroine is frustrated in love.

Films

Are You Ready for Marriage? A young couple who want very much to get married discover what it takes to be ready for marriage, through discussions with a counselor. Coronet Instructional Films. 15 minutes, sound.

The Meaning of Engagement. Shows engagement as a period of developing psychological unity, learning to know each other, and developing plans for the future. Coronet Instructional Films. 15 minutes, sound.

Suggested Readings

Becker, Howard, and Reuben Hill, eds., *Family, Marriage, and Parenthood.* Boston: D. C. Heath and Company, 1948. Ch. IX, "The Engagement."

Bowman, Henry A., *Marriage for Moderns.* New York: McGraw-Hill Book Company, Inc., 1948. Ch. IX, "Wedding and Honeymoon."

Burgess, Ernest W., and Paul Wallin, *Engagement and Marriage.* Chicago: J. B. Lippincott Company, 1953. Entire book, but especially Chs. VIII through XVII.

Cavan, Ruth Shonle, *The American Family.* New York: Thomas Y. Crowell Company, 1953. Ch. X, "Courtship and Engagement."

Christensen, Harold T., *Marriage Analysis.* New York: The Ronald Press Company, 1950. Ch. VI, "Predicting Success or Failure," and Ch. IX, "The Transition into Marriage."

Duvall, Evelyn M., and Reuben Hill, *When You Marry.* Boston: D. C. Heath and Company, Revised 1953. Ch. IX, "Wedding Plans."

Landis, Judson T., and Mary G. Landis, eds., *Readings in Marriage and the Family*. New York: Prentice-Hall, Inc., 1952. Part V, Reading 1, "Marriage Adjustment and Engagement Adjustment," Ernest W. Burgess and Paul Wallin; Reading 2, "Personality and Marriage Adjustment," Robert F. Winch; Reading 3, "A Study of 738 Elopements," Paul Popenoe. Part VI, Reading 1, "Of Weddings," Frank H. Ferris; Readings 2 and 3, "A Hindu Marriage in Bengal," and "A Hindu Wife," D. N. Mitra.

Waller, Willard, *The Family* (Revised by Reuben Hill). New York: The Dryden Press, 1951. Ch. XII, "The Engagement."

CHAPTER XI: *Legal Control of Marriage*

Review Questions

1. What special problems does the state face when it attempts to regulate marriage?

2. How does a marriage contract differ from other civil contracts?

3. What one thing is essential to make a marriage binding?

4. Give some of the most common eugenic regulations of marriage.

5. Why is it difficult to enforce some of the eugenic regulations?

6. What is the most common legal age for marriage without consent? With consent?

7. Folkways and mores rather than the law determine the age at marriage. Explain.

8. Give some of the common regulations of marriages of consanguinity. Of affinity.

9. Why is there great variation among states on marriages of affinity?

10. Summarize the miscegenetic regulations. What is the regulation in your state?

11. Is it possible to marry without a marriage license?

12. Cite evidence to show that requiring a waiting period between the time of application for a license to marry and the marriage is a good regulation.

13. What do authorities think about the policy of recognizing common law marriages?

14. Distinguish between void and voidable marriages. Give an example of each.

15. How does annulment differ from divorce?

16. Give the most common grounds for annulment.

17. What is the legal status of children of void marriages?

18. What changes are taking place to protect children born out of wedlock?

19. Give some additional recommendations for action to protect the children of unwed mothers.

Special Problems and Activities

1. Special report. Have one member of the class consult Vernier's *American Family Laws,* or a statute book from your state, and give a report on the marriage laws in your state.

2. Special report. Gather all available information on your state's policy on children born out of wedlock.

3. Have one member of the class get copies of all the legal forms required for marriage and the registration of births in your state. Post these on your bulletin board.

Suggested Readings

Becker, Howard, and Reuben Hill, eds., *Family, Marriage, and Parenthood.* Boston: D. C. Heath and Company, 1948. Ch. XIX, "What Family Members Should Know About Law."

Truxal, Andrew G., and Francis E. Merrill, *The Family in American Culture.* New York: Prentice-Hall, Inc., 1947. Ch. VII, "The Family and the Law."

Vernier, Chester G., *American Family Laws.* Stanford: Stanford University Press, 1931-38. A complete analysis of American family laws in all 51 jurisdictions.

CHAPTER XII: *Achieving Adjustment in Marriage*

Review Questions

1. Contrast the interaction of courtship adjustment with the interaction of marriage adjustment.

2. How does marriage adjustment in a "mixed marriage" differ from marriage adjustment in a conventional marriage?

3. In what ways is adjusting to a marriage partner comparable to living with a roommate?

4. What are the three chief forms of resolving conflict in marriage adjustment? Illustrate each with cases of marriages you have observed.

5. What are seven potential conflict areas in marriage interaction which may call for adjustment?

6. Which areas seem to require the longest time for adjustment? In which areas are the fewest mutually satisfactory adjustments after some years of marriage?

7. Are marriages happier if mutually satisfactory adjustments are reached early in marriage?

8. Is it possible for a couple to have a happy marriage if they have never adjusted in one area?

9. How does modern living cause tensions to be built up in the individual?

10. Differentiate between productive quarrels and destructive quarrels.

11. Is it possible to have a friendly quarrel? Explain.

12. What might be the effects upon a marriage if one spouse came from a quarreling family and the other from a non-quarreling family?

13. List what you consider are five advantages of the family conference method of handling family differences.

14. Name several wholesome "tension-relievers" which you have found to be effective or which you have observed in your friends.

15. What are "tremendous trifles" in marriage?

16. What is the psychological effect of being "remodeled"?

17. How has the changed status of women affected husband-wife adjustment?

18. What are the most important factors in determining whether a particular marriage will be a success or a failure?

19. Approximately what proportion of marriages are happy?

Special Problems and Activities

1. Write up a case of a family you have observed that uses either quarreling or the conference method of settling family problems.

2. Give a case of a family difference which started as a "productive quarrel" but ended in a family fight.

3. Make a list of "tremendous trifles" which have caused trouble in your family, or some family you know well.

Socio-Dramas

1. The right and the wrong way to settle family differences, two family scenes.

2. "Tremendous trifles" in marriage, a family scene.

3. A scene in a marriage counselor's office; the husband and the wife tell their stories and gain perspective about their problems.

Films

Who's Boss? Use this film here if it was not used at the end of Chapter III.

Marriage Today. Gives a mature concept of marriage and marriage adjustment by showing several couples who have been married for some years. McGraw-Hill Book Company, Inc. 20 minutes, sound.

Suggested Readings

Baber, Ray E., *Marriage and the Family.* New York: McGraw-Hill Book Company, Inc., 1939. Ch. VIII, "The Husband-Wife Relationship."

Bowman, Henry A., *Marriage for Moderns.* New York: McGraw-Hill Book Company, Inc., 1948. Chs. X and XI, "Personality Adjustment."

Burgess, Ernest, and Harvey J. Locke, *The Family.* New York: American Book Company, 1945. Ch. XIV, "Marital Success," and Ch. XV, "Predicting Marital Success."

Burgess, Ernest W., and Paul Wallin, *Engagement and Marriage.* Chicago: J. B. Lippincott Company, 1953. "Marital Adjustment."

Cavan, Ruth Shonle, *The American Family.* New York: Thomas Y. Crowell Company, 1953. Ch. XVI, "Marital Adjustment."

Christensen, Harold, *Marriage Analysis.* New York: The Ronald Press Company, 1950. Ch. X, "Mate Adjustment."

Groves, Ernest R., and Gladys H. Groves, *The Contemporary American Family.* Philadelphia: J. B. Lippincott Company, 1947. Ch. VIII, "Emotional Aspects of Family Life," and Ch. IX, "Behavior Aspects of Family Life."

Harper, Robert A., *Marriage.* New York: Appleton-Century-Crofts, Inc., 1949. Ch. VII, "Learning To Live Together."

Landis, Judson T., and Mary G. Landis, eds., *Readings in Marriage and the Family.* New York: Prentice-Hall, Inc., 1952. Part X, Reading 1, "Psychological Factors in Marital Happiness," Lewis M. Terman; Reading 4, "Time Required To Achieve Marriage Adjustment," Judson T. Landis; Reading 5, "Predicting Adjustment in Marriage," Ernest W. Burgess and Leonard S. Cottrell; Reading 6, "Learning To Live Together—A Case," Anonymous;

Reading 7, "Occupational Factors and Marriage," Meyer F. Nimkoff; Reading 8, "Social Class and Marital Adjustment," Julius Roth and Robert F. Peck.

Truxal, Andrew G., and Francis E. Merrill, *The Family in American Culture.* New York: Prentice-Hall, Inc., 1947. Ch. XXI, "Marital Interaction."

CHAPTER XIII: *Sex Adjustment in Marriage*

Review Questions

1. How important is a good sex adjustment in marriage?

2. In what ways may failure to adjust in spending the family income affect the sex adjustment?

3. What special factors serve to focus attention upon the working out of sex adjustments which do not operate in the making of other marital adjustments?

4. Contrast the attitudes of two generations ago toward sex expression in marriage with the attitudes of today.

5. Name the three broad classifications which include most of the causes of poor sex adjustment in marriage.

6. What are some of the specific circumstances which cause poor sex adjustment?

7. Why is "bull session" information often a handicap to a good sex adjustment in marriage?

8. How does cultural conditioning of the sex response before marriage affect marriage adjustment?

9. Why must the husband show patience and understanding in the early months of marriage if there is to be a good sex adjustment?

10. What is one common difference in sex response of men and women which makes for misunderstanding between husbands and wives?

11. Why does there appear to be a marked difference in the strength of the sex drive of the husband and wife in the early months of marriage?

12. Is there a biological difference in the strength of the sex drive in men and women?

13. If a couple finds they are having difficulty in arriving at a mutually satisfactory sex adjustment, where may they get reliable help?

14. Is there a qualified marriage counselor in your community?

Special Problems and Activities

As a special project, two or three students query all agencies in your community that might be doing marriage counseling to learn what facilities are available to the public. Report to the class.

Suggested Readings

Baber, Ray E., *Marriage and the Family.* New York: McGraw-Hill Book Company, Inc., 1939. Ch. IX, "Husband-Wife Relationships."

Becker, Howard, and Reuben Hill, eds., *Family, Marriage, and Parenthood.* Boston: D. C. Heath and Company, 1948. Ch. X, "Taking Physical Factors into Account."

Burgess, Ernest W., and Paul Wallin, *Engagement and Marriage.* Chicago: J. B. Lippincott Company, 1953. Ch. XX, "The Sex Factor in Marriage."

Butterfield, Oliver, *Sex Life in Marriage.* New York: Emerson Books, Inc., 1937. This book and the one by Stone and Stone are excellent.

Exner, M. J., *The Sexual Side of Marriage.* New York: W. W. Norton & Company, Inc., 1932.

Groves, Ernest, Gladys Groves, and Catherine Groves, *Fulfillment in Marriage.* New York: Emerson Books, Inc., 1943.

Stone, Hannah, and Abraham Stone, *A Marriage Manual.* New York: Simon & Schuster, Inc., 1952. Those about to be married or in the early years of marriage should read this book.

CHAPTER XIV: *In-Laws and Marriage Adjustment*

Review Questions

1. Why are young people often unconscious of the fact that, in reality, marriage unites two entire families?

2. How important are in-laws in marriage adjustment?

3. In what relationships are in-law frictions most common?

4. What is the relationship between the length of time required to adjust to the in-laws, ultimate adjustment with the in-laws, and happiness in marriage?

5. "In-law friction in the early years of marriage is a normal outgrowth of parent-child relationships." Explain.

6. "They give us too much advice." Analyze this tendency in parents-in-law.

7. Why do couples find it difficult to discuss their in-law differences?

8. Give several reasons why the age from 45 to 60 is a crisis period for the average mother.

9. Why is in-law friction more likely if the children live with the parents-in-law?

10. Discuss in-law problems in "mixed" marriages.

11. Why should in-law friction be more pronounced among those who marry young?

12. What three common forms of interaction between the husband and wife develop from frustrations in in-law relationships? Illustrate each.

13. It has been said that most in-law friction is due to two women trying to be first in the affections of one man. What is the basis for this belief?

14. How do in-law problems among middle-aged couples differ from in-law problems of early marriage?

Special Problems and Activities

Make an objective analysis of the in-law relationships in your immediate family. If the in-law relationships are harmonious, why are they? If there is difficulty, who is at fault? Write a paragraph describing an in-law relationship pattern.

Socio-Drama

As a class project write and present a script which will illustrate how the common causes of in-law friction affect the behavior of the husband and wife toward each other.

Cartoons

Collect pictures or make original cartoons and construct a poster illustrating the various situations which make for in-law misunderstandings.

Film

Marriage Is a Partnership. Analyzes the first year of marriage and gives particular emphasis to misunderstandings over and adjustments to in-law relationships. Coronet Instructional Films. 14 minutes. sound.

Suggested Readings

Baber, Ray E., *Marriage and the Family*. New York: McGraw-Hill Book Company, Inc., 1939. Ch. IX, "The Husband-Wife Relationship."

Groves, Ernest R., and Gladys H. Groves, *The Contemporary American Family*. New York: J. B. Lippincott Company, 1947. Ch. XVI, "The Incompatible Family."

Nimkoff, Meyer F., *Marriage and the Family*. Boston: Houghton Mifflin Company, 1947. Ch. XX, "The Happy Family."

CHAPTER XV: *Religious Attitudes and Family Life*

Review Questions

1. What do research studies reveal concerning religion and marital adjustment?

2. How can religious participation serve as a family bond making for family unity? Disunity?

3. What is one of the fundamental contributions of religion to the individual?

4. In what ways does a religious faith fulfill fundamental needs of adults in the modern world?

5. How do you explain the fact that some of the best-selling books in recent years have dealt with religious themes?

6. If it is admitted that religion is an escape, how can religion be defended?

7. What is often the basis of fanaticism in religion?

8. List five ways in which religion should contribute to marital adjustment if one follows Judeo-Christian teachings.

9. How should religion bring about self-discipline?

10. In what ways should religious faith contribute to the general happiness of the individual?

11. The person with a religious philosophy probably has what other characteristics which make for successful marriage adjustment?

Special Problems and Activities

1. Have representatives from the Protestant, Catholic, and Jewish faiths talk to your class on the subject of religion and marriage.

2. Give a book report on one of the current best-selling books with a religious theme. Analyze the book, especially as to why the religious theme has a strong appeal.

Suggested Readings

Becker, Howard, and Reuben Hill, eds., *Family, Marriage, and Parenthood.* Boston: D. C. Heath and Company, 1948. Ch. XX, "Religion and Family Life."

Bro, Margueritte Harmon, *When Children Ask.* Chicago: Willett, Clark & Company, 1940. Tells how to answer children's questions about religion.

Duvall, Evelyn Millis, and Reuben Hill, *When You Marry.* Boston: D. C. Heath and Company, Revised 1953. Ch. XIX, "Family Life and Religious Living."

Eakin, Mildred, and Frank Eakin, *Your Child's Religion.* New York: The Macmillan Company, 1942.

Fosdick, Harry Emerson, *On Being a Real Person.* New York: Harper & Brothers, 1943.

CHAPTER XVI: *Finances and Adjustment in Marriage*

Review Questions

1. What are the basic factors making for misunderstanding between husband and wife over the use of money? Give three illustrations.

2. Why do attitudes toward the spending habits of the spouse sometimes seem to change after marriage?

3. What is the real purpose of a budget?

4. What are some common causes of friction growing out of use of a budget?

5. What are three common family patterns of controlling the family purse?

6. Give some arguments in favor of the wife's having the major responsibility for handling family finances.

Special Problems and Activities

1. Write a few paragraphs describing the "pattern of family spending" in your parents' family. Include: budgeting; who took the chief responsibility for spending; chief values of your family as a unit; chief values of individuals in the family; etc.

2. Give a case history of family friction resulting largely from a difference over values.

Socio-Dramas

1. Present skits showing different methods of controlling the family spending.

2. Present family scenes, one showing how a budget can become a cause of friction in the family.

3. Present a family scene which illustrates family misunderstanding growing out of differences in basic values.

Suggested Readings

Becker, Howard, and Reuben Hill, eds., *Family, Marriage, and Parenthood.* Boston: D. C. Heath and Company, 1948. Ch. XIII, "Financing the Marriage."

Bowman, Henry A., *Marriage for Moderns.* New York: McGraw-Hill Book Company, Inc., 1948. Ch. XIII, "The Use of Money and Leisure Time."

Harper, Robert A., *Marriage.* New York: Appleton-Century-Crofts, 1949. Ch. X, "Economic Adjustment in Marriage."

Jordan, David F., and Edward F. Willett, *Managing Personal Finances.* New York: Prentice-Hall, Inc., 1945.

CHAPTER XVII: *Getting Your Money's Worth*

Review Questions

1. What are the chief advantages and disadvantages of buying on a cash basis? Of using charge accounts?

2. How can a housewife learn to judge the value of goods?

3. What agencies have been organized for the specific purpose of protecting the consumer against buying shoddy goods?

4. What are the chief questions a couple should consider before they borrow money?

5. How do you explain the fact that people will shop around for groceries but not for credit?

6. What questions should a buyer ask before he buys goods on an installment contract?

7. Where does one usually pay a higher interest rate, at a bank or on an installment contract? Why is it difficult to figure the interest rate on installment contracts?

8. What is a small-loan company? How are they controlled?

9. Under what conditions should one consider borrowing from a small-loan company?

10. Why are small-loan companies permitted by state laws to charge such high interest rates?

11. What are the small-loan regulations in your state?

12. Where can one usually borrow money at the lowest rate of interest?

Special Problems and Activities

1. *Special reports.* (a) Give a general over-all report on the method and work of Consumers' Union and Consumers' Research. (b) From a recent issue of Consumers' Union or Consumers' Research give the findings and ratings on some consumer goods.

2. One student "shop" with all the lending agencies in town to see where he can borrow money and at what interest rate. Report findings to the class.

3. Mr. A. wants to buy a new radio but does not have the cash. He decides to borrow the money. He consults all lending agencies in his community in shopping for the credit. Play the role of Mr. A. and ask all the questions that he should ask each lender.

Cartoons and Posters

1. Make a bar chart showing the varying rates of interest charged by lending agencies in your community.

2. Make a chart with labels from canned goods showing the variation in the price for the same grade of article sold under different brand names.

Suggested Readings

Becker, Howard, and Reuben Hill, eds., *Family, Marriage, and Parenthood.* Boston: D. C. Heath and Company, 1948. Ch. XVII, "Designing the Family Home."

Duvall, Evelyn, and Reuben Hill, *When You Marry.* Boston: D. C. Heath and Company, Revised 1953. Ch. XI, "Money Matters in Marriage."

Gordon, Leland J., *Economics for Consumers.* New York: American Book Company, 1944. Chs. X and XI, "Producer Made Wants: Advertising"; Ch. XII, "The Profitable Practice of Fraud"; Ch. XIII, "Price Appeal"; Ch. XXIV, "Producer Aids to Consumers"; Ch. XXVI, "Watch Your Weights and Measures"; and Chs. XXVII and XXVIII, "Government Aids to Consumers."

Jordan, Helen M., ed., *You and Marriage.* New York: John Wiley & Sons, Inc., 1942. Ch. IX, "Money Management."

CHAPTER XVIII: *Buying Life Insurance*

Review Questions

1. Why is a discussion of life insurance pertinent in a book on successful marriage?

2. What is the chief purpose of life insurance? Why are some people confused as to its primary purpose?

3. Name the three chief classifications of life insurance policies.

4. Are industrial insurance and group insurance one and the same thing? How does industrial insurance get its name?

5. What are the chief advantages of industrial insurance? The chief disadvantages?

6. Under what conditions should one buy industrial insurance?

7. Why is group insurance a good buy? What are some of the shortcomings of group insurance?

8. What are the four chief types of policies sold under the heading of ordinary insurance? Which of these is the most commonly sold in face values of policies?

9. What is the chief function of term insurance? Are all term policies convertible? Renewable?

10. What advantages does a straight life policy have over a term policy?

11. Do all straight life policies have a cash or a loan value? Explain.

12. What is the principle of the limited payment policy? Under what circumstances would it be unwise to take out a limited payment policy?

13. Why do many people decide that what they need is an endowment policy? What financial plan might offer more benefits than an endowment policy?

14. Is it wise for families of limited incomes to take out endowment policies on their children for the education of the children? Explain.

15. Do insurance policies which offer the same protection cost the same in different companies? Explain why or why not.

16. How can the consumer of insurance determine the true net cost of an insurance policy?

17. What factors should be taken into consideration in determining one's insurance needs?

18. What is meant by "consumption unit responsibility"?

19. Why have life insurance agents been open to criticism? Who are the C. L. U. agents?

20. What are the chief advantages of having five $1,000 policies rather than one $5,000 policy?

21. Under what conditions should all the insurance of the family be placed upon the life of the breadwinner?

Problems To Solve

1. John and Mary Smith are 25 years old. John is through law school and is starting his law practice. He is in debt several thousands of dollars for his college education and, in addition, must meet the expenses of getting started in his practice. John and Mary have one son, James, who is one year old, and they expect another baby in six months. John has no insurance but is interested in buying some. What would you recommend that he buy?

2. John and Mary Smith are now 40 years old. John is well established in his law practice and all debts have been paid. They have four children now, ages 16, 15, 13, and 10. John followed your advice before and bought the policies recommended. Would you recommend any changes in his policies at this time? If so, what changes would you suggest?

3. An insurance agent has approached you about a policy and has made it sound so good that you feel that you must buy. You have never heard of his company, but he assures you that it is a good one. What should your procedure be before buying?

Socio-Drama

Two scenes between a life insurance agent and a client.
1st scene—Show how life insurance should not be bought or sold.
2nd scene—Show how life insurance should be bought or sold.

Suggested Readings

Gordon, Leland J., *Economics for Consumers*. New York: American Book Company, 1944. Ch. XX, "Buying Protection: Principles of Insurance"; Ch. XXI, "Insurance Practices."

Jordan, David F., and Edward F. Willett, *Managing Personal Finances*. New York: Prentice-Hall, Inc., 1945. Ch. XIII, "Buying

Life Insurance"; Ch. XIV, "Buying an Annuity"; Ch. XV, "Pension Plans and Social Security"; and Ch. XX, "Making a Will."

Upchurch, Garland R., and Bion H. Francis, *Life Insurance from the Buyer's Point of View.* Great Barrington (Maine): American Institute of Economic Research (Latest edition, usually revised each year). One of the best books on the subject from the consumer's point of view.

CHAPTER XIX: *Family Planning*

Review Questions

1. What are some of the factors which have caused young people to change their estimate of the size of the ideal family?

2. How is the birth rate affected by residence? income? educational level? occupation?

3. What is revealed by studies of the birth rates among different religious groups?

4. What are the official attitudes of different religious faiths on the use of contraceptives?

5. What is the legal status of the giving of contraceptive information?

6. What position has the United States Public Health Service taken on the giving of contraceptive information?

7. What are the physical and psychological effects of using contraceptives?

8. How does abortion differ from contraception? Birth control?

9. Explain the difference between spontaneous, therapeutic, and criminal abortions.

10. Why did Russia return to a position of making abortions illegal?

11. What are the chief factors explaining the rapid decrease in the infant mortality rate?

12. How could our infant mortality rate be further reduced?

13. What has brought about the great decrease in maternity deaths during recent years?

14. Explain the differential maternity death rates.

15. Are there any indications that the differential birth rate is contrary to social welfare?

16. Positive and negative eugenicists have the same general goal but hope to achieve it by different means. Explain.

17. What is euthenics? Why does it offer more hope for improving human welfare?

18. Contrast the way in which dependent children were cared for 50 years ago with the policy of today.

19. Name the chief points laid down by the White House Conference on Child Health and Protection.

20. What are some important standards for adoptive parents?

21. What are some questions that prospective adoptive parents should answer before they seriously consider adopting a child?

22. Is it "safe" to adopt a baby? Explain.

23. What will be the most important factor in determining how the adopted child turns out? What mistake did Mr. and Mrs. A. make when they adopted their second child?

24. Does the adopted child have the legal rights of other children?

25. When should an adopted child be told that he is adopted?

Special Problems and Activities

1. Make a tally of what the students in your class consider the ideal number of children in a family. How does it compare with the figures given in the text?

2. From the Vital Statistics reports get the infant mortality rates for your state and county. How do they compare with the rates for other states? If they are out of line, try to find why they are especially high or especially low.

3. Do the same for the maternity death rates.

Cartoons and Posters

Make a diagram of your family tree for as many generations as you can. List the number of children born to each couple for each generation. Do you find a gradual decrease in the number of children in each generation?

Suggested Readings

Baber, Ray E., *Marriage and the Family.* New York: McGraw-Hill Book Company, Inc., 1939. Ch. XVI, "Determinants of Family Size."

Becker, Howard, and Reuben Hill, eds., *Family, Marriage, and Parenthood.* Boston: D. C. Heath and Company, 1948. Ch. XXV, "Larger or Smaller Families for America?"

Fishbein, Morris, and Ernest W. Burgess, *Successful Marriage.* Garden City: Doubleday, Doran & Company, Inc., 1947. Part IV, Ch. III, "Adopting a Child."

Lockbridge, Frances, *Adopting a Child.* New York: Greenberg Publisher, 1947.

Nimkoff, Meyer F., *Marriage and the Family.* Boston: Houghton Mifflin Company, 1947. Ch. XVI, "Parents and Children."

Prentice, Carol S., *An Adopted Child Looks at Adoption.* New York: D. Appleton-Century Company, Inc., 1940.

CHAPTER XX: *Reproduction*

Review Questions

1. Explain the basis of menstruation.

2. Is the "safe period" safe? Why?

3. What seems to be the correct theory as to who is responsible in a sterile marriage?

4. Give some of the most common causes of sterility.

5. What proportion of supposedly sterile marriages may be successfully treated? Does adopting a child affect sterility?

6. What is the principle of the pregnancy tests?

7. Is it possible to determine the sex of an unborn child?

8. How is sex determined? Why are more boys than girls conceived?

9. Explain how twinning takes place.

10. Is twinning more common among Negro or white mothers? Young mothers or older mothers?

11. Where can one find help in choosing an obstetrician?

12. What are some of the common problems facing a couple during pregnancy?

13. Is it possible for a pregnant woman to influence the future behavior of her child by the activities she engages in during pregnancy? Explain.

14. What is the origin of the many old wives' tales about "marking" babies?

15. Draw a diagram on the blackboard showing how the fetus secures nourishment from the mother.

16. Explain the Rh blood factors.

17. What are the three stages in the birth process? At which stage is the mother encouraged to help in giving birth to her child?

18. Explain the theory of "natural childbirth" as you understand it.

19. How are expectant mothers prepared for "natural" childbirth?

Special Problems and Activities

Ask an obstetrician who believes in "natural" childbirth to come to class and give a talk on pregnancy and childbirth.

Film

Human Reproduction. Factual film on human reproductive systems and on process of normal birth. McGraw-Hill Book Company, Inc. 23 minutes, sound.

Suggested Readings

Becker, Howard, and Reuben Hill, eds., *Family, Marriage, and Parenthood*. Boston: D. C. Heath and Company, 1948. Ch. XIV, "Heredity and the Family," and Ch. XV, "Caring for Mother and Child Before and After."

Eastman, Nicholson J., *Expectant Motherhood*. Boston: Little, Brown and Company, Revised 1950. A scientific treatment of the prenatal period by a professor of obstetrics at The Johns Hopkins University and Obstetrician-in-Chief to The Johns Hopkins Hospital.

Farris, Edmond J., *Human Fertility and Problems of the Male*. White Plains: The Author's Press, Inc., 1950. Laboratory research largely on human male, but also on female, to determine real cause of infertility. Should be of interest to all couples having difficulty conceiving.

Goodrich, Frederick W., *Natural Childbirth*. New York: Prentice-Hall, Inc., 1950. A manual containing information on natural childbirth, diet, exercise, relaxation, and the labor experience. For expectant parents.

Heardman, Helen, *Natural Childbirth*. Baltimore: The Williams & Wilkins Company, 1949. A manual describing methods used to prepare mothers for natural childbirth. Includes illustrated instructions for exercises designed to aid in the relaxation necessary for uncomplicated childbirth.

Landis, Judson T., and Mary G. Landis, eds., *Readings in Marriage and the Family*. New York: Prentice-Hall, Inc., 1952. Part IX, Reading 4, "The Rh Blood Factors," Curt Stern; Reading 5, "Effects of First Pregnancy on Sex Adjustment," Judson T. Landis, Thomas and Shirley Poffenberger; Reading 6, "Artificial Insemination," Joseph H. Greenberg; Reading 7, "Effect of Adoption on Fertility," Frederick M. Hanson and John Rock; Reading 8, "Birth Control: The Fortune Survey," Elmo Rock.

Portnoy, Louis, and Jules Saltman, *Fertility in Marriage*. New York: Farrar, Straus and Company, 1950. A guide for childless couples. Discusses methods being tried to help overcome sterility.

Read, Grantley Dick, *Childbirth Without Fear*. New York: Harper & Brothers, 1944. The thesis of this book is that by doing away with fear through knowledge and understanding of childbirth, birth will be the natural, comparatively painless function nature intended it to be.

Thoms, Herbert, and Lawrence Roth, *Understanding Natural Childbirth*. New York: McGraw-Hill Book Company, Inc., 1950. Describes Yale University training program.

CHAPTER XXI: *When Children Come*

Review Questions

1. Almost two out of three couples who divorce have no children. Consequently, the suggestion is sometimes made that it is best to have children early in marriage. Criticize.

2. What are some of the reasons why people desire to have children?

3. Discuss the effect of children upon happiness in marriage.

4. What did Burgess and Cottrell find to be the important factor in determining whether children contributed to the happiness of marriage?

5. Do you feel that your school is giving enough information to prepare you for the responsibilities of parenthood?

6. What readjustments in husband-wife relationships are often required when the first child is born?

7. What seems to be the basic factor underlying conflict between husbands and wives over the training and discipline of their children?

8. What are some of the more common differences concerning child training?

9. Why is it essential for parents to present a united front in child training?

10. What home circumstances seem to be important to the happiness of children?

11. Cite some home situations which make for the unhappiness of children.

12. What are some of the most common fears and worries of children?

13. How can a child be made to feel that his physical features are not a handicap?

Special Problems and Activities

1. Write a case history of parental conflict over the training and disciplining of the children. Bring out the effect of the conflict upon the relationship of the parents as well as the reaction of the children to the conflict.

2. Write an analysis of your own home, bringing out the circumstances which made for happiness or unhappiness and the things which you worried about as a child.

Socio-Dramas

1. Two family scenes, one bringing out a conflict between the parents over the training and disciplining of the children with its effects upon the children, and one showing the desirable way for parents to resolve differences and to present a united front to the children.

2. Two sisters and their husbands and children meet after some years of separation. They make the usual comments about the children with the usual unawareness of the effect of their remarks upon the children.

Films

Preface to a Life. Shows effects of different methods of child training upon the child. 29 minutes, sound. Secured from most film rental services. If only one film is to be used here, we suggest this one. Castle.

Life with Baby. Shows how children grow, mentally and physically, as charted by Dr. Gesell. 18 minutes, sound. March of Time.

Palmour Street. Child care practices in lower-class Negro family. 27 minutes, sound. Health Publication Institute.

Suggested Readings

Baber, Ray E., *Marriage and the Family*. New York: McGraw-Hill Book Company, Inc., 1939. Chs. X and XI, "Parent-Child Interaction."

Burgess, Ernest W., and Paul Wallin, *Engagement and Marriage*. Chicago: J. B. Lippincott Company, 1953. Ch. XXI, "Children and Marital Success."

Christensen, Harold, *Marriage Analysis*. New York: The Ronald Press Company, 1950. Ch. XI, "Parenthood."

Landis, Judson T., and Mary G. Landis, eds., *Readings in Marriage and the Family*. New York: Prentice-Hall, Inc., 1952. Part X, Reading 1, "How Family Forces Affect the Individual," O. Spurgeon English; Reading 2, "The Practical Application of Basic Mental Hygiene Principles by the Cornelian Corner," Leo H. Bartemeier; Reading 3, "Child-Rearing and Social Status," Martha Ericson Dale; Reading 4, "Maternal Over-Protection and Rejection," David M. Levy; Reading 5, "Adolescent-Parent Adjustment," Ivan Nye; Reading 6, "Some Neglected Areas in Family Life Study," Bossard, Boll, and Sanger.

Levy, John, and Ruth Munroe, *The Happy Family*. New York: Alfred A. Knopf, Inc., 1938. Ch. VII, "Children: The Consummation of Marriage," and Ch. VIII, "All Children Have Difficulties."

Nimkoff, Meyer, *Marriage and the Family*. Boston: Houghton Mifflin Company, 1947. Ch. XVI, "Parents and Children."

Truxal, Andrew, and Frances Merrill, *The Family in American Culture*. New York: Prentice-Hall, Inc., 1947. Ch. XVIII, "The Family and the Child."

Waller, Willard, *The Family* (Revised by Reuben Hill). New York: The Dryden Press, 1951. Part V, "Parenthood: Imposing Relationships."

CHAPTER XXII: *Bringing Up Children*

Review Questions

1. What is the most important thing a couple can provide for their children if the children are to grow into well-adjusted people?

2. Why is it hard for parents to see the behavior of their children in its proper perspective?

3. Why do parents often defend the faults of their children to neighbors and relatives?

4. How can one help his child develop initiative and self-reliance? Illustrate.

5. Criticize the allowance systems used by the two families described in the text. Did either of these approach the allowance system you had in your family?

6. Why is a sense of humor important?

7. Why is doing things together as a family important to the development of the child?

8. What questions might a parent ask himself in deciding whether he is pursuing the right course in training his child?

9. Why can't parents fight their children's battles?

10. What should the ultimate goal of child training be?

Special Problems and Activities

1. Give a case from your acquaintance in which the parents always defended the faults of their children.

2. Give a case from your acquaintance in which the parents were careful to train their children on unimportant behavior but permitted the children to engage in other quite serious behavior without comment.

3. Either from your own family or from a family you know, cite how doing things together as a family contributed to the security and happiness of the children.

4. Cite a case of a family pattern in which the parents were constantly trying to fight their children's battles.

5. What bearing does faulty child training have upon marital adjustment?

Socio-Drama

Write a skit on one of the following and have the class act it out:

a. The right and the wrong way to use allowances.
b. A dinner scene which demonstrates the proper and the improper type of conversation.
c. A family with misplaced emphasis upon what is right behavior.
d. A mother fighting the battles of her children with the neighbors or the teacher.

Films

Angry Boy. One of the few films which show the effects of the husband-wife adjustment upon the child. Also shows adequate child-guidance facilities in treating child. 33 minutes, sound. Association Films.

Meeting Emotional Needs in Childhood. Film emphasizes the needs of children for security, complete love, a sense of belonging and independence. 32 minutes, sound. New York University.

Over-Dependency. This is the case history of Jimmy, an attractive young man whose life is crippled by the behavior patterns carried over from a too-dependent childhood. National Film Board of Canada. 30 minutes, sound. McGraw-Hill Book Company, Inc.

Suggested Readings

Aldrich, C. Anderson, and Mary M. Aldrich, *Babies Are Human Beings.* New York: The Macmillan Company, 1938.

Cavan, Ruth Shonle, *The American Family.* New York: Thomas Y. Crowell Company, 1953. Ch. XVIII, "Parents and Children."

Gesell, Arnold, and Frances L. Ilg, *Infant and Child in the Culture of Today.* New York: Harper & Brothers, 1943.

Gruenberg, Sidonie Matsner. *We the Parents.* New York: Harper & Brothers, 1939.

Landis, Judson T., and Mary G. Landis, eds., *Readings in Marriage and the Family.* New York: Prentice-Hall, Inc., 1952. Part XI, Reading 4, "The Stepmother," and Reading 5, "The Stepchild," William C. Smith. Part XII, Reading 5, "Children of Divorce," Kingsley Davis.

Ribble, Margaret A., *The Rights of Infants.* New York: Columbia University Press, 1943.

Spock, Benjamin, *The Common Sense Book of Baby and Child Care.* New York: Duell, Sloan and Pearce, Inc., 1946. A manual on all phases of the physical and emotional development of the infant and young child. A good book for mothers to own.

———, *The Pocketbook of Baby and Child Care.* New York: Pocket books, Inc., 1946. (Pocketbook printing of *The Common Sense Book of Baby and Child Care.*)

Strecker, Edward A., *Their Mothers' Sons.* Philadelphia: J. B. Lippincott Company, 1946.

U.S. Department of Labor, *Your Child from One to Six*. Children's Bureau Publication 30. Superintendent of Documents, Washington, D.C. (Latest revision.)

Wolf, Anna W. M. *The Parents' Manual*. New York: Simon & Schuster, Inc., Revised 1951.

CHAPTER XXIII: *Sex Education*

Review Questions

1. How is the term sex education defined?

2. What was the older theory about giving sex information to children? What were some of the false assumptions of this school of thought?

3. Why is it important for parents to give their children scientific sex information?

4. Criticize the viewpoint of parents who say, "I don't believe children should know about sex; they aren't old enough to know."

5. When is a child old enough to receive his first sex information?

6. What are the most common first questions asked by children about sex?

7. If it is impossible for a parent to answer his child's questions about sex, how else might the information be given?

8. Why do many parents fail to use a scientific vocabulary when talking to their children about sex, reproduction, and bodily elimination?

9. How does a parent establish rapport with his children in discussing sex and reproduction?

10. What are the most common sources of sex information for college students? Would there be a difference for people who did not go to college? Explain.

11. Will knowledge about sex lead to sex experimentation?

12. Why is it so difficult for parents to have the proper perspective on common sex problems of normal children?

13. How can children be prevented from causing a neighborhood riot by giving their scientific information about reproduction to the neighbors' children?

14. What would be included in a complete program of home and family living education at different levels in the school curriculum?

Suggested Problems and Activities

Write your own case history of learning about sex: how it was handled in the home; what you learned from playmates or reading; and your reaction to what you learned.

Socio-Drama

Two family scenes. *The cast:* mother, father, and children ages 4 to 12.

1st scene—The old way of learning about sex. Children ask common questions about sex and the parents give the old type of answers. End with the "woodshed" conference.

2nd scene—The new way of learning about sex. Same as in the first scene except that the parents give correct answers to questions at each age.

(For sample questions asked at each age see Frances Bruce Strain, *New Patterns in Sex Teachings,* pp. xiii-xvi. Ways to answer are given in this book.)

Films

Human Beginnings. Designed to give first-grade children normal attitudes toward reproduction. Probably of more value to use with people approaching parenthood. 20 minutes, sound.

Human Growth. Designed to explain the process of reproductive maturity to children in grades 4 to 6. 20 minutes, sound.

(Association Films. Both are excellent for use with college young people to show them how to handle the sex and reproductive education of children. The films were the outgrowth of the reproductive education program in Oregon.)

Suggested Readings

Bibby, Cyril, *Sex Education. A Guide for Parents, Teachers, and Youth Leaders.* New York: Emerson Books, Inc., 1946.

Hymes, James L., *How To Tell Your Child About Sex.* New York: Public Affairs Committee, 1949. Pamphlet No. 149.

Kirkendall, Lester A., *Sex Education as Human Relations.* New York: Inor Publishing Company, Inc., 1950. Excellent background information on the basic principles of sex education. Description of programs, methods, and materials.

Landis, Judson T., and Mary G. Landis, eds., *Readings in Marriage and the Family*. New York: Prentice-Hall, Inc., 1952. Part XIV, Reading 2, "Sound Attitudes Toward Sex," Lester A. Kirkendall.

Strain, Frances Bruce, *New Patterns in Sex Teachings*. New York: Appleton-Century-Crofts, Inc., Revised 1951.

———, *The Normal Sex Interests of Children*. New York: Appleton-Century-Crofts, Inc., 1948.

Appendix D

SOURCES OF MOTION PICTURES

Association Films	Y.M.C.A. Motion Picture Bureau 347 Madison Avenue, New York, N.Y. 206 S. Michigan Avenue, Chicago, Ill. 3012 Maple Street, Dallas, Texas 351 Turk Street, San Francisco, Calif.
Castle	Castle Films Division, Inc., 445 Park Avenue, New York, N.Y.
Coronet	Coronet Instructional Films, 65 East Water Street, Chicago, Ill.
Health Publication Institute	Health Publication Institute, Raleigh, N.C.
March of Time	March of Time Films, 30 Rockefeller Plaza, New York, N.Y.
McGraw-Hill	McGraw-Hill Book Company, Inc., Text-film Department, 330 West 42nd Street, New York 18, N.Y.
New York University	New York University Film Library, 26 Washington Square, New York, N.Y.

INDEX

A

Abortion:
  criminal, 387-390
  harmful effects of, 139, 389-390
  non-pregnant women and, 388
  Russian policy on, 389
  spontaneous, 387-388
  Swedish policy on, 389-390
  therapeutic, 387-390
Accommodation and marriage adjustment, 256
Adaptability, 100
Adjustment in marriage (*see* Marriage adjustment)
Adolescence:
  mental achievements in, 23-24
  rate of growth in, 19; *figure,* 20
Adoption:
  considerations for adoptive parents, 401-404
  evils of, in past, 400-401
  legal status of adopted children, 406
  premarital pregnancies and, 140
  risks in, 404-406
  standards for, 400-401
  telling child of, 406-407
Affection:
  analysis of needs for, 40-43
  child's need for, 453-454
  grievances in marriage and, 94-95
  needs for, at different ages, 40-43; *figure,* 42
Affinity, marriage prohibitions and, 231-233, 243
Age, maternity death rate by, 396-397; *figure,* 396
Age at marriage:
  annulments and, 246
  divorce and, 108-109; *figure,* 109
  emotional maturity and, 110-112
  in-law adjustments and, *figure,* 311
  marital happiness and, 107-108; *table,* 107
  median, 38-39; *figure,* 38
  reasons for decrease in, 39-40
  socio-economic class and, 106
  time to adjust in marriage and, 107-108
  United States and other countries, 38
  war and, 39-40
Age for marriage:
  legal, 227-231
Age for marriage (*cont.*):
  minimum, *table,* 228-229
  without parental consent, *figure,* 230
Alcaro, Marion Walker, 448
Allowances, children's, 467-469
American Association of Marriage Counselors, Inc., 300, 497-498
American Bar Association, 243
American Board of Obstetrics and Gynecology, 424
American College of Life Underwriters, 372
American Institute for Economic Research, 366
American Medical Association, 385
Anderson, John F., 477
Anderson, W. A., 443
Annulment:
  contrasted to divorce, 245
  legitimacy of children of, 247
  most common grounds for, 246-247
  number per year, 247
  void and voidable marriages, 243-247
Ante-nuptial agreement, 149-150
Ascheim-Zondek test for pregnancy, 417
Assortative mating, 79-82

B

Bachelors:
  death rates of, 59-60; *figure,* 60
  failure to marry, 51-62
  social pressure upon to marry, 48-49
Baber, Ray E., 83, 84, 85, 87, 154, 155, 162, 164, 222, 272, 447, 508
Barlow, Tony, 61
Barron, Milton L., 162
Becker, Howard, 166, 335, 508
Behavior problems, rating of, *table,* 494
Bell, Howard M., 153, 154, 377
Bernard, Jessie, 444
Bigamous marriages:
  annulments and, 247
  legitimacy of children of, 248
  void marriages as, 243-245
Bigelow, Howard F., 334
Birth certificates:
  illegitimacy shown on, 248-251
  short form of, *figure,* 249
Birth control:
  ante-nuptial agreement on, 149-150
  Catholic-Protestant marriages and, 151, 159-160

Birth control (*cont.*):
discussed during engagement, 203, 207
Birth control clinics, number of, 384
Birth rate:
and income, 378-380
by education, *figure,* 379
religion and, 379-380
rural-urban, 378
trends in, 377-378; *figure,* 378
Borrowing money, general considerations in, 347-349
Bossard, James H. S., 81, 82, 509
Bowman, Henry A., 505
Boy-girl relationships, seven stages in, *figure,* 42
Brandeis, Louis D., 370
Brav, Stanley R., 286
Breach of promise, 177, 239
Brooks, Evelyn C., 404
Brooks, Lee M., 404
Budgeting:
as source of friction, 336-337
help in, 337
purpose of, 334-336
Burgess, Ernest W., 50, 79, 80, 101, 102, 105, 107, 158, 173, 179, 184, 200, 212, 279, 285, 321, 326, 416, 447, 508, 509, 510
Burma, John H., 235
Butterfield, Oliver, 202, 292, 507
Buxton, C. L., 414
Buying:
cash, 341, 343
charge accounts and, 342
when to buy, 345
Buying life insurance (*see* Insurance, life)

C

Cannon, Mary A., 382
Caplan, Irwin, 386
Caplow, Theodore, 186, 190, 192, 193, 194
Careers versus homemaking, 27-37 (*see also* Roles)
Cattell, Psyche, 23
Cavan, Ruth S., 508
Central Conference of American Rabbis:
statement on birth control, 382
statement on mixed marriages, 162
Child birth, 433-439
anesthetics and, 435
duration of labor for "natural," 438-439
"natural," 435-439
new theories of, 435-439
pain during, 433-438
Child birth (*cont.*):
training program for, 438
Yale University research on, 438
Child marriages, 230-231
Child Study Association, 488
Child training:
building self-reliance in, 464-466
consideration for others, 470-471
family values in, 467
importance of doing things as families, 473
importance of initiative and self-reliance in, 464-466
money and, 467-468
parental conflict over, 449-452
parental perspective in, 462
possessions and, 469
sense of humor and, 472
sex (*see* Sex education)
trends in practices and, 435
Children:
anxieties of, 455-457; *table,* 457
home circumstances making for happiness of, 452-454; *table,* 453
home circumstances making for unhappiness of, 454-455; *table,* 454
time interval after marriage and, 443
why have, 444
worries of, 455-457
Children's Charter, 400
Choice of a mate (*see* Mate selection)
Christensen, Harold, 115, 118, 387, 505
Church attendance and happiness in marriage, *figure,* 328
Church weddings and marital adjustment, *figure,* 326
Clarke, Helen C., 250
Coitus:
during engagement, 202
frequency of, and age, 295-296
premarital, 130-145
premarital petting and danger of, 67-71
College marriages:
advantages of, 114-115
cost of living in, 118
parental support for, 119-120
parenthood and, 116-117
problems to consider in, 116-120
student attitudes on, 114
success of, 115-116
Commission on Uniform State Laws, 243
Common law marriage, 224, 241-243; *table,* 228-229
age for, 227
states recognizing, *figure,* 242
valid in states, *table,* 228-229
Conflict (*see* Marriage adjustment)

Conception:
sex ratio at, 15, 52, 421
process of, 411-412
Consanguinity, marriage prohibitions on, 231-233, 244
Contraception:
age at marriage and, 39
birth rate and, 380
Catholic position on, 149-151, 380
health and, 384-385
Jewish position on, 382-383
legality of, 383-384
Protestant position on, 381
reliability of, 385-387
religious attitudes on, 149-151, 380-383
sex adjustment and, 385
use of, and social class, 380
Contract in marriage, 223-224
Consumer economics, 342-353
organizations to aid, 345-346
Consumers Research, Inc., 345-346
Consumers' Union, 345-346
Comstock Act, 383
Cost of credit, 347-353; *table,* 353
Cottrell, L. S., 102, 105, 107, 158, 173, 179, 200, 212, 279, 285, 321, 326, 446, 447, 509
Council of Trent, 242
Cousins, marriage of, 231-232
Courtship:
dating and rating in, 74-76
defined, 63-64
desirability and exploitation in, 73
emotional trends in, 190-192; *figure,* 191
exploitation during, 72-74
period of, 63-87
purpose of, 64
suggestions for minimizing sex element in, 71-72
Cultural conditioning, sex response and, 285
Cultural contrasts and broken engagements, 188

D

Dating:
among high-school students, 63
contrasted with courtship, 63-64
defined, 63
rating and, 74-76
Death rates:
by sex, *table,* 15-17; *figure,* 16
infant (*see* Infant mortality)
married, single, divorced, 59-60; *figure,* 60
maternal (*see* Maternal mortality)
of men and women, 15-17
ratio of men to women, *figure,* 16
Deferred marriage, 143-145
Delayed marriage, 143-145
Dewey, John, 324
Dickinson-Belskie birth models, *figures,* 429, 434, 436, 437
Directory of Medical Specialists, 424
Divorce:
adaptability and, 100
age at marriage and, 108-110; *figure,* 109
age differences in spouses and, *table,* 174
attitude toward, and successful marriage, 3-5
court decisions on out-of-state, 222
easy, a hazard to successful marriage, 5
educational differences in spouses and, *table,* 172
failure to adjust and, 262
length of engagement and, 200
mixed marriages of religion and, 152-158; *figure,* 154
personality characteristics and, 93, 100
premarital pregnancy and, 201
ratio of, to marriages, *figure,* 9
religion and, 152-158, 165-166, 322
second marriages and, 128-129 (*see also* Remarriage)
years married and, *figure,* 258
Dollard, John, 256
Double standard, biological basis of, 25-26
Duvall, Evelyn Millis, 464, 505, 506
Dyer, Dorothy T., 509

E

Eastman, Nicholas J., 431
Eberly, Marion S., 357
Economic adjustment in marriage, 330-340
Economic level, age at marriage and, 106
Education:
age at marriage and, 108
divorce and, *table,* 172
family life, 10, 493, 495
for parenthood, 439
happiness in marriage and, 106
marriage adjustment and, 170-172
need for parenthood, 446-447
premarital sex relations and, 132-134
sex (*see* Sex education)
Education for marriage:
in colleges, 10
student demand for, 10
Ego satisfaction and changing roles, 36-37 (*see also* Roles)

Ehrmann, Winston, 70, 72, 132
Eisenstein, Ira, 383
Elmer, M. C., 251
Elopements, marriage success and, 207-208
Emotional immaturity and broken engagements, 187
Emotional maturity:
age for marriage and, 110-112
criteria of, 111-112
readiness for parenthood and, 116-118, 441-442
Endogamy, 164
Engagement:
a contract, 177
becoming engaged, 180-181
breaking of, 196-199
coitus during, 202-203
first date to, *table,* 178
length of, and marriage adjustment, 199-202
length of time to get over broken, 192-196; *table,* 193
nature of, 177-178
percentage ending in marriage, 184; *figure,* 184
permanence of, 184
problems to be discussed during, 203-206
purpose of, 183
reaction to broken, 193-199; *table,* 194
Engle, E. T., 414
Enoch Arden marriages, 245, 247
Epileptics, marriage prohibition of, 224-225
Ethnocentrism, 81
Eugenic regulation of marriage, 224-227
Eugenics:
differential birth rate, 397-398
negative, 398
positive, 398
Euthenics, 399
Exploitation in courtship, 72-74
Exner, M. J., 386, 507

F

Faegre, Marion L., 477
Fallopian tubes, 409, 411, 415
Family buying, 343-346
Family companionship:
child training and, 472-473
happiness of children and, 452-453
Family conference, 269-270
Family life education, 10-11, 493
Family planning (*see* Family size)
Family size:
decrease in, 375-376
Family size (*cont.*):
explanation of decreasing, 377-381
income and, 378-380
religion and, 379-380
rural-urban living and, 379
student attitudes on ideal, *1936, 1947,* and *1952,* 377; *figure,* 376
Farris, Edmond J., 414, 500
Federal Council of the Churches of Christ in America, attitude on birth control, 381
Federal Credit Union Act, 352
Feeble-minded:
marriage prohibition of, 224-225
sterilization of, required for marriage, 244
Feeble-mindedness:
among children of inmates, 245
among parents of inmates, 225
void and voidable marriages and, 243-247
Fetal development, 429-432
Finances and marriage adjustment, 330-340
Fink, Arthur E., 401
Folsom, Joseph Kirk, 43, 60, 508
Force or fraud, as grounds for annulment, 246
Ford, Mary E. N., 69, 133, 443
Francis, Bion F., 366, 509
Frank, Richard, 416
Freehof, Solomon B., 161
Friedman test for pregnancy, 417

G

Genetic incompatibility, 416
Gesell, Arnold, 21, 22, 501
Goldstein, Sidney E., 222, 226, 232
Goldstein, Walter, 181, 197
Gonorrhea and sterility, 415
Govan, C. C., 393
Green, Howard E., 392
Groves, Ernest R., 10, 12, 507, 508
Groves, Gladys H., 507, 508
Guttmacher, Alan F., 339, 419

H

Hamilton, G. V., 170, 444
Hanson, Frederick M., 417
Happiest period in life, *figure,* 6
Happiness in marriage:
adjustment with in-laws and, *figure,* 304
agreement on child training and, *figure,* 451
agreement on religion and, *figure,* 323
agreement on use of money and, *figure,* 333

Happiness in marriage (*cont.*):
  agreement on sex and, *figure,* 293
  children and, 444-446
  church attendance and, 321-322
  duration of marriage and, *figure,* 278
  failure to adjust and, *figure,* 262
  living with in-laws and, *figure,* 316
  summary of studies on, *table,* 279
  time required to adjust and, 257-260; *figure,* 262
Happiness of children, home circumstances contributing to, 452-454
Hart, Hornell, 107
Hattendorf, Katherine W., 482
Health and happiness in marriage, 105
Heardman, Helen, 438, 500
Helle, Ray, 41
Hill, Reuben, 46, 72, 99, 166, 335, 505, 508, 510
Hocking, William E., 324
Hohman, Leslie B., 133
Homemaking versus housekeeping (*see* Roles)
Homogamy, 79
Honeymoon, 210-211
Huffine, Dave, 268
Husband-wife relationship (*see* Marriage adjustment)
Hymen as index to virginity, 409

I

Ignorance and sex adjustment, 286-287
Ilg, Frances L., 21, 22
Illegitimacy, 247-252
Illegitimate children, 247-252
Impotency as grounds for annulment, 247
Incest taboo and marriage laws, 233
Infant mortality:
  anesthetics and, 292, 293
  by sex, 15-16
  parents' income and, 393; *figure,* 392
  premature babies and, 292-293
  reduction in, 390-393; *figure,* 390
Infanticide, 139
Infertility (*see* Sterility)
In-laws, living with, discussed during engagement, 202-204
In-laws and marriage adjustment, 302-320
In-law relationships:
  a problem in marriage, 302-303
  adjustments in, and happiness, 304
  age married and, 311
  case of domination in, 313-315
  friction a feminine pattern in, 304; *table,* 304
  in later years, 319-320
  lack of objectivity in, 306-307

In-law relationships (*cont.*):
  reactions of spouses to friction, 306-307
  successful, 317-318
  time to adjust in, and happiness, 304-305; *figure,* 305
Insanity:
  marriage prohibition for, 224-226
  void and voidable marriage and, 243-246
Installment buying, 349-351
Insurance, life:
  agent, 372-373
  as protection, 354-355; *figure,* 365
  comparative costs, 366-367
  consumption unit responsibility, 368-369; *figure,* 369
  determining needs, 367-368
  endowment, 363-364
  general considerations, 354-355
  group, 358
  industrial, 356-357
  lapse rate of, 356-357, 364, 372
  limited payment, 362
  on children, 357, 364, 374
  ordinary, 356, 359-361
  paying premiums, 373
  savings bank, 370-372
  term, 359-361
  where to buy, 370
  whole or straight life, 361-362
  written on breadwinner, 357, 364, 374
Interfaith marriages (*see* Mixed marriage, interfaith)
Interracial marriages (*see* Mixed marriages, interracial)
Interest rates:
  credit unions, 352
  how to compute, 348-350
  installment buying, 349-351
  on consumer credit, 353
  small loan companies, 351-352

J

Jacobson, Alver H., 35
James, William, 323
Jewish-Gentile marriages, 161-166
Johnson, R. H., 238
Jordan, David F., 364

K

Kavinoky, Nadina, 288, 297
Keate, Jeff, 471
Kennedy, Ruby Jo Reeves, 162
Key, Ted, 208
King, Charles E., 102
Kinsey, Alfred, 132, 133, 291, 296, 299

Kirkendall, Lester A., 503, 504, 506
Kirkpatrick, Clifford, 34, 35, 170, 186, 190, 192, 193, 194
Komarovsky, Mirra, 24, 33
Koos, Earl L., 505, 510
Kraines, S. H., 328

L

Lamson, Herbert D., 78, 79
Landis, Judson T., 6, 35, 46, 75, 84, 96, 103, 107, 114, 117, 170, 200, 258, 259, 262, 279, 292, 305, 387, 418, 426, 453, 457, 505, 507, 508
Landis, Mary G., 35, 505, 507, 508
Landis, Paul H., 509
Lang, Richard O., 279
Latz, Leo J., 414
League of Women Voters, 14
Legal control of marriage, 220-252
Legal status of illegitimates, 248-252
License, wedding, 224
Lichty, George, 68
Life expectancy, by sex and race, 17; *figure,* 18
Life insurance (*see* Insurance, life)
Links, Marty, 58, 80
Living with in-laws, 316-317, 319-320
Locke, Harvey J., 50, 79, 80, 100, 108, 184, 200, 201, 322, 508
Locke, Lafe, 483
Lonely Heart Clubs, 54
Longevity, by sex, 17
Loth, David, 388
Love:
  as a reason for marriage, 43-46
  at first sight, 44-45
Lowrie, Samuel H., 76

M

Mace, Harry, 445
Martin, Clyde E., 132, 291
Marital status:
  longevity and, 59-60
  death rates and, 59-60; *figure,* 60
  happiest period in life and, 6
  insanity, suicide and, 59-60
  of the population, 38-40
Marriage:
  a civil contract, 223-224
  a sacrament, 151
  age at, 38-39
  age by socio-economic class, 106
  age for, 106-109
  arrival of first child after, 443
  as a way of life, 6-7
  as an escape, 50
  between relatives, 231-233
  chances limited by college degree, 55-56
Marriage (*cont.*):
  coeds to classmates, 78-79; *table,* 78
  common law, 241-243
  conditioning men for, 62
  dates preferred, *figure,* 209
  education for, 10-11
  emotional maturity and, 210-212
  failure and premarital pregnancy, 201, 202
  forced by pregnancy, 231
  for economic status, 47-48
  for love, 43-46
  for social status, 46-47
  interracial prohibitions on, 234-235
  Jewish-Gentile (*see* Mixed marriages, interfaith)
  median age at, 38-39
  mixed (*see* Mixed marriages)
  need for matrimonial agencies, 54-55
  on the rebound, 198
  personality needs and, 50-51; *table,* 51
  problems in regulation of, 221-222
  Protestant-Catholic (*see* Mixed marriages, interfaith)
  reason for:
    economic status as, 47-48; *figure,* 47
    escape as, 50
    loneliness as, 49-50
    love as, 43-46
    personality needs a, 50-51; *table,* 51
    social expectancy as, 48-49
    social status as, 46-47
  reasons for regulation of, 220
  the honeymoon and, 210-211
  the sex ratio and, 52-54
  to avoid loneliness, 49-50
  waiting period before, 236-238
  while in college, 113-120
  who is qualified to perform, 239-240
  validity of, 240-241
  void and voidable, 243-247
Marriage adjustment:
  ability to identify and, 100
  ability to work through problems and, 100-101
  accommodation in, 256
  adaptability and, 100
  age at and time to adjust, 107-108
  age at marriage and, *figure,* 107
  age differences and, 173-174
  and the family conference, 269-271
  areas calling for, 254-262
  chief forms of, 255-257
  child training and, 462
  childhood happiness and, 452-454
  conditioning of boys and girls for, 61-62
  conflict on child training, 449-450

Marriage adjustment (*cont.*):
confusion of roles and, 276-277 (*see also* Roles)
contrasted with courtship, 253
courtship behavior in, 274
desire for children and, 444-446; *figure,* 447
difference in economic status and, 172
duration of acquaintance and, *figure,* 179
during pregnancy, 425-427
elopments and, 202
equality and sex drive and, 290-291
factors making for, 96-101; *table,* 97
family background and, 101-104
happiness of parents' marriage and, *figures,* 102, 104
health and, 105
husband-wife grievances, 93-96; *table,* 94
in-laws (*see* In-law relationships)
intelligence and education of spouses and, 169-172
length of acquaintance and, 179
length of engagement and, 199-201; *table and figure,* 199-200
length of time required for, 257-260; *figure,* 259
mutually satisfactory in seven areas, *figure,* 261
parental opposition and, 208-209
personality traits and, 93-101
personality traits of happy and unhappy spouses, 89-92
place married and, *figure,* 326
prediction of, 212-219
quarreling and, 263-269
readiness for children and, 441
religion and, 321-328
remodeling the spouse in, 272-274
required in all marriages, 254-255
sex (*see* Sex adjustment)
sex education in childhood and, 479
similarity in family background and, *figure,* 146
time required and happiness in, 261-262; *figure,* 262
traits predictive of success in, 100-103
when children come, 448
wholesome tension-relievers and, 270-271
Marriage Brokers Association, 54
Marriage counseling agencies (*see* American Association of Marriage Counselors)
Marriage laws by states, *table,* 228-229
Marriage license, required, 235-236
Marriage prediction schedule, 212-219
Marriage prediction, family background and, 101-104
Marriages involving separation:
parenthood and, 124
postponed adjustment and, 121-122
prevalence of, today, 120
questions to consider before making, 121-125
war and, 120-125
Martin, Clyde E., 132, 291
Marvin, Donald M., 81
Masturbation, 492-493
Marry, failure to:
emotional dependence and, 56-57
inability to interest opposite sex and, 55-56
physical reasons for, 59-60
psychological reasons for, 59-60
unequal distribution of sexes and, 52-55
Marsh, Earle, 439
Mate selection:
assortative, 79-80
attitude of parents on, 87
attitudes of students on, 82-86; *table,* 84
factors to consider in, 88-112
personality traits, 89-101
failure to achieve emotional independence and, 56-57
failure to take advantage of opportunities and, 55-56
hindered by physical and psychological factors, 59-60
influenced by loneliness, 49
influenced by the sex ratio, 52-54
limited by college degree, 56
love at first sight and, 44-46
love in, 44-46
occupation and, 81
personality needs and, 50-51
personality traits, *table,* 97
residential propinquity and, 80-82; *figure,* 82
role of matrimonial agencies in, 54
rural-urban sex ratio, 53-54; *figure,* 53
social expectancy as force in, 48-49
social status and, 46-47
student rating of personality traits in, *figure,* 99
Maternal impressions, 482
Maternal mortality:
age of mother and, 396-397; *figure,* 396
hospital care and, 394-395; *figure,* 395
race and, 394-395; *figure,* 394
reasons for reduction in, 393-395
reduction in, 393-395
Mating gradient, 60

Matrimonial agencies, 54
Maturity:
age for marriage and, 110-112
in-law relationships and, 308-312
Menstruation:
and drive, 24
explaining to preadolescent girls, 482
process of, 412-413
Mental achievements of men and of women, 22-24
Midwives, 396
Miller, Uri, 382
Miscegenetic marriage regulations, 234-235
Mixed marriages:
age, 173-175
divorce rate and, 173-175; *table,* 174
happiness in marriage and, 173
economic status, 172
education, 170-172
divorce rate and, 171-172
happiness in marriage and, *figure,* 171
intelligence, 169; *figure,* 170
interfaith:
ante-nuptial agreement in, 149-150
among Protestants, 165-166
attitudes of students toward, 162
birth rates in, 379
chances for, in United States, 147
conflict over children in, 154-160, 164
contrast in beliefs and, 150-152
defined, 127
denominational attitudes on, 150
faith of children of, 155-157, 164
family rejection in, 168
Jewish-Gentile, 161-165
parental policy on training children in, 156-157
problems of, 147
Protestant-Catholic, 147-161; a case, 160-161
internationality, 167-169
a case, 168
interracial, biological and social problems, 166-167
Money and family buying, child training on use of, 467-469
Money in marriage, 330-340
agreement on use of, and happiness, 333-336; *figure,* 333
budgeting, 336
conflict over use of, 330-332
growing together on economic values, 333
Monogamy, 375
Montgomery, Thaddeus L., 440
Mores, 13, 131
Mors, Wallace P., 348
Mortality (*see* Death rates)
Mother-in-law (*see* In-law relationships)
Mowrer, Ernest R., 445
Mowrer, Harriet R., 445
Mudd, Emily H., 509
Multiple births, 421-423; *figure,* 422

N

National Federation of Business and Professional Women, 14
Natural childbirth (*see* Child birth)
New York Maternity Center, 429
Nocturnal emissions, 411, 482
Norway, illegitimacy in, 250
Notestein, Frank W., 106

O

Occupation:
achievement and, 398
age at marriage and, 106; *figure,* 106
divorce and, 104-105
Ogburn, W. F., 53, 54
Olden, Marian S., 225
Orgasm, 293-294
time to achieve in marriage, 291; *table,* 292
Ovulation, 404-412
and the safe period, 413-414
frequency of, 416
sterility and, 416
time of and conception, 416

P

Parent-child relationships (*see* Child training *and* Children)
Parental attachment, 189
Parenthood, readiness for, 441
Parents, evaluating ourselves as, 474 (*see also* Child training)
Paternity and illegitimacy, 247-252
Paul the Apostle, 13
Pearl, Raymond S., 380
Personality traits:
broken engagements and, 187-188
of happy and unhappy spouses, 89-92
successful marriage and, 83-101
Petting, 67-72
opinions of college students on, *figure,* 69
Philbrick, Robert E., 115, 118, 387
Poffenberger, Shirley, 117, 387, 418, 426
Poffenberger, Thomas, 117, 387, 418, 426
Planned Parenthood Federation, 387

Polyandry, 375
Polygamy, 375
Pomeroy, Wardell, 132, 291
Pope Pius XI and birth control, 380
Pope Pius XII and birth control, 380
Popenoe, Paul, 79, 103, 109, 180, 201, 202, 208, 238, 507
Prediction schedule, marriage, 212-219
Predicting marriage adjustment (*see* Marriage prediction)
Pregnancy:
  adjustment of couple during, 425-427
  boy or girl?, 419
  health during, 426-427
  incidence of planning, 117-118
  length of, 430
  maternal impressions, 428
  nausea and, 418
  positive signs of, 418-419
  prenatal care, 423-425
  presumptive signs of, 417-418
  psychology of, 425-427
  sex desire and, 426-427
  tests for, 417
Premarital conditioning and sex adjustment, 285-289
Premarital examination, nature and purpose of, 206-207
Premarital pregnancy, 139-140
  marriage failure and, 201-202
  waives age requirement for marriage, 231
Premarital sex relations:
  attitudes of college students toward, 133-136; *table,* 134
  divorce and, 201, 202
  marital adjustment and, 136-137
  preparation for marriage and, 137-139
  prevalence of, 131-133
  reasons against, *table,* 135
  re-education after marriage, 143
  society's attitude toward, 130-131
Propinquity and mate selection, 81-82
Protestant-Catholic marriages, 147-161 (*see also* Mixed marriages, interfaith)
Puberty (*see* Adolescence)
Puerperal septicemia, 394
Purdue Opinion Poll, 30, 65, 493

Q

Quakers:
  exempted from marriage license, 236
  marriage ceremony of, 240
Quarreling in marriage, 263-267
  effect of, on children, 269, 455-458
  tremendous trifles and, 272
  unhappiness of children and, 454-455; *table,* 454

R

Rabbinical Assembly of America, on birth control, 382
Raines, Shirley, 93
Randall, John H., 324
Ramsey, Glenn V., 478
Race prohibitions on interracial marriages, 234-235
Rape, statutory, 73
Read, Grantley Dick, 500
Reasons for marriage, 43-51 (*see also* Marriage, reason for)
Reed, Robert B., 446
Religion:
  a family bond, 323
  adult needs and, 324
  an escape, 325
  birth rate and, 379-380
  divorce by affiliation, 154
  happiness in marriage and, 321-322; *figure,* 323
  interfaith marriages (*see* Mixed marriages, interfaith)
  non-affiliation and divorce, 153-154, 156
  parenthood and, 328
  proportion of marriages by religious and civil authorities, 240
Religion and family life, 321-329
Religious affiliation and marital success, 321-329
Religious attitudes, marriage adjustment and, 325-328
Religious philosophy and family living, 325
Remarriage:
  factors to consider in, 124
  how differs from first, 126
  success of, 125-128
  why higher failure rate in, 128-129
Repression of sex, 144-145
Reproduction:
  female anatomy of, 408-410
  male anatomy of, 410-411
  need for understanding of, 408
Riemer, Svend, 114, 116
Rock, John, 388
Rockwood, Lemo D., 69, 133, 443
Roles (*see also* Sex differences):
  changing, and courtship, 32-34
  changing, and ego satisfaction, 36-37
  changing, and youth, 30
  confusion in, and marriage adjustment, 276-277
  in transition, 28-29
  wife-and-mother, 30-32
Rooming-in, 439-440
Roth, Salo, 45

Rural-urban residence:
age at marriage and, 106
sex ratio and, 53-54
Russell Sage Foundation, and small loan legislation, 351
Rhythm method (*see* Safe period)

S

Safe period, 380
as a means of birth control, 380, 413-415
religion and, 159-160
Safier, Benno, 489
Savings bank life insurance (*see* Insurance, life)
Schaffner, Bertram, 133
Schatchen, 54
Scheinfeld, Amram, 20, 23, 42, 420, 421
Schmiedeler, Edgar, 148
Scott, W. C., 393
Separation and marriage (*see* Marriages involving separation)
Separations, 151
Sewell, William H., 460, 461
Sex adjustment, 281-301
agreement on, and happiness, *figure*, 293
anxiety over failure in, 297
causes of poor, 285-288
conditioning of children and, 287-289
contrasts in family attitudes on normal and abnormal, 298
during pregnancy, 426-427
during the honeymoon, 210
honeymoon and, 286
importance of, 281-284
length of time required for, 257-259, 289-291
misinformation and, 286-287
mutually satisfactory in 409 marriages, *figure*, 261
not instinctive, 285-286
Sex determination, 419-421; *figure*, 420
Sex deviate behavior, 487-488 (*see also* Sex education)
Sex differences:
conditioning, 287-288
double standard and, 25-26
effect of conditioning upon, 18
having a biological basis, 25-26
in growth rates, 19; *figure*, 21
in muscular strengths, 17-18
in sex response, 289-290
in timing, 293-294
psychological, 21-22
Sex drive, 290-292
Sex education:
at what age, 485
attitudes of children on sex and source of information, *figure*, 489
attitudes on sex and chastity, 489
defined, 476
deviate sex behavior and, 487-488
in the home, 480-485
increase in sex experimentation and, 488-490
marital adjustment affected by, 101, 479
need for, 478-479
senior high school, 495
sources of student information on, 486-488; *tables*, 486, 487
student views on, 485, 493; *table*, 485
types of information given by parents, 487
use of birds, bees, and flowers in explaining, 483-484
vocabulary to use in, 484
Sex knowledge among boys, 478
Sex ratio:
at conception, 15, 52, 421
decline in male surplus, United States, 52
in the United States, 52
percentage married and the, 53-54
rural and urban residence and, 53-54; *figure*, 53
sex exploitation and, 74
Sex relations, premarital, 130-145
Sexual promiscuity, age for marriage and, 221
Source of sex information and promiscuity, 489
Shenk, Pauline, 440
Shields, Wilmer, 107
Sloane Hospital for Women, 414
Slotkin, J. S., 163
Small loan companies, 351
Smith, William M., 75, 76
Social change:
affectional needs affected by, 8-9
marriage and, 7-9
Spinsters:
death rates of, 59; *figure*, 60
changing attitudes toward, 61-62
failure of, to marry, 51-62
social pressure upon, to marry, 48-49
Spock, Benjamin, 459, 502
Steady dating, 64-66
Sterility:
adoption and, 417
causes of, in men, 415-417
causes of, in women, 415-417
contraceptives and, 384-385

Sterility (*cont.*):
  efforts to overcome, 416-417
  postponed pregnancy and, 444
Sterile marriages, percentage of, 376
Steward, Robert E., 440
Stewart, H. L., 430
Stewart, Maxwell S., 355, 360, 361, 362, 363, 371
Stevenson, Robert Louis, 278
Stott, Leland, 427
Strain, Frances B., 476, 503, 504
Strauss, Anselm, 50
Student attitudes on child rearing ability, 447-448
Student marriages, 113-120
Successful marriage:
  a positive social good, 1-3
  achievement of, 3-4
  attitude toward divorce and, 3-5
  concept of, 2
Supreme Court decisions on out-of-state divorce, 222
Syphilis:
  incidence of, in applicants for marriage license, 227
  marriage prohibition on, 224-226

T

Taylor, E. S., 393
Teachers Insurance and Annuity Association of America, 370
Temporary National Economic Committee, 366, 372
Tensions and quarreling, 363-369
Tension-relievers, 370-371
Terman, Lewis M., 23, 24, 89, 90, 93, 94, 100, 101, 102, 107, 131, 169, 170, 173, 179, 199, 279, 280, 291, 293, 294, 398, 444, 510
Thetford, H. S., 328
Thomas, John L., 152
Thomason, Bruce, 291, 292
Thoms, Herbert, 393, 438, 439, 500
Tibbits, Clark, 54
Twins, 421-423
  by age and race of mother, *figure,* 423

U

Upchurch, Garland R., 366, 509
Unhappy husbands and wives, characteristics of, 89-92
Uniform Small Loan Law, 351-352
Unmarried mothers, 250-251

V

Validity of marriage, 240-241
Value systems and conflict over use of money, 330-332
Venereal disease, 205-206
  laws by states, *table,* 228-229
  marriage prohibition on, 224-226
  sterility and, 415
Vernier, Chester G., 223, 224, 233, 234, 239, 243, 244, 245, 251
Vincent, Clark E., 460
Visher, S. S., 397
Void marriages, 242-245
Voidable marriages, 245-247

W

Waggoner, Walter, 133
Waiting period:
  before marriage, by states, *table,* 228-229
  failure to return for marriage license and, 201-202
  for marriage license, 236-237
Waller, Willard, 46, 72, 74, 75, 76, 508, 510
Wallin, Paul, 212, 510
War marriages (*see* Marriages involving separation)
Wedding, planning of, 207-210
Weeks, H. Ashley, 153
White House Conference Children's Charter, 400
Wickman, E. K., 494
Wicks, Donna, 103
Willett, Edward F., 364
Wolfe, George, 47
Women (*see also* Roles):
  changing status of, 27-37
  confusion in roles by, and marriage adjustment, 276-277
  confusion concerning roles of, 27-37
  laws discriminating against, 14
  percentage gainfully employed, *figure,* 32
  proposed amendment for equal rights for, 14
  strength of sex drive in, 290-291
  working outside the home, 14, 32
Woodbury, Robert M., 392
Worries of children, 455-458; *table,* 457
Wyatt, Robert H., 393, 438, 439

Y

Yale University:
  clinic of child development, 21
  rooming-in plan, 439-440
  training for childbirth program, 438
Young, Crawford, 481
Youth, early marriage and divorce of, 108-110